THE AUTHOR

Robert Gibson is Master of Rutherford College and Public Orator at the University of Kent. He is Britain's longest-serving Professor of French Literature and a world authority on *Le Grand Meaulnes*, the haunting novel by the French author Alain-Fournier, of whom he published his first warmly-praised biography as a student in 1953. Subsequently revised in 1975, the biography stands alongside Professor Gibson's critical edition of *Le Grand Meaulnes*, published in 1968. He is currently working on a comprehensive study of Anglo-French relations since the Conquest.

Robert Gibson first came to Ashdon when sent as a London schoolboy to help with the harvest in 1944. This study, "based on seventy interviews and a mountain of archives" is the fruit of a growing involvement and fascination across four decades.

Annals of Ashdon
No ordinary village

Robert Gibson

ESSEX RECORD OFFICE

Published by the
ESSEX RECORD OFFICE
County Hall, Chelmsford, Essex, CM1 1LX

©Essex County Council, 1988

All rights reserved — This book may not be reproduced,
in whole or in part, in any form, without written permission from
the publishers.

ISBN 0-900360-72-0

Essex Record Office Publication No. 99

Printed in Great Britain by
Witley Press, Hunstanton, Norfolk

IN MEMORY OF
JAMES AND MABEL CLIFF

I take delight in history, even in its most prosaic details, because they become poetical as they recede into the past. The poetry of history lies in the quasi-miraculous fact that once, on this earth, once, on this familiar spot of ground, walked other men and women, as actual as we are today, thinking their own thoughts, swayed by their own passions, but now all are gone, one generation vanishing after another, gone as utterly as we ourselves shall shortly be gone like a ghost at cockcrow. This is the most familiar and certain fact about life, but it is also the most poetical, and the knowledge of it has never ceased to entrance me, and throw a halo of poetry round the dustiest record that Dryasdust can bring to light.

G. M. Trevelyan:
Autobiography of an Historian

Contents

	Acknowledgements	viii
1:	Writing about Ashdon	1
2:	The Limits of History	8
3:	The Old Community	33
4:	The Life and Times of the Gentry	68
5:	Annals of the Poor	98
6:	The Rule of Law	137
7:	Unwillingly to School	171
8:	Edwardian Summer	201
9:	The Ashdon Labourers' Strike	250
10:	The Threat of Invasion	268
11:	The End of an Era	289
12:	Death and the Countryman	318
	Select Biography	337
	Index	340

Illustrations

Map of Ashdon	x
The peace of Old Ashdon (lent by Brig. T. Collins)	6
The Bartlow Hills, a curiosity for 18th-century gentlemen (Essex Record Office)	13
Dr. W.M. Palmer with chauffeur Bernard King, in 1923 (lent by Mrs H. Marsh)	31
The Domesday account of the manor of Ascenduna	39
'Daddy' Flack in 1903 (lent by Mrs H. Marsh)	64
One of the countless settlement certificates by which the Poor Law was administered (Essex Record Office)	109
Children's Home boys in 1908 (lent by Mrs E. Buncombe)	132
Ashdon village schoolteachers in 1904 (lent by Mrs M. Eason)	195
Dorothy and Tom Collins displaying hailstones after the great storm of 1913 (lent by Brig. T. Collins)	217
Mr Eason's General Store (lent by Brig. T. Collins)	235
The Ashdon Fire Brigade (lent by Mrs A. Alexander)	242
The end of the Labourers' Strike, 1914 (lent by Mrs H. Marsh)	265
Mrs Luddington distributing prizes at the 1948 Annual Flower Show (lent by Mrs E. Buncombe)	291
Waltons after the fire (lent by Mrs E. Buncombe)	302
'Brother' Joslin in 1953 (lent by Mrs I. Cooper)	327

Acknowledgements

In a complex project of this nature, I have incurred all manner of debts of gratitude and the first of these are to the many past and present inhabitants of Ashdon who, without exception, welcomed me into their homes and dispensed hospitality as generously as they expounded their views. In strictly alphabetical order, they were as follows:

Constance Albon, William Albon, Noreen Allan, Elsie Allgood, Florence Anderson, Bertie Bartram, Lionel Bartram, Joy Bidwell, Lawrence Bidwell, Leslie Bidwell, Eileen Buncombe, Ella Chapman, Germaine Clark, Audrey Clothier, Gerald Clothier, Dorothy Collins, Ivy Cooper, Ronald Cooper, Garry Dale, Brenda Double, John Double, Mabel Eason, Richard Eason, Phyllis Elam, Donald Elsdon, Doris Everitt, Herbert Farrant, Catharine Field, George Fisher, Audrey Ford, Emily Ford, Dennis Ford, Robert Furze, Ethel Gilbey, Mary Goodwin, Dorothy Homewood, Arthur Kemp, Walter Lane, Leila Luddington, William Mallett, Hilda Marsh, Leonard Martin, Frank Moss, Nellie Moss, Charles Peploe, Gemma Rhodes, Kenneth Rhodes, John Stobbs, Susanna Stobbs, Dorothy Steel, Mary Swan, Michael Swan, Michael Chetwynd Talbot, Sir Eric Thompson, James Threadgold, Anne Vestey, Edmund Vestey, Kitty Vinall, James White, Nancy Witty, Barbara Wright, Michael Yorke.

I am very grateful also to the following: to Victor Gray, County Archivist of Essex, for invaluable editorial advice and for seeing the book through the press; the staff of the Essex Record Office, Chelmsford, and Nancy Briggs in particular, for their unfailing courtesy and efficiency in providing much archive material; Mary Whiteman of the Essex County Library, Saffron Walden, for most helpful advice on local books and contacts; Alan Bidwell and Annette Bidwell for the loan of dissertations they each wrote on Ashdon for their Colleges of Education; Andrew Butcher, Patrick Collinson, Gordon Mingay and David Shaw of the University of Kent at Canterbury for invaluable help with the locating and translating of documents; James Styles of the Photographic Unit of the University of Kent Library for skilfully transforming so many faded old photographs into glossy modern prints; Linda Pargeter and Muriel Waring of Rutherford College, together with the Audio-Visual Aids

Department of the University of Kent for their considerable help in transcribing cassette tape-recordings into type; Sheila Hawkins, Mary Thomas and Eve Hurste of Rutherford College for so cheerfully and expeditiously typing fair copies from my elaborate manuscript; my wife and sons for uncomplainingly enduring regular periods of disruption to our family life.

To three other people, I owe a very particular debt of gratitude, not only for so unfailingly opening their own doors to me whenever I needed to visit the village but also because their considerable diplomatic skills succeeded in opening all sorts of other doors for me. Without Ann Alexander, the work would not have been begun; without Tom and Morwenna Collins it would not have been continued and without the regular encouragement and practical assistance of all three, it could never have been completed. Once completed, it could never have been published without the generous financial assistance of the following: the Council of Management of the Marc Fitch Fund, Dorothy Collins, Thomas Collins, H.V. Feldman, Kin McIntosh and Edmund Vestey. I am deeply indebted to them all and hope when they finally read the book they were prepared to back, without even seeing the typescript, they will feel their confidence was not entirely misplaced.

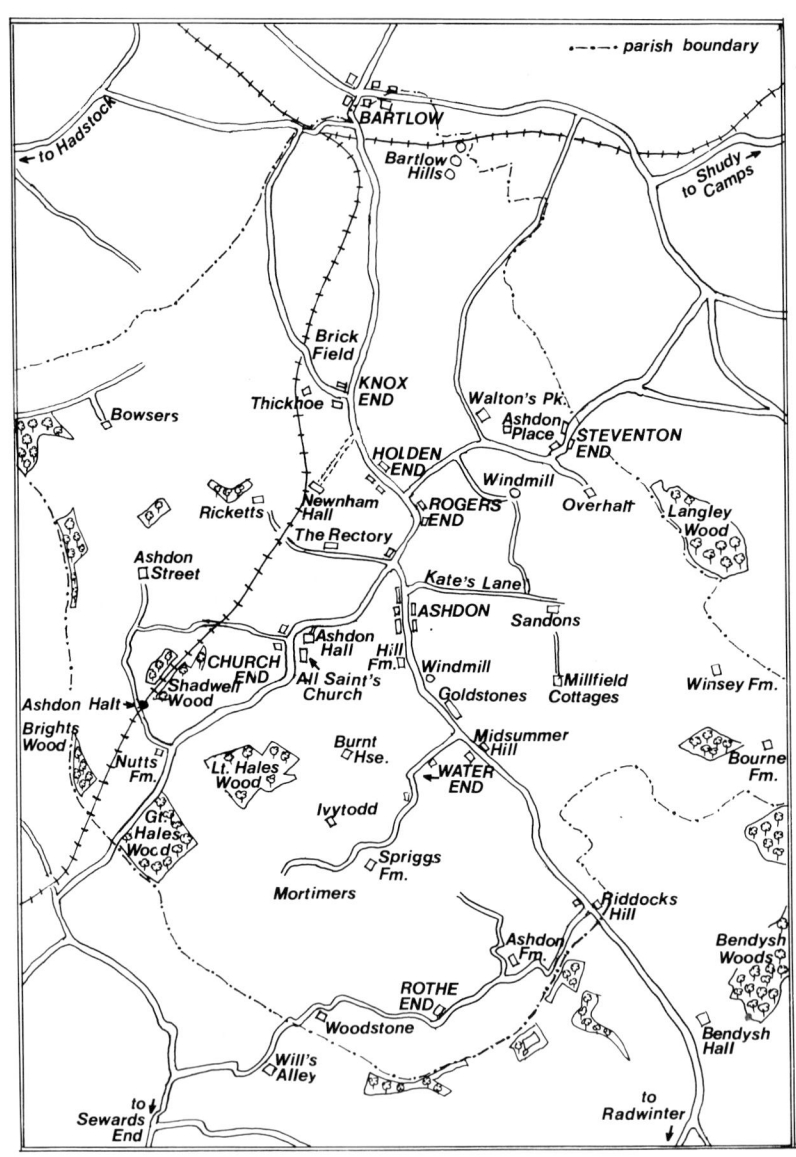

Ashdon in the early years of the century.

1
Writing about Ashdon

> What thou lovest well remains, the rest is dross
> What thou lov'st well shall not be reft from thee
> What thou lov'st well is thy true heritage . . .
>   *Ezra Pound:* Homage to Sextus Propertius

There is a book to be written about my long involvement with Ashdon, about how and why, though I've never been more than a transient visitor, it was once for me the most important place on this earth, about how and why it became so inextricably involved with my equally enduring preoccupation with that unique novel, *Le Grand Meaulnes* — but this is not that book. This is my 'other' Ashdon book, the one completed for a friend who had planned to write it in her own particular way but who died before it was properly begun.

Her name was Mabel Cliff and she was the wife of a farmer to whom I was first sent, as a schoolboy on a working holiday from my London grammar school, to help gather in the harvest in the summer of 1944. She was devoted to Ashdon: she was born there, went to school there, married there, lived and worked there all her life, died there and now lies buried there in the little churchyard up on the hill of the ash trees which gives the village its name. Love of the village and love of words were just two of the many elements which kept our friendship green and growing for nearly a quarter of a century; the two finally came together in November 1966, two years after her husband had retired and their farm had passed into other hands. She wrote to me:

> Now at last I'll be able to do some of the things I've wanted to do all my life. There's plenty of gardening, which you know I love, but you can't do that in the winter. So I thought I'd finally take the advice you gave me all those years ago and write about my past. Can't remember the exact words you said.

> Something about each of us being the World's Number 1 expert on the subject of our own life-story. Well, I got myself a notebook and I've just written the first two sides. That's as far as I've got. Sure there's a lot more to come . . .

On 18th December 1966, she wrote again:

> If ever I can get through with writing down my life-story, I'd like you to correct it for me, perhaps even re-write it . . . Just think, Robert, I can first remember farming when corn was cut with scythes. I can remember Father cutting the corn when we had the small farm I was born on. Midsummer Hill, it was called. Lovely name. From hand-cutting to binder and then to combine. The high old wagons for carting. The 'clonk-clonk' of the wooden wheels. The 'whoa-whoa' and 'Giddup' you could hear all around as the boy leading the cart moved on to the next shock. My mother drawing up water from the well to make her butter. The big bake-up once a week in the big brick oven heated by a faggot of wood. The times I've seen!
> We could make quite a story out of this — Ashdon as it used to be, what it's like now, where it's going next. I lie awake in bed sometimes and think about it all. I can remember my feelings about this and that at various times. If we could only find the right words it would be as good as some of the trash now being made into books. We'll show them . . .

We never did find 'the right words'. On 19 September 1968, after much suffering, she died. James Cliff did not long survive her. At the end of November 1970, he too died of cancer, and was buried beside his wife and his parents in Ashdon churchyard. It was only at that point, trying to come to terms with the realisation that I was not going to see either of them *ever* again, that I resolved to write this book. I very soon found myself confronted with a formidable array of problems, the first of which was how to match the only two pages of the Ashdon book that Mabel Cliff was ever able to write.

They read as follows:-

> A lovely summer's day in the year 1906. I, a small girl not yet old enough for school, was lying face down intently watching a dragonfly emerge from its chrysallis. It had crawled out of

the pound, an ugly, fearsome looking creature and had fastened itself to a swaying piece of grass. Slowly, the sulphur-yellow insect shed its ugly coat and hung there in the sun and gradually, beautiful colours covered its body as though some masterpainter had deftly stroked it with his brush. The wings became transparent; soon it would fly away. The weeping willow branches swayed softly in the breeze, caressing the water as though it too was glad to be alive. On the far side of the pond, knee-deep in mud, stood my Father's two cows, Betsy and Dolly, side by side but facing opposite directions, so that their tails could brush the flies from each other's eyes. The air was alive with the hum of insects. Swarms of bees were busy in the field of beans the other side of the hedge. Larks vied with each other in singing and climbing. Suddenly a voice called:

'An-na! An-na! An-na! where *are* you?'

It was my mother coming to see where I was. How *could* I call back and disturb the magic of it all? . . . It's no use, I'd have to go. Too late, she's found me.

'Why didn't you answer me? I've told you scores of times not to come near this pond. One of these days, an old woman will come up out of the middle of the pond and pull you in.'

I made no reply. I couldn't tell her what a wonderful place it was. She wouldn't have understood. The old woman never frightened me. I knew it would be some days before I could come back again. A careful watch would be kept on my movements. I would play around the buildings, collect hen and turkey feathers and pretend they were families: the wing feathers were the Daddies, the tail feathers the Mummies and the small ones their children. My sisters had shown me how to make houses for them by sweeping dust into little banks for the walls of the rooms. We spent many hours playing thus.

* * *

My mother was churning butter, patiently turning a handle in a wooden churn standing on the kitchen-table. Four wooden arms like a windmill turned the cream inside until the fat separated from the butter-milk. She then came to the well in the garden, let the bucket down on its long chain until it hit the water far below, then slowly wound it up, full of ice-cold water. The butter was washed and washed in this then made into half-pound pats to be sold. The well was another forbidden territory.

Soon I would be able to walk along the road to meet my father who would be coming home from the field furthermost away, where he had been cutting hay. He would lift me on to the back seat and I would hold on to the arms and ride home. Mother was always more worried than usual at hay-time. To gather the hay in good condition meant good winter's feed for the cows. Good food meant good butter. She often quoted: 'You've got to put it into a cow before you can get it out'.

Given that these pages are merely a first draft and conceding that I am strongly prejudiced in their favour, I still feel that they might have grown into yet another successful book about Ashdon. To date, there have been three of these. The actor and novelist Anthony Thorne lived in a cottage on Ashdon's northern border in the thirties and while there, wrote *Cabbage Holiday* (1940) where Ashdon features prominently in the thinnest of disguises. Spike Mays spent his boyhood in the village between 1914 and 1924, in a cottage just five minutes walk from Thorne's, and has recorded his impressions in the widely acclaimed *Reuben's Corner* and the rather less publicized *Five Miles from Bunkum* (1972), written in collaboration with fellow Ashdonian, Christopher Ketteridge, son of the village's master builder. The ideal solution, in my view, would have been to match these books with a collection of Mabel Cliff's writings and/or a biography but this was simply not possible: she had no close confidante, kept no journal, left few letters.

The obvious solution was to attempt the next best thing and compile a *collage* of the period in which she grew up, drawing on the memoirs of her surviving contemporaries. Accordingly, from the autumn of 1971 onwards, solving as best I could the additional problems of having to operate from a base over a hundred miles away in Canterbury and of needing to devote most of my time and energy to teaching and academic administration, I began tape-recording interviews and as wide a cross-section of the Ashdon community as I could persuade to talk to me. In fact, they needed no persuading, there wasn't a single refusal and, in the course of the next five years, I recorded seventy seven interviews. This posed further problems, not only in transcribing, of editing and of shaping and grouping, but also of anticipating the criticism that I was merely copying Ronald Blythe's *Akenfield*. I was and still am ready to counter that charge. I would simply say that while I have always admired Blythe's book, as far as the technique of interviewing country folk is concerned, I feel rather more indebted to the late George Ewart Evans whose comparatively under-valued interviews with some of those same Suffolk villagers were well known to me some years before Blythe's book was published. I would further have observed that, unlike *Akenfield*, which is an adroitly fashioned composite portrait deriving its features from more than one Suffolk village, my own study had been based on interviews with people living within the parish boundaries and that Ashdon, unlike Akenfield, can actually be located on the map.

In the event, I fairly soon decided that my study should not be confined to edited interviews. While these solved the problem of reconstituting Mabel Cliff's Edwardian childhood, they left quite unanswered the whole array of questions about Ashdon's more distant past. When and how was it first settled? How did its ancient inhabitants fill their lives? How, over the centuries, did the community evolve. What evidence is there of continuity? And what of change? The pursuit of answers to these and related questions threatened at first to create more problems than it promised to solve. There rapidly proved to be too much rather than too little archive material, some unearthed for me by ever-helpful Ashdonians, the great bulk of it superbly catalogued and impeccably husbanded in the Essex Record Office at Chelmsford with further documents in the Public Record Office which was, in the early seventies, still in Chancery Lane. The problem of locating and transcribing the village records was fairly readily solved but the problem of appreciating the true significance of all I was amassing and of placing it within the larger context of its time proved more challenging. Such skills as I possess have to do with the communicating of my pleasure in literature; my formal instruction in the techniques of history and historiography was terminated with what used to be called the General School Certificate. I had to manage as best I could with an intensive course of reading prescribed for me by University colleagues and, from almost the very outset, I had to plod on with the daunting knowledge that yet another book on Ashdon was being written by a former resident of the village and a professional historian to boot. This is Angela

Green, former Chief Archivist of the County of Berkshire, who has been working on the official history of Ashdon since 1950. Her study, which is due to be published shortly, clearly cannot fail to be authoritative. Anxious not to trespass too far or too long on her preserves, I have left the legal minutiae to her and drawn, as well as I have been able, the broad outlines. Each time I have transcribed a document, I have tried briefly, not only to evaluate its significance for the evolving Ashdon community but to situate it in the social or legal context of its time. I hope — doubtless vainly — that this will prove neither too simplistic for the specialist nor too fussy for the amateur.

Towards the gratifying large number of more ancient chroniclers of aspects of Ashdon's past, I have obeyed the same self-restricting ordinance that I observed in my interviewing: I have confined myself to the testimony or the case-histories of authentic Ashdon residents. This has enabled me to quote from the writings of Dr. W.M. Palmer because as well as being a distinguished antiquarian, he was Ashdon's general medical practitioner for the first quarter of the present century. The one exception I have made to my self-imposed rule has been in the case of William Harrison who was Rector of Radwinter from 1558 till his death in 1593.

The peace of old Ashdon

In the middle of the eighteenth century, one could apparently still see, painted on a window in Radwinter Rectory, over the initials W.H. and set against a background of 'the sun in his glory', the figure of a hare *couchant*; this was a visual conundrum, the solution to which was 'Hare i' sun = Harrison'. The perpetrator of a pun so appalling is clearly not to be treated altogether lightly but he deserves the attention of posterity for reasons even more significant. He was the author of the *Description of England* (1577) as lively and as informative a work as those other ancient chronicles, Bede's *Historia Ecclesiastica Gentis Anglorum* (731 A.D.), Henry of Huntingdon's *Historia Anglorum* (1154) or Ranulf Higden's early fourteenth-century *Polychronicon*. Harrison has a colourful, often pungent prose style, and a magpie's eye for any bright fragment of arcane erudition; he offers all manner of tart observations on the life and times of his Elizabethan contemporaries. Insofar as many of his comments on the rural scene were based on direct observations made at Radwinter, they are as likely as not to apply to Ashdon, the parish immediately adjoining his own and with the rector of which he shared the pastoral care of more than one manor. I hope I may be forgiven, therefore, in using him to swell my cloud of witnesses. Together, I hope, we may call back yesterday and bid time return.

2
The Limits of History

> What we know of the past is mostly not worth knowing. What is worth knowing is mostly uncertain. Events in the past may roughly be divided into those which probably never happened and those which did not matter.
> W.R. Inge: Assessments and Anticipations

The beauty of Ashdon is, like its character, more than ordinarily elusive. It can boast no opulent stately home or great sweep of formal gardens to attract the tourist trade. It possesses no central reed-fringed pool or cobbled square around which its prize exhibits can be put on display for the delectation of the casual visitor. As you drive through one or other of its main thoroughfares to or from Saffron Walden or Cambridge or Haverhill, you will, at most, receive an impression of neatly clipped hedges, trim lawns and well maintained cottages of mainly modern vintage, between the vistas of prosperous farmlands and wooded slopes. On the other hand, should you decide to alight and linger for an hour or so, any reasonable guide book will direct you to those picturesque features deemed worthy of the antiquarian's notice: the early seventeenth-century 'Rose and Crown' inn at the village-centre, with its showpiece dining-room adorned with authentic Jacobean wall-paintings; the Conservative Club opposite, formerly the 'White Horse' public-house, a seventeenth-century thatched cottage with a three hundred year old strip of delicate floral plaster-work on its west front; the sixteenth-century Tudor Croft, once Little Sandons Farmhouse, less than a hundred yards distant along the road to Radwinter, with all its timber framing dramatically exposed; the mid-eighteenth-century post-mill, meticulously restored in 1973, half a mile out from the village centre on a high field to the north-east; the fourteenth-century church and impeccably restored sixteenth-century Guildhall a mile away up the steep hill to the south; a generous provision of thatched cottages, all two or three hundred years old, dotting each of the main roads and several of the side-lanes close to the heart of the village — all of these are readily visible and well worthy of your close attention but if you then depart, having looked at nothing more, you will have missed quite the loveliest places in the parish.

Nearly all the most picturesque farmhouses, all bearing clear evidence of their seventeenth-century origins are, like Goldstones, some distance from the village centre or, like Bowsers or Ivytodd or Overhall or Ricketts or Ashdon Street, either far out in the fields or, like the gracious, three hundred year old Rectory, attainable only after following the course of a narrow twisting lane. Just such a lane, Kate's Lane, more than a mile in length, winds its way out to Sandons Farm which will be special to me forever because that was where the foot of the rainbow used to touch the earth. The 'Clays', an impressive, basically eighteenth-century residence, is but a few yards from the 'Rose and Crown' but it can only partially be glimpsed behind its high wall of brick abutting the main road to Saffron Walden. The beautiful gardens in front of the cottages out at Water End are permanently on display to anyone prepared to journey out the two miles from the village centre to survey them. The no less lovely gardens of Ashdon Hall, hard by the parish church, with its patrician trees and its proud sweep of lawn sloping gently down to the long, thin rectangle of moat and the shrubbery beyond, is totally hidden from public view behind high hedges and lofty walls. The same is true of the heronry, out at Waltons Park, where, in the dying summer of 1947, I attended my own *fête étrange* and saw my very first kingfisher.

Not only are many of these lovely features well secluded, they are also widely scattered. Because of the curvature of the hills, the profusion of hedges and copses and the serpentine course followed by the main roads and the by-ways, there is no single vantage-point where one can stand on Ashdon earth and survey the parish as a whole. Of the permanent residents, few save the postman or the dedicated pony-trekker perambulates its bounds in the course of the year. Over the past few decades a number of what are obviously ultra-modern houses have been built on either side of the three main roads which radiate from the village centre but these scarcely conceal the fact that, essentially, the community is made up of a rich profusion of isolated farmsteads and little clusters of older cottages called 'Ends': Church End, Holden End, Knox End, Rock End, Rogers End, Steventon End, Water End, each with its distinctive character and idiosyncratic loyalties. Very rarely will habitués of the 'Bonnet' Inn at Steventon End descend the mile into the heart of the village to sup their ale at the 'Bricklayers' Arms' or the 'Rose and Crown'. In the opening decade of this century, while the Baptists held their official service at the Chapel near the village centre, a separate Baptist service, with portable harmonium, used regularly to be held in the open air by the little bridge at Water End. This distinctive separatism has never gone as far as open conflict, but it has been a feature of the Ashdon scene for centuries. It is an authentic historical phenomenon which is best understood in terms of the village's geography.

Four natural features blend together to create the beauty of the Ashdon landscape: river, hills, woods and fields. Of these, the multicoloured patchworks of fields, the principal source of the region's wealth, are the most subject to change, the most recent to appear on the scene and, together with the scattered buildings of various shapes and various ages, they are all man-made. Over the centuries, with infinite patience and untold labour, they were wrested from the woods which once entirely dominated the land and its inhabitants.

Remnants of those woods still survive around Ashdon's borders: stretching along the north-east perimeter of the parish, between Ashdon and Castle and Shudy Camps, is Langley Wood, its wealth of wild nuts and fruit together with small animals and birds all providing an eloquent reminder of the well stocked larder it must have been for the early settlers. In the south, straddling the hilly road from Ashdon to Saffron Walden, are Brights Wood, Little Hales Wood and Great Hales Wood. Till recently, the most venerable trees in the latter were the elms on its southernmost reaches but these have now been ravaged by Dutch Elm disease. Formerly its special glory was its array of truly ancient oak trees but today none of the Great Hales oaks is more than one hundred and fifty years old. The one solitary reminder of that lost magnificence and the oldest tree in the whole of Ashdon is the great oak which stands in the paddock of Ashdon Hall beside the main road at the top of Church Hill. Before it was lopped it was a sight to behold, all of sixty feet high; at a height of five feet it still had a circumference of nineteen feet eight inches. It is today well over five hundred years old, the only Ashdon oak to survive the Great Felling when the great oak trees of the district were all cut down to provide timbers for the roof of the chapel of King's College, Cambridge. Further along the road between Ashdon and Saffron Walden are the seventeen and a half acres of Shadwell Wood (the name means 'the Wood of the Cold Spring'), identifiable as an area of 'ancient woodland' or manorial wood from the Middle Ages by the sinuous ditch and wood bank around the side of it and the oxlip and herb paris that grow within it. Since 1969, it has been maintained by the Essex Naturalists' Trust.

Different sort of evidence that the region was once much more densely wooded is provided in a number of local names. The name Ashdon itself means 'hill of the ash trees' just as neighbouring Bartlow means the 'hill of the birch trees'; Bowsers, name of one of the principal farms in the district, designates 'land cleared by burning', Rothe End signifies 'a clearing', Thickhoe means 'thicket', while Ridducks Hill is a corruption of 'Red Oaks Hill'. When you mount this hill on the road that winds from Ashdon to Radwinter, you will be rewarded with a fine view of the Bendysh Woods which fringe the south-eastern edge of the parish but you will look in vain for any vestige of the lost community of Bendysh itself which, according to the nineteenth-century historian T. Wright (*History & Topography of Essex*, 1836, Vol. 3), vanished clear away sometime during the Dark Ages.

Not far from Ridducks Hill, within the parish of Ashdon, is the source of the River Bourne which flows through the centre of the village on its northward course to join the Granta at Bartlow and flows on into the Cam. If, during my years at Cambridge, I never missed a day's walk through the Backs, it was not merely because of the majesty of the buildings and bridges: it was also because somewhere through those dark waters ran the shy stream from *le domaine perdu*. In the summer, the Bourne is normally little more than a modest trickle, scarcely covering its stony bed but because, in the south of the parish, it provides catchment for the valley slopes of the East Anglian Heights, its character can vary dramatically with the changing seasons. In winter it can be transformed into a *bona fide* river, three or four feet deep and anything up to six feet wide;

before it was properly channelled beneath the new bridge due north of the village centre, it used spectacularly to overflow the main road to Bartlow. It is quite unnavigable and for centuries has in itself had no economic value whatsoever, but in bygone ages its presence must assuredly have been the crucial factor that persuaded nomadic tribesfolk to end their wandering, pitch camp and make the first primitive settlement near its banks. While the surrounding woods offered ample stocks of food and materials for, and the slopes of the valley afforded protection from the vagaries of the weather and the attentions of hostile marauders, the unobtrusive little river with the most unassuming of names — Bourne simple means 'river' — provided all-important drinking-water and a regular bonus of trout. It has been suggested that the widened banks of the Bourne, down in the valley below the church, mark the site of the fish-pond or 'stew' of the original village settlement, fish being a regular supplement for the poorer villagers' diet in the Middle Ages just as deer and pigeons from their private dovecotes were a source of extra food for the rich.

Such tangible evidence as has ever come to light of earlier settlements in Ashdon was unearthed between 1832 and 1852 when parts of the area were intensively investigated by qualified archaeologists. In September 1852, the Honourable R.C. Neville discovered traces of a small Roman villa on Great Copt Hill, part of Bowser's Farm which was then owned by Lord Maynard. It had been much mutilated by its last inhabitants and Neville surmised that it had probably first been occupied and subsequently vandalized by Saxons. A coin of King Alfred was discovered in the same field some years later. In October 1852, Neville uncovered portions of another Roman villa just beyond the Ashdon parish boundary in the grounds of Bartlow House; these could well have formed part of a more extensive building which came briefly to light when the Cambridge-Marks Tey railway-line was unceremoniously driven through the site with cavalier disregard for the priceless historical booty just beneath it. The railway-labourers claimed to have disinterred fifteen skeletons and what were most probably the foundations of an ancient building but no systematic attempt was ever made to follow this up. In the immediate vicinity, Neville discovered three hundred and fifty Roman coins in the course of three weeks, 'almost entirely of the lowest Empire, many exceedingly small, probably imitations of

Roman money by the local tribes'. In 1932, another archaeologist, C.G. Brocklebank submitted to the British Museum three hundred and five coins dug up from the same area, and these proved to range from Claudius to the House of Theodosius. Dr. W.M. Palmer collected twenty seven, ranging from Trajan to Magnus Maximus. The abundance of these particular coins would seem to indicate that there was a settlement in the region somewhere in the fourth century A.D. Other discoveries point to settlements of appreciably earlier date.

Quite the most spectacular survivals from Ashdon's more remote past are the burial mounds in the far north of the parish which have come to be known as the Bartlow Hills. Originally there were at least eight of these but one was destroyed in Elizabethan times and, to serve the needs of agriculture, three more were destroyed in 1832 before they could be examined. The four that survive extend in a straight line running from north to south and they are exactly thirteen feet nine inches apart; the largest is forty five feet high and one hundred and forty four feet in diameter at the base; the smallest is eighteen feet high and eighty feet in diameter at the base. Their present-day appearance is decidedly unprepossessing: they are disfigured by stunted trees and by the ravages of tourists and rabbits but when they were excavated by John Gage between 1832 and 1840 they yielded up some of the most fascinating treasure ever

The Bartlow Hills, a curiosity for 18th-century gentlemen

discovered in Britain. Expert examination of the material, some of which was minutely analyzed by Dr. Michael Faraday (discoverer of electric and magneto-electric induction) established that the barrows were the funeral mounds of important local personages and that they were buried there in all probability between 80 and 100 A.D.

The excavations uncovered fascinating evidence of Roman burial rites. When the dead were ceremoniously buried, milk and wine were offered as ritual libations and the cock, sacred to Apollo, Aesculapius and Mars, was sacrificed to the Lares, once the Roman gods of the farmland. Each of the mounds contained at its centre a regular walled grave. What once had been wooden chests had long since rotted away but still surviving, in an excellent state of preservation, were glass jars full of burnt human bones, urns and pitchers which had once contained the ritual wine and earthenware vessels containing the bones of the sacrificial cock. In one of the barrows was a beautiful spherical container, enamelled throughout with a design of leaves and foliage in red, green and blue, and a magnificent bronze lamp with a bold acanthus leaf rising at the back to form an ornamental handle. In whose honour these sepulchral goods were so reverently assembled and the high mounds so proudly raised, we cannot tell. They are beyond the limits of history where only the novelist or the necromancer will dare to tread.

These are by no means the only questions about Ashdon's more distant past which seem fated never to be given a conclusive answer. Almost as intriguing as what Gage discovered in the heart of the barrows was what he noted about their exterior. In the course of excavating the largest barrow in 1835, he noted that the mound was made up of regular layers of chalk and surface soil. He deduced that the barrow-builders had not quarried chalk specially for the ceremony but had merely scraped up the surface of the surrounding land. In this surface soil were many worked flint chips together with some flint implements and from this he inferred that before the barrows were built, which is to say before 80 A.D., the site had been occupied by more primitive settlers. Who they were and how they lived are matters for conjecture.

Whoever they were, at least the evidence for their existence is incontrovertible. Whether or not they had near neighbours two miles away to the south, on top of the hill where Ashdon Church now stands, is rather less certain. The author of the impressively scholarly church guide, Philip Dickinson F.S.A., does not entirely rule out the possibility. Accepting that it is important to give even an approximate date for the foundation of the settlement beside the church, he comments that its 'position is suggestive of pre-Christian times and that it might be that a pagan temple once stood on the site of the church . . . Special trees were often venerated by the heathen and the place-name [Ashdon] may be a reminder of an ancient cult destroyed by Christianity'. Pope Gregory certainly advised Augustine to adapt existing sacred sites on converting the English so gods other than the Christian one may well once have been worshipped there. The founding fathers of Ashdon's ancient church may conceivably have planned wiser than they knew when they decided to dedicate it to *All* Saints, but what those old gods were, how, when and by whom they were worshipped are questions we are not able to answer any more than we are able to locate with anything like precision the true site of the battle of Assandum.

There have been three crucial battles on English soil in which the prize was the Crown of all England and in which the contenders have been a home-based King and a challenger from overseas. Two of these are well known, or certainly used to be, to every school child: Bosworth, where in 1485, Richard III's body was left dead on the field and the victorious Henry Tudor became Henry VII, and Hastings, where, in 1066, Harold was slain and the Norman usurper, William, Duke of Normandy, became William I of England. The third battle, less well known but no less violent in character and equally decisive in its outcome, was fought at Assandun on 18 October 1016, when the flower of the English nobility was cut down and the Danish path to the throne was left unobstructed.

Cnut's claim to the Crown had been vigorously pressed and as vigorously resisted for some time previously. In 1012, he had overrun Northumbria. Late in 1015, he sailed back from Denmark with a fleet of one hundred and sixty ships determined to conquer the whole of England. After plundering the south coast, he over-ran much of the south-east and laid siege to London. In the course of this siege, on 23rd April 1016, Æthelred (called the 'Unready') died. As though they were impatient to make up for his forty years of vacillating rule, the England powers promptly elected two strong Kings to take his place. A majority of the members of the Witan (or national assembly) met at Southampton and elected Cnut as King;

the remaining members of the Witan met in beleaguered London and, in conclave with its leading citizens, offered the crown to Edmund Ironside. In the months that followed, each of these formidable adversaries strove to eliminate his rival.

Edmund had decidedly the better of the opening exchanges: first at Selwood (in Somerset) then at Sherston (in Wiltshire), the Danes were put to flight. Next, Edmund's forces succeeded in raising the siege of London and once again, in driving the Danes before them, but conclusive victory still eluded them. What happened after that is best described in the nearest thing we have to a contemporary report, the account provided in the *Anglo-Saxon Chronicle* (1961 version, translated by Professor Dorothy Whitelock):

> King Edmund collected all his army for the fourth time and crossed the Thames at Brentford and went into Kent. And the Danish army fled before him with their horses into Sheppey. The king killed as many of them as he could overtake and Ealdorman Edric came to meet the king at Aylesford. No greater folly was ever agreed to than that was. The army went again inland into Essex and proceeded into Mercia and destroyed everything in its path.
>
> When the king learnt that the army had gone inland, for the fifth time he collected all the English nation; and pursued them and overtook them in Essex [the original Chronicle next states *ae^t paere dune pe man haet Assandun* which Professor Whitelock translates as 'at the hill which is called Ashingdon' but which for the moment, I prefer to render as 'Assandun'] and they stoutly joined battle there. Then Ealdorman Edric did as he had often done before: he was the first to start the flight with the Magonsaete [the people of Herfordshire] and thus betrayed his liege lord and all the people of England. There Cnut had the victory and won for himself all the English people. There was Bishop Eadnorth [of Dorchester] killled, and Abbot Wuflsige [of Ramsey] and Ealdorman Aelfric [of Hampshire] and Godwine, the Earldorman of Linsey and Ulfcetel of East Anglia, and Aethelweard, son of Earldorman Aethelwine [of East Anglia] , and all the nobility of England was there destroyed.

King Edmund survived but, in the words of another translator, with 'all the flower of the Angle race destroyed', the only course left open to him was flight. He made for the west, Cnut gave chase and caught up with him at the Isle of Olaney, in the Severn, near Deerhurst, in Gloucestershire. They agreed, quite amicably by all accounts, to divide the Kingdom between them, but a few months later, Edmund was dead. Some believed he was poisoned; one chronicler, William of Malmesbury, reported that he was assassinated by two of his servants who 'drove an iron hook into his posteriors as he was sitting down for a necessary purpose'. Whatever the manner of his untimely end, it was universally believed that his brother-in-law Eadric was the instigator, by common consent, the most avaricious and most treacherous man of the age. Soon afterwards, Eadric himself was killed in London — 'very rightly' in the view of the *Anglo-Saxon Chronicle* — and his body was thrown over the city wall or into the Thames without compunction. Cnut, whose degree of involvement with Eadric's machinations has never been established, was left as undisputed ruler of the whole kingdom.

Historians have long been agreed on the importance of the battle of Assandun — it confirmed Cnut in power and brought nineteen years of firm and effective rule — but, to this day, they remain bitterly divided over where precisely it was fought. For centuries, there have been two principal contenders: Ashdon, near the north-west frontier of present-day Essex and Ashingdon, some thirty five miles to the south, on the southern side of the River Crouch. The supporters of each site have sometimes seemed as bitterly opposed to each other as those of Cnut and Edmund Ironside, but so far neither has won a truly decisive victory. The Ashingdon cause would, for the moment, seem to be in the ascendant, with a State visit from the King of Denmark in the mid-seventies to the supposed site of his illustrious ancestor's spectacular victory but, with the greatest possible respect, one has to say that this merely demonstrates that he and his royal advisers have been rather too readily persuaded. The only truth that emerges from centuries of disputation is further confirmation of the old adage that 'while History may or may not repeat itself, historians undoubtedly repeat one another'.

The root of the problem is the unreliability and the vagueness of the earliest evidence on which all subsequent arguments have had to be based. The *Anglo-Saxon Chronicle* creates more problems than it solves: all it indicates is that the battle took place on or near to the 'hill of the ash-trees' or, much less likely, 'the hill of the asses', somewhere in Essex; no mention is made of either a river or proximity to the sea. One may reasonably infer that Edmund's armies overtook Cnut's while these were still on their way to Mercia, or even in the act of plundering, and this would point to a site far inland, some considerable distance from Cnut's base on Sheppey or by the River Crouch. The chronicles written by monks later in the eleventh century provide a number of details not to be found in the *Anglo-Saxon Chronicle* but no clues that are truly conclusive. Thus, Florence of Worcester reports that when Edmund had gone back into West Saxony, 'Cnut led his forces into East Saxony and again went into Mercia to pillage, ordering his army to commit greater enormities than before. They were not backward in obeying his orders; and after having beheaded all who fell into their hands, burnt numerous vills and laid waste the fields, returned laded with spoil to their ships. Edmund Ironside, king of the English, pursued them with the army which he had collected from all parts of England, and came up with them on their march at a hill called Assandun which means "The Ass's hill".' An almost identical account is provided by another eleventh-century monk, Simeon of Durham in his *Historia Regum Anglorum* who describes Cnut's soldiers hastening to 'return to their ships enriched with great abundance of plunder' and being overtaken 'as they were escaping at the hill called Assandun, that is, "The Ass's Hill".' What needs noting about these two accounts is that while in some respects they are close enough to suggest they derive from the same common source and are both quite wrong in translating 'Assandun' as 'the Hill of the Asses' — something it never has meant — there is one crucial difference between them. Had Cnut's men indeed 'returned to their ships' or were they 'overtaken on the march'? Were the Danes advancing into Mercia or retreating towards the estuary of the Crouch? If the latter question is answered affirmatively, then where were they retreating *from*? Ashingdon is *south* of the river.' To opt for one rather than the other would seem to be, in the last analysis, an arbitrary matter into which the 'professional' historian has no clearer insight than the layman. One can merely observe that in electing to stand and fight, Cnut was acting out of character. On four previous occasions, when faced with Edward's forces he had chosen to withdraw. Here, at Assandun, when his troops were laden with 'great abundance of plunder', he must have had compelling reasons to do so. Common sense surely suggests that he fought because he was obliged to do so, and that he was obliged to do so because he was beyond the reach of his beach-head beside the Crouch, because he was, in fact, closer to Ashdon than to Ashingdon.

The eleventh-century scribes provide another clue, once again tantalizing for being inconclusive, when they describe the aftermath of the battle. One version of the *Anglo-Saxon Chronicle* relates that Cnut decreed that a 'mynster' be constructed at 'Assandun', 'built of stone and lime' for the souls of the men who were there slain'. William of Malmesbury amplifies this by describing how Cnut tried to restore peace throughout this Kingdom by doing all that was in his power for the living and the dead:

> He repaired, throughout England, the monasteries which he had partly injured and partly destroyed by the military incursions of himself or of his father; he built churches in all the places where he had fought and more particularly at Assingdon, and appointed ministers to them who, through the succeeding revolutions of ages, might pray to God for the souls of the persons there slain.

Doubtless because it was meant to mark the greatest of all his victories, the church at 'Assandun' was designed to be no ordinary church and it was consecrated with considerable ceremony. The *Anglo-Saxon Chronicle* reports that in 1020:

> the King went to Assandun and [with him went] the Archbishop Wulfstan [of York — the see of Canterbury being at that time vacant] and Earl Thorkell, and many bishops and also abbots, and many monks with them, and they hallowed the Mynster at Assandun.

One version of the *Anglo-Saxon Chronicle* adds that Cnut then gave the 'mynster' into the keeping of one of his priests, 'whose name was Stigand'. Again this was no ordinary gesture because Stigand is said to have been Cnut's personal chaplain who went on to achieve particular eminence. In 1038, he became Bishop of Elmham; in 1047, he became Bishop of Winchester; in 1052, he became Archbishop of Canterbury; in 1066, it was he, in all probability, who crowned Harold king just before the invasion of the Normans. He is mentioned by name on the Bayeux Tapestry — 'Stigant Archiep[iscopu]s'

— and is represented thereon, in full archiepiscopal attire, blessing the newly crowned King.

No tapestry was ever woven to commemorate Assandun. No weapons have ever been unearthed that would help us locate the battlefield or the mighty *mynster* erected to commemorate it. The only testimony we have that the battle was ever fought or that the *mynster* was ever built is the set of records, sketchy and inconsistent, of a handful of devoted monks, distant in space and time from the events they sought to describe and doubtless dependent on hearsay evidence and the rudiments of legend. It is small wonder that the one fact on which they are all agreed, the name of 'Assandun' is a signpost pointing towards mystery — and, as events were to prove, towards mystification.

No further references of importance are extant on the subject of the great battle till near the end of the sixteenth century when William Camden proceeded to identify the site with some precision. Writing in 1586 in his famous *Britannia* (which bore the grandiloquent subtitle *A Chorographical Description of Great Britain and Ireland together with the adjacent lands*), he declared in his section on southeast Essex:

> Hard by [Billiricay] is *Ashdown*, formerly Assandun — i.e. as Marianus inteprets it, *The Mount of Asses*; famous for a desperate battle in which Edmund Ironside at first had the better of the Danes but afterwards, through treachery, lost the day, together with a great number of his Nobility. In memory of which, we read, that Canutus the Dane built a church here: when, repenting of all the blood he had occasion'd to be spilt, he erected some kind of Religious structure wherever he had engaged in fight.

This passage, the first attempt on record to give Assandun a precise location, calls for a number of comments: no proof is offered for identifying Assandun with 'Ashdown' (what is now Ashingdon); he does not indicate which of the by now ancient chronicles he has consulted and he provides no hard evidence that he even visited the site in person. Though later historians came to treat his work with the unquestioning reverence normally reserved for holy writ, one would do well to bear in mind that when pronouncing on the battle of Assandun he was more remote from the events he was describing than we are today from the Spanish Armada.

Much the same reservations may be made of Raphael Holinshed who published his equally influential *Chronicle* just one year after Camden's *Britannia*, proposing a totally different location for the battle at the extremity of Essex farthest removed from Ashingdon thirty five miles to the north-west:

> Then Cnute with his armie passed over the Thames into Essex and there assembled all his power togither, and began to spoile and waste the countrie on each hand. King Edmund advertised thereof, hasted foorth to succour his people, and at Ashdone in Essex three miles from Saffron Walden, gave battell to Cnute, where after sore and cruell fight continued with great slaughter on both sides a long time, duke Edrike fled to the comfort of the Danes and to the discomfort of the Englishmen . . .

After describing the progress of the battle and calling the roll of the illustrious English dead, Holinshed then proceeds, unlike Camden, to provide some sort of proof for his confident choice of Ashdon as the likely battle-ground:

> In the place where this Field was fought are yet seven or eight Hills, wherein the Carcasses of them that were slain at the same Field were buried, and one of them being dug down of late, there were found two Bodies in a Coffin of Stone, of which one lay with his Head towards the Other's Feet, and many chains of Iron like the Water-Chains of the Bitts of Horses.

The hills, which have for so long been known as the Bartlow Hills, are still a most striking group of tumuli even though only four survive. One can readily appreciate how much more impressive they must have appeared when there were eight of them and how readily it was assumed that they must have been erected to commemorate some out-of-the-ordinary event like an ancient battle. The bodies laid ceremoniously end to end and, more particularly, the accoutrements of the horses must have seemed to clinch the matter and for the next two hundred and fifty years, the Bartlow Hills constituted the prime 'proof' that Ashdon and ancient Assandun were one and the same. Newcourt voiced the convictions of all the Ashdon supporters when he declared, in 1710, in his *Repertorium Ecclesiasticum Parochiale Londinense*:

> Mr. Camden tells us of a place called Barklow, near Cambridgeshire, not above two miles from Ashdon, and therefore not improbably within the verge of these two great Armies, when they fought, famous for four great Barrows, such as our Ancestors us'd to raise to the Memory of such Soldiers as were killed in Battle and their Bodies lost . . . Now, there being no such Monuments of a Battle mentioned by Mr. Camden, or any other Author, that I have read, to be found about Ashdon in Rochford Hundred, I am apt to believe, that this our Ashdon, in the Hundred of Freshwell, and not Ashdowne in the Hundred of Rochford, was the Place . . .

In point of fact, there are (or were) also a number of man-made mounds quite close to Ashdown (or Ashingdon), on the salt-marshes, on the further (north) bank of the River Crouch, and, in the course of time, these were adduced as 'proof' that Ashingdon was the site of the battle after all. The claim was first made in 1789 by Richard Gough in his 'Additions' to Camden's *Britannia*. He began by expressing astonishment that so many antiquaries could be so deluded as to believe that Ashdon could conceivably have been the site of the battle and that 'though they had the authority of Camden against them, they have carried it quite across the county, to the northern extremity, as far from the sea as possible, and in defiance of every circumstance that could fix it there'. As far as Gough was concerned, the evidence for identifying Assandun with Ashingdon was clear for all to see and hear: Ashingdon adjoins the parish of Canewdon (pronounced locally Canewdon) which contains a mound with traces of an ancient camp on the top; five and a half miles to the west of Ashingdon, at the head of navigation on the River Crouch, stands *Battles* Bridge and the mounds on the salt-flats (of which there were then twenty two) were quite obviously the burial grounds of dead warriors.

Gough's peremptory dismissal of Ashdon as the battleground seemed well justified half a century later when the Bartlow Hills were at last properly excavated and proved to contain Anglo-Roman remains. This seemed finally to dispose of Ashdon's claim not only in the 1830s, but a hundred and fifty years later, when the two quite unrelated historical events were juxtaposed in an essay by Angela Green, 'The Bartlow Hills and the Battle of Assandun' (published in Volume 63 of *The Essex Review* in 1954). One remains at a loss to understand how demonstrating that the Bartlow Hills were connected with an era much earlier than the famous battle could quite so conclusively have proved that Ashingdon must have been the battle-site. And confusion was worse confounded in 1925, when Ashingdon's mounds were eventually excavated by Professor Miller Christy and proved to belong to a period several centuries later than Assandun and to have been somehow connected with the salt-making industry. To this day, no adequate explanation has been forthcoming for the two bodies said to have been found near Ashdon in Tudor times together with the 'bitts of horses'. That they have vanished without trace is the more disconcerting because the Romano-British human remains that were excavated from the Bartlow tumuli had been *cremated*. The bodies said to have been dug from those same tumuli, or from tumuli which disappeared in the course of the seventeenth century (but how? and whither?), could conceivably have belonged to another age.

Confusion and contradiction have attended all the other efforts made by antiquarians to settle the controversy. In every case, the arguments advance to establish or refute the claims of one side can be turned against the other. Thus, while it can be strongly argued that the Ashdon area must have been densely wooded in 1016 and so have constituted a most unlikely battleground, it can be reasonably counter-argued that the field beside the Crouch claimed as the Ashingdon battle-site by J.R. Green in his *Conquest of England* was a grass-marsh when he wrote his history in 1883 and must, in the eleventh century, have been a tidal mud-flat on which men would scarcely have been able to walk, let alone engage in mortal combat.

One might have expected that the etymologist might by now have settled the issue once and for all but this is by no means the case. Dr. P.H. Reaney, one of our leading authorities and compiler of the Essex volume for the English Place Name Society argues that 'The identification of Assandun with Ashingdon is, on the whole, consistent with the later development of the name. Assandun cannot lie behind the forms of Ashdon with which it has alternatively been identified'.

This would seem to place excessive trust in the particular form of the name of the battleground that has come down to us via the *Anglo-Saxon Chronicle*. We have been warned to treat that chronicle with some caution by no less an authority than Dorothy Whitelock, latterly Professor of Anglo-Saxon in the University of Cambridge and one of the most recent translators of the ancient history on which the textual arguments are founded:

> In spite of its importance as our oldest manuscript, the value of [the most complete version of the Chronicle] even for the period in which it is a full record must not be overstressed, for it is rather carelessly written and is at least two removes from the original work.

Other documents written at a time quite close to the actual battle serve only to complicate the issue: the Norse poem *Knutsdrapa* by Ottar Svarti (Ottar the Black) praises Cnut for fighting 'beneath the shield' at Assatunum; another work of the same period, written to eulogize Cnut's dead wife Emma speaks of a great battle fought *in Aescenduno loco quod nos Latini montem fraxinorum possum interpretari*. Already, then, we have three variant spellings of the battle-field — Assandun, Assatunum and Aescendum — and, with due respect for Dr. Reaney's formidable erudition, at least one of these, the latter, points more positively towards Ashdon than towards Ashingdon. In the Domesday Survey of 1086, Ashdon is registered as 'Ascenduna' while Ashingdon is listed as 'Nesenduna'.

The firmness with which Dr. Reaney discounts the possibility that Ashdon might have been Assandun or Aescendum is the more surprising in view of the remarkable number of variant spellings he has been able to cull for each of the contending sites from such mediaeval legal documents as charter rolls, assize rolls or the so-called Feet of Fines which were agreements made after disputes over land ownership. What is particularly striking about these variants is not only their rich profusion in each case but the very close similarity between them. Thus, at various times, present-day Ashdon features as Essenduna, Essyndone, Eston, Aston, Assindene, Assyndone, Essedon, Hashedon, Aysshedon and Essyngton; present-day Ashingdon features as Assatunum, Assendon, Essendon, Asington, Assingdon, Assington and Ashendon. On at least one occasion (in 1337) Ashdon is spelled Asshingdon while on another (in 1406) Ashingdon appears as As(s)h(e)don. Quite evidently, any proponent of either cause seeking to found his hypothesis on etymological grounds is building on shifting sands. This is especially true of those who have sought to buttress their arguments with supporting 'evidence' based on the etymology of other places in the vicinity.

Professor Freeman, one of the most enthusiastic of Ashingdon supporters, sought a connection between Canewdon and Canute in his massive *History of the Norman Conquest of England* which was first published in 1867. Speaking of what he describes as the two hills beside the alleged battle-ground on the banks of the Crouch, he declared that 'one still retains the name of Ashington, an easy corruption of the ancient form, while the other, in its name of Canewdon, perhaps preserves the memory of the Danish conqueror himself'. This turns out to be fanciful. Canewdon is listed in the Domesday Book as 'Carenduna' and variously, thereafter, as 'Canendon' or 'Kenewdon': its likeliest derivation is from the name 'Cana', the name meaning 'the hill of Cana's people'. As for 'Battlesbridge', the site favoured by Richard Gough, it would seem to have little or nothing to do with any specific battle but to be associated instead with a once prominent local family named Bataille. Ashdon supporters seeking the assistance of etymology have fared no better: John Oliver the cartographer who wrote 'The Battle Hills' over Bartlow on his map of Essex in 1696 seems to have been indulging in a flight of fancy as was the Ashdon stalwart in 1971 who assured me, in all sincerity, that 'Bartlow means "brought low" on account of the famous battle'!

Attempts to identify Cnut's *mynster* have been marginally more convincing than the arguments to locate the battlefield but they have inevitably included various exercises in whimsy. Holinshed regarded Bartlow Church as Cnut's *mynster* partly because he felt that Ashdon Church was simply too far from the Bartlow Hills and partly because Bartlow Church has a round tower which conveyed what he took to be an authentic Danish flavour. This notion was still being entertained nearly two centuries later by such county historians as Philip Morant who declared in 1768 in his *History of Essex* that Cnut's *mynster* 'could not be the present Church of Ashdon because it stands too far from the field of Battle. Therefore it is with great reason supposed that it was Bartlow Church, which stands near the Hills and hath a round Steeple, being the Danish way of building'. Proximity to the battlefield did not, however, impress Richard Gough as a particularly important criterion because in his 'Additions' to Camden's *Britannia*, he situated Cnut's church at Hockley, some two and a half miles west of Ashingdon, three miles from Battles Bridge where, he argued, the fighting had taken place and two miles south of where he insisted the dead warriors had been buried. As if in conscious reaction to this extravagant wanderlust, other antiquaries have seen in the fabric of their own local parish church Saxon features which have escaped the notice of the accredited experts: in 1867, Benton, a local historian and champion of the Ashingdon cause, asserted that parts of Ashingdon parish church were unmistakenly Saxon; in 1889, addressing members of the Essex Archaeological Society in Bartlow, the then Rector of Ashdon, Dr. H.B. Swete, had the temerity to suggest that Bartlow Church, round tower notwithstanding, might not be Cnut's *mynster* after all. He spoke of 'an old font long disused, until lately forming a door step, and the arch over a stoop for holy water, also recently disclosed [in 1886], of early Norman or pre-Norman workmanship ... The existing Church of Ashdon contains features which point to a much earlier building and which may be due to the Minster which Cnut and all England consecrated in 1020'.

But this was not all. He also described what he had found on the slope which falls quite steeply away immediately below the east window of Ashdon church down into the valley known as Water Lane or Rock Lane:

> Some sixty years ago, as I have learned from old inhabitants, in digging for gravel, graves were found, lying north and south — in large numbers, it was stated, and rude weapons were turned up together with (Roman?) pottery. Of these remains, unfortunately, nothing has been preserved. But in 1882, observing a very large mound at the bottom of the field, I obtained permission from the owner to cut it open; and it was found to consist of tons of lime, containing organic remains, chiefly the bones of the sheep, sheep, ox and horse, mixed with oyster shells and the shells of esculent crawfish or the like. The quantity of these remains was so large as to preclude the idea that the food which they represented had been consumed by the villagers; and it had been suggested, not I think unreasonably, that such a vast heap agrees well with the sup-

position that the army of Cnut just come back from their raid into Mercia discussed their good fare on Ashdon Hill the night before the battle or after the victory was won.

Not an extravagant supposition, certainly, but expert opinion now tends towards the view that the site Dr. Swete describes, with its clearly delineated terraces and its fish-pool in the depths of the little river-valley, marks the site of the original village settlement before Ashdon transplanted its heart to the bottom of Church Hill.

There is, in fact, a very promising candidate for the rôle of Cnut's lost *mynster* and it is none of the churches so far mentioned: it is the parish church of Hadstock, some two miles to the north-west of Ashdon which is to say much the same distance away as the once much favoured Bartlow tumuli. It is incontrovertibly older than any of the rival claimants, parts of it undoubtedly dating from at least the eleventh century, and it is dedicated to St. Botolph, a seventh-century East Anglian abbot who was later canonized. In 1916, it was described in the *Report of the Royal Commission on the Historical Monuments of Essex* as 'a remarkable cruciform church, of pre-Conquest date, with peculiar ornament'. In 1974, when the north transept of the church was excavated, twenty floor levels were uncovered. It was noted that the inpost blocks and outer arch-moulding of the monumental north doorway are decorated with palmette ornaments dating from the early eleventh century and that at the 'crossing' of the nave, highly ornate archways once led into the four arms of the church. In its original form, it must have been quite spectacularly imposing for its humble setting: there was once a central tower of unknown height, which collapsed in the thirteenth century; it was a hundred feet long and sixty feet wide across the transepts. Quite clearly, it was an edifice of considerable importance. There are ground for thinking it was once the church of the lost settlement of Icanho, which was destroyed by marauding Danes in 870 A.D. The lower halves of both the north and south walls of the nave are undoubtedly pre-Danish, and no less undoubtedly were once subject to intense burning which reddened the montas and calcined the flints. Against the last wall of the south transept, an early Saxon grave was discovered which was large and so shallow that the two metre long stone coffin it once contained must mostly have been above ground level. This suggests that the body within must have been that of an important personage, later exhumed, and it is known that this was the fate of St. Botolph's corpse in 970 when it was disinterred, dismembered and distributed to the reliquaries of various monasteries. None of which precludes the Church's having been Cnut's *mynster* or obviates the need convincingly to explain why a church on this scale was constructed in this remote spot before 1066.

In his magisterial essay on 'The Site of Assandun' (*History Studies*, Pergamon Press, Vol. I, 1968, pp. 1-12), Dr. Cyril Hart argues, I think persuasively, that Hadstock Church has by far the most convincing claim yet advanced to have been Cnut's 'church of stone and lime'. Deploying all his authority as one of our leading specialists on early wills and charters, he establishes an impressive number of connections between Ashdon, Hadstock and the monastery of Ely. About 1036, Ashdon was bequeathed to Ely which had purchased the adjacent estate of Hadstock in 1008; many monks from Ely were slain at Assandun, together with their bishop, Eadnoth, and Abbot Wulfsige of Ramsey; one of Cnut's doughtiest warriors, Thurkill the Tall, was made Earl of East Anglia after the battle, built the *mynster* at Assandun and was present at its dedication; soon after being assigned there, Cnut's nominee, Stigand, witnessed a land agreement at Wimbish, the estate immediately south of Ashdon; within a few months of becoming Bishop of Elmham, a diocese embracing Norfolk and Suffolk, he was bequeathed a large sum of money by one Thurstan whose estates comprised Ashdon and many other properties in the region; he retained considerable interests in the border county of Essex, Cambridgeshire and Suffolk and remained connected with Ely throughout his life. No such links with Ely can be established for Ashingdon which is forty two miles further away from East Anglia than is Ashdon. While all this evidence may not be quite conclusive, it requires a deal of answering.

There is one further piquant detail connected with Hadstock Church: if it provides positive proof of anything at all, it can only be of the tenacity of folk-memory. All the same the particular form of that folk-memory is not without significance. It is generally accepted that the north door of this church and the iron work over it are original, which is to say that they date from the early eleventh century. There seems little doubt that for centuries, the door beneath that original iron work was covered by a skin which local tradition insisted was that of a Danish king or warrior. The skin survived intact for centuries but was removed, piece by piece, by curio-hunters. In 1847, the last surviving fragment was given by the then rector, the Reverend C. Townley to Lord Braybrooke; he in turn presented it to Saffron Walden Museum where it is still preserved. It was examined by an expert in 1847 who pronounced that it was unquestionably human, and that, on the evidence of three microscopic hairs still attached to it, it had been taken from the back of a fair-haired man. In 1925, in a very well documented and occasionally pungent article on the Battle of Assandun, rejecting the claims of Ashingdon and supporting those of Hadstock, Professor Miller Christy speculated on the identity of the person from whom the skin had been stripped:

> It is not easy to see how this fragment of skin can have been taken from a Dane, still less from a Danish King: for in the battle fought at Hadstock, the Danes were victorious and had no king killed, and there were no later fights with Danes on English soil. In all the circumstances of the case, it is not altogether fantastic to suggest that the skin may be that of the traitor Eadric, retrieved from the City ditch or the Thames and nailed by Cnut's order on the door of his new *mynster*, erected on the very spot where the arch-traitor perpetrated his worst act of treachery, as a perpetual warning to all other traitors. Unfortunately, however, evidence is lacking.

'Unfortunately', indeed. And if evidence were forthcoming to enable one to prove that the skin were Eadric's, one would be bound to conclude that Cnut's feelings must have been perculiarly mixed when the warning was nailed to the door: Eadric's untimely defection cost Edmund Ironside the battle of Assandun and his subsequent act of treachery cost Edmund his life. As far as Cnut was concerned, the moral was rather less 'crime doesn't pay' so much as 'The end justifies the means — and to hell with conscience'.

It now seems unlikely that the mysteries surrounding the battle and the *mynster* can ever be definitely resolved: the events are too remote, the evidence too sketchy, the work of the earlier antiquarians too rudimentary for anyone to pronounce today with conviction of authority. Ever and anon, as one examines what passes for 'evidence' one is tantalized by clues that can never be quite conclusive just as one is irritated by the spectacle of scholars muffing their opportunities. If only Camden, for example, the first to advance the claims of Ashingdon had followed up the trail which opened up so promisingly before him in the Ashdon area at the opposite end of the county. Writing of the Bartlow Hills, he reported:

> The Country-People have a Tradition that they were rais'd after a Battle with the Danes in that place. And the *Wall-wort* or *Dwarf-elder* that grows hereabouts in great Plenty and bears red Berries, they call by no other Name but *Danes-blood* from the Multitude of Danes that were slain there . . .

Oral testimony is notoriously difficult to evaluate and popular myths are not necessarily trustworthy for being widespread or enduring — The Angels of Mons which many soldiers were reputed to have seen with their own eyes in the skies above their retreat from Mons in August 1914 actually derived from a short story by Arthur Machen, *The Bowmen*, in which the ghosts of the English bowmen, victorious at Agincourt, returned from the dead to slay the foe with arrows which left no mark. For all that, Camden's account of Bartlow folklore should not be dismissed out of hand. It evidently derived from local oral tradition and it was through that same oral process, the recounting of tales by one man to another, that the eleventh-century chronicles came to be written in the first. When the eleventh-century scribes — and certainly when the Tudor antiquarians — put quill to parchment they too were writing of 'old unhappy far-off things and battles long ago'.

A further argument in favour of Ashdon as the more likely site has been advanced by P. Croxton-Smith (in a letter to *Essex Countryside*, Vol. 15, 1965-66, p. 319) who suggests that when, as the Anglo-Saxon Chronicle relates, Edmund and Cnut both moved from the battlefield into Gloucestershire, it was most probably along the old trackways from north Essex to the west. Had the battle been fought at Ashingdon, Edmund's logical escape-route would have been south to London which was ever-loyal to his cause. It has also been pointed out that the roll of the illustrious personages slain on Edmund's side were all East Anglian ealdormen. While they might readily have involved themselves in a battle at Ashdon, right on the Suffolk-Cambridgeshire border, it is scarcely conceivable that they would have been drawn as far as Ashingdon, in central Essex which was never part of East Anglia and had quite a different set of ealdormen.

One final anecdote will doubtless do nothing to convince the (rightly) quizzical professional historian but it may win a convert or two to the Ashdon cause from those who do not insist that for evidence to be valid it must derive from documents. In July, 1923, the Cambridge Antiquarian Society paid an official visit to Waltons Park. This was subsequently described in an official report written by Dr. William Palmer. He concluded his general description of his survey of the manor house at Waltons which looks out towards Bartlow and Hadstock and the general area which, over the centuries, has been claimed as the likely site of the Battle of Assandun:

> A house like this with double ceilings, walled up gables and fearsome attics is likely to have a peculiar psychic effect on special temperaments, and the owner [Mrs Leila Luddington] tells of a visitor who, looking across the valley at midnight, saw fierce fighting going on in a field near the home of the Cloptons, Newnham Hall, where many skeletons have been found.

Mrs. Luddington recounted this same story to me when I interviewed her in 1971, frail but still very alert in her ninety fourth year. What is to be made of it is for the individual reader to judge. For my part, I see it not as conclusive evidence, one way or the other,

Dr. W.M. Palmer with chauffeur Bernard King, in 1923

so much as emblematic of the mystery which continues to enshroud that battle won and lost so long ago. The only surviving witnesses are the stars which looked down on the victors and the vanquished when the fighting finished, but they are just as mute in answer to our questioning as the gravestones beside the south door of the church, worn so smooth by centuries of wind and rain that not a mark on them remains to speak for those who sleep so soundly out there in the peaceful earth.

3

The Old Community

> Only a man harrowing clods
>   In a slow silent walk
> With an old horse that stumbles and nods
>   Half asleep as they stalk.
>
> Only thin smoke without flame
>   From the heaps of couch-grass;
> Yet this will go onward the same
>   Though Dynasties pass ...
>   *Thomas Hardy:*
>   In Time of 'the breaking of Nations'

In the Venerable Bede's Latin history of the English people, there is an often anthologized incident which most vividly captures the ethos of that bleak lost age. A sparrow is flying through the darkness of a storm-wracked night. Suddenly it happens to fly through the open eaves of a great warrior hall and for a few seconds only it is surrounded by light and warmth and the sounds of revelry. Then the bird flies out through the opening in the wall opposite and pursues its untracked course through the cold and the dark. At this point, Bede comments 'So is the life of man revealed for a brief space, but what went before and what follows we know not'. Repeatedly, that image and those words came to mind as I turned up unrelated documents from Ashdon's more distant past, so exciting because they have survived for so long, so tantalizing for affording such a brief moment of brightness between great tracts of darkness.

Just such feelings are inevitably aroused by the earliest documents in Ashdon's recorded history, two wills which date from near the end of the Saxon era. One of these has long since been lost but it is mentioned in the archives of Ely Abbey to which, in about 1036, a certain Lustwine left the lands he held in various parts of north-west Essex, not only in Ashdon but also in Pentlow, Wimbish and

Thaxted. Who he was, where he made his family home, how extensive his estates were, whether his life was serene or embittered are questions we cannot answer. In the other will, dated between 1046 and 1056, a rather more prosperous landowner named Thurstan lists his extensive Essex estates. He held land in Wimbish, Harlow, Pentlow, Henham, Little Dunmow, Ongar as well as in Ashdon. The bulk of the property is left to his wife Aethelgyth whose name is transcribed as Ailid in the Domesday Book from which we also learn that the estate she inherited at Ashdon was the Manor of Ashdon Hall.

The settlement at what is now Ashdon Hall, clustered beside the church and the ash-trees on the hill, was one of the four hamlets already in existence in Saxon times. They consisted of a few cottages only, set up on patches of ground cleared from the still extensive forest, the walls built from the branches of trees, the roofs thatched with straw from the small areas given over to the growing of corn in the large common fields. There were no separate farms on the scale or pattern of the present day. Under the 'open field' system, each man tilled a number of isolated strips, separated by 'baulks' of turf and allotted to each man according to the number of oxen he contributed to the communal ploughing-team. Pigs were kept in large numbers, originally left free to graze in the public forest but later looked after by a swineherd specifically appointed for that task. Other specialist duties were, in the course of time, allotted to officials elected by the community: shepherd, oxherd, bee-keeper, hayward (who tended the hedges which marked the boundaries of the fields and meadows) and woodward (in charge of the forest lands).

Within any Saxon settlement of more than a few dwellings only there was an elaborate social hierarchy. At the top was the *thane* who held his land from an overlord or from the King directly and was, in effect, the lord of the local manor. In one of four highly readable articles he contributed to the *Cambridge Chronicle* between April and June 1924, Dr. W.M. Palmer argued persuasively that one might picture the conditions in which a thane used to live by inspecting the magnificent barn beside the sixteenth-century farmhouse of Ashdon Place, the home farm of Waltons Park. Because it so authentically evoked a past long since lost, Dr. Palmer had no hesitation in pronouncing it the most outstanding specimen of domestic architecture in the whole neighbourhood:

Adjoining Ashdon Place, and close to the stables at Waltons, is a barn framed in oak and tiled, of a type once universal in Cambridgeshire and its borders, if one may judge from the wide distribution of surviving examples. It is of seven bays with aisles like the nave of a church; the resemblance is drawn closer by the fact that from the massive oak posts, which support the roof and which form an arcade on either side of the central open space, spring diagonal brackets in the plane of the axis of the building. Each bay of the arcade thus presents an arched outline — as does also each bay of the nave. . . . An English house or hall was, originally, there is little doubt, no more or less than an English barn; new ideas of comfort and demands for privacy led to the construction at either end of subsidiary rooms and thus the 'H' or modified 'H'-shaped plan of the central hall type of wooden house was evolved. It requires little effort of imagination to picture the dwelling of a Saxon Thegn in this corner of East Anglia in the time before local historical record begins. Take the Ashdon Place Barn and surround it with subsidiary buildings; add lean-tos at each gable and reduce the size of the doors. You must then put louvres in the roof, for a fire of logs is burning on a hearth extending for some distance along the centre of the hall. The aisles will not at first sight be apparent, for each bay is closed in, the spaces being used for bedrooms, store-rooms, garderobes. At each end, the main cross beams carry a floor. The upper rooms thus made are reached by ladders and are lighted by small openings in the gables . . .

Under the thane's protection, but able to cultivate his lands independently was the *Ceorl* (or freeman). He might be called upon to perform some light menial duties for the thane above him, but he was free to sell his allegiance and his services. Beneath him came various grades of tenant enjoying less and less freedom and obliged to discharge more and more duties as they descended in the hierarchy. The *villeins* (or villagers) might well hold land of their own but if they did so it was at the will of the lord who could depose them from it whenever he pleased. They were obliged to carry out a number of seasonal tasks for him such as ploughing the land on his demesne (the lord's own holding); sowing it with seed they themselves had to provide, mowing the meadow, cutting and carting timber; their daughters could not marry without the payment of a fine; upon their death, a fine had to be paid to the lord by the heirs. Beneath the villeins came the *bordars* and the *cottars*, smallholders living some little distance outside the village in their cottages on the outer borders of the enclave; they held less land than the villeins and were expected to do considerably more work for their lord. Lowest of the low were the *servi* or slaves (*theow* in Anglo-Saxon) who could be either conquered natives or felons: they had no land, no oxen and no rights whatsoever. This, in brief, was the agricultural and social system that was still in being when, in 1085, William I decreed that a survey should be made of all the English territories he had conquered.

So detailed and authoritative was this survey that it was quickly nicknamed the Domesday Book. Like Domesday or Judgement Day there was no escaping it and, fortunately for our purposes, all the separate settlements that were subsequently to be united into the village of Ashdon were ensnared in its meshes.

One cannot say for certain where the local officials foregathered to compile their return to William's survey because what is today regarded as the village 'centre' was, in 1085, no more than a ford or bridge over the Bourne. As likely a place as any must have been up on the hill, somewhere near the present site of the parish church where the first villagers would seem to have settled. What is as clear and unambiguous today as the day it was drawn up is the list of questions put to every community in England by William's team of Royal Commissioners. They asked the same questions in the same sequence at every meeting:

(i) What is the name of the manor?

(ii) Who was the tenant T.R.E. [Tempore Regis Edwardi = in the time of King Edward the Confessor]?

(iii) Who is the tenant now, T.R.W. [Tempore Regis Willelmi = in the time of King William]?

(iv) How many *hides* does the manor contain?

— The *hide* as a unit of 'rateable value' for tax-purposes dated from long before the Norman Conquest. For Domesday specialists, it is — together with the no less controversial 'Carucate' — a particularly controversial term. I shall adhere to the commonly held layman's view that the 'hide' represented the area of land which could be tilled with a single plough in a year.

(v) How many inhabitants are there, divided into the classes villeins, bordars, [or small-holders] cottars, freemen, serfs and *sokemen*?

— Soke was a Danelaw county term for a jurisdiction over a number of estates and villages. It is thought that the original sokemen were Danish soldiers who owned personal allegiance to their own particular overlord. Any such overlord was entitled to hold his own Soke Court and could exercise his lordship over the inhabitants of other lords' villagers and farms.

(vi) How much woodland is there? How much meadow? How much pasture?

(vii) How many mills and fishponds are there? What is their annual value?

(viii) What was the total value of the manor, T.R.E. and what is its present value, T.R.W.?

The answers from the Ashdon community are to be found in the so-called 'Little Domesday Book', the volume dealing exclusively with Essex, Suffolk and Norfolk, and they are listed separately amongst the estates of William's tenants-in-chief who between them exercised lordship not only over the parish of Ashdon but of vast areas of the eastern counties. I shall deal with the overlords in the following chapter; my immediate purpose is simply to describe the resources of the Ashdon manors at the time of the Domesday Survey and the uses to which they were being put. To simplify proceedings, I have accepted that *carucata* should here be translated as plough or plough-team.

In *Ascenduna* [later to become Ashdon Hall] there were 14 villeins in King Edward's time; now [i.e. in 1086] there are 20. Then, there were 3 bordars, now there are 9. Then there were 2 serfs, now there are none. Both then and now there are 2 plough-teams on the demesne and 4 plough-teams belonging to the tenants. There is enough woodland for 100 swine, 6 acres of meadow and 1 acre of vineyard (one of only nine vineyards listed in the Essex Domesday folios, no doubt planted in order to provide wine for the Norman lord himself). Then there were 2 runcini (usually translated as packhorses), 5 cows, 60 swine, 200 sheep and 10 hives of bees (in considerable demand in the eleventh century as they provided not only the sole sweetening agent then known but also wax for Church candles). Now there are 1 packhorse, 7 cows, 60 swine, 65 sheep and 3 hives of bees. Then it was worth £6, now it is worth £8. And there are 2 sokemen holding 15 acres in free tenure.

Similarly detailed answers were provided for each of Ashdon's other settlements, still sufficiently detached from 'Ascenduna' to count as autonomous communities.

The Domesday account of the manor of Ascenduna

Newnhan (later Newnham Hall), a settlement on the more open, chalky ground, toward the northern extremity of the present parish, was no doubt so called because as a hamlet it was 'new' in relation to the original settlement of Ashdon.

In the time of King Edward there were 6 villeins, now (under King William) there are 9. Then there were 2 bordars; later and at present there are 7. Now, as then, there are 6 slaves on the lord's estate and 3 plough-teams. Then the tenants had

4 plough-teams; now there are 3. There is enough woodland for 20 swine and 5 acres of meadow. There are 14 swine, 56 sheep and 1 packhorse. To this manor belonged 5 sokemen, holding half a hide of land, and a further 35 acres which remained in sokeright; they used to have 3 plough-teams, now they have 2; they have 5 acres of meadow. The whole use to be worth £11; now it is worth £12.

There was a third hamlet called *Steventuna* (meaning the 'tun' or manor of Styfa, no doubt the most powerful of the earliest overlords). It was subsequently to become known as Stevington End or, alternatively, Bartlow Hamlet, and became the site of Waltons Park, now the largest estate in the parish. The lands were shared out in rather complicated fashion as will be described in the next chapter.

Now, as then, there are 2 plough-teams on the lord's estate. Previously there was 1 bordar; now there are 3. Now, as then, there are 4 slaves. There are 5 acres of meadow. Then there were 5 cows, 5 swine, 10 sheep and 2 hives of bees; now there are 5 cows, 1 packhorse, 30 swine, 50 sheep and 1 hive of bees. Previously it was worth 40 shillings; now it is worth 100 shillings and 1 ounce of gold.

Also in the manor of Steventuna were two men, Renold and Orderic, who used to be in the king's *soke* but he gave them to Aubrey de Vere [one of the tenants-in-chief]. On this part of the manor, now as previously, there are 3 villeins, 2 bordars and 1 plough-team. There is woodland for 10 swine and 3 acres of meadow. Previously it was worth 20 shillings; now it is worth 30 shillings. There is also a certain Englishman who has leased 40 acres from Aubrey which used to be held by Alvric the *sokeman*. He had the right to sell this land but the 'sac and soc' [i.e. the right to hold a court and to receive manorial profits and services] belonged to the land and not to the vendor. Now, as then, there are 2 bordars and enough land for one plough-team. It is worth 10 shillings.

Frodo, brother of the Abbot [of St. Edmunds] has hitherto held 2 freemen in Steventuna who were seized by Orgar [his predecessor]. They dwell in the king's *soke* and hold 20 acres. Now, as then, there is land for half a plough team and it is worth 4 shillings.

Finally, there was yet another hamlet, more remote and secluded than any of the others, but still within the boundaries of the parish. This was in a clearing in the forest close to Water End, near the source of the River Bourne.

> Now, as then, there is half a hide of land. There is woodland for 8 swine and ½ acres of meadow. Then it was worth five shillings; now it is worth 10 shillings.

* * *

Between the Ashdon community of the Domesday Survey and that of the nineteenth and twentieth centuries which copious documents and numerous eye-witness accounts have done much to illuminate, there are a number of striking similarities as well as important differences. Unlike the modern Ashdon farmers who have concentrated, with conspicuous success, on corn production, those whose activities are recorded in the Domesday book were pre-eminently stockmen, clearly devoting more of their time and energy to their pigs, cows and sheep than to arable husbandry. The forests continued to dominate the Norman landscape and the lives of its inhabitants just as they had done in Saxon times. The small but not insignificant increase in the number of *bordars* between King Edward's and King William's reigns possibly indicates a modest effort to extend the perimeters of the first forest-clearings but the four settlements were to remain relatively small and cut-off from one another for generations. Finally, what seems emphatically true of Domesday Ashdon remained characteristic of the Ashdon community down the centuries: wealth and privilege was concentrated in the hands of those fortunate or powerful enough to be in control of the land. The landowners are granted the dignity of their names and titles in the Domesday Survey; the tenants and serfs are mere statistics.

This point is made even more emphatically in the next document in chronological sequence concerned with the Ashdon community as a whole, the Lay Subsidy return for 1327: the well-to-do are listed by name and their tax-liability specified, the poor are neither named nor numbered.

Levying taxes on the better-off's personal property or movable goods became a regular practice among England's mediaeval kings though from the reign of Edward I onwards, Parliament's assent had

THE OLD COMMUNITY

to be secured on each occasion. In 1327, following the abdication of the chronically indecisive Edward II and the accession of Edward III, who was then still a minor, extra revenue was urgently required to defend the realm against the increasingly turbulent Scots. Once the rate of tax had been fixed at one twentieth of the value of the citizen's property, each county selected two or three of its most prominent men to appoint a clerk. In Essex, the three wise men were Thomas Gobion, Ralph Giffard and Nicholas de Storteforde. They proceeded to enlist the help of from four to six trustworthy men from each vill who had to swear that they would make full inquiry into the goods owned by their fellow citizens at Michaelmas 1327. This time was no doubt deliberately chosen because at Michaelmas the harvest would just have been gathered in and the community would have been at its most affluent.

Some possessions were exempt from tax: the armour, horses and treasures of knights and gentry; for lesser fry, such items as a bed, a table, a chair, tools and a quantity of food adjudged to be adequate for the needs of the individual household. Surplus grain believed to be available for sale was taxed though this, together with live-stock, was often given a notional rather than a market valuation. In 1327, the taxable minimum was ten shillings worth of goods which produced a levy of sixpence. The two sets of 1327 tax-returns for Essex, more complete than for any other county, survive in the Public Record Office on twenty-four membranes, inscribed in Latin on the back and front of the parchment in double columns. They have been superbly edited by Jennifer Ward and it is on her introduction that this summary account has been based.

8,326 Essex taxpayers are grouped under 356 separate vills which are arranged under their respective 'hundreds' (administrative subdivisions of the county, each with its own court). Ashdon is listed in the Hundred of Uttlesford though, strictly speaking, it was in the Half Hundred of Freshwell. This name derives from St. Pris's Well, a rivulet which had its source in a valley near Radwinter and contained a large number of frogs (Anglo-Saxon: *frocga, froso*, German: *Frosch*).

The entry for Ashdon reads as follows:

Villata de Asschendone/Asshendone

(Where alternative forms of spelling are given, it means that each of the two surviving copies was written by a different clerk. One copy had to be sent to the Exchequer while one was stored locally. It is interesting to note that in 1327, there was still uncertainty about how to spell the name of the village — one further demonstration of how unreliable is etymological evidence for locating the site of the Battle of Assandun.)

	s	d			s	d	
De Elena de Darnaston/			Galfrido Cayly		xvj		
Darnardeston	iiij	v	Roberto Barnard		xxiiij	ob	
Edmundo de Durem/			Johanne Frebern		vj		
Dureme	iij		Adam Steynild		vj	ob	
Johanna de Westone	iiij		Johanne Prike		vj	qr	
Johanne de Bousser/			Willelmo Astyn		vj	ob	
Boussier	v	j qr	Ricardo le Cartere		vj		
Roberto de Wautone	iij	x	Waltero le Rede		vj		
Roberto de Bilkemor	iij	v	Lora de Shaldeforde/				
Matilde de Sampforde	iiij	ix	Schaldeforde	iij		ob	
Horemma de			Galfrido de				
Holmstede/Holmestede		xj	Loundres/London		xxiij		
Johanne de Roksswelle		xij	Johanne Gobet		xviiij		
Johanne le Waleys		xij ob					
Rogero Cordy	iiij	v					

Summa xlixs vd qr

The following points are worthy of note. Ashdon, at this moment in its history, would seem to have been amongst the lower-to-middle reaches of the county's vills. The average tax for the whole county was 11.4 shillings per square mile; the wealthiest hundred was Chafford which yielded 14.2 shillings per square mile, the lowest Thurstable 7.1 shillings per square mile; the average for Uttlesford and Freshwell, Ashdon's hundred, was 9.6 shillings per square mile. Unlike the vills of Great Bardfield (where the assessment of the lady of the manor, Elizabeth de Burgh, was over twice as high as the next figure on the list) or Castle Hedingham (where the assessment of Robert de Vere, Earl of Oxford, was considerably higher than that of all the other tax-payers), Ashdon's wealth was evenly spread. Only one Ashdonian had to pay over five shillings, five paid between four and five shillings, three between three and four shillings, five between one and two shillings and nine paid under a shilling, seven of these paying the very minimum or a fraction over it. At this time, Ashdon numbered no conspicuously wealthy individuals amongst its members: the five shillings and a penny farthing paid by John de Boussep seems a modest amount when set aside the sum of £1 regularly paid by knights and affluent gentry. Some of the names may indicate the tax-payer's occupation — Carter or Reeve (leader of the villagers). The preposition 'de' before a surname does not designate an aristocrat as it would in French usage, but the person's regular or sometime domicile, London or the villages of Roxwell, Sampford or Shelford. Two place-names have come down over six centuries and survive in Ashdon at the present-day: Waltons (Park) and Bowser's (Farm). Five of those assessed in Ashdon were women, almost certainly widows, by no means the only time in the village's history when they achieved local eminence (see pages 55-6).

Informative though the 1327 tax-return undoubtedly is, it leaves important and tantalizing gaps as do all English official documents until the nineteenth century. Churchmen were exempt from the Lay Subsidy so are not listed; the poor, on this occasion, were not required to pay. How many of them there were, how large were their families and how small were their earnings and possessions we cannot tell. All that is known for certain is that twenty one years after what is generally agreed to be a high peak in the nation's economic fortunes, the country's population was cut brutally in half by the Black Death.

We are unlikely ever to know the names or numbers of Ashdonians who were stricken by the Black Death. What does now seem fairly generally accepted is that round about this time, possibly in an attempt to escape the worst ravages of the plague, large numbers of parishioners moved from the original village-site, clustered around the church on the hill, to a new location at the foot of Church Hill, athwart the river where the Radwinter road meets the road that runs between Saffron Walden and Bartlow. The Church of All Saints remained where it had been from the very beginning of the village's history on top of the 'hill of the ash-trees' and from the scattered settlements of the district rich and poor alike came each Sunday to form one congregation. Because it remained for centuries the most important unifying influence on the community, it is entirely appropriate that it should still today contain more tangible evidence of the distant past than any other building in the village.

The long spacious chancel is thought to have been erected in the thirteenth century. Early in the fourteenth century, the North East and South Chapels were added and the south aisle rebuilt on the site of an earlier aisle which cannot be dated. About 1375 the square west tower was built with its distinctive crenellated parapet and small slender spire rising diffidently above. The North-west chapel and north aisle were also built in the fourteenth century while the present roof of the chancel was set in place about the time of the Battle of Agincourt in 1415. The walls throughout were built of flints collected from the local fields though this is regrettably not readily apparent since the exterior of the whole edifice was covered over with cement early in the nineteenth century when several of the larger windows were blocked in. Of the original stained glass which must have been one of the glories of the building long years ago, only isolated fragments survive: in the tracery of the eastern window, some early fourteenth-century ornamentation and fifteenth-century flower, in the fine south window, the golden wing of a lost angel.

The next Lay Subsidy of which reliable records have survived, that for 1524-25, during the reign of Richard II, indicates both how the nation had prospered since the ravages of the Black Death and how ingenious and rapacious the royal taxers had become. The assessment of 1524-25 was made on lands, personal property ('goods') or wages. No man was assessed on all three but on whichever category produced the most revenue for the exchequer. On this occasion, when the tax was levied at the rate of four shillings in the pound on land and two shillings and sixpence in the pound on goods, some fifty Ashdonians were liable to pay. The amounts of tax demanded ranged from twenty shillings in the lowest reaches, where there were eight contributors, up to a maximum of twenty pounds, where there were three: William Claydon, John Webb and William Willowes. Precisely how many Ashdonians were too poor to be liable for taxes in 1524-25 one again cannot tell though it is possible, with some degree of accuracy, to calculate the size of the village population a couple of decades later.

In 1547, when Henry VIII demanded a detailed account of all the properties and funds of the churches up and down the land, the Chantry Commissioners reported that 'The town of Asheton is a grete and populous town having in yt to the nombre of cccc (i.e. 400) of howslynge people and more'. If this figure is anything like accurate, and there seems little reason to doubt it, Ashdon in the mid-sixteenth century was indeed 'populous'. 'Houseling people' means 'communicants' and represents the number of inhabitants aged about fifteen and over. According to Professor W.G. Hoskins (in his *Local History in England*, Longman, 2nd edition, 1972, p.171), it can be fairly assumed that children under fifteen account for some 40% of the whole community at any time, so the total population of Ashdon in 1547 must have been in the region of six hundred and seventy. This is not markedly short of the population of present-day Ashdon which, since 1685, has regularly included for census puposes the figure for Bartlow Hamlet. If it was also roughly similar to the figure for 1524-25, the indications are, unsurprisingly, that comparatively few of the villagers enjoyed reasonable material comforts and were taxed for the privilege while the great majority were not considered well enough off to need to pay taxes at all. This particular division remained for centuries and, if anything, grew wider with the passing years.

For a comprehensive account of the whole Ashdon community one has to wait till the middle of the nineteenth century when, more or less by chance, within the space of six years, it became the focus of a succession of bureaucratic investigations which, in other communities, were often separated by decades. It was reviewed by the Tithe Commutation Assessors in 1845, by the Enclosure Commissioners in 1847, by the Census Enumerators in 1851 and the Ecclesiastical Census investigators in the same year. From the reports of each of these officials, one can construct a picture of the Ashdon community more detailed and more extensive even than that provided by William I's great Survey.

Over the span of centuries separating the Norman and the Victorian investigations of the village, the inhabitants of the Ashdon settlement had dedicated the whole of their working lives to agriculture. While dynasties rose and fell, while armies marched and counter-marched, while vast new lands were being discovered and colonized, while the nation's laws were several times being rewritten, generation after generation of countryfolk were dutifully following the ritual and the rhythm of the seasons, as fixed and as regular in their earthly course as the constellations above them. For hundreds of years there was no dramatic change in either agricultural methods or equipment and the same rotation system was practised in the large open common as had been followed in the time of the Saxons: two fields were cultivated in any one year while a third was left fallow, to be grazed and fertilized by the cattle. It was only in the eighteenth century that the inefficiency of these traditional methods was demonstrated, most effectively of all by Charles

Viscount Townshend who, from 1730 on, adopted the Norfolk four-course rotation system which has since become standard. While the benefits of the innovations were readily apparent, it was perhaps not so widely appreciated that they spelt the end of the age-old open-field system. The inflexibility of this ancient rotation-system could not accommodate the introduction of the vital new crops such as clover and sanfoin, while the herding together of all the community's beasts on the same common fields facilitated the spread of diseases and prevented selective breeding, the self-evident virtues of which were demonstrated by such eighteenth-century pioneers as Thomas Coke and Robert Bakewell.

We cannot say with any precision when Ashdon farmers began to adopt the Townshend system, whether in pure or modified form, but it is clear that, for whatever reason, the agricultural scene in Ashdon was not effectively transformed until well into the eighteenth century. Even when it was so transformed the local community continued as it had done since the time of the first settlements to live off as well as for the land. Proportionately, markedly more time and land was given over to corn production since the time of the Domesday Survey but in other important respects, the structure of the community had not effectively changed: while most of the inhabitants tilled the land, only a few owned it and because of this they continued to enjoy, as they always had done, a virtual monopoly of power and privilege. How little conditions had changed in this regard over the course of eight centuries may be judged from examining the clutch of surveys undertaken of the Ashdon community in the middle of the nineteenth century and the first of these in chronological sequence, though not necessarily in importance, is the activity which followed the passing of the Tithe Commutation Act in 1836.

The effect of this Act was to transform a system which had remained an integral feature of village life since time immemorial, probably since as long ago as the age of the Romans when one tenth of all the produce of any community had to be yielded up as tribute. For centuries, every parish had been obliged to pay tithes to its local church: every year, its members had to donate a tenth part of their main produce from the land (their corn, their oats or their wood) together with a tenth part of their labour and produce of their stock (wool, milk, pigs etc.). The account books of successive Ashdon rectors have survived from the beginning of the eighteenth century onwards and these offer revealing glimpses of how the system worked. In 1704, one finds entries like the following, showing how the rector was paid in cash or in kind and how part, at least, of the income was spent:

Composition Tithes

			£	s	d
1704	Mr. Stocks	2 quarters of oats	1	0	0
	J. Whitby	for an acre of wheat	0	4	0
	April 6	Paid up for malt	8	2	2
	Ap[ril] 12	Put up for brewing	1	6	0
	May 19	Put up for brewing	1	0	0
	June 22	Put up for brewing	1	0	0
	July 5	Put up for brewing	1	0	0
	July 26	Put up for brewing	1	0	0
	Aug 14	Put up for brewing	1	0	0
	Sep 20	Put up for brewing	0	2	0

These entries should not be taken to mean that Ashdon's rector was at this time 'a parson much bemused in beer'. It is conceivable that the product of the brewing was 'Church ale', sold and drunk to raise funds for the fabric of the Church as is more commonly done nowadays by means of the fête or the bazaar.

Piggs Anno 1704

Wm Coe	a pig	Pd 18^d
Tho Smyth	a pig	Pd in kind
Tom Cowell	6 piggs	9^d not paid
Thos Barker	6 piggs	9^d unpd.
Thos Bucke	a pig	not pd
Thos Goss	a pig	pd in kind
J Slogrove	a pig	
J Day	a pig	in kind
Thomas Pettit	4 cows away	Dec. 7th

The incumbent's personal stipend could be further supplemented by his parishioners' seasonal offerings which were quite separate form the tithe; for example:

Easter Offerings 1705
Richard Wolland

	£	s	d
2 years offerings	0	1	0
5 cows	0	2	1
5 lambs	0	0	2
Churching your wife	0	6	6
[i.e. bringing her to church to render thanks for the delivery of a child]		3	9

	£	s	d
Thomas Cowell	0	0	6
6 cows	0	1	8
4 lambs	0	0	2
Eggs	0	0	2
		2	6

Casual Payments 1809

		£	s	d
Manor. Court Dinner		1	17	6
To widows of Essex Clergy		1	1	0
To Labourers Club			12	0
To Curate	Salary	54	12	0
	Sermon on Fast	1	1	0
	Surplice Fees	1	10	0
To Ringers on 5 Nov			2	6
To Psalm-singers on Tithe Day			10	6

This entry is immediately followed by a detailed list of emoluments received from parishioners, arranged in alphabetical order, including entries for wood and for sheep; under this last head, Anne Giblin of Goldstone's Farm donated £1.12s.6d and Joseph Giblin of Bowser's Farm £1.1s.0d.

For the Rector, collecting his tithes was doubtless a most satisfying occasion, well worthy of some genteel celebration, so his account book for 1814 includes the characteristic entry 'Dinners £4.12s.6d. and Bowl of Punch 5s.6d. on Tithe Day'. Given such details, one can the more readily appreciate both the fact that village parsons were among those privileged to receive nightly visitations from Shakespeare's Queen Mab and the means she used to set them dreaming of their heart's desire:

> ... sometimes comes she with a tithe-pig's tail,
> Tickling a parson's nose as a' lies asleep,
> Then dreams he of another benefice.

Not unnaturally, the payment of tithes had long been resented by the rest of the community and there was no call for rejoicing when the age-old system of tribute in goods or in service was transformed into an annual payment in cash. Commissioners surveyed every parish in the land, assessed the value of every holding and calculated the amount of rent payable each year. It was, in this way, as thoroughgoing an investigation as the Domesday Survey, and for the local historian, the minutely detailed map and descriptive commentary which accompanied each Commissioner's Award constitute an invaluable and fully comprehensive record of who owned which lands in every parish and the use to which they were put.

The Tithe Apportionment for Ashdon was sealed and signed by the Tithe Commissioners on 26th September 1848 though the survey was in fact concluded on 5th February 1845. It was conducted by the Assistant Tithe Commissioner, John Maurice Herbert of Lincoln's Inn, who reported that the total area of the parish was 4825 acres and 33 perches. Of these, 3737 acres and 24 perches were designated as arable land, 661 acres and 2 rods and 7 perches as meadow and pasture and 426 acres as woodland. The Award was complicated by the fact that the Rector of neighbouring Bartlow was entitled to tithes deriving from certain lands in Bartlow Hamlet (which, despite its name, had administratively been part of Ashdon since 12th September 1650, the decision to unite the two having been taken after a Parochial Inquisition held in the 'Saracen's Head' at Great Dunmow) plus a half share of some lands in Ashdon. The total annual sum awarded to the two rectors was £203 for the lands they shared, £909 to the Ashdon rector for all of his Ashdon lands plus a further £35 for his Ashdon glebe lands. The total sum allotted to the Ashdon rector was £944 per year and to the Bartlow rector £210 per year. Crucial figures in computing these awards were the current values ascribed to the grain crops and these were estimated at $7s.0\tfrac{1}{4}d.$ per bushel for wheat, $3s.11\tfrac{1}{2}d.$ per bushel for barley and $2s.9d.$ per bushel for oats. The annual wage of an Ashdon farm labourer would, at this period, have been between £26 and £39 per year.

At the time of the Tithe Commissioners' Award in the late 1840s, when the total population of the parish was about 1200, the ownership of the lands of Ashdon was divided between 111 different parties many of whom owned merely a 'cottage and garden' or 'tenement and orchard'. In fact, the great bulk of the land was quite unevenly divided. Of the 4825 acres in the parish, no fewer than 2110 were owned by the Right Honorable Viscount Maynard and the sum of his annual tithe-rents was assessed at £507.15s.1d. At the time of the assessment, he owned and occupied Waltons Park, then as now the most opulent house and grounds in the parish, and he also owned the eight largest farms. The second largest land-owner was an absentee proprietor, the Right Honorable Lord Braybrooke of Audley End, whose 261 acres included the extensive woods across the south-western borders of the parish and whose annual rental was fixed at £30.17s.2d. There follows a list of the next twenty wealthiest land-owners which is particularly noteworthy for the number of parsons who feature in its upper reaches, even excluding the Master and Fellows of Caius College, Cambridge at a period when the Anglican prerequisite was still paramount in all Oxbridge colleges. Thirteen of the twenty did not live in Ashdon though some lived in close proximity, such as Lord Braybrooke at Audley End or the Reverend Thomas Dayrell who lived in the adjoining parish of Shudy Camps. By the time of the 1851 Census, Viscount Maynard had vacated Waltons Park so it would be true to say that in the middle of the nineteenth century, some two-thirds of the parish belonged to owners who occasionally set foot in it: to this extent, there had been no significant change since Domesday almost nine centuries before. One dramatic change, very slow indeed to be effected since Domesday, was about to be finalised in Ashdon in the middle of the nineteenth century and this was the shape and ownership of its fields.

For centuries, as more and more land was cleared from the forest, the rural communities persisted in cultivating large open fields. These were divided into separate strips and the ownership of them was distributed amongst a wide range of individuals. The crops and stock were regularly controlled by the community as a whole following ancient rights and customs and the shared interest of everyone in the large fields that they tilled was made explicit in such fields being called 'the Commons'. In the course of time, as ownership of the land passed from the many to the few, it came to be recognized that farming could be made more profitable and more efficient if what formerly had been small and isolated strips of land could be purchased or exchanged and then amalgamated to form much larger single units. Rights of ownership over the newly enlarged fields were then emphasized by enclosing each with a hedge in much the same way as the right to hunt or shoot within the seclusion of one's private estate were established with wall or deer-leap. The process went on continuously, with variations in pace and emphasis, from the Middle Ages onwards. In Elizabethan times, William Harrison complained that large tracts of the English countryside were being effectively depopulated through the insistence of powerful lords on claiming part of their estates for the pleasures of the chase. Writing in the *Annals of Agriculture* in 1800, the then Rector of Ashdon, John North, noted that in his parish 'a number of farms have been laid to other forms, a practice which has been very frequent since the year 1730 and of which instances have occurred very frequently during my incumbency of near nine years, and are occurring in the present year; and some others will still be so laid together as soon as certain existing contracts are terminated'. In the terrier he himself drew up in 1810 of all the Ashdon Rectory lands and benefices, he noted 'The Glebe lands belonging to The Rectory consist of a Pasture and arable Lands all enclosed', one further small but significant indication that the process of enclosing in Ashdon, as in countless other parishes, was not suddenly achieved by the dramatic flourish of a pen but had been proceeding insiduously over many long years.

While many enclosures were effected by private arrangement between individual proprietors, it became standard practice to conclude the enclosure of the community as a whole through having a private Act passed through Parliament: 900 such Acts were passed between 1760 and 1770, a conspicuously busy period of activity, and a further 2000 during the Napoleonic war, between 1793 and 1815. Though the notoriously complex legal procedures were simplified in 1801 by a General Enclosure Act, it was still necessary for any parish seeking enclosure to secure the authority of its own private Act of Parliament. In 1836, the procedure was streamlined still further by another General Act which allowed negotiations for enclosure to be initiated provided that the proposal to do so was supported by local owners of at least two-thirds of the land, calculated by value and by area.

As in many other parishes in north-west Essex, the Enclosure of Ashdon came relatively late. The first formal steps were taken on 1st April 1845 when a number of prominent land-owners in the parish assembled in the 'Rose and Crown' and secured the necessary two-thirds majority allowing them to proceed. The plans to redistribute the Ashdon common lands were completed in 1847 but not revealed till early in 1851 when the Enclosure Award was made public. An announcement was inserted in the *Chelmsford Chronicle* and a notice fixed to the principal outer door of the parish Church convening a public meeting in the 'Rose and Crown' on 24 January. There, in the presence of all the interested parties, the details of the award were formally read out and the large Enclosure Map first displayed, making clear who had been allotted which holdings in the surviving common fields. There were as many as fourteen of these: Burnt House Field, Bramble Breed Common, Church Field, Falldown Common, Gore Field, Great Bartlow Field, Great Copt Hill, Great Stalentine Common, Holden Common, Longmeadow Field, Mill Field, Moor Field, Turft Common and Woodmore Common. Thirty six people were allotted lands in these large fields, thirteen plots being allotted to Lord Maynard, seven to the Reverend Thomas Dayrell and — an interesting curiosity — six to the Reverend Charles Keene on account of six separate areas of land he had inherited from six different parishioners. In addition, it was revealed that there were sixteen instances of persons prepared to exchange one plot of ground for another, doubtless with the object of fashioning fields of a more acceptable shape. Thirteen of these exchanges involved Lord Maynard, four involved the Reverend William Hammond, two involved Lord Braybrooke and two the Reverend Benedict Chapman, at that time the Rector of Ashdon.

All persons allotted land had to accept within two months of the Award's being promulgated. Within three months, their plots had to be 'inclosed, hedged, ditched and fenced at the proper costs and charges'. The allottees were directed to 'make the fences with good and proper thickset hedges and with good and substantive posts and rails and other sufficient guard-fences' and with ditches 'of a necessary and sufficient breadth for the whole extent of their boundary fences for conveying and carrying off the water from the contiguous and adjoining allotments'. As a result of such directives, the whole appearance of the landscape up and down the country was

THE OLD COMMUNITY

transformed. It is only latterly, with the progressive taking-over of smaller farms, that the Enclosure hedges have been grubbed up and, in many instances, in Ashdon and elsewhere, the fields are being restored to something like the shape and size of the old Commons.

All the indications are that the consequences of enclosure for Ashdon in 1851 were not conspicuously dramatic. Over the preceding years, as has already been demonstrated, Ashdon's fields were progressively being enclosed in any event; poverty was a chronic problem for many of the villagers by the end of the eighteenth century and, as will be seen later, this was due to a complexity of factors. It is not possible to calculate how many Ashdon villagers owned their own personal cow and were deprived by enclosure of their right to graze it but one can, with some degree of accuracy, estimate how many of them had at least a small plot of ground in which to cultivate their own fruit and vegetables. In 1851, the Census Enumerators reported that there were some 249 inhabited dwellings in the parish. Three years previously, the Tithe Commissioners found that in addition to thirty farms in the parish, there were as many as 91 cottages and tenements with either a garden or an orchard adjoining. All of which would seem to suggest that while the nineteenth-century Ashdon cottages may well have had to content themselves with meagre wages and doubtless a monotonous diet, there was no serious danger of mass-starvation.

*   *   *

A clearer and deeper insight into the character of the Ashdon community in the middle of the nineteenth century is provided by the return compiled by Enumerators when they conducted the Census inquiry for 1851. The documents pertaining to this particular census remain the most informative extant for the local historian: they provide the exact ages and birthplaces of everyone resident in the parish as well as each person's occupation, marital status and relationship to the head of the household.

At the time of the 1851 Census on 7th April, there were resident in Ashdon and Bartlow Hamlet together a total of 1195 persons; the oldest inhabitant was an 84 year old widow, the youngest was the one week old son, still unchristened, of an agricultural labourer, John Andrews. The following table will enable us to see the significance of this figure in relationship to Ashdon in the nineteenth century and to population trends in England as a whole (last two columns of figures from Phyllis Deane and A.W. Cole: *British Economic Growth 1688-1959*, Cambridge, 1962, pp.142-3):

Year	Population of Ashdon and Bartlow Hamlet	No. of persons in agriculture, forestry and fishing	Percentage of total labour force
1801	873	1.7 million	35.9
1811	1009	1.8 million	33.0
1821	1014	1.8 million	28.4
1831	1103	1.8 million	24.6
1841	1164	1.9 million	22.2
1851	1195	2.1 million	21.7
1861	1192	2.0 million	18.7
1871	1174	1.8 million	15.1
1881	1030	1.7 million	12.6
1891	965	1.6 million	10.5
1901	800	1.5 million	8.7

From these columns of figures, the following may be fairly inferred: the rise to a high peak in the village's population in the middle of the century followed by a fall to below the figures of the beginning of the century runs parallel to trends in the country as a whole; the chronic problem of poverty in the village, as in rural communities generally for that matter, would seem to be related more directly to the growth in population than to the incidence of enclosure. Certainly, as far as Ashdon is concerned, the steady then fairly rapid fall in population followed the formal enclosing of the parish in 1851 but there is no necessary casual link between these two. The relatively steep fall in Ashdon's total population between 1871 and 1901 had little if anything to do with enclosure and a great deal to do with the catastrophic depression which affected English farming from the late 1870s on.

By the middle of the nineteenth century, most of the eastern lowland region of England had gone over to 'mixed' farming, combining the raising of livestock with the cultivation of crops. In Essex, however, considerably greater emphasis was placed on growing wheat and barley, while clover, beans and root crops were also grown to provide fodder for livestock. In this respect, with more than three

quarters of its acreage given over to arable husbandry (see p.)
Ashdon was not untypical of the county as a whole, and inevitably,
when the great depression so blighted the Essex agricultural scene
in the late nineteenth century, Ashdon was blighted too. The force
of the impact may be the better gauged when it is demonstrated just
how throughly the village was committed to agriculture. With this
particular depression, enclosure had nothing to do: indeed, by providing the parish with a more rationally ordered field-system,
enclosure mitigated the force of the disaster.

In fact, the major cause of the depression was a catastrophic fall
in wheat prices. This was due, in part, to a succession of disastrous
harvests but even more to the inflow of huge quantities of the
dramatically expanding granaries overseas. Because of improved
methods of bulk harvesting, transport and storage, American and
Russian corn could be bought in London more cheaply than corn
grown in Essex, for so long one of the capital's chief sources of supply.
Imported wheat represented 25% of the annual whole in England
in 1850; by 1900, this figure had risen to 75%. From 1875 to the
end of the century, the price of corn fell by 50%. The population
of the country as a whole, becoming ever more urbanized as the extreme right-hand column in the table above so clearly indicates, was
much more interested in buying its food at the cheapest price than
in ensuring the economic survival of its own country cousins and
it needed the traumatic shock of the First World War to redress the
balance. By that time, technology had intervened as a potent new
feature of the agricultural scene, all manner of new machines had
begun to do the work of whole battalions of farm labourers, like
Cyrus McCormick's self-binder invented in 1878, and none of the
country's rural parishes was ever as populous again.

If the 1851 Census shows Ashdon at its most crowded, it also shows
it at its most single-mindedly agricultural. At the time of the
Enumerators' Return, there were 32 farmers in the parish, no fewer
than five of whom were women, one (Hannah Giblin, a fifty year
old widow) farming the 310-acre Goldstones Farm with a labour force
of fourteen men, and another (Elizabeth Haylock, a seventy one year
old spinster) farming the 160 acre Ashdon Place Farm with a labour
force of six men. There was also a female blacksmith, Martha Green.
These details recall that an interesting feature revealed by the Domesday Survey was the extent to which estates had been controlled by

women before the Norman Conquest, the Ashdon owners Ailid and Edeva being in this respect the rule rather than the exception.

There were a few Ashdon residents not living directly from or having formerly worked in agriculture — the Baptist Minister, the Church of England curate, six schoolteachers and a pupil teacher, one postman, one police officer, two Chelsea pensioners and one 'annuitant', Philip S. Parker, married to a lady twenty five years older than himself and one of the signatories of the petition in favour of Enclosure. All the rest of the population worked on the land, was supported by those who worked on the land or ministered to the needs of those who worked on the land. There were 243 agricultural labourers, the eldest, still at work, aged 78, the youngest listed, a boy aged 11 and two girls aged 7 and 8. (It was only in 1873 that the Agricultural Children's Act banned all children under eight from working on farms.) In addition, there were 3 farm bailiffs, 10 carpenters (one of whom was living in the Rectory and employing 6 men and an apprentice), 7 blacksmiths, 7 boot and shoemakers, 7 plaiters, all girls under twenty, preparing straw for the hat trade, 4 bricklayers (all named Kitteridge), 3 thatchers, 2 shepherds, 1 wheelwright, 1 collarmaker, 1 dairywoman, 1 cooper, 3 millers, 2 journeymen millers, 2 drovers, 2 gamekeepers, 2 sawyers, and 1 cattle dealer. Their goods and services were supplied by 4 dressmakers, 3 butchers, 3 tailors (one employing two men), 3 general storekeepers, 1 grocer, 1 hawker, 1 innkeeper and 2 licensed victuallers.

The 1851 Census also provides eloquent evidence of the contrast in lifestyles between the Ashdon well-to-do and the paupers. The most opulent establishment in the parish, then as now, was Waltons Park, at the time of the census occupied by a 49 year old merchant Henry Hewston, his wife, Mary, aged 50, his 19 year old son and his 12 year old daughter. To tend to their needs, they employed and provided living quarters for the following establishment: 1 governess, 2 servants, 2 housemaids, 1 cook, 1 coachman, 1 gamekeeper and 1 general handyman. Nearly all the farmers employed at least one house-servant who lived in: Abraham Saward, aged 42, who farmed the 237 acre Bowsers Farm, had a 26 year old wife, three children under five, and employed a house-servant, a nursemaid and a 12 year old errand boy to help run the home while, to till his fields, he had ten men and three boys. George Jonas aged 23, was married to a 23 year old wife and had a seven month old daughter. He employed two house-servants and one groom, listed his occupation as 'farmer' but seems at this stage in his clearly not unpromising career to have had no farm. The largest farm in the parish was Newnham Hall, its 400 acres being cultivated by 65 year old Devereux Hustler. He employed twenty men and had three house-servants living in. The smallest farm was a holding of four acres owned by a 62 year old bachelor, John Ford, who farmed it with his 60 year old bachelor brother. They had no other labourers and no house-servants.

At the farther end of the social scale were the 59 parish paupers. Of these, the twenty males had all worked on the land including fifteen agricultural labourers and one former farmer; the eldest was 83, the youngest 43 and the one in greatest need of parish relief, a 48 year old with a wife and six children to support. Of the 39 female paupers, 27 were the widows of former agricultural labourers, the oldest being 79 and nine others being over 70; the youngest married female pauper was 23 years old with two children aged 2 and 6 months, and no comment on the whereabouts of her husband; the youngest unmarried female pauper was 19 years old living with a female lodger who also qualified for parish relief.

As striking a statistic as any is the number of Ashdonians who can fairly be numbered as dependents: the number of persons over 60 in the parish in 1851 was 99; the number of children under 12 was 398; the number of households with children under 12 was 119, so it would not be unreasonable to add say 100 mothers to the total of 600 persons in the community of 1200 unable because of their age or their domestic role to contribute to their own upkeep. Not all these dependents were the children of labourers: the two most prolific fathers in Ashdon were both farmers: John Cro, aged 45, farming the 120 acres of Midsummer Hill with the help of 5 men and 2 of his teenage sons, had five other children aged 5 or under. Fuller Tredgett, aged 39 and married to a 35 year old wife, owned 130 acres at Winsey Farm, had 4 men and a boy to help him and eight children under 11 to support. To introduce these statistics is not only to make the point that employers as well as employees had dependent children to support but that they were each required to support the other. The farmers, the labourers, their young children, their aged parents, the shopkeepers who supplied their food and clothing all had a powerful vested interest in agricultural prosperity. However wide the gulf that separated Ashdon's wealthy from its poor, they were all united in their dependence on the nation's willingness to pay a fair price for the corn which Ashdon's fine soil has always produced in rich abundance. When the chill winds of agricultural depression blew, they all shivered.

If the profitability of farming was one issue which both united and divided the Ashdon community in the middle of the nineteenth century, commitment to the Christian faith was emphatically another. For hundreds of years, the parish church was by far the most important single building in the life of the community. It was where the parishioners came to be christened and to be married, where they were brought to be buried and into which, at every Sunday Service, everyone processed and was seated according to the time-hallowed dictates of a very strict social hierarchy: the gentry preceded the tradespeople who preceded the farmers who preceded the labourers, and this processional order survived well into the twentieth century. For hundreds of years, whatever the quality of the parishioners' convictions, they all worshipped before the same altar and they all, nominally at least, subscribed to the same faith. Only after the Reformation in the sixteenth century and the bitter internecine secular and religious strife of the seventeenth, did the Church authorities feel it incumbent to check periodically to ensure themselves that each little local flock was still safely confined in the Anglican fold. It was for this reason that in 1642, all males aged eighteen and over in every parish were called upon to subscribe to the Oath of Protestation. Unfortunately, the returns for Essex cover but a small proportion of the county and the Clerk of the Records of the House of Lords Record Office, where all the original returns are stored, reports that the relevant document for Ashdon has not survived. What has survived, however, is the reply to a further request for similar information demanded in 1676, the so-called Compton Census, a complete copy of which is kept in the William Salt Library at Stafford. The entry for Ashdon states that at this time, there were in the parish 131 conformists, no papists and 9 non-conformists, the figures in each category being for males and females over the age of sixteen. The faith of some of these non-conformists was certainly Quaker because it has been established that there were at least four Quakers in Ashdon during the Restoration Period: Thomas Day (in 1664), Grace, wife of Thomas Buck (in 1681) and Edward Stanton and his wife (in 1681) (See Felix Hull: 'Essex Friends of the Restoration

Period', *Essex Review*, Vol. 57, 1948, p.68). There may conceivably have been others circumspect enough to keep their religious sympathies discreetly concealed because the Quakers were being actively persecuted at this time. In Saffron Walden, subsequently an important centre of Quaker power and influence, the corporation books contain such entries as the following: 'Spent when the proclamacyon came out against the Quakers, 1/2' (1664), 'Paid at the Bell when the Quakers were committed, 3/-' (1683), 'For nailing up the Quakers' door — twice, 4d' (1683). The Saffron Walden Church Register includes the following entry for 1669: 'Anthonie Peniston, Quaker, buried his mother like a dog in his garden.'

The same unmistakable whiff of bigotry is all too apparent in the way successive Bishops of London regularly worded the questionnaire they sent out to all incumbents in their diocese before they embarked on their periodic Visitation. After asking such routine questions as the extent of the parish, where the incumbent resided, the number of times on which he performed Divine Service and how often he catechized the young, the Bishop would invariably demand:

> Are there any Papists in your Parish? How many, and of what Rank? Have any Persons been lately perverted to Papery? By whom and by what Means? Is there any Place in your Parish in which they assemble and where Mass is performed? Doth any Papist Priest reside in your Parish or resort to it, and what is his Name? Is there any Papish School in your Parish, to which Protestant Children are admitted? Hath any Confirmation or Visitation been lately held in your Parish by any Papish Bishop? The Visitation replies which have survived from eighteenth-century Ashdon were invariably negative and almost identical: 'I know of no Papist in the Parish' (1766), 'I know of no Papist in the Parish' (1778), 'There are not any Papists nor any place in which Papists assemble' (1790). However, answers to another question in the later eighteenth-century Visitation returns from Ashdon provide clear indications of the dramatic developments that were to transform the religious scene.

In seeking so persistently for evidence of Papist perversion in rural England in the 1770s, the Bishop of London was pursuing recusancy in quite the wrong quarter. The threat to the monolithic rule of the Anglican Church at this time came not from the Roman Catholics but from the Methodists, fired by Wesley in full cry, and from the Baptists, founded in 1609 by John Smythe, repressed under James I and Charles II, set free by the Toleration Act of 1689 by William and Mary, but remaining in decline till the general revival of nonconformism in the middle of the eighteenth century. The appeal of both was emphatically, indeed stridently, to the yeoman and to the cottager, to men and women 'who were just climbing out of the utter poverty by the dint of their own thrifty endeavour' (J.H. Plumb: *England in the Eighteenth Century*, Penguin Books, 1950, p.95). There was no shortage of such men and women in Ashdon at the turn of the eighteenth century or of others who felt no particular compulsion to subscribe to the beliefs of the Squire. Sooner rather than later, religious nonconformity was bound to manifest itself in Ashdon in tangible form and the first signs of it are to be seen in the rector's replies to the seventh question in the Visitation return:

> 'Are there in your Parish any Dissenters from the Church of England, and of what Denomination? Have they any Meeting-Houses? Are they duly licensed and are their Teachers qualified according to the Law? Have you any who call themselves Methodists or Moravians, and has their Number lessened or increased of late Years?' In 1766, the rector's reply was: 'There are some few Presbyterians, Anabaptists and Quakers and I am afraid they are rather increased than lessened among us of late years'. In 1790, the reply was: 'There are some dissenters from the Church of England in the parish, though of what denomination I know not. They go to a Meeting House in Saffron Walden about four miles from this place. I cannot tell whether the Number is lessened or increased. I have been Curate [the section here has been eaten by rodents]. On account of the loss of his eye sight the Rector is incapable of performing the Duty of Parish . . . [the rest is illegible].

It was not long after this that the non-conformists in Ashdon were freed of the obligation to travel into Saffron Walden in order to worship. On 17th December 1809, the Reverend Matthew Walker and eleven members of his congregation formed themselves into 'The Particular Baptist Church of Christ being Protestant Dissenters'.

Before 1809, the Baptist Gospel had been preached to those Ashdon villagers who would listen in cottages or by the roadside by Ministers from the High Street Baptist Church in Saffron Walden. The Particular Baptist Church of Ashdon held its meetings near the village centre in a barn standing in a meadow beside what is now Chapel Farm. For the next thirty one years, until a new brick building was constructed largely from savings raised by the congregation, the Baptist faithful continued to meet, without heating or organ, in their wooden shed, the walls of which began to give way in the early 1830s. The principles of their faith were set out in the Church book. Some would have been readily accepted by many if not all Christian denominations:

> Faith is the gift of God and is wrought in the heart by the Holy Spirit of God;
> That it is appointed that all men once to die and after this the judgement;
> That the Book which we call the Bible . . . is the word of God and was given to us by the influence of the Holy Ghost.

Some were peculiar to Baptists in general:

> That Christ has appointed two positive Ordinances in His Church, Baptism and the Lord's Supper. By Baptism, we mean water baptism, to which only true believers have right, and that immersion is the only scriptural mode.

Some were confined to Particular Baptists of the persuasion which had set up its chapel in Ashdon:

> That God chose a certain number of the posterity of Adam in Christ *before* the foundations of the world, to everlasting life to be called in Time and received under the influence of the Holy Ghost and to be made wise by salvation.
> That Christ has died for the elect only.
> That those who were chosen by the Father, and redeemed by the Son, shall be called by Grace, and sanctified by the influence of the Holy Ghost.

In those Particular pioneering days, the Ashdon Baptists were clearly in no mood to compromise with those of any other persuasion. In 1834, Thomas J. Middleditch showed that he was, in spite of his name, no middle of the road man by having the following rules promulgated:

> That since Christians are commanded to watch over one another in the Lord, and since the honour and consistency of the Church as a body greatly depended upon the proper conduct of the individual members, when any of our number shall be guilty of immoral conduct, it is desirable that it should be communicated to the Church, and such steps to be taken as may appear advisable to maintain the honour and Christian character of the Church.
>
> That since the institution of a Church is designed to promote the union and intercourse of its members, if any one shall be absent from the Ordinance of the Lord's Supper three successive times, he or she shall be visited by persons appointed by the Church, and if no satisfactory reasons for such absence can be given shall be considered no longer a member.
>
> (All details and quotations are from A.L. Bidwell: *Ashdon Baptist Church - 1809-1959*, published privately in 1959 to mark the Chapel's ter-jubilee).

The Ashdon Baptists practised what they preached: in 1836, one of their members was suspended from the Church for six months after having been found guilty of intoxication; in 1845, a married lady was excluded for six months for 'very immoral conduct' and there are several references in the records to members being excluded from the congregation for failing to give a satisfactory explanation for not attending the Lord's Supper. It was two hundred years or more since the established Church in Ashdon had punished its adherents for reasons of this nature (see pp.153-5), so in choosing, as they did, to make a particular issue of this in the middle of the nineteenth century, the Baptists were adding an anachronistic barrier to the array of essentially social differences which separated them from their Anglican brethren in Christ.

On 8th May 1836, the Ashdon Baptists held their first recorded Baptism, the two persons concerned being John Freeman and a Mrs R. Graves. It is not known where the act of baptism was carried out, possibly in the River Bourne, possibly in one or other of the numerous ponds in the near vicinity. Between 1843 and 1846, 63 persons were baptised in Ashdon in the Baptist faith, and in 1847, its Church membership attained its highest membership ever recorded of 124. These figures need to be compared with those returned in yet another of the fact-finding inquiries in which the mid-nineteenth century authorities in England seem to have so delighted, in this case, the Ecclesiastical Census of 1851. The Commissioners sought to establish the total number of attendances at Church of England services on Sunday 30th March and, at the same time, asked for an estimate of the average attendances over the course of a year. The Ashdon return was as follows:

	On 30th March 1851			Average over twelve months		
	Morning	Afternoon	Evening	Morning	Afternoon	Evening
Men	184	329	—	200	400	—
Women	128	128	—	137	137	—
Total	312	457	—	337	537	—

Edward Hanson, the curate of Ashdon, reported that there were 125 Anglican communicants in total and that the average Sunday attendance of these was 89. In this respect, the figures quoted for 30th March 1851 seem to err distinctly on the side of wishful thinking. He justified his arithmetic in a letter he appended to the official return stating that the houses in the parish were 'scattered in all directions, many of them being 2½ miles from the Church', that 'the land is a heavy clay land' and 'the roads so bad that it [was] almost impossible for females to get to Church in wet weather'. He admitted that his figures were, accordingly, notional but nonetheless claimed that at the afternoon service, in fine weather, 'the Church [was] well filled with upwards of 400 people present'.

*   *   *

One outstanding set of statistics which emerges from the Government Census of 1851 are those for the birthplaces of the Ashdon inhabitants. Out of a total population of 1195, no fewer than 893 are listed as having been born in Ashdon or Bartlow Hamlet. Of the remainder, a striking number were born either in immediately adjoining parishes — 49 in Radwinter, 37 in Saffron Walden, 29 in Castle Camps, 9 in Linton, 4 in Bartlow — or in parishes within a

'Daddy' Flack in 1903

six mile radius — 16 in Sampford, 10 in Wimbish, 7 in Steeple Bumpstead, 5 in Hempstead, 3 in Debden. Those born in parishes rather further afield, such as Cambridge or further away still, such as Sheffield or Wallingford (Surrey), were almost invariably those supplying professional services, such as the schoolteachers and the ministers of religion, or the gentry. It is wholly symptomatic of the Ashdon community that the occupants of its most spacious home and grounds should have changed so frequently: in 1845, at the time of the Tithe Commissioners' survey, Viscount Maynard was designated as both the owner and the occupier of Waltons Park; in the 1848 edition of *White's Directory of Essex*, it is described as 'unoccupied'; in 1851, as has been shown, it was occupied by the family and retinue of 'Henry Hewston, Merchant'; in the 1863 edition of *White's Directory*, the occupier of Waltons is designated as a 'William Henry Betts, Esquire'.

Given this rate of change in the space of a mere eighteen years, it is by no means surprising that in the course of something like two centuries, the names of the well-to-do in the Ashdon community should have changed entirely. The most affluent of Ashdon's gentry in 1845 are listed in the Tithe Commissioners' Award documents; their counterparts in 1327 and 1524 are listed in the Lay Subsidy rolls and in 1664 in the Hearth Tax returns. No single surname appears in more than one document and none of the names will be found anywhere in the Ashdon graveyard. But for the fact that they were once adjudged wealthy enough to be assessed for tax purposes, they might never have existed.

What is more surprising than the lack of continuity in the surnames of Ashdon's better-off families is a similar lack of continuity in the surnames of its labouring class. Given the severe restrictions on poorer people's movement between parishes in the eighteenth century and the evidence of apparent geographical stasis in the statistics concerning inhabitants' birthplaces in the 1851 census, it is indeed remarkable how few family surnames recur in the variety of village records from age to age. A few that are still on the electoral rolls for the 1970s appear in the parish registers for the middle of the sixteenth century: Kytriche (the Tudor form of Kitteridge or Ketteridge), Cowper, Cornyll, Gooddinge (Goodwin), Page, Petytt and Thayke. In the middle of the eighteenth-century volumes, one regularly encounters Chapman, Flack, Ford, Marsh, Moss, Swann,

Webb, Woodley, names familiar to the Ashdon villager of today, but a whole muster-roll of surnames compiled from other sections of this book could be proclaimed today in the centre of the village and nobody would come forward in answer. It is a popular delusion, in fact, that in the past the great majority of country families stayed on in the same spot for centuries on end. A few remained rooted, especially if they were small freeholders or, as in the case of the Ashdon Kitteridges, they handed on a particular craft like bricklaying from generation to generation, but the great preponderance of countryfolk seem to have moved about from century to century, to a much greater degree than is commonly supposed. They did not engage in dramatic migrations from one end of the country to another, they mostly moved within a radius of ten miles or so, but all too rarely did a family and its descendants linger for more than a hundred years in the one place.

While, over the centuries, Ashdon would seem to have been no more static a rural community than any other, the one conspicuous quality which has always characterized it is its very real sense of seclusion. The reasons for this are not hard to find. The community was some distance from any of the country's main highways. For all essential goods and services it was self-sufficient, so there was no pressing need for any of the parishioners to travel. With its separate settlements scattered across hilly and, in places, heavily wooded terrain, its own local road-systems left much to be desired. This, at any rate, was the view of a surveyor in the 1770s who reported:

> ... the [Ashdon] roads [are] both bad and exceedingly intricate, there being scarce a direction-post to be seen, or a track to be depended on, the commons over which you pass being more worn by the neighbouring inhabitants in passing from their ground to their respective farmhouses than by travellers in their passage from parish to parish'.
> (From *History of Essex* by a Gentleman, quoted in A.F.J. Brown: *Essex at Work — 1770-1815*, Essex Record Office, 1969, p.77)

Only in the nineteenth century were concerted attempts made to improve Ashdon's internal system of communications and its links with the outside world. Brick bridges were built to replace the ages-old system of fords, all of which were impassable when the normally modest River Bourne asserted itself, burst its banks and flooded the surrounding terrain. After the rates had been increased and public subscriptions, one bridge was built in 1836 at the centre of the village by the 'Rose and Crown' and another was built nine years later over the road to Stevington End. Raising the money, planning and overseeing the planning of this second bridge was the responsibility of the Parish Surveyor, John Ruse, of Hill Farm. When the bridge was opened, the Rector of the day, Benedict Chapman, announced that it should for ever after be known as Ruse's Bridge, a more commendable way of achieving immortality than many another.

Over these new bridges, omnibuses and merchants' carts began to travel regularly between Ashdon and the outside world. White's Gazetteer of the County announced year by year that an omnibus left the centre of Ashdon for Audley End at 9 a.m. each day and that two separate carriers travelled to Cambridge every Wednesday and Saturday. In 1865, a single track railway line of standard gauge was built from Audley End via Saffron Walden to Bartlow Junction; a bundle of newspapers used to be lobbed from the engine footplate each morning as the train bridged Rectory Lane but it was not until 1910 that the trains began regularly to stop at Ashdon Halt. Exactly why they did so in that particular year we shall explain when we present our detailed picture of Ashdon in Edwardian times. Even then, as we shall see, and indeed until surprisingly far into modern times, twentieth-century Ashdon retained the most distinctive features of the ages-old community: secluded, self-sufficient, devoted to as it was dependent on its agriculture, its wealth inequitably divided between the wealthy few and the impoverished many. To explore the contrasting lifestyles of each will be the business of the following chapters.

4

The Life and Times of the Gentry

> Whosoever studieth the laws of the realm, whoso abideth in the university (giving his mind to his book), or professeth physic and the liberal sciences, or besides has service in the room of a captain in the wars, or good counsel given at home, whereby his commonwealth is benefited, can live without manual labour, and thereto is able and will bear the post, charge and countenance of a gentleman, he shall for money have a coat and arms bestowed upon him by the heralds, and thereunto, being made so good cheap, be called master, which is the title that men give to esquires and gentlemen, and reputed for a gentleman ever after.
>
> *William Harrison:* Description of England

(i) The overlords of Ashdon

Following his dramatic victory near Hastings in 1066 and his subjugation of the north over the four years which followed, William of Normandy was well able to enforce his claim that England had become his by might as he believed it was by right. He reserved a quarter of the Kingdom for his own use and distributed the rest among some hundred and seventy of his land-hungry henchmen. Ten of the most powerful of his noblemen shared half of these spoils between them and acquired up to seven or eight hundred confiscated manors apiece. At the lower end of the scale, humbler tenants-in-chief were rewarded with twenty manors or less, sometimes scattered across the shires. Whether his benefactions were vast or modest, William made it clear to the recipients that they were merely holding the lands on trust and that they, in return, were expected to provide him with men or money to garrison the royal castles and to staff the King's army. Over the centuries that followed, successive Kings viewed the lands of England with the same proprietorial eye and from the reign of Henry III onward, whenever a royal tenant-in-chief died, a detailed investigation was conducted into the possessions and services he was felt to owe the Crown to establish who had rights of inheritance. From these documents, the *Inquisitiones post mortem*, carefully stored and often calendared at the Public Record Office, and from other sources such as the Domesday Survey or the Red Book of the Exchequer, it is possible, with some accuracy, to establish who inherited what from whom and when.

There were, for hundreds of years, four main manors in the parish of Ashdon, Ashdon Hall, the Rectory Manor, Newnham Hall and Waltons and the account of their complicated conveyancing has principally to do with how, by a series of mischances and manoeuvres, they came into the possession of a single family and then at the very end of the nineteenth century were sold away.

Ashdon Hall was taken over from the Saxon widow, Ailid by Ralph Baignard, a powerful personage, who, in his time, served as Shire-Reeve (Sheriff) for the whole of Essex, which meant that he was chief officer of the Crown with fiscal and military responsibility for all of the county. No doubt he spent little or no time in Ashdon because his family seat was at Little Dunmow and his power-base, the massive Baynards Castle, on the banks of the Thames, where King's College and Somerset House now stand. His one act of lasting consequence for Ashdon was, in conjunction with his brother, Geoffrey Baignard, to donate the Manor of the Rectory to the Priory of Lewes in Sussex in 1096. The Abbot and Convent of Lewes retained the advowson (right of appointing the rector) of Ashdon Church till the Dissolution of the Monasteries by Henry VIII in the sixteenth century. At that point, Henry granted the Lordship of the Rectory Manor to Thomas Cromwell and, when he fell from grace, it reverted to the Crown. In 1552, it was given by Edward VI to Richard Tyrrel of Waltons (about whom there will be more anon). Thereafter, it passed through the hands of a succession of self-styled 'Gentlemen' or City merchants for the next hundred and fifty years till it was finally purchased by the Master and Fellows of Gonville and Caius College, Cambridge. It was the only significant part of the Ashdon scene which did not become one of the Maynards' possessions.

The Baignards did not retain the lordship of Ashdon Hall for long. In 1111, William Baignard, Ralph's grandson, conspired with one William Malet to replace King Henry I by Robert Duke of Normandy. I had hoped to establish that this personage was a very distant ancestor of William Mallett, the present-day, highly successful Ashdon fruit-farmer and Chairman of Ashdon Parish Council, but to date my researches have not enabled me to establish any connection. The twelfth-century Malet was Baron of Eyre and Great Chamberlain of England and apart from his relationship with Baignard, would seem to have had no connection with Ashdon. Neither did Baignard after the conspiracy was uncovered, because he was stripped of all his estates. They were given to Robert, younger son of Richard Fitz-Gislebert, ancestor of the noble family of Fitzwalter who were lords of Ashdon Hall for ten generations.

Their overlordship was not entirely without incident. The Patent Rolls reveal that in 1299, in the twenty seventh year of the reign of Edward I, Robert Fitzwalter 'complained that while he was on the King's service in Gascony and under his protection, Simon de Bradenham ejected him from the manor of Esshedon in the County of Essex'. A similar fate befell Edmund Bendysh whose lands lay across Ashdon's southern boundaries and were subsequently to become part of the Maynard estate. According to Holinshed, while Bendysh was attending Edward III at the siege of Calais, he mortgaged his manor at Bendysh Hall to the monks of Faversham. The siege dragged on and the mortgage lapsed before Bendysh could get back to confer with his creditors. The monks assured him that since he was absent on the King's service, payment could quite properly be delayed beyond the day assigned for settlement. When eventually he returned from the wars, he found that the monks, notwithstanding their assurances, had secured the estate to themselves. 'This induced Edmund Bendysh constantly to warn his contemporaries and to leave written admonition to posterity not easily to be persuaded to trust the fair promises of knave monk or knave friar.'

All that Edmund Bendysh lost for his pains was his estate; this is less than can be said of Sir John Ratcliffe who succeeded to the lordship of Ashdon Hall at the end of the fifteenth century after his mother, Anne, heiress to the Fitzwalter estate, married Thomas Ratcliffe. After being summoned to Parliament in 1485, Sir John was persuaded to support Perkin Warbeck in his bid for the throne of

England. He was brought to trial, convicted of high treason and beheaded. His estates were forfeited but all honours were restored to the family in 1505; Sir John's son Robert not only became Viscount Fitzwalter in 1525 but was made Earl of Sussex the year after. Almost five centuries after the Domesday Survey which provides proof positive of the way in which a victorious monarch could dole out lands to his henchmen for services rendered, it is interesting to observe that honours and an estate like Ashdon Hall could still be given or taken away by a powerful monarch to encourage the habit of loyalty.

After the Earl's death in 1542, the Ratcliffes retained possession of Ashdon Hall till 1619 when the estate was conveyed to William Bramston, *Esquire*, a term with more specific application in the class-conscious seventeenth century than it has in the egalitarian world of today. In the mediaeval era, the term designated the attendant of a Knight who accompanied him to the wars and rendered him personal services. In the course of time, its use was extended to include the sons of peers, and the firstborn sons of baronets and knights. Towards the end of the sixteenth century, its meaning was relatively restricted once more as William Harrison made clear in his *Description of England*:

> We in England divide our people commonly into four sorts, as gentlemen, citizens or burgesses, yeomen, and artificers or labourers. Of gentlemen the first and chief (next the King) be the princes, dukes, marquises, earls, viscounts, and barons, and these are called gentlemen of the greater sort, or (as our common usage of speech is) lords and noblemen; and next unto them be knights, esquires, and, last of all, they that are simply called gentlemen ...

In the course of the seventeenth century, Ashdon Hall was conveyed from one set of 'Esquires', by Harrison's reckoning, comparatively modest sprigs of the nation's gentry — to another, from an assortment of Bramstons on to a succession of Richers and subsequently, in the first half of the eighteenth century, to the Kings (or Sclater Kings). Eventually, Thomas of that ilk sold the manor to Henry, Lord Maynard, then the oldest surviving son of a family which already owned a goodly portion of Ashdon and which, over the next century and a half, was to come into possession of considerably more.

Before describing how this came about and the rather less than glorious final outcome, we first ought to provide a brief chronicle of the other two principal Ashdon manors and the major personages and incidents therein.

Newnham Hall was just one of the many prizes awarded to Count Eustace of Boulogne for the part he played in William's victory at Hastings. He appears in the Bayeux Tapestry, next to the Conqueror himself, pointing histrionically towards his leader who has tilted back his helmet and displayed his face in order to scotch the rumour that he had been slain. Eustace was rewarded with vast estates and indeed became the greatest lay baron in the whole of Essex and Hertfordshire. In addition to Newnham Hall, he also became overlord of Bendysh Hall now within the parish of neighbouring Radwinter but centuries ago part of a separate hamlet which was partly in Radwinter and partly in Ashdon.

In 1210, Newnham was still part of the Honor of Boulogne, a so-called 'Knight's Fee' which meant that in return for his being allowed tenure of land which was technically the King's, the holder had to provide the Crown with a fully armed Knight and his retinue of servants for forty days each year. For the next century and a half, Newnham was occupied by members of the de Lacy family, a branch of the ennobled family of Lacys, Earls of Lincoln. In 1347, John de Lacy sold the manor to Sir William de Clopton, Commissioner of Array for the County of Suffolk, and the family remained in residence for almost three hundred years. For reasons about which one can only speculate, Sir William de Clopton and his sons were ordered in 1366 not to leave the country with the threat that all their lands would be forfeit if they disobeyed. For other reasons almost as problematic, Newnham Hall was willed to Sir William's second son, Edmund, about whom little is known except that he married a Blanche Fitzeustace, left the estate to his son William and died in 1389. Rather more is known about his oldest brother, Walter de Clopton who rose to high eminence in the legal profession and in 1388-89, in the twelfth year of the reign of Richard II, became Chief Justice. On retiring from his legal career, in the course of which he collected and arranged the evidence of complicity of John Hall in the murder of the Duke of Gloucester, and tried all manner of petitions from England, Ireland and Wales in the Parliament of 1399, he was induced by the 'piety, integrity, and commendable example' of Robert

Coleman D.D. (Chancellor of Oxford University in 1419) to enter the monastery of the Grey Friars in Norwich where he wrote several treatises which have vanished without trace. The elder of his two daughters married Thomas Bendysh of Bendysh Hall.

Long after their association with Ashdon had ceased, the Cloptons continued to be commemorated in the parish. Cloptons remained an alternative name for Newnham. After close on three centuries of their occupation of Newnham Hall, as is not uncommon in account of land-tenure bound up with genealogy, the Clopton family found itself with no surviving male heirs. When yet another Sir William Clopton died in 1618, the estates were inherited by his daughter Anne who married Sir Symonds d'Ewes. Of their several children, all but two daughters died in infancy and when Sybil, the younger of these, married Sir Thomas Darcy, Baronet, he became lord of the Newnham Manor. From him it passed to Lord Maynard who also acquired possession of Mortivaux or Mortimers, part of the Newnham demesne which was owned by the Bendysh family from 1381 till 1545 when they sold it to one Stephen Cobb, a London haberdasher.

The main remaining area so far unaccounted for in Ashdon parish is Steventon End and the story of its various overlords is not the least interesting. In the wake of the Norman Conquest, this area was shared between two immensely powerful owners, Alberic de Vere, progenitor of the Earls of Oxford who were also allotted half of Radwinter, and Tihel Brito alias Tihel the Breton, also known as Tihel de Herion (or de Helion). He was one of the Bretons who served in the rear of William's armies under Alan the Red. The name Helion derives from Helléan in the Morbihan region of Brittany, and it still survives today in the form of Helions Bumpstead, a small village four miles due east of Ashdon. The Helion Barony also included a settlement at what is now called Thickhoe. There was also within the Ashdon parish boundaries a 'parcel of land' which was let by Count Alan the Red to Hervey Hispania, that same Hervey of Spain whose family name is still perpetuated in Essex in the village of Willingale Spain. This settlement, some forty acres in extent, is now known as Rothe End; it was formerly called Roda and immediately before the Conquest, it belonged to a lady with — what is for me — the second most evocative of all the names in Ashdon's long history, Edeva, alias Edith the Fair, otherwise known as Edith Swan Neck.

In 1259, a lease of Tihel's land was bought by Sir Richard de Walton (sometimes also found in the forms Wanton or Wawton) and from him derives the name by which the most extensive estate in the parish has ever since been known, Waltons Park or sometimes plain Waltons. This is by no means the only property in Ashdon to continue to bear the name of one of its earliest occupiers. According to Dr. P.H. Reaney, compiler of the authoritative *Place-Names of Essex*, others include Bourne Farm (home of Eudo Ateburne, 1278), Goldstones Farm (home of John Goldston, 1407), Hill Farm (home of Walter atte Hille, 1288), Sandons Farm (home of John de Sandon, 1303), and Winsey Farm, on the parish outskirts (home of Humphrey de Wyneleshey, 1553, of Willesey, 'just over the border').

It is not known how long the de Walton family retained possession of the estate which bears their name though we know that William de Walton was one of the knights representing the County of Essex in Parliament in 1304-5 and in 1310-12 and also that Robert de Walton presented a service-book to Bartlow Church about 1350. Tihel's line ended in a single heiress who married a Tyrell and this family took possession of Waltons in the early part of the fifteenth century.

The Tyrrells were an ancient Essex family and amongst the ancestors of various branches of the family they could number several individuals conspicuous either for murky or for glittering public deeds. The family claimed descent from Walter Tirel, the reputed killer of William Rufus; Sir John Tyrel, sheriff of Essex in 1423 and sometime Speaker of the House of Commons, was present at Agincourt in the retinue of Henry V who appointed him surveyor of the carpenters of the new works at Calais; his grandson Sir James Tyrell was the alleged murderer of the Princes of the Tower. If the Ashdon Tyrrells were not quite so exemplary either in virtue or in villainy, they nonetheless experienced chequered fortunes.

The first Tyrrell of whom details are extant for the Ashdon neighbourhood is Robert Tyrel, Esquire, who in 1524 was lessee of the Park at neighbouring Castle Camps, a small and ancient village in Cambridgeshire where Aubrey de Vere built himself a castle soon after the battle of Hastings. Robert Tyrell's name appears in a letter amongs the official State papers. It was written by Thomas Cromwell, Henry VIII's Minister, to the widowed Countess of Oxford and is an interesting mixture of blandishment and threat. Cromwell desires the Countess to continue to be his good friend and restore Master Tyrrel to the Park of Castle Camps whom she had wronged in expelling therefrom. It would, he stressed, be dishonourable to have the case tried in open court 'and the King is minded to have justice done in this cause without respect in persons'. The Countess has endorsed it 'a letter direct from my Master'.

This same Robert Tyrrell probably built and lived in the mansion house at Waltons while his son Richard lived in the adjoining farmstead of Ashdon Place. Robert was succeeded by Richard and he by his son Edward who was made Warden of the Fleet Prison in London as well as Keeper of the Palace of Westminster and of the shops and stalls in Westminster Hall. This was an office of profit which, since at least as far back as the reign of Richard I, the King had been accustomed to grant to persons of high estate. The profits consisted in the amount the first grantee could get by sub-letting, usually to persons of low degree so, as Dr. W.M. Palmer observed in a most informative article in the *Cambridge Chronicle* of May 21st 1924, 'it is true to say that some of the comforts which the Tyrrels enjoyed at Waltons were derived from the groans of the prisoners in the Fleet Prison'.

Edward Tyrrel's eldest son Robert succeeded him and was knighted in 1607. He married Susan Millicent of Barham Priory. The marriage was not a success because we find in 1612 Sir Robert's trustee paying over a large sum to Lady Susan's brother for the maintenance of her and her children. The capital Mansion House, otherwise called the King's Gaol of the Fleet, was also handed over to Sir Robert Millicent as a security. A long list of the plate, furniture and clothing which Lady Millicent took with her from Waltons, has survived. There were fifty pieces of silver, including a silver perfuming pan. There were also one great jewel of diamonds and rubies, a cloth riding coat lined with watchet velvet and trimmed with gold and silver lace and buttons, a watch and a 'larm' and a fair pearl hat band. Dr. Palmer suggests that 'perhaps the cause of the family discord in this case may have been Sir Robert's great love for the fair sex. His moral lapses were several times the subject of presentments at the Ecclesiastical Court. Perhaps that is why he changed his residence so often. From Ashdon he emigrated to Bartlow Hall, then to Shudy Camps and in 1633 he was living at Linton'.

When Sir Robert moved to Bartlow early in the sixteenth century he sold Waltons to William, Lord Maynard, and, together with the greater and certainly the more prosperous part of Ashdon, it remained in the possession of the Maynard family for virtually the next three centuries. The Maynards (Mainards or Maignards) were a family of considerable antiquity who, before putting down their roots deep into Essex soil, were seated in Kent and at Brixham in Devon. Why specifically Sir William was created a baronet in 1611 is not clear. Honours were not hard to come by immediately after the death of Queen Elizabeth who had been notoriously niggardly in distributing them. James I and successive Stuart monarchs were, in contrast, positively profligate: any landowner with an annual income of £20 (subsequently raised to £40) was expected to become a knight and Charles I actually fined all those duly qualified who had not come forward to have themselves knighted at his coronation. The newly created title of baronet was jealously restricted at first but rapidly declined in status as the Crown's financial needs led to increased sales. James I reduced its price from £700 in 1619 to £220 in 1622 and Charles I in his turn created many more baronets in the later 1620s in order to raise much needed revenue.

None of which is meant to mean that Sir William Maynard, Baronet, was any more or less unworthy than his peers, or that there was anything particularly noteworthy, for either good or ill, about his being created Baron Maynard of Wicklow in 1620 or a Baron of the realm by Charles I in 1627. The title he chose was Maynard of Estaines Parva and Little Easton (near Dunmow) and this remained the family seat until the 1930s. All that can be said about this particular member of the family is that he would seem to have done nothing conspicuous enough in his lifetime to warrant an entry in the *Directory of National Biography* unlike his younger brother Sir John Maynard who 'danced the admired of all beholders in the Court masque on Twelfth Night, 1619', who composed a masque for Buckingham on 16th November 1623 which was 'performed with no great approbration', and who, on being impeached by Parliament for his blatant Royalist sympathies on 1st February 1648, refused to make any defence, refused to kneel or in any way recognize the jurisdiction of the House of Lords and, for his pains, was fined £500 and incarcerated in the Tower. With the exception of Baron Maynard's son William, born in 1622 by his second wife, who went on to become a Privy Councillor and Comptroller of the Household of James II, the rest of the Maynards kept discreetly out of the public eye and devoted themsleves to country pursuits in the depths of their Essex heartlands.

It seems to have been no easy matter to ensure the family succession and, with it, the continuing connection of the Maynard name with the rich estates. William can be said to have done his best: he married firstly Dorothy née Banastre, by whom he had two sons, Banastre and William, and secondly Margaret, daughter of James Murray, the Earl of Dysart, by whom he had a son, Henry, and a daughter, Elizabeth. In 1698, Banastre became third Baron and when he died in 1717, the estate and the honours passed to Henry, the eldest surviving son. He died in 1742, unmarried, at the age of seventy, and he was succeeded by his brother, Grey, who died also unmarried, aged sixty five, in 1745. He, in turn, was succeeded by his youngest brother Charles, the sixth Baron and last direct male descendant of the first Baron Maynard; he was created Baron Maynard of Much Easton in 1766. When he died, unmarried like his brothers before him, in 1775, the baronetcy and the English baronies of 1620 and 1628 became extinct but the new title, created in 1766, passed to a third cousin, Sir William Maynard of Waltons Park, the great grandson of Charles Maynard, third son of Henry. We shall return to him later.

The Maynards remained overlords of most of Ashdon till 1896 though their empire contracted slightly when Ashdon Hall and its manor was sold to the family of the Reverend William Hammond early in the nineteenth century. Colonel Maynard, the last male heir, died before his father, and when the last surviving Maynard, the beautiful and vivacious Frances Evelyn, married the Earl of Warwick, the still very extensive estates became linked with another family name. The name of the Countess of Warwick was soon romantically linked with that of Edward Prince of Wales and he became a regular visitor to her country seat at Little Easton. At the outset, she would meet him with her coach and four at Elsenham Station and in the 1960s there were still people living in the Dunmow area who could remember how 'Darling Daisy' would personally take the reins to drive her Prince Teddy home. Later, a special railway halt was set up between Bishops Stortford and Dunmow where she would regularly meet his train. There was never anything clandestine about the relationship. On one occasion, the couple paid a quasi-State visit to Thaxted's magnificent parish church and listened to the Town Brass Band outside the mediaeval Guildhall as it played 'God Bless the Prince of Wales'. In his engaging book of reminiscences, *The Mayor and the Matron*, Stanley Wilson records that he once conversed with some of those bandsmen who testified that when the Countess asked the Prince for his assessement of the rendition, he replied, 'Not too bad, though not yet quite up to the standard of my Brigade of Guards'.

Doubtless it was because another set of pipers finally had to be paid for an endless round of rather different tunes that the Maynards' Ashdon estates finally had to be sold. They comprised the eleven largest farms in Ashdon as well as Bendysh Hall in Radwinter, all manner of messuages, the advowson of the Rectory and Ashdon's stateliest home, Waltons Park. It was all purchased in 1896 by an Irish gentleman whose stay in the district seemed, from the outset, likely to be fairly brief. The local newspaper reported:

> In our last issue we reported that an Irish gentleman was the purchaser for £38,000 of Lady Warwick's Ashdon and Radwinter estate, which was disposed of by private contract a few days before the date fixed for public auction. It was now transpired that the gentleman is Mr Ernest T. Hooley, who has also just purchased Lord Ashburton's Wiltshire estate. Mr Hooley is said to be an energetic Churchman and a generous supporter of all ecclesiastical and charitable funds of the Ilkeston of Derbyshire where, it is stated, he is to stand as Conservative candidate against Sir B. Foster M.P.

While this particular purchaser left no impression whatsoever on the life of the Ashdon community, the same is not entirely true of the colourful vendor. On being dramatically converted to the Socialist cause following a scathing attack on her extravagant lifestyle by Robert Blatchford of the weekly *Clarion*, the Countess of Warwick pledged her considerable energies and what was left of her once considerable wealth to the Labour movement. Because she also retained a lifelong affection for Waltons Park and Ashdon, where she spent a brief and happy period in her teens, she readily rallied to the side of the Ashdon labourers when they came out on strike in the summer of 1914 and was conspicuously active in their support.

(ii) The Rectors

In Ashdon, as in most other parishes over the centuries, the wealthiest and most influential member of the community after the squire was consistently the village rector. In addition to what he might earn from the sale of property and farm-produce, he could be assured of a regular, and often handsome, income through the exercise of all manner of ancient rights and privileges. The Rector received a payment whenever he christened his parisioners, whenever he married them and whenever he buried them. Often, though not invariably, he was entitled to a *Soul Scot* (the second best beast or chattel after the Lord's *heriot*) but, most important and rewarding of all, he was entitled to his tithes, the annual payment from everyone in the community of a tenth part of their produce and in certain cases, their services. The Rector of Ashdon was not only the parish priest, he was also Lord of the Rectory Manor. Given that in addition, for hundreds of years, he could rely on the support of affluent and important patrons, it is not altogether surprising that among the long line of reverend gentlemen who can be identified as having held the benefice over the last seven centuries, some have been particularly distinguished.

Of these, undoubtedly the most powerful was Rowland Lee who was Rector of Ashdon from 1522 until 1533. The amount of time he actually spent in the village is likely to have been strictly limited indeed, he might rarely have set foot there and may well have appointed a vicar to officiate on his behalf. He was a conspicuously hungry office-seeker. By virtue of bulls from three successive popes, he held simultaneously the livings of Banham, in Norfolk (from 26th October 1520), Ashdon (from 24th July 1522) and Fenny Compton, Warwickshire (from 1st October 1526). While still retaining these three posts, he became Prebendary of Lichfield, Archdeacon of Cornwall and Archdeacon of Taunton. Most of these preferments, it is assumed, he owned to Cardinal Wolsey but after the fall of Wolsey, he played an important part in the rise of Thomas Cromwell. He helped suppress a number of monasteries and priories, including Felixstowe and Mountjoy in Norfolk. While still nominally Rector of Ashdon in 1533, he officiated at the private wedding ceremony between Henry VIII and Anne Boleyn in a 'garret' in Whitechapel on 25th January. It is doubtless no coincidence that in the same year, he was elevated from the Rectory of Ashdon to the Bishopric of Coventry and Litchfield. He went on to become Lord Resident of the Welsh Marches and before his death on 28th January 1543, he had according to A.L. Rowse (in *The England of Elizabeth*), 'hanged thieves in hundreds, right and left', without, on his own admission, making theft any whit the less frequent in the notoriously lawless areas he had been charged with administering.

While Rowland Lee was by far the most powerful personage ever to have been associated with Ashdon Rectory, the most eminent in terms of high office was no less certainly his contemporary Matthew Parker. Born in 1504 and educated at Cambridge, Parker was Rector of Ashdon from 1542 to 1544. In December 1544, he was elected Master of Corpus Christi College, Cambridge, and was commended to its Fellows 'as well for his apparent learning, wisdom and honesty, as for his singular grace and industry in bringing up youth in virtue and learning, so apt for the exercise of the said roome [i.e. office] as it is thought very hard to find the like for all respects and purposes'. A month later, at the age of 41, he became Vice-Chancellor of Cambridge University and in 1559, he was made Archbishop of Canterbury. Clearly, at this stage in its history, Ashdon Rectory was a living reserved by those in charge of the Church's affairs for its favourite sons, whether or not they actually took up residence there.

Though the names of Lee's and Parker's Ashdon predecessors are known as far back as 1285, their personalities and accomplishments are shrouded in almost total obscurity. On one occasion, it would appear, 'William Jones, parson of Ashdon', was denounced as 'a scandalous minister' in a report to the Earl of Manchester, though whether the scandal was of a doctrinal or of a moral nature, one cannot say. It is somehow characteristic of Ashdon Rectory's own Dark Ages that when, in 1710, the venerable antiquarian Richard Newcourt came to compile his list of Ashdon rectors, the only one besides Lee about whom he could provide any details of consequence was one John Upton, rector in 1396: he notes that about this time, there was a John Upton of the Order of Carmelites, a Doctor of Divinity of Oxford, and subsequently a preacher in London 'who was in great Esteem with Thomas, Duke of Clarence, and his Confessor, and grew daily in great Esteem with the People, and also with the Prince. He wrote much and published one Book of learned Sermons . . . but whether he was the same with *our* John Upton, I know not'. Something else he seems not to have known is Matthew Parker's link with Ashdon: it does not receive a mention.

Ashdon's other sixteenth- and seventeenth-century rectors remain almost as shadowy as the mediaeval ones and it is only from the eighteenth century onwards that one can begin to supply some of the Rectors' names with anything like a *curriculum vitae* or a personality. While none of them could match the academic distinction of Benedict Chapman, Rector of Ashdon from 1818 to 1852, who became Master of Gonville and Caius College, Cambridge, or of Henry Swete, Rector of Ashdon from 1877 to 1890, who became Regius Professor of Divinity in the University of Cambridge, many of them reveal a bureaucratic preoccupation with statistical *minutiae* far beyond the call of duty. The words clergyman, cleric and clerk all belong to the same etymological family and while one may reasonably wonder whether each and every one of the long line of Ashdon rectors has always possessed the devout attributes popularly associated with the first two of these terms, study of the parish records again and again reveals that loving care for book-keeping, legal transactions and list-making which characterizee the third. As a direct consequence of this, and because so many of the Ashdon rectorial documents have been lovingly preserved, we know more about the domestic surroundings, chattels and accoutrements of the church and its officers than we do of any other set of parishioners.

An inventory of the Ashdon Church goods, made in 1552-53, in the sixth year of Edward VI, provides clear evidence of the opulent style in which ceremonial had to be conducted at a time when the great majority of the local population were living in comparative penury:

> Goods not alienated delyvered into the hands and custodie of William Odle and John Freman [described as 'presenters' but, in fact, the Churchwardens]
>
> ii challices of xxii ounces weight. A cope of red velvet and a vestment of the same. A cope of white satten and a vestment of the same. A blue vestment of velvett. i black vestment of velvett. A vestment with tunacles to the same of blue satten silke. A tunacle of blue silke with a cros of Imagery wrote. A herse cloth of black velvett with a cros of white damask. A canopie clothe or blacke satten. A alter clothe with flower

> delies [de lys] of clothe of golde and iii other clothes silke. ii pillowes of blue silke and i of black silke satten. iiii corporas cases. ii corporas clothes. A cote of crymsen satten and another of red velvet. A cros clothe of silke. ii banners of silke. i towels that were for the rodelofte. ii howseling clothes. vi towels. A rodeloft clothe. A clothe that did hang before the Image of all halowes. A hollywater stock of bras. A paire of censers, a ship and a basen of brass. iii trivetts and a crismytorie of pewter. iiii bells in the steple of lviii. A sanctus bell. A little bell at the Chauncel ende. iii hande bells.
> Goods . . . solde
> A crosse of silver; a paire of censers, a pix box, a paxe, a pair of cruetts of sylver for £xxxi which is in the hands of John Coll and Thomas Cleydon of the saide parishe.
> Goods alienated and taken away.
> By Mr Sylesdon, the gilde stock — £30 — vi — viii. A pair of andirons worth iiis[hillings] . ii spitts worthe xs[hillings]. A pott worth xxs. By what authoritie we knowe not.

One would like to know more about this enigmatic Mr Sylesdon and whether he was ever brought to account.

Some notion of the desirability of the Ashdon living can be gauged from the list of possessions which went with it. A Terrier (or descriptive list of property) belonging to the Rectory in 1610 consisted of the following:

> A Parsonage-House, and other Houses of Office, two Barns, a Stable, a Hay-House, and a Gate-House, with Rooms above and below, a Dove-House, an Orchard, a Whiting-Yard, and a Pasture containing four Acres, lying on the West-side of the Parsonage House; as also 54 Acres more of Glebeland, besides a Close of Pasture called *Parsonage-Wodehill*, the quantity not set down; and 20 Acres of Arable-Land, which were granted by Copy of Court-Roll in 21. Hen. VIII (i.e. the 21st Year of the reign of Henry VIII — 1529-30) by Rowland Leigh, then Parson . . .
> (Newcourt: *Repertorium Ecclesiasticum Parochiale Londinense*, Vol. II, 1710).

Another Terrier was drawn up in 1810 by the then Rector, John North, who listed the 'Lands Houses Tenements and the Lights and

Emoluments belonging to the Rectory of the Parish of Ashdon in the County of Essex and in the Diocese of London'.

> One tiled Dwelling House called the Parsonage House which has been considerably repaired and improved by the present Rector with its Offices also tiled together with a Cottage adjoining now occupied by Joseph Lofts Labourer — and also two thatched Barns — a Cowhouse — Chaisehouse — two thatched Stables built by the present Rector in 1796 — a tiled Dove house and two thatched cottages — and also a Farm Yard — a Cow Yard — a Stackyard — a Wood Yard — a Courtyard before the House — a walled Garden and small Plantation near it. One tiled Cottage adjoining to the Church Yard called the Vicarage occupied by Richard Marsh Labourer and a Garden containing one Rood and a quarter of Land. The Glebe Lands belonging to the Rectory consist of a Pasture and arable Lands all enclosed.

He then proceeds to enumerate all his fields, identifying them by name and minutely describing their boundaries in relation to those of the adjoining properties. He then notes that

> to the Rectory also appertains a Manor called the Manor of the Rectory ... At this Time the Number of Tenants is about 30 — The Number of Parcels of Land is about 45 — several of which are the site of mere Cottages inhabited by Labourers with very small Gardens adjoining — The Number of Acres of Land amount to 60 acres more or less — The Rental of the whole amounts to £3-2-8 — All these Lands as well as the Manor annexed are free from any Fines Rates or Services to any other Lord of a Manor.

(iii) The Gentry at play

Such was the Norman Kings' passion for hunting that a third of all England was decreed to be one vast game-reserve and a harsh set of special laws was enacted to ensure that at all times the royal court might be able to pursue 'the beasts of the forests', the red and fallow deer, the roe and the wild boar. Offences were numerous: not merely poaching the game for oneself but cutting down any forest, woods or thickets suitable for feeding animals, clearing or cultivating land that might have provided cover for breeding or being found in the forest with an unslung bow or with a dog which had not been 'law-ed' by cutting three claws from each of its forepaws. The laws were enforced by an elaborate hierarchy of officers appointed for that specific purpose: local foresters on foot or horseback were responsible for the *verderers* (four for each county) who served under the wardens (regularly appointed at the King's pleasure), who were, in turn, commanded by the Chief Forester. From the early Norman period onwards there were severe penalties for those offending against the greenwood or against the venison or for having the temerity even to resist the forest law-enforcers. The penalties ranged from having to pay a heavy fine to losing one's hand, one's skin or one's life. The penalties remained almost as savage between Norman and Tudor times during which period much of what had begun as exclusively royal control over the forests passed to the aristocracy and thence to the landed gentry. One can see this transfer of rights taking place in the various transactions that were negotiated for hunting rights over Ashdon lands.

In 1204, the 'men of Essex', the knights and freemen who attended the Shire Court, were already sufficiently keen on their hunting to offer King John 500 marks and 5 palfreys if he would renounce his legal jurisdiction over 'the forest of Essex which is beyond the causeway between Colchester and Bishops Stortford'. Over the years, successive monarchs granted 'free warren' to a variety of favored personages, thereby permitting them to kill all game and beasts on the estates specified other than the precious deer: in 1293, Edward I granted Walden Abbey free warren at Ashdon; in 1315, Edward III granted Bartholomew de Badelsmere and his heirs the right to hold a weekly market on Fridays in their manor of Ashdon, to hold a yearly fair there 'on the Vigil, the feast and the morrow of the Translation of St. Nicholas' 'and also free warren in all their demesne lands'; in 1330, Edward III also granted free warren in all their demesne lands in Ashdon to Robert de Bousser and his heirs while in 1348, the same monarch, 'by a grant of special grace', allowed William de Clopton and his heirs free warren in their demesne lands at Newnham Hall in Ashdon. In August 1533, Rowland Lee visited his parish in Ashdon then moved on to Broomhill in Norfolk where he and Gregory Cromwell 'killed a great buck' and from where he sent a gift of partridges to Thomas Cromwell.

When, in the second half of the sixteenth century, William Harrison came to describe the state of England, he could not fail to comment on a feature as prominent as hunting. About contemporary developments in this age-old pursuit, he clearly had mixed feelings. He did not expatiate on the by now defunct sport of jousting but he had no doubts that the hunting classes of bygone times were markedly more heroic than their Elizabethan successors. 'The beasts of the chase were commonly the buck, the roe, the fox and the marten. Those of venery in old time were the hart, the hare, the boar and the wolf' (*Description of England*, pp.259-260). Such creatures, in Harrison's view, were well worth pursuing but times and practices had changed:

> The fallow deer, as bucks and does, are nourished in parks, and conies in warrens and burrows. As for hares, they run at their own adventure, except some gentleman or other (for his pleasure) do make an enclosure for them. Of these, also, the stag is accounted for the most noble game, the fallow deer is the next, then the roe, whereof we have indifferent store, and last of all the hare, not the least in estimation because the hunting of that seely [defenceless] beast is mother to all the terms, blasts and artificial devices that hunters do use. All which (notwithstanding our custom) are pastimes more meet for ladies and gentlewomen to exercise . . . than for men of courage to follow, whose hunting should practise their arms in tasting of their manhood and dealing with such beasts as eftsoons will turn again and offer them the hardest [danger] rather than their horses' feet, which many times may carry them with dishonor from the field (*loc. cit.*, pp.327-328).

Harrison also criticized his contemporaries for their growing tendency to fence or hedge off their estates rather than hunt across the open Chase or through the forests as the King and the gentry had done since time immemorial. He reminded his readers (who were inevitably of the well-to-do class) that it was 'trespass and against the law for any man to have or make chase, park or free warren without good warranty of the King by his charter or perfect title of prescription. To hive off land for private hunting, he declared, not only risked offending the King but also threatened to depopulate vast areas.

These strictures apart, Harrison had no reservations about the activity of hunting as such. He was not only an eclectic scholar, he was also a country parson and it was quite in character for him to write so enthusiastically of the gentry's pursuit of game while maintaining an eloquent silence on the morality of the punishments meted out to those of the lower orders rash or hungry enough to want to partake of it too. The landed gentry watched over their preserves with the same jealous vigilance as their royal predecessors. The Forest Laws gave way to the Game Laws and attempts to enforce them or to contravene them became a form of class warfare that was waged for three centuries. One suspects that when, on 1st September 1591, the following charge was brought against William Berry, husbandman of Ashdon at the Quarter Sessions, it had almost as much to do with his non-possession of property as with his possession of an offensive weapon:

> Not having lands etc. to the value of £100 yearly, charged with shooting twelve shots with a fowling piece in a certain parcel of land at [Ashdon] called Sames, and killing five ring-doves, also for shooting eight shots in the parish of Radwinter and killing six doves, contrary to the statute of 33 Henry VIII.

The Acts for protecting game in England did not become really ferocious until after the accession of George III. Under the Game Act of 1770, anybody who unlawfully killed game of any kind between sunset and sunrise, or used any gun, or dog, snare, net or other engine for destroying game at night was, on conviction by one witness before one Justice of the Peace, to be punished with not less than three months or more than six months imprisonment. For a subsequent offence he was to be imprisoned for not less than six months or more than twelve, and to be whipped publicly between the hours of twelve and one o'clock. It was in this legal climate and with much of this legal phraseology that Nathanael Salter, Rector of Ashdon and Lord of the Rectory Manor, drew up a document in his own copper-plate hand in 1772, appointing William Haylock junior as his new gamekeeper and authorizing him 'to take and sieze [sic] all such Guns, Greyhounds, Setting Dogs, Lurchers or other Dogs and all such Trannells, Hayes, Netts, Snares or other Engines whatsoever as shall be used or kept for the taking, killing or Destroying of hares, phessants, partridges or other Game within [his] said Manor or the precincts thereof'.

In 1800, a fresh Act to curb poachers was passed decreeing that when two or more persons were found in any forest, chase, park, wood, plantation, paddock, field, meadow, or other open or enclosed ground, having any gun, net, engine, or other instrument, with the intent to destroy, take or kill game, they were to be seized by keepers or servants, and on conviction before a J.P., to be treated as rogues and vagabonds and punished by imprisonment with hard labour; an incorrigible rogue, that is a second offender, was to be imprisoned for two years with whipping. If the offender was over twelve years old, he might be sentenced to serve in the army or navy.

In the circumstances, when on 15th November 1801, 'Thomas Day of Ashdon yeoman was convicted at Quarter Sessions for 'keeping and using a gun to kill and destroy game' or when, on 3rd March 1804, Thomas Hall and James Hall, labourers of Ashdon, were found guilty of the same offence, all three might be considered to have escaped lightly when each was fined £5. The J.P. who sentenced Thomas Hall was one William Lee and while he may possibly have been merciful on this occasion he would not seem to have been particularly realistic. When, in January 1801, the Ashdon Overseers sent in their statutory list of the poor to the Justices, Thomas Hall had a wife and two children under 12 to support and his total weekly wage was 14 shillings. One wonders how or if the £5 was paid.

Whatever the unfortunate Hall's fate, he could count himself fortunate that he was not convicted under the Game Act of 1817. This decreed that any person found at night in any forest, chase or park, armed with gun, crossbow, bludgeon or any other offensive weapon was to be tried at Quarter Sessions and, if convicted, to be sentenced to transportation for seven years; should a person so convicted be found back in England before this seven year term, he was to be transported for the rest of his life. This Act was softened eleven years later when transportation was reserved for a third conviction, the first and second meriting three and six months respectively. Nonetheless, if three men were found in a wood and one carried a gun or bludgeon, all three were liable, even on first conviction, to be transported for fourteen years.

Down the centuries, no single issue generated more bitter feelings in rural areas than the contested right to hunt game and in no area is the forging of the law as a social weapon surely quite so blatant. The reverberations from that conflict went on, as will be seen, into the Edwardian age in Ashdon and well beyond.

Not all the leisure pursuits of the Ashdon gentry were so sanguinary even though, on occasion, they might have been pursued as fanatically as the hunt. There was, for example, gardening. William Harrison, sometime Rector of Radwinter, describes how, in the late sixteenth century, he and his peer-group could be no less concerned than their present-day counterparts with embellishing the gardens around their homes. He waxes positively lyrical over the horticultural bounty being shipped back from across the oceans by Elizabethan voyagers who were then so actively exploring the other side of the world:

> If you look into our gardens annexed to our houses, how wonderfully is their beauty increased, not only with flowers ... and variety of curious and costly workmanship, but also with rare and medicinable herbs sought up in the land within these forty years; so that in comparison of this present the ancient gardens were but dunghills and laystows to such as did possess them ... It is a world also to see how many strange herbs, plants and annual fruits are daily brought us from the Indies, Americans, Taprobane [Ceylon], Canary Isles, and all parts of the world; the which, albeit that in respect of the constitutions of our bodies they do not grow for us, because that God hath bestowed sufficient commodities upon every country for her own necessity, yet for delectation sake unto the eye and their odoriferous savors unto the nose they are to be cherished and God to be glorified also in them, because they are His good gifts and created to do man help and service. There is not one nobleman, gentleman or merchant that hath not great store of these flowers, which now also do begin to wax so well acquainted with our soils that we may also account of them as parcel of our own commodities.
>
> Thanks be given unto our nobility, gentlemen, and others for their continual nutriture and cherishing of such homeborn and foreign simples in their gardens; for hereby they shall not only be had at hand and preserved, but also their forms made more familiar to be discerned and their forces better known than hitherto they have been.
>
> And even as it fareth with our gardens, so doth it with our

> orchards, which were never furnished with so good fruit nor with such variety as at this present. For besides that we have most delicate apples, plums, pears, walnuts, filberts, etc., and those of sundry sorts, planted within forty years past, in comparison of which most of the old trees are nothing worth, so we have no less store of strange fruit, as apricots, almonds, peaches, figs, corn trees [cornelian cherry] in noblemen's orchards. I have seen capers, oranges and lemons, and heard of wild olives growing here, beside other strange trees brought from afar whose name I know not . . .

After eulogizing the nation's gardeners for their unending virtuosity in the arts of grafting, he turned to the subject of his own modest garden beside Radwinter Rectory:

> For mine own part, good reader, let me boast a little of my garden, which is but small and the whole area thereof little above three hundred foot of ground, and yet, such hath been my good luck in purchase of the variety of simples that, notwithstanding my small ability, there are very near three hundred of one sort and other contained therein, no one of them being common or usually to be had. If therefore my little plot, void of all cost in keeping, be so well furnished, what shall we think of those of Hampton Court, Nonsuch [the royal palace near Cheam in Surrey], Theobalds [Lord Burghley's manor in Hertfordshire] or Cobham Garden [the seat of Harrison's patron in Kent]?
> *Description of England*, ed. cit., pp.265-271.

One finds the same delight in gardening together with a detailed account of the life-style of the Essex country gentry in the diary of another cleric in the middle of the eighteenth century. The Reverend William Cooper was curate of Thaxted in the 1750s. He attended Trinity College, Cambridge and was brother of Sir Guy Cooper, Secretary to the Treasury in the North Administration. The diary he kept was first published in the *East Anglian* (New Series, X, Nos. 152-7) and is liberally quoted by A.F.J. Brown in his highly informative *Essex People 1750-1900* (Essex Record Office, Chelmsford, 1972). The diary-entry for June 12th 1759 is both characteristic and revealing and suggests that while Cooper may not have been the archetypal Young Man in a Hurry, he was consistently aware of life's glittering prizes:

> As ye several offices and duties of my Parish demanded by strictest care and attention, ye greatest part of my time was taken up in a constant and punctual performance of them; every morning I visited ye sick and ye poor, and, to ye utmost of my Abilities and Power, aided and assisted them both; every afternoon (without some particular business prevented me) I rode out to Easton, Dunmow or Ashdon, or some of ye Neighbouring seats, where I agreeably spent my time with those whose Integrity and good Sense might be of Service to me in my further progress through ye World [Note: Clearly his time was not entirely wasted because he eventually became Archdeacon of York].
>
> Here let me remark that I never before or after, have been so perfectly happy as I was during my residence at Thaxted, being conscious to myself that I was doing all ye good that men in my profession ought to do; that I was not (as God knows too often is ye case) avariciously hoarding up ye income or profits of my Cure, but at intervals disposing of it to those whose needs and distress, as they came under my own eye, more particularly required my help and assistance.

Cooper praises Lord Maynard, then in his sixty eighth year, and stresses his generosity to the poor. He describes Easton Lodge, with its 'very large and extensive park containing upwards of three hundred head of Deer', the chapel, with 'some paintings wonderfully well executed upon glass and ye Library, which contains a very fine collection of books . . .'. He then proceeds to describe some of his own particular friends, including 'ye Reverend Mr Forester who is a very good natur'd well-bred man, not overstocked with polite literature yet serves properly enough for ye office of a Country Rector: His house is situated in Lord Maynard's Park from whence you have ye same views as from Easton Lodge. He has in his garden a very pleasant Arbour in which he sometimes reads a piece of Divinity and sometimes a News-paper; also a fish-pond well supply'd with Tench, which however he is not remarkably expert in catching. His House contains six Bedchambers, a Parlour, Drawing-Room, Hall, Kitchen, and other conveniences'.

Other Essex friends with whom he had spent 'many a cheeful and agreeable Hour' included Sir William and Lady Maynard of Waltons Park, Ashdon:

> Sir William Maynards seat at Ashdon is most beautifully situated: it is nine miles distant from Thaxted, and fourteen from Cambridge: from Sir William's you plainly see Lord Godolphin's house upon Hogmagog [sic] Hills. Ye Walks, ye Partirres, ye Avenues are laid out with great taste and judgement; ye whole house is very elegantly furnished; in it there is one room which cannot fail of attracting ye Eyes of ye beholders, as ye furniture of it is remarkably splendid, and ye Paper ye finest India paper I ever saw. In this room you see a very good picture of Ld Maynard, done by Wills, who some years afterwards, being touch'd in his *pericranium*, quarrell'd with his Art, and commenced a Parson.
> > *Qui fit, Maecenas, ut nemo, quam sibi sortem*
> > *Seu ratio dederit seu fors objecerit, illa*
> > *Contentus vivat . . .*
>
> [The opening of the first poem in Horace's first book of Satires: 'How comes, it Maecenas, that nobody lives contented with that place in life which his reason has chosen or chance has set before him?']
>
> Here, by way of anecdote, let me observe that if any Person at any time should take it into their heads to say 'You play well upon ye Guittar, Billy', such a person, making such and so very judicious an observation, must immediately be informed 'that it is by no means to be wonder'd at, as ye Player had ye honor of receiving his first Instructions necessary to his Improvement or that sweet, delicate Instrument, from ye pretty mouth, and fair hand of Lady Maynard, one of ye Handsomest Women he ever beheld'.
>
> *op. cit.* pp.52-3.

Another glimpse of the life-style of the local gentry is provided by letters and documents belonging to the Dayrell family and described and analyzed by Dr. W.M. Palmer. The Dayrells lived at Shudy Camps, the parish adjoining Ashdon to the north-east over the Cambridgeshire border, and at the time of the Tithe Commissioners' survey of Ashdon in 1845, they owned 188 acres of it (see p.50). They numbered some highly distinguished and colourful personalities amongst their ancestors including the grandmother of King Edward VI, the so-called 'Wild Dayrell' of Queen Elizabeth's reign and Thomas Dayrell who was born in 1603, was sent to London to study law and was 'so comely a person' that he was chosen to lead the masque given at the Banqueting Hall in Whitehall on Candlemas Day, 1633. He went on to become one of the most austere of Royalists and died bewailing 'the luxury and idleness of these worst of times'. Amongst the Dayrell papers described by Dr. Palmer was an account book of personal expenses for the period 1717 to 1742 kept by Mistress Elizabeth, wife of Francis Dayrell, who is described as 'a very worthy gentleman tall and thin, of a great state and ceremony. The account book reveals that she lost a deal of money at cards (the expression 'put in my play purse' occurs quite frequently), she paid £5.15s.0d. for a lutestring nightgown with silver 'tosils', 2s.6d. for being blooded and 5s. for having her hair cut. Towards the end of the eighteenth century, the head of the Dayrell family married Henrietta Tempest, 'a fine black West Indian woman' whose extravagant spending was, apparently, on such a scale that Shudy Camps Park had to be let to strangers. The property returned to the Dayrells early in the nineteenth century and the Reverend Thomas Dayrell acquired it after his elder brother died without an heir. According to Dr. Palmer some of the Rev. Thomas's letters written in 1826 to his brother Francis, who was doing the Grand Tour, are good reading. The Rev. Thomas was ordained by the Archbishop of York and stayed at Bishopthorpe where he and other young divines made desperate love to the Archbishop's daughter, Georgina. In another letter he says, 'Crawley is still curate of [Shudy] Camps. He is as good a fellow as ever. He keeps good cigars and good brandy at the Parsonage House, so we shall have a room to smoke in when you return instead of the bank of the Island Pond . . .'. It looks as if the young men were not allowed to smoke in the Hall. It seems rather hard that the Lord of the Manor's sons should smoke the cigars and drink the brandy of the poor curate. The Rev. Thomas went on to have a large family, including many daughters, and he would seem to have impoverished the estate and dramatically deforested it to provide each of them with a portion.

In 1884, another cleric came to Ashdon on a tour of inspection. His eye for detail was no less sharp than that of Radwinter's William

Harrison or Ashdon's own John North but his field of inquiry was considerably more specialized than theirs. He was exclusively interested in church bells and in 1884, the *Essex Review* published his essay 'A Brief Account of the Bells in some of the Parishes in North Essex'. Ashdon was one of the parishes he visited and he described its church bells as 'a superb six, in excellent ringing order; the fifth and sixth remarkable for their tone'. He noted that the fourth bell, cast in 1787 by W. & T. Mears of Whitechapel, was regularly rung at 9 o'clock on Sunday mornings 'probably a reminiscence of the priest's bell for High Mass', that it was rung for deaths and funerals and was also used during Harvest, at nine in the morning and five in the afternoon — doubtless to signal the beginning and ending of the period when gleaning was officially sanctioned; the second bell, cast in 1842 at the same Whitechapel foundry, was tolled on Sundays; the sixth or tenor bell, reserved for use on Good Friday bore the inscription 'Miles Graye made me, 1668', Graye being, in Mr Deedes's estimation, 'the maker of one of the finest bells in England at Lavenham, in Suffolk'. In his view, the most noteworthy of the Ashdon bells was the fifth, made about 1500 by Thomas Church of Bury St. Edmunds, 'a most interesting bell with several escutcheons upon it and deserves another visit'.

With his nagging concern for the bells he inspected (and he provides his own approximate measurements of each and every one of them), Mr Deedes manifests that preoccupation with minute detail which is wholly characteristic of all authentic campanologists. Ever since the art of change-ringing was first invented in England at the start of the seventeenth century, its practitioners have devoted themselves to it with a single-mindedness which is matched by only the most fanatical of collectors. Your truly dedicated bell-ringer would travel the length and breadth of his ever-expanding region, seeking out fresh spires to climb, meticulously recording in his notebook the number of bells in the tower and the age, size and weight of each. He would not rest until he had heard a full peal with his own ears, or better by far, helped ring it with his own hands, then noted the precise details in his ringing-book. Just such a book was kept in the first half of the nineteenth century by John Carr, leader of the Cambridge Company of Bell-ringers, and his account of a visit to Ashdon in 1843 provides an interesting sign not only of the bell-ringing fraternity at their devotions but something of the flavour of a quieter age. It may help the layman to know that 'Bob' is simply the term used to designate a peal of courses or set of changes and that the maximum range of permutations which can possibly be run on any given number of bells can be calculated by geometric progression. Thus the maximum possible of different sequences in which four bells can be rung is $1 \times 2 \times 3 \times 4 = 24$, the maximum of five bells is $1 \times 2 \times 3 \times 4 \times 5 = 120$ and the maximum for six is $1 \times 2 \times 3 \times 4 \times 5 \times 6 = 720$. Change-ringing on five bells is called 'Doubles'. Change-ringing on six bells is called 'Bob Minor', on seven 'Triple Bob', on eight 'Bob Major', on ten 'Royal' and on twelve 'Bob Maximus'. The Richard Miller in question was not, strictly speaking, to be numbered amongst Ashdon's gentry though in the difficult times of the early nineteenth century he was comparatively well-to-do. His farm of Ashdon Street covered 124 acres, he employed four men and a boy and, like most of his farming contemporaries in the village, he had a house-servant living in. He features in *A Narrative of Various Peals in Change-Ringing*, printed at the office of the *Cambridge Advertiser* in 1847 and written by John Carr, leader of the Cambridge Company of Bell-Ringers and formerly of Waltham Abbey, Essex.

> *October 1843.*
> The next morning early, I felt most anxious to see my old friend Richard Miller, and after walking four miles, I arrived at his farmhouse, Ashdon Street; he came when I knocked at the door, but had not the least knowledge of me until I spoke, when he knew me instantly; we were both of us much affected and did not speak for some time. When I recovered myself, I was introduced to Mrs Miller, a most worthy person, she was in truth both mother and sister to me, and indeed the family together made it their chief study to make me comfortable.
> I stopped here several weeks, working on the farm, and making myself useful as far as I could; in the evening we met over their wood fire, and spent many hours together. Sometimes I played a little on the violin, at another on the handbells, sometimes we had a song, and on Sunday evening we sang some sacred psalms and hymns. The first Tuesday of my visit we went to Walden with Mr Miller and rung 1,000 Treble Bob and Double Norwich Court Bob Major. I also rang several 720

on the six bells of Ashdon Church and on Sunday, to the great surprise of the villagers, I chimed some sacred tunes on the church bells and 120 Grandsire Five with some Bob Major . . .

Having been to Cambridge on the occasion of the Queen's visit, I returned to Ashdon, where I was received with as much kindness as had hitherto been shewed me. I had resolved in my own mind to start to Soham, but the whole family insisted on my staying till after 5th November; on that morning I rang 720 at Ashdon, and in the afternoon, I rang at Walden, the best piece of Treble Bob and Norwich Court, I think I ever did ring and Mr Miller was much pleased. On the Monday evening following I accompanied him to Ashdon Tower where I met old friends Rumball, Francis and Mr Wright of Walden. With them I rang 360 of Plain Bob, after which we adjourned to *The White Horse Inn* where a good supper was provided; subsequently I commenced the evening by tapping a course of eightsome tunes. After which Mr Smart and his son played most delightfully on the bugle and trumpet, we had near thirty in company . . . altogether we spent a merry and pleasant evening, keeping up mirth and harmony till a late hour.

On November 15th my brothers, William and Charles, came over to Ashdon, when we rang 720 Plain Bob with Ashdon Ringers, after which we went to the inn where my brother and myself rang a course of Treble Bob Major, some touches of Grandsire Triples, tunes etc., to the great amusement of those who had never before witnessed this arduous task . . .

In December, John Carr duly made his visit to Soham where he told the churchwardens of his performances at Ashdon:

> I spent several happy hours with these gentlemen, talking over my travels at which they were much amused, they being ringers, and when I related to his son the task which my brother William and myself had performed at Ashdon (I mean our ringing on the handbells some Treble Bob) he was much surprised and could not imagine how we could hold them.

Richard Miller's exploits are further eulogized by E. Morris in *The History of the Art of Change-Ringing* where he is described as 'a very eminent ringer' who composed and conducted a number of outstanding peals: on 6th June 1807, 6832 changes, Bob Major, in four and a half hours; on 15th December 1813, 5040 changes, Bob Major, in three hours, twenty one minutes; on 4 June 1815, 6112 changes, Oxford Treble Bob, in four hours two minutes; on 4th February 1817, 5040 changes, Double Norwich Court Bob in three hours twenty five minutes; 21st February 1826, 5040 changes, Grandsire Triples in three hours eighteen minutes and on 29th January 1828, 5120 changes, Oxford Treble Bob, in three hours, twenty six minutes. Of these, the 1807, 1815 and 1817 peals, all composed and conducted by Miller, are commemorated on a peal-board in the Saffron Walden belfry where his picture is also displayed. The 1813, 1826 and 1828 peals, also conducted by Miller, are recorded on the fly-leaf of his Ringing Book in which the opening entry is dated 23rd December 1804. He had a long and illustrious ringing career and it was largely due to his skill and enthusiasm that the Saffron Walden ringers established their reputation for excellence in the first half of the nineteenth century. He died on 7th January 1862 at the age of 81.

Be all of that as it may, one must concede that in the nineteenth century bell-ringing was just as much a minority activity as it is today and, then as now, not one peculiar to the gentry. The evidence strongly suggests that for the Ashdon gentry, as for their counterparts elsewhere, the principal leisure pursuits were shooting and hunting. One has to assume that they played cards and occasionally also made music but the hard evidence for this is sketchy. In this regard, the Reverend William Cooper's account leaves tantalizing gaps: he fails to give any detail of the paintings on his host's walls, or of the books in the library or of the music to which Sir William liked to listen at Waltons Park.

Of one thing we can be certain: very few Ashdonians would ever — like William Cooper, the visitor from Thaxted — have been privileged to enter the drawing-room at Waltons which, for centuries, was, with Ashdon Hall and the Rectory, one of the bastions of the Ashdon gentry. As has been seen, amongst these, in the course of the village's long history, can be numbered some highly colourful personalities but, at any one time, they were distinctly thin on the local ground. There was never any shortage of farmers or millers or tradespeople but however prosperous these may have become, they would never have expected to be asked to make up a four at whist with Squire or Rector. It would simply not have done for such denizens of the gentry to socialize with those over whom, at local and sometimes even at national level, they legislated. As will be seen, these conditions were to prevail in Ashdon till well into the present century.

5

Annals of the Poor

> The poor when manag'd, and employed in Trade, —
> Are to the publick Welfare, usefull made;
> But if kept Idle, from their Vices spring
> Whores for the Stews, and Soldiers for the King.
> *Verse on the back of 1720 playing card.*

Though a strict social hierarchy had existed in England's rural communities from well before the Conquest, it was from the fifteenth century onwards that the rich began to grow spectacularly richer and the poor emphatically poorer. The growth of the nation's wool trade made merchants and farmers prosperous and spinning in their own small homes provided many a cottager with welcome additional income but it also created considerable hardship. Many fewer workers were needed to tend flocks of sheep than to till fields of corn so there was a dramatic increase in unemployment. The progressive enclosing of common fields robbed labourers of grazing and of their traditional supplies of wood for fuel or building and the Dissolution of the Monasteries by Henry VIII deprived them of their age-old alms and doles. For this complex of reasons, the Tudor law-makers found themselves confronted with a vast and ever-growing army of poor and they and their successors in the following centuries spent considerable time and ingenuity seeking to distinguish between those who could not work and those who would not work.

Wholly characteristic of their not always consistent thinking and feeling was the Elizabethans' attitude towards illegitimacy. Distinctive ambivalence is apparent in the Act promulgated in 1576, the eighteenth year of Elizabeth's reign, when they seemed as much concerned about the financial consequences for the parish, faced with the prospect of having to support husbandless wife and fatherless child, as they were by the flouting of divine law:

> Concerning bastards begotten and born out of lawful matrimony (an offence against God's law and man's law) the said bastards being now left to be kept at the charges of the parish where they be born, to the great burden of the same parish, and in defrauding of the relief of the impotent and aged, *true poor of the same parish*, and to evil example and encouragement of lewd life, it is enacted that two justices of the peace, upon examination of the cause and circumstance, shall, by discretion take order as well for the punishment of the mother and reputed father, as also for the better relief of every such parish in part or in all; and for the Keeping of every such child, by charging such mother or reputed father with the payment of money weekly, or other sustentation, for the relief of such child in such wise as they shall think convenient: and if after the same order by them subscribed under their hands, the said persons, viz., mother or reputed father, upon notice thereof, shall not, for their part, observe and perform the said order, every such party so making default to be committed to gaol, there to remain, except he, she, or they shall put in sufficient surety to perform the said order, or else personally appear at the next general sessions of the peace, and also to abide such order as the justices of the peace then and there shall take in that behalf.

Although, in the wake of this Act, the Churchwardens of Ashdon seem to have been intermittently vigilant, and to have brought several reports of suspected illicit fornication before the Archdeacon's Court (see pp.149-153), only one case got as far as the Quarter Sessions. On 13th December 1583:

> Recognizance [was] taken before George Nicholls and Matthew Bradbury, esquires, of Thomas Patericke of Ashdon, bricklayer, John Odell and Robert Quye of the same, yeoman [a term normally applied to a freeholder farming his own land, normally worth forty shillings or more a year], for the said Thomas to answer for the child begotten of the body of Philippa Pledger, whereof he is the reputed father, and to stand to the order hereunto annexed or such order as the justices shall

set down touching the same.

Upon the appearance of the said Pattrick (sic) the court ordered that the former order, made by the aforesaid justices and certified to this Sessions shall stand in force and the said Pattrick can lawfully discharge himself of the said crime.

Order: that Thomas Pattrick, reputed father of Thomas begotten of the body of Philippa Pledger, shall weekly contribute to the said child 10^D a week till the same child shall be able to relieve himself with his labour or otherwise. And the same Philippa shall be at the like time. And their further punishment referred to the spiritual function (see pp. -) And in their default to be further ordered by us.

Not for the first time in the history of the human race, the father did not for long honour his obligations. The Quarter Sessions files reveal that on 22nd April 1585:

> Thomas Pattrycke (sic) of Ashdon (was) handed in bail to John Odell and Christopher Wylson of the same, yeomen, for refusing to stand to the order of Mr Niccolls and Mr Bradbury for a bastard child.

What happened thereafter to him, to Philippa Pledger and to young Thomas we can only speculate, but that the Act of 1576 was in general ineffective may be fairly inferred from the appearance of a fresh Act in 1609, in the seventh year of the reign of James I. This proposed to visit the full vigour of the law not on the often elusive father but on the more readily identifiable mother:

> Because great changes ariseth upon many places within this realm by reason of bastardy, besides the great dishonour of Almighty God ... every lewd woman which shall have any bastard which may be chargeable to the parish shall be committed to the house of correction, there to be punished and set on work, during the term of one whole year; and if she shall eftsoons offend again shall be committed to the said house of correction as aforesaid, and there remain until she can put in good sureties for her good behaviour, not to offend so again.

Had the letter of this particular law actually been put into effect, vast regiments of unmarried mothers would have remained in occupation of the nation's prisons for the greater part of their lives. In the event, it was circumvented by one or both of the parents running away, often leaving their children in the charge of the parish where they had been born. To counter this, churchwardens and overseers of the poor were empowered to take so much of the goods and chattels, if any, of the putative father as were necessary for bringing up the child. Just as frequently, the unmarried mother would be left behind, and no small part of the time and energy of officialdom was spent in trying to establish proof of paternity and, this having been achieved by whatever means, then in seeking to locate the father. Some colourful instances of this are to be found in the Ashdon records.

On 13th December 1641, a Suffolk J.P. wrote to one of his Essex counterparts (unspecified):

> Noble Sir,
> I perceyve by yor letter that a wench hath brought a chylde from London and hath left it in a hedg betwixt Ashden and Campes [the adjoining parish, in Cambridgeshire] and is gone her waye, and she hath reported that it should be gotten in my house by a falconer of myne one Scutt. I doe presume this wench is one Alic Hodgkin who was a servant to one Mistress Leet an Aunt of myne that lived in my house this tyme twelvemonth this wench was at my howse in Sturbridge fayer tyme last [Stourbridge Fair, outside Cambridge, in September] and did charge this John Scutt to be father of her chyld, I required suertyes of Scutt for his forth comminge but this wench goeine a waye before she was fully examyned [i.e. legally cross-examined] I did not bynd him but I have now sent for the Constable and will take suerties for his appearance at the next Sessions which is all I can doe/
> And thus with my servis unto yow I rest
> Your assured frende and servant
> George Lehunte
> Sr I did forgett to tell yow that I did never threten to send her to the howse of correcon for I did know her to be sendable to the place where she was setteled as a servant but to no other place which was at London/

The Quarter Sessions provides further instances, the first of which suggests that the gentry were not always above the law:

16th July 1644.
John Killingworth of Ashdon, gent., is called upon to answer the inhabitants of Debden (by Saffron Walden, Essex) touching a bastard child of Kath. Hammond.
Defaulted.
Entreated.
7th April 1646.
Geo. Whitmarsh, Ashdon, labourer, is charged with begetting a base child on Alice Webb, Ashdon, a singlewoman.
John Packer is alleged to be the father of the base child of Ann Ockman, singlewoman.
10th January 1654.
Tho. Bullet, married man, is indicted for begetting a bastard child with Margt. Dover, singlewoman.
Tho. Quy, bachelor, charged with fathering bastard child on Alice Adams, widow of Ashdon.

Further legislation was passed in 1732, in the sixth year of the reign of George II. This put further pressure on the mother by obliging her to declare she was pregnant with an illegitimate child and state the name of the father. Once again, what seems uppermost is the need to spare the rest of the community undue expense:

> If any single woman declare herself to be pregnant, and charge any person with being the father, it shall be lawful for any justice of any division, on the application of the overseers (of the poor), or of any substantial householder, to issue his warrant for the immediate apprehending of such person, and he is required to commit such person to gaol, unless he shall give security to indemnify the parish, or enter into a recognizance, with sufficient surety to appear at the quarter sessions, and to perform the order to be then made.

It seems doubtful whether these reiterated legal threats were very much of a deterrent. Blank forms of the following description were printed in the eighteenth century, doubtless in considerable bulk, and supplied to local authority officials up and down the country. The following examples pertain to Ashdon and the italicized words are printed on the official forms:

> *To all Constables, and other His Majesty's Officers of the Peace for the said County to wit. These are in His Majesty's Name to command you, and every of you, upon Sight hereof, to take hereof, to take and bring before me, or some other of his Majesty's Justices of the Peace for the said* County *the Body of* Elizabeth Woodley Singlewoman the Daughter of James Woodley *of whom you shall have Notice* to be Examined touching the Reputed Father of a Bastard Child of which she hath lately been delivered in the said parish.
>
> *Hereof fail not at your Peril. Given under my Hand and Seal, this* 10th *Day of* September *in the Year of our Lord* 1774.
>
> Jas. Raymond. Essex.

(After Birth)
To the Constable of Ashdon and to all other Constables *in the said* County.

WHEREAS Phoebe Cowell of the Parish *of* Ashdon aforesaid *single Woman, hath by her Examination, taken in Writing upon Oath, before me* Thomas Wolfe Esquire *one of his Majesty's Justices of the Peace in and for the said* County *declared, that on the* twenty fifth *Day of* May *now last past at* Ashdon *aforesaid, she the said* Phoebe Cowell *was delivered of a* Male *Bastard Child, and that the said Child is likely to become chargeable to the said* Parish *and hath charged* John Overall of Arkesden *in the said* County, Servant,*with having gotten her with Child of the said Bastard Child*: *And whereas* Thomas Day *one of the Overseers of the Poor of the* Parish of Ashdon *aforesaid, in order to indemnify the said* Parish *in the Premises, hath applied to me to issue out my Warrant for the apprehending of the said* John Overall *and to bring him before me, or some other of his Majesty's Justices of the Peace for the said County to find Security to indemnify the said* Parish of Ashdon *or else to find sufficient Surety for his appearance at the next General* Quarter *Sessions of the Peace to be holden for the said* County *and to abide and perform such Order or Orders, as shall be made in Pursuance of an Act passed in the Eighteenth Year of her late Majesty* QUEEN ELIZABETH, *concerning Bastards, begotten and born out of lawful Matrimony. GIVEN under my Hand and Seal the* 14th *Day of* November *in the* thirtieth *Year of his Majesty's Reign, and in the*

Year of our Lord One Thousand Seven Hundred and eighty nine.
Tho. Wolfe
Sold by J. Coles and Son, Stationers, Fleet Street.

We do not know whether John Overall was brought to book. Neither he nor Phoebe Cowell appear in the full list of Ashdon residents compiled by the parish overseers twelve years later. It requires but little effort of the imagination to fashion a plausible sequel to their shadowy life-story or to conceive of the mixture of feelings which another Ashdon mother must have experienced when the Rector, like a discreet but omniscient Recording Angel opened his brand-new Parish Register in 1756 with the following two lines:

6th February 1756. Frederick, son of Mary Wornham. Baseborn.
21st March 1756 Frederick, son of Mary Wornham. Buried.

*   *   *

Those fathers who tried to evade their parental and civic responsibilities by fleeing from the parish at once found themselves ensnared in a tangle of other legislation more ancient and even more menacing designed to protect the respectable members of society from its vagabonds and beggars.

The earliest law discouraging beggars is an Act of 1349, promulgated in the twenty third year of the reign of Edward III, while the Black Death was at its height, punishing with imprisonment the giving of alms to anyone physically capable of working. In 1388, in the seventh year of his reign and seven years after the Peasants' Revolt, Richard II concentrated attention more directly on the beggars themselves by ordering the 'impotent' to be sent back to their place of birth carrying 'letters testimonial' to prove that they had a valid reason for travelling across the country. The Beggars Act of 1495 considerably intensified the pressure by punishing vagrants capable of work with a range of penalties from whipping to loss of their ears or hanging. Nonetheless, the problem was no nearer solution in 1531 when, in the twenty second year of the reign of Henry VIII, yet another Beggars Act was passed, allegedly because 'in all places throughout this realm of England vagabonds and beggars have of long time increased and daily do increase in great and excessive numbers, by the occasion of idleness, mother and root of all vices, whereby hath insurged and sprung and daily insurgeth and springeth continual thefts, murders and other heinous offences and great enormities, to the high displeasure of God, the inquietation and damage of the King's people, and to the marvellous disturbance of the common weal of this realm'. To combat this menace, all Justices of the Peace were commanded to make an example of anyone convicted of vagrancy (i.e. 'being whole and mighty in body' but being without work or without the prospect of work) by having 'every such idel person brought to the next market town or other place where the said Justices of the Peace shall think most convenient . . . and there to be tied to the end of a cart naked and be beaten with whips throughout the same market town or other place till his body be bloody by reason of such whipping'. After being whipped, the vagrant was then ordered, under oath, to return to the place of his birth or 'where he last dwelled before the same punishment by the space of 3 years and there put himself to labour like as a true man oweth to do . . .' No arrangements seem to have been made to ensure that work was available back at the birthplace of the duly chastened idler; presumably this was left to Providence. In any event, Henry VIII's Act seems to have done little to diminish the 'great and excessive numbers' of vagrants because in 1547, in the very first year of the reign of his successor, Edward VI felt obliged to bring in even more ferocious legislation. On conviction, rogues and vagabonds were branded 'in the breast' and reduced to slavery for two years. If they escaped from slavery and were recaptured, they were branded 'on the forehead or the ball of the cheek' and were then made slaves for life; the penalty for a second successful escape-bid was death. The more savage features of this Act were repealed by yet another Act passed in 1598 'for the punishment of Rogues, Vagabonds and Sturdy Beggars' though it retained the penalty of stripping the felon naked to the waist and applying the whip 'until his or her body be bloody'. This new Act was promulgated in the thirty ninth year of the reign of Elizabeth and the novel insertion of the feminine third person singular possessive suggests that in her regime, women were not to be accorded any favours. The Act also allowed for Houses of Correction to be set up for vagrants and dangerous rogues. They were equipped for carding, combing, spinning and weaving and they remained in being till 1865 when they were merged into the prison system and vagrants were set to pick oakum in the casual wards of the Union Workhouse.

In his *Description of England*, Harrison was especially scathing about the great variety of 'dangerous rogues' who, in ever-growing numbers, were preying on the public. He especially disliked 'counterfeit Egyptians', people pretending to be authentic gypsies who, in his time, were believed to have originated from Egypt (but, in fact, came from India and spoke a language related to Hindi). He listed twenty three distinct categories of rogues, the most colourful being 'hookers and anglers' (thieves stealing from open windows), 'priggers of prancers' (horse thieves), 'whipjacks' (beggars pretending to have been shipwrecked), 'dummerers' (sham deaf-mutes), 'jarkmen' (forgers of licences), 'doxies' (prostitutes who begin with upright men) and 'dells' (under-age, incipient doxies). 'What notable robberies, pilferies, rapes and stealings of young children, burning, breaking, and disfiguring their limbs to make them pitiful in the sight of the people I need not rehearse', he complains, concluding gloomily, 'the punishment that is ordained for this kind of people is very sharp, and yet it cannot restrain them from their gadding . . .'.

There is sufficient, unwonted indignation in this section of Harrison's survey, presumably written in his study at Radwinter Rectory, to lead us to assume that it must, at least in part, have been inspired by direct observation and experience. What was observable in Radwinter would have been little different in Ashdon, just a few miles along the winding lane. For all that, the surviving Ashdon records for this time contain no instances of the more colourful criminals listed by Harrison.

While there are several instances of horse-stealing among the Ashdon records (see pp.161-2), the culprits were identified as local labourers who doubtless acted on impulse rather than 'priggers of prancers' who would seem to have followed a calculated and no doubt wide-ranging plan of campaign. There are no recorded cases of visitations from 'Egyptians', presumed real or patently counterfeit, and given 'the great routs and companies' of sturdy beggars alleged by the Tudor law-makers to be roaming the length and breadth of the land, the instances of run-of-the-mill vagrancy reported are remarkably few. At the Epiphany Quarter Sessions in 1614, 'Sarah Betts, late servante to Miss Browneburde of Saffron Walden' was indicated for 'running from her mistress and being taken at Ashdon as vagrant and much suspected for pilfering of linen there', while on 6th July 1630, 'Thomas Stedder and his wife were arrested in Ashdon for wandering and begging'. They were duly punished, one presumes in accordance with the statutes, then 'sent to Southwark near London where they dwell (as they confessed)'. Since there is ample evidence available that Ashdon was not, in other respects, a conspicuously law-abiding community in the late sixteenth and early seventeenth centuries, one has to conclude either that the full legal records of vagrancy in the area for that period have not survived or that the law-officers did not enforce the letter of the successive Beggars' Acts with all the fearsome rigour that was repeatedly called for.

The same is not true of the Laws of Settlement passed later in the seventeenth century, the energetic enforcement of which made life busy for parish officials and wretched for the poorer parishioners. Modelled on the vagrancy legislation formulated in 1388 by Richard II (see p.104), the Settlement Laws were founded on the premise that every person had one parish and one parish only in which he had a 'settlement' and in which, if he was sufficiently destitute, he had a theoretical right to parish relief. The preamble to the first of the two seventeenth-century Settlement Acts, passed in 1662, in the second year of the reign of Charles II, explained that fresh legislation was necessary because 'by reason of some defects in the law, poor people are not restrained from going from one parish to the other, and therefore do endeavour to settle themselves in those parishes where there is the best stock, the largest commons or wastes to build cottages, and the most woods for them to burn and destroy; and when they have consumed it, then to another parish; and at last become rogues and vagabonds; to the great discouragement of parishes to provide stock, when it is liable to be devoured by strangers'.

By the provisions of the 1662 Act, any stranger staying in the parish could be removed by an Overseer of the Poor if, within forty days of his arrival, he had no prospect of work or was not renting property worth at least £10 per year. A temporary resident, staying to help with the harvest, had to come provided with a certificate from his home parish guaranteeing to take him back. After residing in the parish for forty days, the newcomer could claim he was 'settled' which meant that if the need arose, he or she could become eligible for relief. Officialdom's ready awareness of this led to many a swift removal, especially if the stranger was an obviously pregnant woman. Persistent vagrants could be punished by the newly devised penalty of transportation across the seas.

The 1662 Act was modified by a further Settlement Act passed in 1697, during the ninth year of the reign of William III. To prevent parish officers from summarily rejecting newcomers to the parish, it was decreed that if the new arrival brought with him a properly drawn-up certificate from another parish accepting responsibility for him, he could not be moved on till he made a claim for poor relief. Settlement could henceforward be acquired in four further ways. Bastards acquired a settlement by birth, although the parish was able till 1810 to enjoy the satisfaction of punishing the mother with a year's hard labour; legitimate children acquired a settlement by birth if their father's, or failing that, their mother's legal settlement was not known; women gained a settlement by marriage; persons with an estate of their own, however small it might be, could, if they occupied it, not be moved on. At the same time, the 1697 Act decreed that paupers and their families should wear a capital P on their clothing and that the punishment for failing to comply would be loss of relief, imprisonment, hard labour or whipping.

It is difficult to assess whether the laws really achieved their object but they certainly succeeded in generating a vast amount both of human misery and of bureaucratic activity. While the sons of the well-to-do were free to undertake the fashionable Grand Tour of the European continent without benefit of passport or visa, eighteenth-century England was, in the words of J.L. and Barbara Hammond, 'like a chessboard of parishes on which the poor were moved about like pawns', (*The Village Labourer*, p.108).

The Essex Record Office at Chelmsford has a rich store of Settlement documents including many for Ashdon and for all manner of other parishes besides. While the following examples provide a clear indication of the standard procedure, one can, even with a moderate degree of empathy, feel one's way through the legalistic jargon to the human drama beyond.

Each request for a legal settlement or protest against threatened removal necessitated an 'examination' by two Justices of the Peace, educated men who seem regularly to have been confronted with individuals who were obliged to sign documents with a simple cross. One is bound to wonder how, without the aid of a solicitor or a social

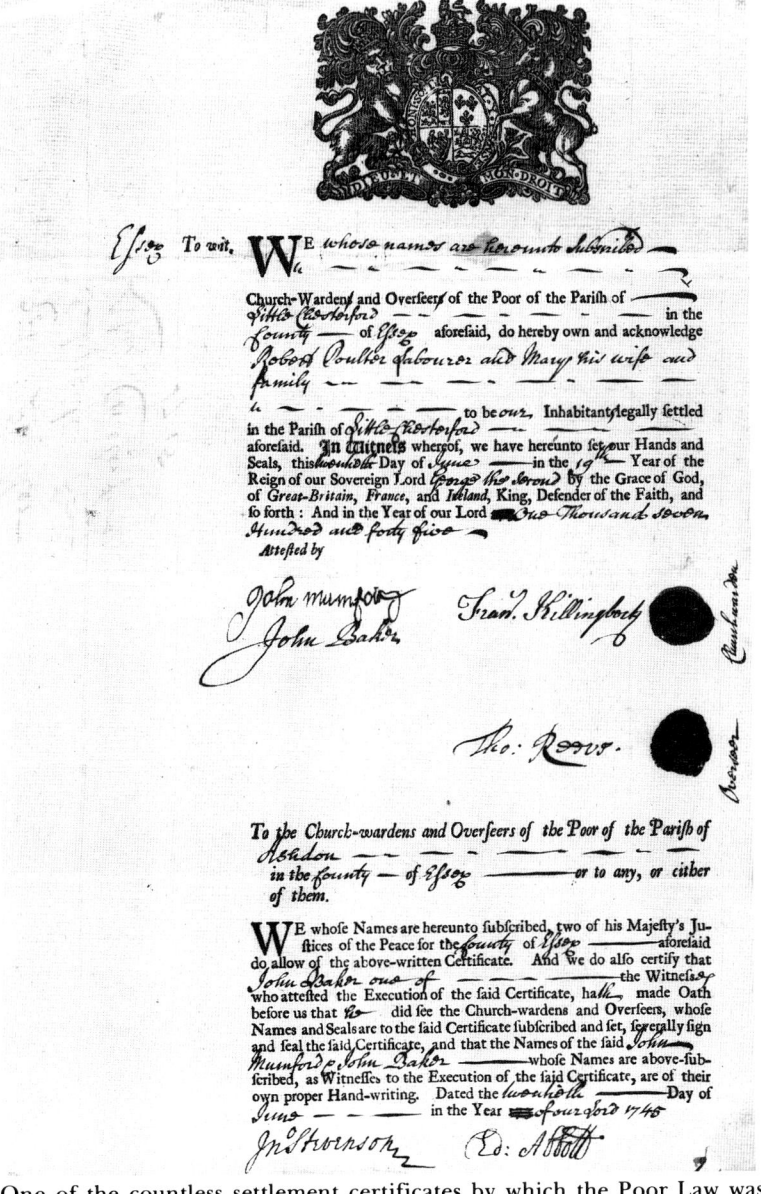

One of the countless settlement certificates by which the Poor Law was administered

worker the would-be settler was able to plead an effective case.

> The Examination of Mary Chapman taken this 2nd day of September 1758 before us two of his Majesties [sic] Justices of the Peace in and for the County of Essex.
>
> This Examinant on her Oath saith that She is the wife of John Chapman now at Sea on board the Prince Edward privateer (armed vessel privately owned but authorized by the government to attack the ships of a hostile nation) and that the lawful Settlement of her said Husband is in the parish of Ashdon in the said County of Essex where her said husband was born and bred and where the settlement of her said Husbands Father John Chapman is as she is informed and verily believes. And saith that her said Husband hath not gained any Settlement since his Birth to her Knowledge or beliefe either by Service Apprenticeship or otherwise howsoever and saith she hath only one Child named John aged four years who is now with his Grandfather at Ashdon aforesaid.

While Mary Chapman's case rested on the fact that her absent husband had a legal Ashdon settlement, William Brazier's, which follows, is that he had been employed in the parish for a full calendar year. Like many other servants and labourers, he would seem to have put himself up for hire at a local Statute Fair which were held once a year at Michaelmas:

> Examination of William Brazier now residing in the Parish of Ashdon in the said County of Essex touching the place of the last legal Settlement taken on Oath before us the underwritten two of his Majesty's Justices of the Peace in and for the said County this 14th Day of May 1792.
>
> Who deposeth that he was born in the Parish of Hempstead (near Saffron Walden) in the said County as he has heard and believes, that he has lived as a Yearly Servant in several places but the last person he served a whole year was Thomas Barnard of Bartlow Hamlet in the said County Farmer to whom he let himself about 17 years agoe the day after Michaelmas and entered on his said Service the same day and served the said Thomas Barnard till the day after Michaelmas following and earned his full Years Wages, since which time he hath

not done act whereby to gain a Settlement elsewhere.
Amy Brazier his wife.
Charlotte aged 6 years.
James aged 2 years.

It seems to have been even more difficult for the following applicant to secure a settlement than it was for William Brazier because although he could claim he had been born in Ashdon he had lived a somewhat chequered career beyond the parish boundaries:

> Richard Freeman, a Private in the 5th Regiment of Dragoon Guards, appeared before the statutory two J.P.s on 18th October 1800 following a complaint from the Ashdon Churchwardens and Overseers of the Poor. He testified on oath that he was born in the parish of Ashdon where his Father was a legal Inhabitant as he was heard and believes, that about eleven years ago, with the consent of his Father he bound himself Apprentice by Indenture to James Doo of Linton in the County of Cambridge, Carpenter, to serve him for five years his Master agreeing to allow him five shillings a week for the first year, six shillings per week for the second year, seven shillings per week for the third, eight shillings for the fourth and nine for the fifth to enable him to find and provide himself with Board Lodging and Cloaths, but as no Consideration was given to the said James Doo for taking him as an apprentice he believes his Indentures were not inrolled. And this Examinant saith that he served the said James Doo under such Indentures in the said Parish of Linton for about four years and a half when he inlisted into the Cambridgeshire Fencibles [Army Defence Force against the threat of Napoleonic invasion] *and that he has done no other Act whereby to gain as Settlement and that he has one child by his late wife named Ann aged about five years and a quarter.*

Like the previous applicants, Freeman was unable to sign his name and there is no indication in the files that any of the pleas persuaded the Justices to allow the plaintiffs to settle in Ashdon. While not all the records have survived, the indication would seem to be that Ashdon was a 'close parish', one which at this time was particularly reluctant to permit fresh settlement within its borders. The Essex

Record Office's Calendar of Removals has record of only three pleas for settlements being granted though the number may have been a little higher since the names listed in the Calendar do not correspond with those on the copies of the certificates actually issued. Much more numerous are those documents like the following in which the officers of one parish dispute with those of another over who is going to accept the legal and financial responsibility of the hapless poor in search of a settlement to call their own:

> To the Church-Wardens and Overseers of the Poor of the Parish of Ashdon in the said County of Essex and to the Church-Wardens and Overseers of the Poor of the Parish of Saffron Walden in the county aforesaid,
> and to each and every of them.
> Upon the Complaint of the Church-Wardens and Overseers of the Poor of Ashdon in the County of Essex unto us whose Names are hereunto set and seals affixed, being two of his Majesty's Justices of the Peace . . . that Robert Miller and Ann his Wife, Nicholas their son aged Nine Years, Robert their son aged eight years, James their son aged six years, William their Son aged four years, Prudence their Daughter aged two years, and Hannah their Daughter aged One Year did lately come to inhabit in the said Parish of Ashdon not having gained a legal Settlement there, not produced any Certificate owning them to be settled elsewhere, and that the said Robert Miller his said Wife and Children are likely to be chargeable to the said Parish of Ashdon. We the said Justices upon due Proof made thereof, as well upon the Examination of the said Robert Miller upon Oath . . . do adjudge the same to be true; and we do likewise adjudge that the lawful Settlement of them . . . is in the Parish of Saffron Walden in the said County of Essex. We do therefore require you the said Churchwardens and Overseers of the Poor of the Parish of Ashdon or some or one of you to convey Robert Miller and his said Wife and Children from and out of the Parish of Ashdon to the Parish of Saffron Walden and them deliver to the Churchwardens and Overseers of the Poor there or to some, or to one of them, together with this our Order; And we do also hereby require you . . . to receive and provide for them as Inhabitants of your

Parish. Given under our Hands and Seals the Second Day of January in the Year of our Lord One Thousand Seven Hundred and Seventy Eight.

There are quite literally hundreds of such forms extant for the County of Essex alone, empowering one set of officials, after a deal of argument and counterargument, to transfer families to the care of another set of officials. More often than not, the parishes were contiguous, or, at most, a few miles apart. Given that, on balance, each parish would seem to have ended up by acquiring just about as many poor families as it managed to off-load, the whole exercise would seem to have been as futile as it was cruel and complicated. It virtually came to an end in 1834 when the Poor Law Amendment Act decreed that the much larger Union rather than the single parish thenceforward constituted the administrative unit for settlement purposes. Poverty was in no way reduced, however, and towards the end of the nineteenth century, after the decade of acute agricultural depression in the 1880s, once again, vagrants reappeared in the countryside in appreciable numbers and as will be seen, stalked the imagination of many a respectable householder and more than one impressionable child . . .

*   *   *

In concentrating as I have done so far in this chapter on the more oppressive of our ancestors' policies towards the poor, I have been less than fair both to those who devised the laws in earlier centuries and to those charged with the responsibilities of putting them into effect. At the same time as they were passing their Acts concerned with Bastards, with Sturdy Beggars and with Settlement, successive governments were also trying to devize ways and means of creating employment, protecting apprentices, improving working conditions and of supporting those members of the community who, because of infirmity or old age, were unable to support themselves.

There had been earlier attempts to legislate on employment and wages, most notably the 1349 Ordinance of Labourers and the 1351 Statute of Labourers, but the most thorough-going and epoch-making was the Statute of Artificers, Labourers, Servants in Husbandry and Apprentices, passed in 1563, in the fifth year of the reign of Elizabeth. Those who drafted the Statute declared in their preamble that their object was to 'banish idleness, advance husbandry [i.e. agriculture] and yield unto the hired person both in the time of scarcity and in the time of plenty a convenient proportion of wages'. It recognized the labourer's right to work and threatened to impose a fine of 40$s.$ on any employer who, without reasonable cause, dismissed his employee before the end of what was normally a one year contract. At the same time, it emphasized the labourer's obligation to work, and threatened him with imprisonment if he departed 'from his master, mistress or dame before the end of his or her term'. It decreed that all persons between the ages of 12 and 60, not being otherwise employed, were compellable to be yearly agricultural labourers. Hours of work were established as 5 a.m. to 7 or 8 p.m., between mid-March and mid-September, and from dawn till dusk during the rest of the year. Wages were to be reassessed periodically by Quarter Sessions.

A brief glimpse of this system at work is provided by the following two Ashdon entries in the Essex Quarter Sessions files for a few years later. On 22nd December 1573, Robert Claydon and John Cowell, the Ashdon constables, reported that 'Michael Gardyner of the same, labourer of the age of thirty years and unmarried (who had a competent farm whereupon he lived and employed himself until the feast of St. Michael last past, being expired at the said feast) is willing to be retained with any and "to do his dylygent servis to his power" and further that all is in good order'.

On 5th April 1602, at the Statute Sessions held at Great Sampford before John Westley, Chief Constable, the jurors reported that 'William Page, Thomas Freake, Robert Freake and Thomas Mansfeilde are within the age of 12 and 60 years, inhabitants of Ashdon, singlemen, and are not retained in anyone's service; and that Agnes Porter, Jane Cornell, Elizabeth Cornell, Grace Highmarshe and Margaret Crooke are likewise inhabitants of the same within the age of 12 and 40 years, singlewomen, and are not retained'.

These entries point to practical flaws in what, in theory, was quite a sensible system. While employers could not be legally compelled to provide employment, labourers were legally obliged to work. Should they fail to get themselves hired at the annual Michaelmas Statute Fair or should they not be retained at the end of their year of service, they could not fail to commit the heinous Elizabethan sin of idleness. Once they moved on from their native parish to seek employment elsewhere, they no less inevitably ran the risk of being treated as 'rogues and vagabonds'.

In an attempt to counter this, the Poor Relief Act of 1576 had been passed with the express purpose of 'Setting the Poor on Work and Avoiding Idleness'.

> To the intent youth may be accustomed and brought up in labour and work, and then not like to grow to be idle rogues, and to the intent also that such to be already grown up in idleness, and so rogues at present, may not have any just excuse in saying they cannot get any service or work and then without any favour or toleration worthy to be executed, and that other poor and needy persons being willing to work may be set on work: Be it ordained and enacted ... That in every city and town corporate within the realm a competent store and stock of wool, hemp, flax, iron, or other stuff [i.e. materials] by the appointment and order of the Mayor, Bailiffs, Justices, or other head officers having rule in the said cities or towns corporate ... shall be provided.

The wool or flax was to be made into yarn, the poor paid 'according to the desert of the work', the yarn sold in the market place and the proceeds used to purchase more wool or flax to be made into yet more yarn. In this way, the poor would have no need 'to go abroad either begging or committing pilferings or other misdemeanours, living in idleness'.

The more famous Elizabethan Poor Relief Acts of 1598 and 1601 reiterated these principles and, among other things, tried to ensure that the children of poor parents would 'secure employment in later life by binding them as craft apprentices'. Persons proceeding to practice a craft without being properly apprenticed were duly punished. So, on 5th July 1605, 'Thomas Ansell of Ashdon was indicted at Brentwood for exercising the art of a tailor for 8 months without having been apprenticed thereto for seven years'.

With their habitual regard for social efficiency combined with rigorous moral standards, the Tudor legislators did their best to ensure that the apprentice's years of training were not wasted. Henry VIII's Act of 1495 reveals sharp awareness of the ways of likely temptation:

It is ordained and enacted that none apprentice nor servant of husbandry, labourer nor servant artificer, play at the tables [backgammon] . . . but only for meat and drink, nor at the tennis, closh [a game in which a ball had to be driven through a hoop with a spade-shaped instrument], dice, cards, bowls, nor any other unlawful game in no wise out of Christmas, and in Christmas to play only in the dwelling-house of his master or where the master of any of the said servants is present, upon paid on imprisonment by the space of a day in the stocks openly . . .

This wish to safeguard the moral welfare of the trainee and to ensure that the employer honestly discharged his contractual obligations remained enshrined in apprenticeship documents for centuries. It is strikingly evident in the following Indenture of Apprenticeship drawn up in 1867 for William Cater Smith who when his apprenticeship was completed, worked as one of Ashdon's blacksmiths for more than fifty years:

> This Indenture witnesseth that *William Cater Smith* of his own free will and with the consent of *Samuel Cater Smith* and *John Cater Smith*, Trustees of the Will of the late David Smith his father testified by executing these presents, doth put himself Apprentice to *Edward George Podd* of *Debenham* in the County of Suffolk, General and Shoeing Smith, to learn his Art, and with him, after the Manner of an Apprentice, to serve from the twentieth day of November, one thousand eight hundred and sixty seven unto the full End and Term of Four Years from thence next following to be fully complete and ended During which Term, the said Apprentice his Master faithfully shall serve his secrets keep his lawful commands everywhere gladly do, he shall do no damage to his said Master nor see to be done of others but to his Power shall tell or forthwith given warning to his said Master of the same, he shall not waste the Goods of his said Master nor lend them unlawfully to any, he shall not commit fornication nor contract Matrimony within the said Term, he shall not play at Cards or Dice Tables or any other unlawful Games whereby his said Master may have any loss with his own goods or others during the said Term without Licence of his said Master — he shall neither

buy nor sell, he shall not haunt Taverns or Playhouses nor absent himself from his said Master's service day or night unlawfully, But in all things as a faithful Apprentice he shall behave himself towards his said Master and all his during the said Term. And the said Edward George Podd in consideration of the sum of Fifteen Pounds one moiety or half part thereof being this day paid by the above named Trustees, and, the remaining moiety or half part thereof to be paid at the end of two years from the date hereof, his said Apprentice in the Art of a General and Shoeing Smith which he useth by the best means he can shall teach and Instruct or cause to be taught and instructed Finding unto the said Apprentice sufficient Meat, Drink, Work and Lodging and all other Necessaries during the said Term save and except Medical Attendance and Medicine. They, the said Trustees convenanting to find the same and also all necessary and proper clothing and washing for him the said Apprentice during the said term.

William Smith was fortunate enough for the cost of his apprenticeship to be met from money put in trust by his father. Poorer boys were provided with their apprenticeships either by private charity or from public funds raised by their native parish.

The bulk of these funds, however, were regularly expended on the poorest parishioners of all, the widows with families, the elderly or the chronic sick. Like so much English social legislation from the sixteenth century to the present day, the community's acceptance that it had a responsibility to provide for the destitute and the inadequate was promulgated in legislation of the early Tudors and indelibly underlined in the reign of Elizabeth. The Beggars Act of 1531 made the crucial distinction between 'aged, poor and impotent persons' who, provided they first secured a magistrate's licence, were authorized to beg, and those who were 'whole and mighty in body and able to labour' who were to be harried by the law. The Beggars Act of 1536 introduced the principle that each parish should be held responsible for the care of its own impotent poor, ordaining that 'the churchwardens or two others of every parish of this realm shall in good and charitable wise take such discreet and convenient order, by gathering and procuring of such charitable and voluntary alms of the good Christian people within the same with boxes every Sunday, Holy Day, and other Festival Day or otherwise among themselves, in such good and discrete wise as the poor, impotent, lame, feeble, sick, and diseased people, being not able to work, may be provided, holpen and relieved, so that in no wise they nor none of them be suffered to go openly in begging; And that such as be lusty or having their limbs strong enough to labour may be daily kept in continual labour, whereby every one of them may get their own sustance and living with their own hands . . .'. To ensure that the undeserving were not rewarded, the giving of private alms was forbidden by law, the penalty for disobedience being ten times the amount illegally donated.

An Act of 1552 further stressed the 'intent that valiant beggars, idle and loitering persons may be avoided, and the impotent, feeble and lame provided for, which are poor in very deed'. It decreed that Two Collectors of Alms were to be chosen from the inhabitants of every town parish yearly in Whitsun Week, 'which Collectors, the Sunday next after their election . . . when the people is at the church and hath heard God's holy word, shall gently ask and demand of every man and woman what they of charity will be contented to give weekly towards the relief of the poor'. The contributions so promised were to be entered in a register containing the names of the inhabitants and of the impotent poor of the parish who needed sustenance; the Collectors were to make a weekly distribution of the alms to the poor on the register. An interesting innovation was to enlist the influence of the Bishop should any well-provided parishioner prove recalcitrant: 'if any person or persons being able to further this charitable work do obstinately and frowardly refuse to given towards the help of the poor, or do wilfully discourage other from so charitable a deed, the parson, vicar, or curate, and churchwardens of the parish where he dwelleth shall gently exhort him or them towards the relief of the poor; and if he or they will not be persuaded, then upon the certificate of the parson, vicar or curate of the parish to the Bishop of the diocese the same Bishop shall send for him or them to induce and persuade him or them by charitable ways and means, and so according to his discretion to take order for the reformation thereof'.

One notes with interest that if, at the same time, an Ashdon householder expressed his charitable impulses by allowing a vagrant to sleep in the hay or gave shelter to an unmarried pregnant woman, he incurred the grave displeasure of the Archdeacon's Court (see pp.156-7).

The Act of 1563, passed in the fifth year of Elizabeth's reign, introduced an innovation of historic importance by applying the principle of compulsion to the collection of funds for poor relief. Persons unmoved by the Bishop's exhortations were to be sent by him to Quarter Sessions where the Justices would, in their turn, 'charitably and gently persuade and move the said obstinate persons to extend their charity towards the relief of the poor in the parish where he or she inhabiteth and dwelleth'. If gentle judicial persuasion was unavailing, the Justices were empowered to 'cess, tax and limit upon every such obstinate person so refusing, according to their good discretions, what sum the said obstinate person shall pay weekly towards the relief of the poor'. Continued refusal to pay would result in a prison sentence. This Act was also the first to decree that the richer parishes should given financial aid to the poorer parishes. Further important developments, instituted in the Poor Relief Acts of 1598 and 1601, were to provide for the welfare of the poorer members of each parish by imposing a local tax on the relatively well-to-do and for the relief of the poor to be administered by individual parishes through Overseers, nominated by each vestry and confirmed in office by the County Justices. The main features of this scheme continued virtually unchanged till the Poor Law Amendment Act of 1834.

From the middle of the sixteenth century when the English Poor Law was being progressively evolved until the middle of the eighteenth century, it operated in the way its progenitors had intended. The Overseers were selected from the ranks of the yeomanry or local crafts or tradesmen and every one or two weeks, they dispensed small sums of money or useful goods to the paupers of the parish. In the meticulously kept Ashdon Overseers' account-books, the most regular entries are 'Allowed — being sick 1s.0d.' or 'Allowed — 1s.0d. (without a reason given)' or '— 5 faggots (bundles of firewood) out of the barn'.

The following is a typical entry dated 12th May 1759, just a month before the Reverend William Cooper's diary entry that same year (see p.p.89-91).

	£	s	d
Bought a Lock for Mary Chapman	0	1	2

Paid for George Taylors Discharge from being a Soldier	3	9	0
Paid for Letter for him	0	3	6
Allowed John Barker to pay ye Doctor	1	1	0
Paid John Kittridge he and man for splents	0	2	6
& nails & small beer	0	1	2
Bought John Marsh Boy a piece of cloth when he was Bound aprentice	0	9	9
for a pair of Breeches and a Hat and a pair of Stockings and two Shirts	0	8	5
pair of Shoes	0	3	8
Paid for making a Coat & Wescote & Triming	0	4	6
Paid Wm Cole for taking John Marsh's Boy a Prentice	3	3	0
Paid Mr Baker for the Indenters	0	7	6
Paid Expenses at the same time	0	5	0
Paid John Freeman for Thatching	0	4	0
Paid Mr Kent for Straw	0	3	0
Paid the Glasiers bill	0	5	1½
Paid John Green for a pound of Nails	0	0	4½
Paid Mr Kent for Qt Rent dew 1759	0	0	4
Paid for Expences	0	5	0
	10	18	0

A whole world of social and economic change separates that entry, recording routine payments to or for the service of paupers, within the meaning of the Elizabethan Acts, and the Return prepared by the Ashdon Overseers of the Poor for transmission to the Justices of the Peace on 17th January 1801. It lists all the persons in the village receiving Poor Law Allowances, thier (sic) employment, the number of children under 12 years of age, the weekly earnings of the family and the money paid over to them by the Overseers. The list includes 7 widows, 69 farm labourers, 5 carpenters, 3 cordwainers (shoemakers), 2 bricklayers, 1 brickmaker, 1 wheelwright, 1 gardener, 1 higler (travelling salesman) and the village schoolmaster, John Darcy, earning 8 shillings per week. In addition there is just one person described as living in the parish workhouse. The Overseers calculated that to each of these they had paid 4s.6d. per week and sold 62 bushels of corn at a reduced price, each bushel thus sold constituting a loss of 4s.6d. to the parish. Of the people on the list, only the seven widows and the workhouse inmate would have begun to be considered for poor relief earlier in the eighteenth century. None of the rest was aged or infirm or even unemployed; all were apparently able-bodied and actively employed in a full-time occupation. What had happened in the intervening forty two years?

What happened in Ashdon happened in rural England generally. Fewer deaths in child-birth, the virtual absence of major epidemics and an increase in fertility brought about a dramatic increase in the population. The progressive enclosure of the rural commons made the prosperous few even more prosperous and the poor poorer at the same time as they were becoming more numerous. Many small-scale tenant-farmers found it increasingly difficult to pay their rent and either left the land altogether or became labourers in their turn. All this while, the price of corn was inexorably rising, an absolutely crucial item in the poorer countryman's budget since he virtually lived on bread. From 1715 to 1774, the price of corn rose from an average of 34s.11d. to 51s. a quarter; though it fell back again temporarily, it never dropped below 35s. a quarter; from 1795, when England was at war with Revolutionary France (see pp.270-1), the price climbed to an average of 75s. per quarter. Over this period, agricultural wages rose by only 20% when, to keep in line with food prices, they ought to have doubled. In point of fact, many farmers discovered that the easiest way to reduce their production costs was to increase the number of working hours and lower the wages. This tactic seemed to receive official blessing with the historic decision taken at Speenhamland in 1795 when the Berkshire Justices allowed the current price of bread to determine the extent by which wages should be supplemented from the poor rates. Many employers are believed to have deliberately underpaid their employees, confident in their expectation that the wages would be made up by the parish.

A variant of this device may be seen in the way a prominent Colchester baymaker, one Isaac Boggis, relied on the Ashdon Vestry to make up the low wages he paid his cottage spinning-women and to reimburse him for his transport costs. Boggis conducted his profitable business of exporting baize from his house near Colchester

Castle. He collected his wool each year from Stourbridge Fair, had it stored, cleaned and combed in Colchester, then sent it out to a number of 'spinning houses' in the Essex villages of Belchamp Walter, Helions Bumpstead and Ashdon and the Cambridgeshire villages of Hinxton and Abingdon. The spinning was carried out by the wives and daughters of agricultural labourers in their own homes. The yarn was collected by his carriers, brought back to the Colchester repository where it was stored till it was needed by his weavers who worked in their own homes in or near Colchester. His average weekly output in 1790-91 was 33 pieces of baize, each measuring some 40 yards by 2 yards, and this provided employment for about 50 weavers and up to 350 spinners and combers. He compensated himself for the transport costs incurred in using distant villages for spinning by exacting from the parish vestries concerned a subsidy of 4*d.* for every shilling earned by the spinners. The vestries apparently found it preferable to pay the subsidy and so keep the spinners in work than to take away their employment and maintain them from the poor rate. A surviving letter from one of Boggis's agents provides a glimpse of the scheme in action:

Colchester, Jan 7th, 1791.

Mr Parkis,

Please to carry the wool to Hinkson and tell Mr Moore to put it out and for he to tell the spinners that I shall be there on the 27th inst. about 2 o'clock and that he must put it out at 4^d in the shilling. And that of Ashdon, please to carry to Mr Youngs at the [Rose and] Crown and enquire for Mary Lowts to assist in the weighing it out and tell the spinners I shall be there on the 28th inst. about 2 o'clock.

I am etc.,

J. Browne

(Details from A.F.J. Brown: *Essex at Work, 1700-1815*, Essex Record Office, 1972, p.84)

Whatever the ethics of Boggis's accounting methods, his wages quite clearly provided a welcome addition to the income of many a labourer's family and when, in the course of the nineteenth century, the introduction of new machinery put an end to the cottage spinning industry, the poor of many a village were significantly impoverished.

One further response to the chronic problem of nationwide poverty was to provide a workhouse. Parishes were first encouraged to adopt this tactic by the Poor Law Act of 1598 which permitted 'convenient houses of dwelling' to be erected for the impotent poor at the ratepayers' expense. The Ashdon Vestry elected to involve its ratepayers in such expense in 1775 by making a workhouse from the village Guildhall. This building was so named because it once housed the Ashdon Parish Gild of St. Mary the Virgin. Gilds, which flourished in England after the Conquest, served both a spiritual and a practical purpose. They normally functioned in the parish church, where an altar would be dedicated to the Gild's patron saint and where the Guild's own priest would say masses for its members, both the living and the dead. In this respect, they were the poor man's equivalent of the Chantry Chapels endowed by the rich for the betterment of their souls. The more earthly function of the Gild was to serve as a mutual benefit organization similar to the Friendly Society founded at the beginning of the nineteenth century by a number of Ashdon's farm labourers. Members contributed a small sum each year or each quarter and their communal fund could be drawn upon should any individual be in need. In Saffron Walden, a special Gild, 'Our Lady of Pity', was formed in 1400 chiefly to maintain an almshouse for thirteen poor men to live in 'such as be lame, crooked, blind and bed-ridden and most at need'.

Gild funds were occasionally augmented by benefactions. When Ashdon's Gild of St. Mary the Virgin was originally founded is not known. It does not feature in a list of religous gilds compiled in 1388 (and listed in H.F. Westlake: *The Parish Gilds of Mediaeval England*, S.P.C.K., 1919) but it is named in the will of a local man, Roger Bryght in 1501, when he left it a tenement with two houses built upon it. The Gild was left 6*s*. 8*d.* by Robert Cleydon in 1505 while John Cleydon, who then occupied Goldstones Farm, donated the revenues of a pasture near Brights Farm on the periphery of the parish. In 1547, when some 2400 chantries and gild chapels were suppressed all over the country, the Chantry Commissioners noted that the Ashdon Gild Chapel, which they designated as Our Lady Brotherhood, had received a bequest from Sir John Chalne, clerk, to provide a priest for the Gild, the current holder of the office being one 'Sir Phillipe Fawdon, Clerk', whom they described as being 'literatus and of good conversacion'; they reported that his bequest was also being used to 'discharge XX [i.e. twenty] of the poore beynge contributory ther . . .'.

When the Ashdon Gild was suppressed at the Reformation, the Hall where its members had held their meetings passed through various vicissitudes, being described as 'ruinous' in 1570, serving as the parish 'Town House' in the middle of the seventeenth century then being divided into several tenements in the earlier part of the eighteenth. When, in 1775, it became the parish Workhouse, it once again became associated with the social welfare which had been prominent amongst the preoccupations of its original founders. The separate tenements were converted into a communal building. According to an inventory drawn up in 1788, there was a buttery, a large kitchen with fireplace and a room known as the Ward downstairs, while upstairs, directly above the Ward, was a dormitory containing six beds with a separate single bedroom leading off. Those Ashdon paupers who were not able-bodied and who had nowhere else to go, and who therefore qualified for 'indoor relief', lived on these premises and, as laid down in the sixteenth-century Statutes (see p.115), spun wool to pay for their keep.

The Suffolk poet George Crabbe is reputed to have immortalized the principal features of the archetypal workhouse in his starkly realistic poem *The Village* (1783).

> There is yon House that holds the parish poor,
> Whose walls of mud scarce bear the broken door;
> There, where the putrid vapours, flagging, play,
> And the dull wheel hums doleful through the day;—
> There children dwell who know no parents' care;
> Parents, who know no children's love, dwell there!
> Heart-broken matrons on their joyless bed,
> Forsaken wives, and mothers never wed;
> Dejected widows with unheeded tears,
> And crippled age with more than childhood fears;
> The lame, the blind, and far the happiest they!
> The moping idiot and the madman gay.

Ashdon's paupers may conceivably have suffered some of these tribulations during the short period of its workhouse's existence but if they did so, it was in a setting more congenial than Crabbe's. It did not bear a threatening inscription above its front door like the eighteenth-century Workhouse in Walthamstow which announced to the doubtless illiterate paupers 'If any would not work, neither should he eat'. It was conceived on a modest scale and set in sylvan surroundings up on the airy hill beside the ancient church and though it is difficult to conceive of anyone's forming much of an attachment to an institution such as the workhouse, the inmates are more than likely to have resented the change when, five years after the Poor Law Amendment Act of 1834, they were all compulsorily transferred to the Union Workhouse at Saffron Walden. For the remainder of the nineteenth century, it was official policy to make workhouse conditions as unpleasant as possible so as to persuade the inmates to get out and find work elsewhere.

A particularly perceptive commentary on the causes and effects of changes in administering the poor law in the eighteenth century was produced by the Reverend John North, Rector of Ashdon from 1791 till 1818. He both described and tried to analyze what he had observed in his own parish in a lengthy article, 'State of the Poor in the Parish of Ashdon, Essex' published in volume 35 of the reputable journal *Annals of Agriculture* in 1800. Having noted the vast increase in the Overseers' disbursements to the poor of the parish in the course of the century, an average of £112 per year in the period 1731-1734 rising to £663 10s. per year in the period 1794-1799, the increase in the number of the parishioners needing to be relieved and the change in their nature, from bona fide paupers to able-bodied workers being paid an inadequate wage, he deplores the fact that 'persons who are able and willing to work and who really do work' can still work 'even to the utmost of their power and are not able to maintain themselves'.

> When I hear it asserted in general terms 'that the price of labour will always find its level', I cannot help thinking there is some mistake even in *ordinary* times. In *extraordinary* times, or in sudden changes of prices of necessaries of life, the position must be evidently false; for if the ordinary wages of a day labourer in this parish, which are 7s. a week, is only sufficient and barely sufficient to maintain a labourer and his wife and a child when wheat is 6s. a bushel, and we choose to say it has then found its level, we can not but confess that the level is lost if the wages remain without augmentation when wheat

is at 16s. a bushel; and as the farmers are in general greatly averse from raising of the wages, and the great farmers are more averse than any others, little hope remains that such a level will be found, or even sought for, by them. 'Can you let me have any work?' (says a labourer to a farmer) — 'Come on Monday morning' (says the farmer) 'and I will employ you.' — 'What will you give me?' — 'You shall fare as the rest.' Less than this generally passes in the contract between the farmer and the labourer. Let us endeavour to supply the conditions of the contract in the circumstances of each party. In the farmer's mind, something further passes of which this may be the sum:— 'I have made an agreement with all my neighbourhood to pay only 7s. a week for labour. If the labourer call this a combination of masters against labourers, I do not know that such a combination is contrary to law; and if it should, what evidence can the labourer produce of it? He neither has money nor courage to prosecute, and he knows he never would be employed again in this parish'. At the same time there pass in the labourer's mind some reflections similar to the following. 'Seven shillings a week are but a poor compensation for six days' labour, and by no means a sufficiency for seven days' maintenance; but if I refuse those wages for a single day, I must deprive my family of subsistence for a day, and on the day following, I must accept the same wages either from this master or some other. If I induce the other labourers to refuse to work, the farmers will bring us to justice for unlawful combinations. [The 1799 and 1800 Combination Acts prohibited workers from forming combinations or, as we would now say, Trade Unions. They were repealed in 1824.] I must, therefore, take what he offers and I must do all I can to induce my master to become my friend and advocate at the vestry whenever I may stand in need (as I do now) of rent for my house, of wood, and clothing, and occasional assistance of every kind from this parish'. On terms like these, either expressed or understood, the contract begins and proceeds. For my own part, I can see little in this kind of transaction which promises that the wages of day labourers will ever find the level above mentioned.

The effect of this mode of wage-bargaining, North found wholly deplorable for employees and employers alike. 'The labourers are hereby taught that the great part of their maintenance does not depend upon industry but upon begging. They are hereby taught that the habit of laying anything aside for a further day is of little use; for it is impossible to lay aside anything for sickness, old age, or even for paying their yearly rent, or to buy wood or coals for fuel; nothing remains but to throw those cares upon the Overseers.' The farmers, for their part, were more than likely to allow the parish to furnish the labourers' required additional income which by rights ought to have been provided in the form of an adequate wage, and the effect of this would inevitably be that 'the ties of *Kindness* and its concomitant *gratitude*' would 'be loosened, if not totally dissolved'. Observing that the rate burden was unevenly distributed, he concluded pessimistically 'as the little farmer is a loser in proportion to his littleness, the great farmer is, by this administration, a gainer in proportion to his greatness; and as the great farmers govern the parish, the increase of the wages of labourers will always be opposed by great farmers; and as great farms are daily increasing in number and size, the hope of seeing the wages of labourers ... become more adequate to their daily wants seems to me not to be drawing near ...'.

North's style is sometimes fussy, and his manner regularly tends towards labouriousness, but he seems to me to have been rather more in touch with rural realities than his much more famous contemporary Arthur Young who, for all his reputation as a humane agricultural theorist, could still declare:

> Everyone knows that the lower classes must be kept poor or they will never be industrious ... they must (like all mankind) be in poverty or they will not work.

To be fair to Young, he was by no means always as crass in his utterances as this quotation might suggest. His most famous single quotation reveals a rather more sympathetic and perceptive attitude towards the symptoms and the causes of rural poverty at the end of the eighteenth century:

> Go to an alehouse kitchen of an old-enclosed country, and there you will see the origin of poverty and the poor rates.

For whom are they to be sober? For whom are they to save? For the parish? If I am diligent, shall I then have leave to build a cottage? If I am sober, shall I have land for a cow? If I am frugal, shall I have half an acre of potatoes? You offer no motives, you have nothing but a parish officer and a workhouse. Bring me another pot,' (Quoted in Chambers & Mingay, *op. cit.*, p.102).

Unlike Young, who contrived to be both a prolific and regularly perceptive commentator on the English agricultural scene and a failure as a practical farmer, North was in daily contact with the poor. He would have seen, if not helped draw up, the Ashdon Overseers' list of allowances to the poor families of the parish on 2nd December 1799. 110 families are enumerated on the list, including 8 widows (4 with 3 children to support), 16 families with 3 children, 9 with 4 children, 9 with 5 children and 3 with 6 children. The Overseers have appended to the columns of names the allowances they granted on this occasion: For a man and wife with 2 children under 12, 1s. 0d.; for a man and wife with 3 children under 12, 1s. 6d. and so on up to a maximum of 4s. 0d. for a man and wife with 6 children under 7. The Overseers have noted 'Allowances granted on Account of high Price of Corn'.

As long as the price of corn remained high, the poor benefitted from the advantages of the 'Speenhamland' system; it was only after the end of the French Wars, when the price of corn began to fluctuate wildly, that the serious disadvantages of the system became apparent. Not for the first time in our nation's history, peace failed to bring prosperity. The high wartime prices had not only made farmers rich but through their higher rate contributions, enabled the parishes to afford the Speenhamland payments. The Corn Law of 1815 was designed to keep corn prices high: it allowed foreign corn to be imported and warehoused duty free at all times but wheat could be sold only when the home price reached 80 shillings a quarter. This price was indeed exceeded in 1817 and 1818 thanks to poor harvests in England and in Western Europe but with a marked improvement in the continental yields thereafter, large imports flooded in, there were exceptionally large home harvests in 1821 and 1822, and the home prices sank to 44s. 7d. Prices remained low thereafter throughout the 1820s and farmers and labourers both suffered: landowners and farmers were bankrupted, a very low rate of relief was paid out under Speenhamland and the invention of new machines virtually put an end to the cottage industry of spinning in which well organized labouring families had been able to engage to supplement their chronically low wages. Unrest became rife across the English countryside and 1830 brought a spate of riots and rick-burning. On this, the *Times* carried a remarkably compassionate leading article, declaring:

> Let the rich be taught that Providence will not suffer them to oppress their fellow creatures with impunity. Here are tens of thousands of Englishmen, industrious, kind-hearted but broken-hearted beings, exasperated into madness by insufficient food and clothing, by utter want of necessaries for themselves and their unfortunate families.

The rich were not impressed by such rhetoric: 6 labourers were executed, 400 sent to prison and 457 transported to Australia.

If the labourers of Ashdon were not involved in these disturbances or in the wave of machine-wrecking organized over the south of England in the 1830s by the still mysterious 'Captain Swing', it should not be taken to mean that they were more affluent or more docile than their counterparts elsewhere. From such diverse records as the parish Overseers' accounts, John North's essay and the array of law court indictments (see p.87), it is evident that they had to suffer the same pressures of poverty as anyone else. That there was a limit to what they could endure was finally demonstrated when they withdrew their labour at the very beginning of harvest-time on the eve of the First World War.

* * *

With the implementation of the Poor Law Amendment Act of 1834, caring for the poor became at once a more professional and more impersonal affair. The unpaid parish overseers were replaced by a salaried reviewing officer answerable to a Board of Guardians, 'guardian' being the term traditionally used by the well endowed when providing for their own orphans. The smaller parishes were encouraged to combine into unions to provide a single workhouse for a larger geographical area. Essex established seventeen such unions and, in the process, Ashdon became part of the Saffron

Walden Union. 'Outdoor' relief was virtually abolished for those able to exist in homes of their own but it was re-introduced towards the end of the nineteenth century when an offical 'Relieving Officer' was empowered to give a weekly allowance of bread and two shillings per week at the pay station. There are account of this system in operation in the interviews of Mrs Anderson and Mrs Ford (see pp.205 & 210). Until 1908 and the introduction of Old Age Pensions, even the strongest, ablest and proudest of farm workers were, at times, dependent on Poor Law Relief. Throughout rural England, in the nineteenth century, the great majority of the workers labouring to produce the nation's food were for much of the time ill fed if not half-starved. In the meantime, individual parishes provided what supplementary relief they could from their Charities.

From early in the sixteenth century till the middle of the nineteenth, the poor of Ashdon benefitted from a number of modest benefactions, usually the fund accumulating from the rent on property or land. In 1517, John Charles (or Chalne) left the parish money raised from the sale of his lands in Wethersfield in Suffolk and directed that part of the proceeds should be used to pay 'at the next tax to be levied and paid to our soveraigne lorde the King' on behalf of twenty of the poorest parishioners in Ashdon. Edmond Sherbrooke, rector of Ashdon from 1565 to 1584, left in his will, dated 3rd September 1589, the rent charge deriving from part of the estate at Newnham Hall; the sum amounted to 10 shillings per year and the money was to be spent on bread, distributed to the poor once a year about the end of January. John Freeman, by a will dated 11th October 1639, gave a rent charge of ten shillings payable from an enclosed field on Ashdon Street Farm. Thomas Saward, by a will dated 10th October 1696, gave half an acre of pasture, the rent from which had to be paid on St. Thomas's Day to 'as many poor Persons of the parish as the amount will allow one shilling each'. In 1691, the sum of £5 accumulated in the Guildhall Charity was handed over to the Overseers and 'was disposed of as followeth: three pounds fourteen shillings was expended in the putting forth of William and Mary the children of William Page of this parish, the boy to Thomas Cole of this towne, the girle to Mr Moore of Linton, the remaining Twenty six shillings goeth towards the putting out of — Wishbie, sonne of Tho. Wishbie of this parish who is placed with Richard Mascall ... and it is ordered that wt money shall arise out of the towne houses and lands for the future shall be imploied to no other use than the putting out of poore Children' (i.e. to be apprenticed). One 11th February 1796, a 'double Tenement' near Mill Field was conveyed to the parish from an unknown source. In 1837, the Rector, Dr. Benedict Chapman, noted '(The two buildings) have hitherto been occupied by poor Persons who pay no rent. They are called "Pest Houses" as Poor Persons are sent there in case of their having the small pox, or any infectious disorder. These have been sold under the new Poor Laws (of 1834)'.

From the sixteenth century onwards, when charitably minded persons bequeathed money to the poor they commonly also left money to the upkeep either of the Church or of their own funeral monument. Sometimes these interests came into conflict as they did when the time came to administer the benefaction of Robert Freeman. Second son of Richard Freeman, an Ashdon tailor, Robert worked for some years in Cambridge as servant to Dr. Torkington, Master of Clare College. In his employ and through inheritance, he acquired some property and after his death in 1817, it was discovered that he had left £100 in stock to the parish of Ashdon, the annual dividends to be used partly to keep his 'gravestone and the inscription thereon in good order and condition', and partly to purchase books to the value of ten shillings per year to be distributed to 'such poor children of the parish of Ashdon by the Minister at his discretion as shall have been instructed by him in the Church Catechism on Easter Sunday yearly'; any residue was to be used for 'placing out such poor children of the said Parish of Ashdon to school as the Minister shall from time to time appoint'.

A further benefaction was provided by Dr. Benedict Chapman, some time Rector of Ashdon, who willed eight acres of land in perpetuity in trust to Caius College Cambridge on condition that the rents be used for the upkeep of the church organ which, he reminded his executors, he had erected in 1821 at the personal expense of £130, and towards the maintenance of the National Schoolhouse to which he had personally contributed the sum of £200 for it to be erected on waste ground within the Rectory Manor; any residue from the trust was to be applied towards giving places in the Ashdon National School to poor children whose parents were members of the Church of England.

Noteworthy though Dr. Chapman's contribution was to the Ashdon

Children's Home boys in 1908

poor of his day, it was surpassed in terms of beneficence and of vision by that of one of his Victorian successors, Dr. Henry Swete. Before becoming Regius Professor of Divinity in the University of Cambridge, Swete was Professor of Pastoral Theology at King's College London, and it is doubtless because of this London connection that he had been able to observe at first hand the way in which the pauper children of the capital were obliged to exist. In Victorian times, hundreds of poverty-stricken children spent their lives in the streets. By day, they would sweep crossings, sell lace, sing ballads or perform acrobatics before theatre queues; at night, they would sleep beneath railway arches, in empty wagons, under sacks or tarpaulins, in dustbins or ashpits, in cellars or on staircases. The nightmarish dark world into which Oliver Twist is transported when he reaches London may have been transfigured by Dicken's lurid imagination but it was essentially based on grim reality and it was to rescue children from such dire conditions that, in 1881, Edward Rudolf founded 'The Church of England Society for Providing Homes for Waifs and Strays'.

Up till then, provision for destitute children had taken three main forms. They were either kept in the Poor Law workhouse or industrial school where their lives were industrialized to a degree, from which they emerged, in the words of one observer, 'just like deer let out of a cart before the hunt, looking about vacantly in every direction'. They could be housed in orphan asylums some of which had existed since the eighteenth century and many of which were upgraded in the course of the nineteenth in such a way as to restrict entry to 'persons respectably descended' or to the offspring of particular social groups such as the Clergy Orphan Asylum or the Railway Benevolent Institution; Thomas Coram's Foundling Hospital limited itself to admitting only the *first* of a mother's illegitimate children. Finally there were a number of voluntary societies founded by such dedicated philanthropists as Lord Shaftsbury or Dr. Barnardo. The combined resources of all these institutions were inadequate to meet the increasing pressures of the trade depression of the 1870s and a rapidly expanding population and it was to provide something more and something different that, at Edward Rudolf's insistence, the Church of England was moved to fund homes for waifs and strays. Dr. Swete, who had become Rector of Ashdon in 1877, was one of many Anglican clergymen to respond to the appeal for practical help.

His own childhood had been wretched: his mother died when he was one month old and he was brought up by an overbearing stepmother; when, in later life, he was occasionally taxed with being overindulgent to children, his explanation was always that he wanted to ensure that they did not suffer as he had done. As Lord of the Ashdon Rectory Manor, he was able to provide a four hundred year old cottage rent free; he paid half of the cost of furnishing it and appointed his own sister as Matron. The first six town boys arrived in the summer of 1885. Their ages ranged from three to seven: two were illegitimate, one had been abandoned by both his parents, one was from a family of nine children whose father had killed himself and the remaining two were brothers about whose background nothing is known; three more infants arrived shortly after. Dr. Swete was delighted. 'No country parish is complete without its waifs and strays', he observed. 'The children bring fresh blood and ideas into the village school, and they are a constant source of interest and delight to the parish priest.'

In 1889, the Bishop of Colchester visited the Ashdon Home and shook hands with each of the boys. Soon afterwards, the following report appeared in the Church of England Waifs and Strays Society *Journal*:

> The little home at Ashdon for nine boys is very successful. The house, a thatched cottage, stands in a great open field of which a small piece is enclosed as a garden and playground. Each boy has a tiny garden and the elder ones keep them as a model of neatness ... However, the inside of the cottage is not very promising, for it is very old and worn out. Sometimes the leg of a bedstead goes through the floor, much to the boys' amusement, but it is very roomy and airy and with occasional patching will last many years.

Dr. Swete was not much taken with the notion of 'occasional patching'. He proceeded to build a completely new and decidedly more spacious home just down the lane from his elegant Rectory, on land rented from Gonville and Caius College. On St. Michael and All Souls Day, 1890, there was a service of benediction for the new building and after the service, the procession, singing hymns, walked the half mile across the glebe back to the new building. Thereafter it was officially known as All Saints' Home (Cottage Home for 12 Boys from 8 to 13).

After starting as an intimate family concern run by Dr. Swete and his sister, the Home was administered by a local committee who met once a month to hear the Matron's report, pass the accounts, deal with current problems and consider which new boys to admit and possible careers for those about to leave. Prominent among those who carried on Dr. Swete's work after he had left for Cambridge were Mrs Brocklebank, wife of the immensely rich Reverend C.H. Brocklebank of Bartlow Hall, who served on the Committee from 1904 to 1934. She would always arrive by Rolls Royce, and every Christmas Day, would give each boy a freshly minted half crown. He was allowed to keep it for the whole day after which it was put away in a sealed money box. Her record of long service in the cause of the Home was surpassed only by Miss Ellen Whitehead who was appointed as Matron at a salary of £20 per year in 1895 when she was twenty nine years old. She remained as Matron for thirty seven years. Each Sunday, after dinner, she would explain the Collect for the day which the boys had to learn by heart. Prayers were said in the dormitory every day. On Sundays, all the boys were taken to morning service and the elder ones, most of whom were in the church choir, returned again in the evening. During the week, on their return from the village school, the boys could play the routine indoor and outdoor games, snakes-and-ladders, dominoes, halma, ludo and what one offical report on the Home cryptically called 'cricket and football of a sort'. No games were permitted on Sundays although, on returning from their regular walk around or across the fields, the boys were allowed to knit or to read bound copies of the *Illustrated London News*.

Over the years, a number of the Home boys were successfully apprenticed to various crafts, quite regularly at the Society's own printing works at Frome in Somerset; inevitably, some joined the Services, naval training-ships being consistently popular, and several emigrated to Canada; one former pupil joined the police, became personal bodyguard to the Prince of Wales then Commander of a Metropolitan district; one became a journalist and moved to Alexandria to join the editorial board of the *Egyptian Gazette*. Even though few chose to settle quite so far away, the horizons of all of them must have significantly widened when they were moved from the drearier regions of London to Ashdon's hills and fields. There were regular excursions to Clacton, Frinton, Walton-on-the-Naze or to Cambridge and after just such a visit in 1890, the following letter appeared in the Church of England Waifs and Strays Society *Journal*:

> Dear Sir,
> Dr. Swete took four of us and Matron to Cambridge, and he showed us some of the Colleges — St. John's, King's, Queen's and Trinity. We went through some of them and the libraries; we went to King's College Chapel for evening service; we saw the museum and the mummies; we went through the Bridge of Sighs; we went on the water in a boat; and Dr. Swete bought each of us a little book all about Cambridge. We saw a heathen altar and a temple made of ivory and all kinds of beautiful things; we all think it is a pretty place. We went to the Senate House and saw the Chancellors Chair; we saw the printing the prayer book and the Bible; and we saw the great engine at work; and we had such a nice dinner and tea, and Miss Swete invited the other five to the Rectory, and

they did enjoy themselves, and so did we, and I am sure we shall never forget it.

From your loving boys at Ashdon.

There may well be some doubt about the authorship of that letter because the adroit use of that reiterated semi-colon is a talent not normally given to children quite so young, but of the authenticity of the deep affection generated amongst generations of boys for their Matron and their Ashdon Home there can be no doubt whatsoever. They wrote back warmly long after they had left and sometimes returned to spend their adult holidays there.

At the end of a chapter in which much evidence has had to be provided of official insensitivity to the causes and effects of deprivation, it is both pleasant and poignant to conclude with the brief chronicle of one Home boy whose experience of institutional living moved him to write just before the First World War 'Ashdon Home was *my* home and Ashdon was *my* village'. This was Thomas Deradour, whose first appearance in the village records is in the Discipline Book of the village school when the Headmaster noted 'Detained till 4.30 this afternoon for kicking and throwing gravel on to the School garden'. On 1st October 1913, his future career prospects were reviewed by the local Home-committee and on 6th May 1914, he left the Home for Canada. In November 1916, Private T. Deradour visited the Home and donated £1 to be spent on behalf of the Home boys: the money was used to buy a wheelbarrow. In June 1917, he was killed in action; his name can still be seen on the Ashdon War Memorial which stands in front of the village school. He was seventeen years old.

6

The Rule of Law

> The law is the witness and external deposit of our moral life. Its history is the moral development of the race.
> *Oliver Wendell Holmes, Jr.,*
> speech, Boston, 8th Jan. 1897.

In the world of our distant ancestors, laws and law-enforcers were almost as thick on the ground as the forests which, in bygone times, all but covered the face of England. If the ordinary citizen managed his affairs so as never to be haled before those charged with administering the law of the land or what purported to be the law of God, in his day-to-day existence he could not avoid being affected by the laws of his local manorial court. With the waning of the Middle Ages, the manor may well have lost most of its significance as an economic unit, but at local level, it continued to exert considerable judicial and administrative influence throughout the Tudor era. It did so through the agency of its two courts, the Court Baron and the Court Leet.

The Court Baron was the court of the lord of the manor and its principal function was to settle questions pertaining to his manor lands. It served to register changes in tenancy, to deal with the minor infringement of property rights, to collect rents and other dues, to claim escheats (lands reverting to the lord of the manor when a tenant died without an heir or was required to forfeit his estate after conviction for a felony), to maintain watch against minor enclosures, illegal tree-felling or the stealing of wood, to consider boundary disputes, to impose fines on copyholders (tenants protected by title written into the manor court rolls) who had transgressed against the immemorial customs relating to the commons, the open fields and the meadows. In theory, the lord could insist on his court's convening every three weeks; in practice, meetings were rarely held more than once or twice a year.

The following are typical examples of Court Baron business. They are taken from the meeting of a Court Baron, held on 5th September 1589, presided over by Henry, Earl of Sussex, who was making his first appearance as Lord of the Manor of Ashdon Hall. This is the only pre-1600 manorial record to have survived:

> — It is presented by the homage [assembled body of the Lord's tenants] that Thomas Freman outside the court and after the last court surrendered into the lord's hand by the hand of John Odell unfree tenant of this manor in the presence of William Perkyn also unfree tenant of the said manor, witness, according to the custom of the said manor: 1 piece of land containing 2 acres in Paynes cockfield, 1 headland [untilled land at the head of strips on which the plough turned] abutting on to Grenestrete to the west, and another headland abutting on to the lord's land called Colman Brede and one other piece of land containing, by estimation 1½ acres more or less in the field called Brodestreet or Lyttlefalle downe, which holding the said Thomas Freman has to himself and to his heirs from the Lord, having possession on Wednesday on the feast of St. Andrew the Apostle on 30th November 12 Elizabeth [1597] and which he had before to himself and his heirs by hereditary right after the death of John Freman ... Fine paid and fealty done, and admitted to the holding.
> — The homage say on oath that Robert Dalton sold to — Sutton, gent, and his heirs 2 acres of land called Richards Crofte and surrenders it. And because no one come to take it up it is held over.
> — And that John Odell conveyed to John Pettyt and his heirs 4 acres of land called Costards and surrendered it.
> — And that Robert Bentley conveyed to Robert Freman 8 acres of free pasture and woodland.
> — And that John Odell sold to Jeremy Johnson and his heirs three acres of free pasture.
> — And that Richard Wyllowes bought of Ferdinand Parrys, armiger [one entitled to bear heraldic arms] 12 acres of free land.

In public and private archives throughout the country, there must be literally miles of manorial rolls containing items of this nature, now entirely void of any sort of human interest but, in their day, doubtless as likely to generate powerful feelings of satisfaction or frustration as compulsory purchase orders or the granting of planning permission do today. Such transactions, however, affected only those fortunate enough to be able to buy or sell or rent land. The existence of the ordinary villager was much more likely to be affected by decisions taken by the Court Leet which was supposed theoretically to meet twice a year, within a month after Easter and Michaelmas, but which, by Elizabethan times, tended to meet annually. Its routine business was to deal with 'nuisances' and 'misdemeanours' not grave enough to go forward to the County Assizes: disorders in ale-houses, trade offences and all manner of little local difficulties such as failing to keep the highways clean or polluting the air with an obnoxious privy. Any offender proved guilty was warned that failure to remedy the nuisance or repetition of the misdemeanour would result in a forfeit or an amercement (fine). Those who offended persistently or were unable to pay their fine were put in the pillory or the stocks in keeping with our ancestors' view that a necessary part of judicial punishment was public humiliation; that same view was also instrumental in causing immoral or nagging women to be ducked in the village pool or stream.

It was also the business of the Court Leet to elect the manorial officers: the Reeve (who ran the day-to-day business of the manor), the hayward (who looked after the commons), the pinder (whose responsibility was the manorial pound for strays) and the surveyors of the highways. The upkeep of the local roads proved as chronic a problem in the Ashdon area as it did throughout the length and breadth of the kingdom and there is no shortage of evidence in the legal records to bear this out. The road between Ashdon and neighbouring Radwinter passed through the Manor of Bendysh Hall which, as late as 1836, was still a separate hamlet partly in Radwinter parish and partly in Ashdon: entries in its Court Roll for the mid-sixteenth century give some indication of the nature of the problem: in 1551, just one year after the inhabitants of Bendysh Hall were reprimanded for allowing their stocks and pillory to fall into a 'state of decay', Thomas Mountford, the Lord's bailiff, and another tenant were censured because 'the Queen's highways [were] a nuisance because of default in scouring ditches and cutting down branches of trees'; in 1564, because the inhabitants of Bendysh Hall had 'frequently pastured their beasts in the Queen's highways and broken their neighbours' hedges, the manorial court banned them from the roadside verges and fined the culprits 4*d.* for each beast, one half to be paid to the *pinder* (or empounder) the other half to the lord of the manor who was at that time Lord Cobham, Warden of the Cinque Ports.

Some of the inhabitants of Ashdon were no less delinquent in the discharge of their civic responsibilities and were from time to time brought before the Justices of the Peace at Quarter Sessions: on 30th September 1574, one can still read in the Quarter Sessions Calendar at the Essex Record Office, 'within the township of Ashdon, the constables find a noyous plot in the Queens highway before John Bades gate by reason that the water cannot have the right course, which should be amended by the township aforesaid'; on 8th June 1607, 'Anthony Colton of Saffron Walden, gent, is indicted for that he hath hedged in and diged up a common highway lying in Saffron Walden leading from the same up to Ashdon and thence towards London, by reason of which hedge and ditch the Kings liege people are not able to have free passage by and across the same highway as they were wont to have'.

In the seventeenth and eighteenth centuries, roads were the responsibility of individual parishes which, under threat of a Quarter Sessions fine, had to maintain them by six days of 'Statute labour' performed by all able-bodied men; a small rate was paid to the parish once the Justices were persuaded that the 'Statute Labour' had been adequately carried out. It was not always possible to rely on the co-operation of every parishioner and occasionally the parish constables were obliged to report the fact to the local Justices. In 1612, they provided 'a note of such persons as have refused work in the King's highway in the parish of Ashdon. Keepers of teams or drafts refusing to do their work: 'Keeling Branton hath done two days work and refuseth to do any more, saying that he will answer for it; Wm Fremlin refuseth to make any carriage for the highway'. On 30th June 1614, 'Thos. Purkis of Bartlow, yeoman, having 7 or 8 score acres of arable land and pasture in Ashdon is indicted for not doing any of his six days work'. On 1st May 1660, 'Tho. Greene of Ashdon, yeoman, is indicted for fencing and hedging in of half an acre of land called

Overhall Greene in Ashdon, being the highway from Ashdon to Saffron Walden'; on 11th January 1686, 'the Hamlet of Bartlow is (collectively) indicted for not repairing the highway for three rods from Ashdon to Bartlow; on 2nd October 1688, 'the inhabitants of Ashdon are charged with not enclosing a well lying in the highway called *le three want way*, (presumably what is now Crown Hill, the junction of the Saffron Walden-Bartlow and the Ashdon-Radwinter roads).

The local Surveyors of Highways had received no professional training. They were recruited year by year from the ranks of the ratepaying parishioners and had reluctantly to supervise their less than enthusiasic neighbours to carry out operations for which their own enthusiasm was seldom likely to get out of control: the job was unpaid. The records do not provide much evidence of any coherent policy or 'forward planning', merely a pragmatic response to problems as they arose: ruts might occasionally be filled in, ditches unblocked in times of flooding, ice and snow cleared from the main street. The 'surveyors' ought not to have found it necessary to handle money since the local inhabitants were supposed, in theory, to provide labour and carts but in practice, many of them compounded for these obligations. Some indication of the system in operation is offered by the following 'account of the Several Disbursements made by us Robert Swan, James Wells and Wm Sparks, Surveyors of the Highways of Ashdon from Christmas 1734 to the 12th of December 1735':

P[er] Robt. Swann 1734		£	s	d
March 20	pd Tho. Symonts for picking two Load & a half of stones	0	2	6
21	pd for my return at the Sessions	0	0	6
1735 June —	pd John Marsh & Jn Warren for diging of Gravel six days a peice at 2s 2d p[er] day	0	13	6
Octo^r —	pd Henry Sale for putting down the Stiles in Stephen Adams fields that were taken vp to carry Gravel into the Road	0	0	4

In addition to the surveyors of the highways, further important manorial officers were the tasters of bread and ale whose duties are clearly defined by the oath they had to swear on taking up their office:

> You shall truly see that all bread do contain such weight according to the assize (a periodic announcement by which, from 1266 onwards, the civic authority of each locality laid down the price of bread and ale), and take care that all brewers do brew good and wholesome beer and ale, and that the same be essayed by you, and at such price as it shall be limited by the justices of the peace; and all offences committed by brewers, bakers and tipplers you shall present to this court.

The Elizabethans' fondness for their ale is the subject of a characteristically trenchant comment by William Harrison. Having noted their habit of criticizing the quality of the bakers' bread when they attend the local market, he continues:

> Howbeit, though they are so nice in the proportion of their bread, yet in lieu of the same there is such heady ale and beer in most of them as for the mightiness thereof among such as seek it out is commonly called huffcap, the mad dog, father-whoreson, angels'-food, dragons'-milk, go-by-the-wall, stride-wide, and lift-leg etc. And this is more to be noted, that when one of late fell by God's providence into a troubled conscience, after he had considered well of his reckless life and dangerous estate, another thinking belike to change his color and not his mind, carried him straightway to the strongest ale as to the next physician. It is incredible to say how our maltbugs lug (suck) at this liquor, even as pigs should lie in a row lugging at their dam's teats till they lie still again and be not able to wag. Neither did Romulus and Remus suck their she-wolf, or sheperd's wife, Lupa, with sharp and eager devotion as these men hale at huffcap till they be red as cocks and little wiser than their combs.'

In the course of time, the enforcement of the laws governing the conduct of alehouses passed to wider authority and to higher courts. On 13th December 1565, the Ashdon constables felt able to report to the Quarter Sessions 'Our alehouses keep good roull and are bound according to the statute'; on 6th July 1571, they reported that 'a typpeler whoos name is Robert Overye beyng a verye poore man suffereth menes servants to use in his house verye much playing at dyse and cards'. In the following century, alehouse offences were being regularly reported at the Assizes: on 26th February 1634, 'Robert Hymnis, labourer, Joseph Sutbury and Rob. Clarke, all of Ashdon' were reported for 'keeping a common alehouse without a licence'. On 19th July 1654, 'John Claydon of Ashdon [was] charged [because he] kept a tippling house without a licence'. Whatever his punishment, it seems to have been anything but a deterrent because the following year, on 11th August 1655, the Assize Court was called upon to pass judgement on 'John Claydon, Hen: Mathew, Tho. Parkin, victuallers, Eliz. Splitimber, widow, all of Ashdon, who all kept tippling houses without licence'. Claydon was charged with the same offence on 24th March 1656, together with 'Widow Warren' and again on 5th April 1658, when 'Eliz. Splitimber, widow', was also charged once more. One is bound to infer that either the punishment was minimal or the profits from illicit tippling were more than adequate to cover the annual fine.

The most important local officials appointed by the Court Leet were the constables. Each Manor elected two each year and their legal writ was supposed to run only within the confines of their particular manor. Before the judicial powers of the lord of the manor passed to the wider community as a whole, the lord enjoyed the rights of inganenthief (the right to try and punish a thief caught within the confines of the manor) and outfangenethief (the right to pursue a thief beyond the manor boundary and bring him back to the manor court for trial). As recently as 1731, the proceedings of the Court Leet of Newnham Hall were still being set down in abbreviated legal Latin.

At that particular meeting of the members of the Court Baron of Newnham Hall, they proceeded to appoint for the year to come two manorial Pinders, manorial officers in charge of the pound or pinfold into which straying animals were put, and two manorial Constables. By 1731, the *manorial* Constable was a purely honorary officer. The Constables who actually did the work were chosen by the parish. Their duties were many and various and would be likely to include some, though rarely all, of the following. They were expected to maintain the peace throughout the manor (a term which has been reactivated by Metropolitan Police Stations to designate their area of jurisdiction), to accept responsibility for keeping *watch* (vigilance by night) and *ward* (vigilance by day), to execute the Justice's warrants for arrests, to ensure the upkeep of the stocks, the whipping-post, the cucking-stool and the 'cage' (village lock-up), to keep the archery butts in a state of good order and repair, to collect the rates and taxes, to care for the manorial bull, to oversee arrangements for the apprenticing of pauper children, to supervise the removal of beggars out or of strangers denied a 'settlement', to inspect alehouses and to suppress gaming-houses. Should a law-breaker from another district be suspected of fleeing across their territory, he was expected to raise the *hue and cry*, a judicial bush-telegraph system colourfully described by Harrison:

> For the better apprehension of thieves and man-killers there is an old law in England very well provided, whereby it is ordered that if he that is robbed or any man complain and give warning of slaughter or murder committed, the constable of the village whereunto he cometh and crieth for succor is to raise the parish about him and to search woods, groves, and all suspected houses and places where the trespasser may be or is supposed to lurk; and not finding him there, he is to give warning unto the next constable, and so one constable, after search made, to advertise another from parish to parish till they come to the same where the offender is harboured and found. It is also provided that if any parish in this business do not her duty but suffereth the thief (for the avoiding of trouble sake), in carrying him to the jail if he should be apprehended or other letting of their work, to escape, the same parish is not only to make fine to the King but also the same, with the whole hundred wherein it standeth, to repay the party robbed his damages and leave his estate harmless. Certes, this is a good law; howbeit, I have known by mine own experience felons, being taken, to have escaped out of the stocks, being rescued by other for want of watch and ward; that thieves have been let pass because the covetous and greedy parishioners would neither take the pains nor be at the charge to carry them to prison, if it were far off; that when hue and cry have been made even to the faces of some constables, they have

said, 'God restore your loss! I have other business at this time.' And by such means the meaning of many a good law is left unexecuted, malefactors emboldened, and many a poor man turned out of that which he hath sweat and taken great pains for toward the maintenance of himself and his poor children and family.

Description of England, pp.194-5.

Given that Harrison's jaundiced attitude is based on his own experience within his own parish of Radwinter, one wonders whether those constables he found half-hearted in their judiciary zeal were based just across the boundary in Ashdon. In contrast, his Ashdon contemporaries, on one occasion at least, pronounced themselves well satisfied. In the Quarter Sessions records we find the following entry for 28th September 1574:

> John Cowell and Robert Claydon, petty constables of Ashdon, report that the township is in such good order that there is nothing in default.

More than a century later, on 28th April 1685, the constable submitting his report felt able to paint a more detailed and even rosier picture:

> *Petty constables' Presentment for Ashdon:—*
> — No papish recusants;
> — Rob. Freake, Rich. Miller, Tho. Miller, Rich. Mannfield, John Medcapp, Roger Palmer reported for not coming to Church;
> — No unlicensed or disorderly alehouses;
> — No common swearers or drunkards;
> — No unlawful weights or measures;
> — All hues and cries duly executed;
> — Highways and bridges in good repair;
> — No cottages lately erected;
> — No young persons out of service;
> — No destroyers of game with nets and guns nor any who keep greyhounds or setting dogs but 'quallified';
> — Search made for rogues, idle and suspicious persons but none found.
> Signature of: Richard Woolward

These particular Ashdon constables would seem to have been more than usually fortunate or more than usually complacent because over the century or so between their reports, as we shall presently observe, the village was just as troubled by crime and sometimes of a particularly violent sort as anywhere else in a particularly violent Kingdom.

A post nearly as venerable as that of the village constable which impinged no less consistently on the everyday activities of the local community was that of Churchwarden. Elected by the parish Vestry, usually on Easter Thursday, his duties included the following: allocating the pews for worship in such a way as not to offend the susceptibilities of a hierarchy-conscious congregation; ensuring that parishioners attended church regularly and brought their children for baptism; supervising the education and the relief of the poor; arranging for the burial of unknown strangers and the baptism of foundlings; supervising the parish arms and the payment of soldiers; attending to the extinction of vermin; reporting to higher authority on any failing of the incumbent; maintaining the Church property in good order and accounting for the income and expenditure of the Church rate. A clear insight into these latter activities is provided by a number of pages bound into the back of the Ashdon Register for Births, Marriages and Deaths for the period 1553-1595 and transcribed by R.H. Browne of Stapleford Abbots, Essex, in 1898:

> Received of Thomas Claydon and John Coule in the year of our Lord 1557, 23s. 4d. and of John Coule 20d. We Churchwardens of Ashdon John Freman and Thomas Numan.
> It[em] To ye Glacer [i.e. Glazier] 10s. and for a piece of lyme a peny
> It[em] To John Hace for ye Lampe XVIII^D.
> It[em] For ye Glase. 11^d.
> It. For a pyn therefor 1^d.
> It. Halfe a quart of ayle 111^d.
> It. For a Procession 11^D.
> It. For a Procession 11^D.
> It. For Making of ye Belle Whyll XII^D.
> It. For Mending ye Sanctus Bele 11^D.
> It. To Robert Qui for such yren & nayls 11^D.
> It. For Quart of Oyle for ye Lampe VIII^D.

It. For Thred to Mende ye Copes & Vestments 11^D.
For setting up ye Alter
It. For vi Busshels of Lyme xx^d.
It. To ye Workman ix^D and for his meate & drynke viii^D.
It. To Thomas Smyth for his worke meat & drynke viii^D.
It. for two lods of stons gatheryng III^D.
It. for Mendyng ye Church dore key IIII^D.
It. for a quart of Ayle IIII^D against Christmas III^D.
It. for a bowke of ye litany in englyshe II^D.
Imprimis to Master Bawtry for a Communion Booke 11^D.
It. at [Bishops] Stortford beying (?) befor ye Quenes Visitors
It. for a booke of ye Artycles & Injunctions.
It. for a makying one lyst & Inventory 11^D.
It. and ye delyveryng up of ye same Byll 11^D.
It. to John Hache for ye mendying ye ledd betwene the Chancell & the Chappell 11^D.
Item for a Lyne [rope] for ye Sanctus Bell III^D.
It. to Robert Qui for a pin of yron, a colare, yron & Nayles for ye great bell Whele VIII^D.
John Freman did laye out Seven shylings of his own monye to ye workmen for makyng of ye whele.
Prayer book VIII^D & another book of injuctions & interrogations IIII^D.
Thomas Burton of Thaxted glasier for mendynge of ye wyndowe of the belfry and also byndynge & emendynge the other wyndowes and aboute the Churche VIII^D
It for a pecke of Lyme for the same glasier P. ob.
Item to Wilyam Woodroofe tyler for thre days worke mendyng the chapel toward the southe and the two porches & halfe a bushell lyme for whiche III daies he founde hym selfe meate & drynke 11^s 6^D
Item to George Goose hys servar [mate] for ye same thre daies fyrynge and fetchynge ye halfe bushell of lyme afore observed and fetchynge of sande 11^s
Item for thre busshels of lyme fetched at Walden XV^D
It. a penyworthe of lathe a pennyworthe nayles & a pennyworthe tyle pynnes III^D
It. we had of Mr Richarde Tyrell half a thousande tyle not yet paide for

It. I gave to John Hampton for laying the same tyles 1^D.

One needed to be particularly public-spirited or more than ordinarily officious to assume the offices of village constable or churchwarden because as well as being onerous they were, for centuries, unpaid. At the beginning of the nineteenth century, many a parishioner was at pains to acquire what came popularly to be known as a 'Tyburn Ticket', a certificate granted by the Clerk of the Peace to any person successfully prosecuting a felon. Possession of such a certificate exempted the possessor from the responsibility of holding any parish office or from jury service and 'Tyburn Tickets' were, not surprisingly, highly valued and eminently saleable. The following are examples of awards of this nature from the County records:

> 2nd August 1805. (Enrolled 9th October 1805). To John Lovett, on the conviction of Ann Overall, 31st July 1805, for housebreaking and stealing goods worth 17s 8d. on 9th July 1805 at Ashdon.
>
> 11th March 1815. (Enrolled 23rd March 1815). To Rob. Driver Thurgood, on the conviction of Jas. Robinson for housebreaking and stealing a bank-note and money worth £6. 4s. from John Marsh at Ashdon.
>
> 11th March 1815. (Enrolled 4th April 1815). To John Marsh, on the conviction of Ishmeal Cutler, 6th March 1815, for stealing a bank-note and money worth £6. 4s. from John Marsh at Ashdon.

Concern for the rule of law and the self-interest of the citizen here conveniently coincide with mutually beneficial results. The same is not immediately apparent when one reviews the activities of the parish churchwardens centuries earlier when one of their most important functions was to report their fellow citizens for suspected dereliction of their Christian duty to their superiors at the Church Court.

While the manorial courts concerned themselves primarily with the conveyancing of property and alleged infractions of the local lord's proprietorial rights, the local church court addressed itself to and on many an occasion involved itself in all manner of aspects of the parishioners' intimate private life. While crimes of violence or theft were normally dealt with by the secular court, for centuries after the Norman Conquest the Church Courts remained preoccupied with the nation's morals. In 1253, inquiries were made in every diocese of England concerning 'the life and conversation of priests and laity ... whether any layman has committed adultery with the wife of any other. Whether any layman has committed incest with or in any way defiled sister or daughter or any other female relative. Whether any layman frequents the house of any of those above without good reason. Whether any layman is a drunkard or a frequenter of taverns, or a practiser of usury ... Whether any layman or woman gives hospitality to the concubine of any man or to those who are adulterers and whores ... Whether adultery and public crime and misdeeds of the laity are corrected by the archdeacon' (H.R. Luard (ed.): *Annales Monastici*, Vol. I, Rolls Series, 1864).

The archdeacon of the diocese was supposed to visit the parish at least once and sometimes twice a year to ensure that the physical fabric of the church and the moral fabric of the parishioners' bodies and souls was in good repair. Chaucer immortalized his archetype in the *Friar's Tale* at the end of the fourteenth century:

> In my district once there used to be,
> A fine Archdeacon, one of high degree,
> Who bravely did the execution due
> on FORNICATION and on WITCHCRAFT too,
> BAWDRY, ADULTERY and DEFAMATION,
> BREACHES OF WILLS AND CONTRACTS, SPOLIATION
> OF CHURCH ENDOWMENT, FAILURE IN CHURCH
>   RENTS
> AND TITHES, and DISREGARD OF SACRAMENTS.
> — All these and certain other sorts of crime
> That need no mention at this time,
> Like SIMONY or USURY. But he would boast
> That LECHERY was what he punished most ...
> And ere the Bishop caught them with his crook
> Down they went in the Archdeacon's book;
> For he had Jurisdiction, after Detection,
> And Power to Administer Correction.
> (translated by Nevil Coghill and quoted in P. Hair: *Before the Bawdy Court*, Elek, 1972, p.33).

Some time before his Visitation, the archdeacon would ask the parish churchwardens to collect evidence of a wide range of moral transgressions. The list was more or less standard and the following terms of reference, sent to the parish officials of Wislow in Yorkshire by the Archdeacon of York in 1587, were identical to those addressed by all dioceses to all parish ministers and churchwardens across the length and breadth of the land:

> *x* Item: whether there be any married man in your parishe that doth live from his wife or she from him or any that are married together the bannes of matrimonie beinge not three solemne days asked before, or any that are married furth of their own parishe Churche or no ...
>
> *xiii* Item: whether there now be or at any time within this twelvemonthe last past have bene in your parishe any fornicators or adulterers or any man or woman either married or unmarried which are judged or suspected to have lived in fornication or adulterye together and if there be any suche presented, their names and where they nowe remain ...
>
> *xiv* Item: whether there be any woman in your parishe which is withe childe or hath borne a childe in fornication and hath not named the father thereof then by vertue of your othes who have heard named or suspected to be the father therof ...
>
> *xi* Item: whether there be any man or woman in your parishe which hath a childe begotten in fornication or adulterie with theis vii yeares last past and after the gettinge or bearinge thereof did flee furth of youre parishe before he or she did penance for the same and is now comed into your parishe again ...
>
> *xvii* Item: whether there be within your parishe any bawdes or receyvers of noughtie companye or suspected persons into their houses or have harboured any woman begotten with childe furthe of matrimony and have suffered them to departe unpunished and if there be any suche presente their names ...
>
> *xix* Item: whether there be any fornicators or adulterers within your parishe which have bene putt to pennance by the deane of the deanrie since Easter last past was a twelvemonth

and what be their names.

xx Item: whether there be any somoner or under-somoner which have taken any bribes or rewards or any fornicators adulterers or other offenders within your parishe for bearinge with them or overseinge their offences or for any other things whatsoever ...

J.S. Purvis (ed): *Tudor parish documents of the diocese of York*, 1948.

In response to these questions, the parish churchwardens prepared their Bill of Detection in which they reported or 'presented' the transgressors. For the most part, they relied on proven fact but they could and, as will shortly be apparent, sometimes did report parishioners simply on the strength of local gossip. The churchwardens' reports were sent to the church court where they were considered and where a list was drawn up of the persons required to answer any charges. A notary or his clerk would write out the 'citation' (or summons) against any suspect ordering him to appear before the court on a given day. The citation was delivered by the 'apparitor', invariably a well-known local figure whose arrival at the house of the suspect could be guaranteed to keep wagging the tongues which may well have caused the charge to be brought in the first place. If the accused had been alerted of the apparitor's approach and had the wit to make sure he was not at home, the summons was conveyed to him by alternative 'ways and means' such as fixing it on his front door, or on the door of the Church or by having it proclaimed from the pulpit of the church just before Sunday morning service.

When the accused appeared before the archdeacon and the rest of the assembled court, the charge was 'objected' [or named] to him. He then took the oath and either admitted the charge or denied it. Should he admit the charge, he was either dismissed with a 'monition' [warning] not to repeat the offence or ordered to do penance. Penance normally took the form of a full confession of the offence either before the Minister and church officials or before the whole congregation at the Sunday morning service. The penitent was obliged to confess his sin in intimate detail, standing on a stool in the middle aisle near the pulpit, sometimes wearing ordinary clothes, sometimes, for more serious offences, draped in a white sheet, bare foot and bare-headed, holding a white rod. Some penitents had to remain standing for the whole length of the service, some only till the end of the sermon or the second lesson; some had to do penance on more than one Sunday, some had to undergo more protracted humiliation by standing in a white sheet in full view in a public place. The public confessing ritual punishing would seem to have been regular events and, as far as the congregation was concerned in a largely illiterate age, constituted a flesh and blood substitute for the more sensational case-reports and criminals' autobiographies which have long been the staple content of the popular Sunday papers of our more educated times.

If the accused denied the charge, he would be ordered to 'purge' (or clear) himself either on his sworn oath alone or backed by the evidence of a number of 'compurgators' (defence-witnesses). When purgation was proposed, due notice had to be proclaimed in the parish church at least six days in advance, summoning all those who intended to oppose the accused and his 'compurgators' to appear with their counter-evidence before the court on a specified day. On the day of the hearing, the proclamation had to be repeated three times in a loud voice summoning the objectors to appear. If the objections were accepted or the accused failed to produce his compurgators, he was adjudged guilty and ordered to do penance. Should the accused disobey the summons to appear on the specified day, even after his name was called three times in a loud voice, he was formally pronounced to be 'contumacious' (disobedient). For contumaciousness, the penalty was either minor excommunication (the exclusion of the offender from church services and sacraments) or major ex-communication (which meant not merely exclusion from the communion of the faithful but from all commercial dealings and the protection of the law). Should a guilty person still remain excommunicated after forty days, his offence was said to be 'aggravated' and he was liable to be handed over to the secular authorities for imprisonment or worse. The ban of excommunication could be removed only by formal Absolution. To obtain this, the culprit had humbly to petition the judge and take a solemn oath 'to obey the law and stand by the commandments of the Church'. If he then carried out the court's requirements, he would be absolved and dismissed.

To judge by the entries in the court books of the Archdeaconry of Colchester, for which the series is virtually complete for the period 1569 to 1603, the churchwardens of Ashdon were no more or no less energetic than their counterparts elsewhere in the diocese. Over the years, they seem to have 'presented' parishioners for most of the moral lapses all churchwardens were exhorted to detect though their zeal seems to have been spasmodic. This may have been due to varying degrees of enthusiasm among successive churchwardens or to the occasional spate of punitive activity designed to impress a new incumbent. Fluctuations in the volume of 'presenting' could also be due to changes in official policy towards the Church's laws, for example in observing the Sabbath. Well before the advent of Calvin, there were particularly strict rules about keeping the Sabbath: shopkeepers were prohibited from engaging in business, drinking was not allowed in alehouses or even in one's private home, games, fishing and music-making were proscribed activities, attendance at church was compulsory. In this regard, the regime of Elizabeth was noticeably repressive and it is only under James I that any noticeable relaxation is apparent. His *King's Book of Sports* encouraged the playing of games once Sunday service was over and he positively commended such activities as archery, leaping and vaulting for men, dancing for both sexes, May games and whitsun 'ales'. in 1633, there was considerable Puritan uproar when Charles I re-issued his father's book and even before the Civil War, the Puritans condemned all Sunday sports and the observance of Saints' days as public holidays. After the Civil War, they continued to forbid the playing of games on Sundays, as well as music-making, dancing on the village green and even Christmas feasts. The furore has not entirely subsided even now.

A taste of our ancestors' attitudes to these matters is afforded by the Ashdon Churchwardens' 'presentments' of offenders accused of dereliction in their Sabbath duties. In 1584, Margaret, wife of John Claydon senior, pleaded that she had 'not wilfully nor negligently [been absent from Church] but sometimes by reason of her own sickness and sometimes by reason of the weakness of her mother, an old blind woman, who in duty she hath been enforced to attend upon and comfort'. Whether or not the Court was sympathetic is not known; she was ordered to attend more often. In 1587, William Bowtell, one of the churchwardens, was numbered amongst those that 'do not send their youth to be catechized'. In 1588, John Odell was one of nine people found guilty of non-attendance at Holy Communion. He offered himself for Communion at Christmas 'but his pastor would not permit him because at the Assizes holden at

Chelmsford on 14th July he did wilfully take a false oath, to the great offence of the congregation, until he had acknowledged his fault with repentance to the satisfaction of the congregation'. He was excommunicated. In 1595 Widow Fitch was absent from church and Andrea Whitehand reported for not receiving Communion. In 1598 Robert Smith was absent from church; his defence was that he was at Mildenhall with his daughter, Ellen Pettit, widow, where he attended church. In 1617 Mr Gilbert Habor was 'presented for suffering his servants to go to plough upon our Lady Day in service time; and in 1620, Thomas Turner was presented for not resorting to his parish Church 'according to the Canon'. Non-attendance at Church was also treated as a secular offence and could end with the offender's appearing before the Justices at the Quarter Sessions or the Assizes.

On 16th May 1603, Widow Willows appeared at the Quarter Sessions 'for not having attended Ashdon parish church by the space of two years' and on 1st November 1607, as if to demonstrate that their vigilance extended to the gentry as well as to the labouring class, 'Thomas Freman and William Swann, churchwardens of Ashdon, presented Anne, wife of John Claydon, gent, for refusing to attend Church these three years past'. On 11th July 1654, at Chelmsford General Sessions, 'Edward Rayson of Ashdon, victualler', was charged 'with suffering on 23rd April, Wm. Hynes, Nich. Hynes, John Freacke and Tho. Swann, all of Ashdon, to sit drinking and tippling in his house on the sabbath day during the sermon' and at the same Sessions 'Henry Mathews senior of Ashdon [was] charged with keeping many drinking in his house divers times on the sabbath days'. There is no record of the verdict.

Later in the century, parishioners failing to keep the Sabbath appeared at the Assizes. On 26th July 1671, the Ashdon constables, Henry Barker and Eustace Wakeling, reported that Thomas Miller had not been to church for six months. The same Thomas Miller was again reported on 10th October for still refusing to go to church and 'proclamation was made'. Whatever its effect, it does not seem to have taught him the error of his ways because on 31st August 1685, 'Richard Miller, Roger Paymer, Thomas Miller, Robert Freacke, and Rich. Mansfield, all of Ashdon, had not been to church for three days', and again, on 21st February 1686, these same worthies plus one John Medcapp, 'all of Ashdon', were reported for not going to church at all. The regular repetition of the offence suggests that either some sort of vendetta was being conducted against Miller or, if it really was fair and just to make an example of him that the sanctions against him were not punitive enough to be effective.

A strictly church law that might occasionally be broken was one in force after the Reformation which prohibited as 'superstitious' the ringing of church bells on holy days or on the eve of holy days. For ignoring this prohibition, Robert Flacke, John Stubbing and James Maye were 'presented' in 1584 for ringing the Ashdon church bells 'in All Hallows Night'. The outcome of their case is not on record but one feels they would have found it no easy matter to produce evidence that would stand up in court. This is no less true of William Overed who, three years later, 'being a man appointed to kepe the Churche clean', was presented because on 24th March of that year 'he did go into the Chapel and there pissed'. His defence was that 'he went into the Chapel to make water upon his hands, being sore'. The Court was not impressed by the invocation of this reputedly traditional remedy for this ailment and he was ordered to acknowledge his guilt in church on the following Sunday. Evidently, with this particular set of churchwardens in office, it was a testing time for the male members of Ashdon: in 1588, Richard Walker alias Pigton was presented on the grounds that 'he did set his windows open and was abusing of pricke'. He pleaded guilty and was ordered to confess his guilt before the full congregation in church on the following Sunday.

As well as punishing parishioners for succumbing to moral temptation, the Archdeacon's Visitation was meant to check that the church's own house was in order. Sometimes it manifestly was not: in 1562, Thomas Davyes was ordered by the Archdeacon to repair the chancel and the 'parsonage house'; in 1587, a specially active year for the Ashdon churchwardens, they reported not only that the 'porches were not so well in reparacion as they should be' but also that one of the preceding churchwardens had 'gone out of the towne and carried away with him the book of accounts and certain money which he gathered in the parish for the use of the Church, as his fellow Churchwarden sayeth' (this was not the only time this had happened in Ashdon's history because in 1562, when an inventory of the church goods was taken, it was noted that a Mr Sylesdon had 'taken away' the gild stock of £3. 6s. 8d., a pair of andirons worth four shillings, two spits worth ten shillings and a pot worth twenty shillings, 'by what aucthoritie we knowe not'). The authorities were more fortunate in 1619 because they succeeded in presenting Eustace Wakeling for 'detaining money from the Church'. Whether Wakeling was detained in turn is not known.

For all that, to judge by the frequency with which the charges are brought, the major preoccupation of the church court officials over the years was consistently fornication. Parishioners could be accused of fornication plain and simple if they were not married to each other and 'ante-nuptial fornication' if a bride was obviously pregnant at the solemnization of her marriage or gave birth to a child within the space of six months thereafter. Instances of the latter were not uncommon because in earlier centuries, marriage was formalized in two acts: a private betrothal, often involving the exchange of various tokens, and the public solemnization of the marriage by the priest in church. Provided that the contract had been freely entered into, the act of betrothal in itself created a permanent bond so, strictly speaking, to accuse partners of 'ante-nuptial fornication' was to charge them with consummating what was, to all intents and purposes, already a marriage. Doubtless because they had the good sense to realise this, the churchwardens presented parishioners for 'ante-nuptial fornication' comparatively infrequently. In the period in question, there are only three entries under this head for Ashdon, each recorded in abbreviated Latin: in 1620, 'John True incoit ante nupt, Richard Flisher incòit ante nupt'; in 1621, 'William Quy et uxor [and his wife] incoit ante nupt'.

Cases of straightforward 'fornication', or what we would now call adultery, are rather more numerous. In 1587, 'Audrey Whitehand, single', was 'vehemently suspected of incontinence with Robert Coote, a single man from Radwinter on the testimony of Mr Hole of Ashdon' who reported that the churchwardens had 'not presented the same in their quarterly bills'. There may well have been a deal of internecine rivalry within the parish church at this time because two years later the churchwardens presented this same Mr Hole for marrying 'Henry Yeomans alias Emerson' without a licence at a prohibited time. In that same year of 1587, John Whitehand was reported because he had a woman with child in his house, doubtless an unmarried mother whose sin he was presumed to be condoning by offering her hospitality. Parishioners do not seem to have been allowed to give hospitality even to their own kinsfolk because in 1596,

Richard Rutter of Ashdon was reported 'for receiving Anne Rutter into his house and suffering her to depart unpunished'.

Also in 1587, John Noble was 'presented' because of fornication with Alice Willowes but the authorities seem to have experienced some difficulty in bringing him to book: in 1588, appearing before the Archdeacon's court, 'Joanna Noble deposed that about Shrovetyde last past that her brother John Noble dwelt in London in St. Martins or thereabouts, with a taylor, otherwise she cannot tell where the said John Noble is'. In 1588, the churchwardens were instructed to make inquiries 'touching a matter in Ashdon of a taylor lying in one Cornell's house' and 'suspected of leading an incontinent life there with the wife of the said Cornell'.

In 1595, John Whitehand again appeared before the court, this time suspected of 'being incontinent with Maria Stacie'. He insisted that 'he was of good fame and there was no cause of suspicion but only in going to her house to demand his debt in the evening'. He was ordered to exculpate himself. Accordingly, at the next session, he appeared with William Hanna, the curate, and Gabriel Barker, churchwarden, who affirmed 'that in their opinion the said Whitehand was not at fault but that it was spread upon evil will'. He was enjoined to donate five shillings to the poor but not to purge so he probably considered himself exonerated. Gabriel Barker, the defence witness, must have had a forgiving nature because three years earlier, on 14th August 1593, 'Thomas Whitehand, John Whitehand and Robert Whitehand', all described as yeomen, had all appeared before the Justices at the Quarter Sessions, accused of 'breaking into the close of Gabriel Barker at Ashdon'. At the same time, they were charged with assaulting and beating William Flacke at Ashdon, 'so that he despaired of his life'. All three were ordered to be of good behaviour 'upon apparent matter to the corte'.

Of all the Ashdon inhabitants who feature in the various law reports, Thomas Whitehand is virtually unique in that, as his will clearly indicates, he was well provided with worldly goods. In 1601, when his son John Whitehande indicted the village constables 'John Cornell, husbandman, and Robert Cornell, labourer, for assulting him on Christmas Day and unlawfully imprisoning him for one hour', he was described in the Quarter Sessions records as a Gentleman. Nearly all the other cases which we shall now consider concern petty larceny or robbery, with or without violence, and were allegedly committed by the poorer members of the community. Such crimes were the specific concern of the secular authorities and the guilt or innocence of the accused was determined either at Quarter Sessions or the Assizes.

The Quarter Sessions were held four times per year. They were regularly attended by the high constables, who represented the Hundreds of the County and by the petty constables, who represented the villages but the most important dignitaries present were the Justices of the Peace. The office of Justice derived from the *Conservatores pacis* first instituted in 1195 by proclamation of Archbishop Hubert, justiciar (or Chief Justice) of Richard I. The office was further strengthened by a statute passed in 1360 by Edward III, in the thirty fourth year of his reign which, throughout England, 'assigned for the keeping of the peace one lord and with him three or four of the most worthy in the county, with some learned of the law' and authorized them not only to arrest and imprison offenders but also to 'hear and determine at the King's suit all manner of felonies and trespasses done in the same county'. Through the Tudor reconstruction of local government which, at one and the same time effectively centralized the administration of the nation and, as far as possible, ensured that power at county level was exercised by local men with special local knowledge, the Justices of the Peace became key officers. In his treatise *De Republica Anglorum*, completed in 1565 and first published in 1583, Sir Thomas Smith declared:

> The Justices of the Peace be those in whom at this time for the repressing of robbers, thieves, and vagabonds, of privy complots and conspiracies, of riots and violences, and all other misdemeanours in the common wealth the Prince putteth his special trust. Each of them hath authority upon complaint to him made of any theft, robbery, manslaughter, murder, violence, complots, riots, unlawful games, or any such disturbances of the peace and quiet of the realm, to commit the persons whom he supposeth offenders to the prison ... till he and his fellows do meet. A few lines signed with his hand is enough for that purpose: these do meet four times in the year, that is, in each quarter once, to enquire of all the misdemeanours aforesaid ...'

At these quarterly sessions, from 1531 on, the Justices administered the Poor Law and from 1601 on, they formally confirmed the appointment of the Overseers of the Poor on the recommendation of the individual parish vestry concerned.

The Quarter Sessions normally tried 'trespasses', minor robbery and petty larceny (the theft of goods valued under a shilling). More serious crimes, felonies such as murder, treason and witchcraft, were generally tried at the Assizes, held at the county towns in England three or four times each year and usually presided over by a judge of the High Court from London. The variety of felonies on which they were called upon to pronounce judgement and the range of punishments they normally meted out are colourfully described by William Harrison in Chapter XI of his *Description of England* entitled 'Of Sundry Kinds of Punishments Appointed for Malefactors':

> In cases of felony, manslaughter, robbery, murder, rape, piracy and such capital crimes as are not reputed for treason or hurt of the state, our sentence pronounced upon the offender is to hang till he be dead ... The greatest and most grievous punishment used in England for such as offend against the state is drawing from the prison to the place of execution upon an hurdle or sled, where they are hanged till they be half dead and then taken down and quartered alive; after that, their members and bowels are cut from their bodies and thrown into a fire provided near-hand and within their own sight, even for the same purpose. Sometimes, if the trespass be not the more heinous, they are suffered to hang till they be quite dead ... If he be convicted of willful murder done either upon pretended malice or in any notable robbery, he is either hanged alive in chains near the place where the fact was committed, or else, upon compassion taken, first strangled with a rope, and so continueth till his bones consume to nothing ... When willful manslaughter is perpetuated, beside hanging, the offender hath his right hand commonly stricken off before or near unto the place where the act was done, after which he is led forth to the place of execution and there put to death according to the law ...
>
> If a woman poison her husband, she is burned alive; if the servant kill his master, he is to be executed for petty treason;

he that poisoneth a man is to be boiled to death in water or lead, although the party die not of the practice; in cases of murder all the accessories are to suffer pains of death accordingly. Perjury is punished by the pillory, burning in the forehead with the letter P, the rewalting [overthrowing] of the trees growing upon the grounds of the offenders, and the loss of all his movables. Many trespassers also are punished by the cutting of one or both ears from the head of the offender, as the utterance of seditious words against the magistrates, fray-makers, petty robbers, etc. Rogues are burned through the ears; carriers of sheep out of the land by the loss of their hands; such as kill by poison are either boiled or scalded to death in lead or seething water. Heretics are burned quick; harlots and their mates, by carting, ducking, and doing of open penance in sheets, in churches and marketsteads, are often put to rebuke. Howbeit, as this is counted with some either as no punishment at all to speak of or but smally regarded of the offenders, so I would wish adultery and fornication to have some sharper law. For what great smart is it to be turned out of a hot sheet into a cold or after a little washing in the water to be let loose again unto their former trades? . . .

Rogues and vagabonds are often stocked [put in the stocks] and whipped; scolds are ducked upon cucking stools in the water. Such felons as stand mute and speak not at their arraignment are pressed to death by huge weights laid upon a board that lieth over their breast and a sharp stone under their backs, and these commonly hold their peace, thereby to save their goods unto their wives and children, which if they were condemned, should be confiscated to the prince. Thieves that are saved by their books and clergy for the first offense [i.e. gained exemption from certain first offences by demonstrating that they were able to read], if they have stolen nothing else but oxen, sheep, money, or suchlike, which be no open robberies as by the highway side, or assailing of any man's house in the night without putting him in fear of his life or breaking up of his walls or doors, are burned in the left hand upon the brawn of the thumb with an hot iron, so that if they be apprehended again that mark bewrayeth them to have been arraigned of felony before, whereby they are sure

at that time to have no mercy . . .
Description of England, pp.187-192.

Tudor England seems to have been at least as violent as parts of the inner cities of England and the United States have now become. Soon after Henry VII had ascended the English throne, the Venetian envoy reported: 'There is no country in the world where there are so many thieves and robbers as in England; in so much that few venture to go alone in the country excepting in the middle of the day, and fewer still in the towns at night, and least of all in London' (quoted in G.M. Trevelyan: *History of England*, Longmans, 1943, p.273). Had he proceeded to seek refuge in the Ashdon countryside then or later in the Tudor period, he would have found no haven of calm: the sheer volume of crime was inevitably less striking but the range and regularity of its incidence strongly suggest that the villagers needed no lessons from the capital in how to fall foul of the manifold laws of the land.

The following selection of Ashdon cases, drawn from the Quarter Sessions and Assize files of the Essex Record Office, may serve not only to indicate sixteenth- and seventeenth-century attitudes to crime and punishment but also to provide a glimpse of how the villagers lived their lives in the world we have lost. The letter *A* indicates the charge was heard at the County Assizes and the letters *Q.S.* indicate Quarter Sessions.

STEALING ANIMALS

19th March 1575 (A): John Totenham of Ashdon, labourer, on 18th November 1574 stole there a horse worth £5 belonging to Tho. Newman. Pleads not guilty: guilty — to hang.

4th March 1590 (A): John Marshe of Ashdon, butcher and Hugh Wrighte of Stoke-by-Clare, Suffolk, labourer, 12th October in the thirty second year of the reign of Queen Elizabeth, stole two sheep worth 8s. and a lamb worth 2s. belonging to Barnaby Rand. Marsh pleads not guilty; guilty; clerk. Wright not in prison.

The same, 12th October, at Ashdon stole 'a hayfer' worth 30s., belonging to Allen Chapman. Marsh pleads not guilty; guilty; clerk. Wright not in prison.

4th July 1608 (A): Jas. Mathew of Ashdon, labourer, on 16th May, there stole a black Gelding worth £3 belonging to Henry

Kingesberry. Pleads not guilty; guilty; hanged. Witness: Hen. Kingesberry.

26th February 1634 (A): Henry Knight of Ashdon, labourer, 1st December 1633, there stole a white ewe worth 6s. belonging to Thos. Jackson. Pleads not guilty: guilty; hanged; did not read. Witnesses: Rob. Freeman, John Freeman, Tho. Jackson.

13th July 1658 (Q.S.): Giles Phillips of Ashdon, labourer, stole a wether sheep worth 5s. of Rob Lagden. Guilty. No goods. Read and is cauterized.

19th August 1704 (A): John Addams of Ashdon, labourer, 8th June in third year of reign of Queen Anne [1704], there stole a bay mare worth £7 belonging to Jas. Hammond. Guilty. To be hanged.

OFFENCES INVOLVING CROPS

29th November 1561 (Q.S.): Robert Fox, Nicholas Webb, Robert Gardiner and John Holder, all of Ashdon, husbandmen, indicted for breaking into the close of John Cornell, called Grygges, in the same place and cutting down and taking away 15 cartloads of firewood.

Each fined 2s.

1st June 1562 (Q.S.): Richard Wyllowes and Edward Wyllowes, both husbandmen of Ashdon indicted for breaking into the close of William Wyllowes called Barthelmwe Felde at Ashdon and wasting and destroying with horses and ploughs, four acres of oats and peas called bullymonge then growing there.

18th March 1566 (Q.S.): Ralph Page, bailiff of Richard Tirrell, esquire, found 5 steers belonging to Thomas Wyllowes, of Ashdon, husbandman, on the land of the same Richard Tirrell called Le Thre Trowes, trampling upon and depasturing the crops upon the said land, and the same Ralph as bailiff took the same five steers to empark them in the Queens park in Ashdon for an amercement [i.e. fine] on account of the said damage.

The said Thomas Willowes and William Willowes the younger, all of Ashdon, husbandmen, forcibly took and rescued the said animals from the lawful custody of the said Ralph and with a pitcheford [sic] violently assaulted him. Each fined 8d. by George Nycolles, R. Amys & E. Barrett.

1615 (Q.S.): Keling Brampton, yeoman, Wm. Quys, blacksmith, and Geo. Stonnard, husbandman, all of Ashdon, broke into the close of John Cornell at Ashdon and carried away two cumulos [heaps] of barley worth 12*d.* belonging to him.

There is likely to have been a direct connection between this charge and the one brought at the Epiphany Sessions of 1615 when it was alleged that 'John Cornell, junior, husbandman of Ashdon, assaulted Keling Brampton, gent., Wm. Quye and Geo. Stonnard, servants of Brampton, there wounding and ill-treating them so that their lives were despaired of. Witness: Kelling Brampton'. This was not the first time Brampton's name had featured at the Quarter Sessions: in 1612, he was reported for having refused to work in the King's highway in the parish of Ashdon even though he owned a team of horses and was therefore legally obliged to contribute to the upkeep of the road; the constables noted: 'Keling Brampton hath done two days work and refuseth to do any more; he will answer for it.' One assumes that this meant that Brampton was ready with an explanation rather than that the constables were resolved to take the law into their own hands.

Epiphany 1627 (Q.S.): Hen. Kempe of Ashdon, yeoman, is indicted for cutting 400 'staddels or storers' of oak in 5 acres of woods of which he was possessed in the wood called Four Acre Grove in Ashdon between 1st February 1626 and 1st October of which straddles none was ten inches square three foot above the ground, contrary to the Statute.
Forfeits £66. 13*s.* 4*d.*, viz. 3*s.* 4*d.* for each straddle so cut.

The Statute here referred to was passed in the thirty fifth year of the reign of Henry VIII, 1544, and was intended to curb the alarmingly rapid destruction of the nation's woodlands. Where any coppice wood of less than twenty four years growth was cut down, twelve standles or staddels [saplings] were supposed to be left for further growth. The statutory fine for breaking this law was the fine here imposed of 3*s.* 4*d.* for each staddle. William Harrison complained that the Statute was more honoured in the breach than the observance:

Within these forty years, we shall have little great timber growing above forty years old: for it is commonly seen that those young staddles which we leave standing at one-and-twenty years' fall are usually at the next sale cut down without any danger of the statute and serve for firebote [Old English term for the right to take wood from the commons for fuel] if it please the owner to burn them.

Description of England, p.283.

THEFT OF GOODS AND CHATTELS

18th March 1593 (A): Hen. Wakefield, carpenter, Rob. Mynsted and John Williamson, labourers, all of Ashdon, 27th January, there stole fower peces of porck worth 10*d.* belonging to Wm. Hymfrye. Acknowledge the petty larceny. 'Whippe'.

26th February 1611 (A): Rob. Himnis of Ashdon, labourer, 1st September 1610, there stole xxiii sheaves or barlie worth 10*d.* belonging to John Baker clerk. Confessed. Witness: John Baker.

15th March 1613 (A): Eliz. Johnson of Ashdon, spinster, 18th September [1612], there stole one childs coat (*tunicam*) worth 4*d.*, one paire of stockins (*calligarum*) worth 4*d.* and a packcloath worth 3*d.* belonging to Wm. Cockerton. Confessed for 7*d.*; whipped. Witness: Wm. Cockerton.

11th January 1615 (Q.S.): Tho. Hills of Ashdon, labourer, stole a purple cloak (color de roy) worth 19*s.* there belonging to Josias Pyggn, gent. Guilty. No chattels. Reads and is branded.

24th March 1656 (A): Alice, wife of Nich. Ball of Ashdon, labourer, 1st November 1655, there stole 2 lbs. of bacon worth 16*d.*, 2 lbs. of butter worth 8*d.*, 10 lbs. of cheese worth 20*d.*, a peck of oats worth 8*d.*, a peck of barley worth 5*d.*, half a peck of wheat worth 4*d.*, 10 eggs worth 3*d.* and a bag worth 1*d.* belonging to Wm. Whiskyn. Pleads not guilty; guilty to the value of 10*d.* only. To be whipped.

24th March 1656 (A): Tho. Hempstead of Ashdon, labourer, 13th October 1655, there on the highway assaulted Margaret Smith and took from her a hat worth 3*d.* and a petticoat worth 14*d.*

No true bill [i.e. prima facie case not established]. Witness: Marg. Smith.

OFFENCES AGAINST THE PERSON

14th March 1565 (A): Wm. Willowes of Ashdon, yeoman, 15th July 1564, assaulted there, Alice Stonerde aged nine years, violently striking her with a 'walking staffe' as a result of which she languished from that day until 1st August when she died. Pleads not guilty; not guilty.

17th July 1581 (A): Inquisition taken at Ashdon, 4th June, twenty third year of reign of Elizabeth, before Hen. Longe, gent., Coroner, upon the view of the body of Wm. Hammond, servant of John Odell of Ashdon, yeoman. 15 jurors say upon their oaths that on 1st June it happened that Gaven Hargrave of [illegible], butcher, and Geo. Taylor, John Reder & Geo. Parker, all of Ashdon, labourers, were crossing a piece of land with a cartload of wood from a wood called Shadwell Grove which, the said John Odell objecting to, went to prevent them and they withdrew. But the next day they returned with the cart and Gideon Mercye of Ashdon, and peacably went to cross the land but John Odell, John Cranford and the said Wm. Hammond with bows, arrows and pitchforks prevented their passage, and the said Odell shot at them with his arrows and the said Hargrave and the others closed with the said Odell, Cranford and Hammond and in the struggle Hammond was mortally wounded on the top of his head from which he languished from 7 a.m. until 9 p.m. when he died. Gaven Hargrave pleads not guilty; found guilty of killing in self-defence. Gideon Mercye pleads not guilty; not guilty. Geo. Taylor pleads not guilty of felony but that he withdrew; tried in August 1852, he was found guilty of killing in self-defence.

24th July 1587 (A): Inquisition taken at Ashdon, 28th June, before Hen. Longe, Coroner, upon the view of the body of Geo. Parker of Ashdon, husbandman. The jurors say that on 27th June the aforesaid Geo. Parker and John Newborne of the same, labourer, then serving Edm. Sherbrooke, Master of Theology [and Rector of Ashdon], Parker was angry with Newborne because he made two lez taypinnes against his, the said Parker's wish, so he gave Newborne 'a layshe' with a 'carte whippe' by reason by which the said Newborne being moved by wrath assaulted Parker with a knife, worth 1d., which he threw at Parker so that 'the poynt' of it gave him a mortal wound on the upper part of his breast one [illegible], whereof he instantly died. Pleads not guilty; guilty.

10th January 1628 (Q.S.): Rich. Strachy, gent., Eustace Waklinge and Wm. Gaye, yeomen, all of Ashdon, brought to trial: Strachy to answer for beating and wounding Martha Newman.

24th April 1656 (Q.S.): John Hayward of Ashdon, carpenter, before and since 3rd February is a common *barretor* and disturber of the peace and sower of quarrels among his neighbours.

[*Barratry* was a particularly common charge in sixteenth- and seventeenth-century England. It covered all manner of disorderly acts including malicious (usually female) slander and gossip. According to F.G. Emmison, the court rolls of the Elizabethan period regularly contain references to such nuisances as *communis rixatric* [brawler], *garrulatrix* [babbler] or *fabulatrix* [talebearer], usually coupled with a gloss like 'common disturber of the peace' or 'scold'. The normal punishment awarded was a short term in one of the instruments of humiliation: the stocks, the pillory, the cucking-stool or the tumbril.]

16th March 1697 (A): Tho. Rust and John Ward, of Ashdon, labourers, 22nd July, in the ninth year of the reign of William III, there on the highway assaulted John Byam and took from him a pair of gloves worth 6*d.*, a knife worth 6*d.*, one 'inknorne' worth 4*d.* belonging to the said Byam, a leather portmantle worth 2*s.*, a paper book worth 2*d.*, two linen bags worth 4*d.* and £20 in money belonging to Peter Coveney. Rust acquitted. Ward pleaded guilty, To be hanged.

27th July 1697 (A): Wm. Vievart, Tho. Reed, Alex Vievart, Adolphus Vievart, yeomen, Sara Harrell, spinster, Geo. [illegible] yeoman and Eliz. Head, spinster, all of Ashdon, on 20th June in the fifth year of the reign of William and Mary assembled there and assaulted Andrew Turner. Witnesses: Tho. White, Wm. Deeks.

One is left to speculate what Andrew Turner could conceivably have done to incur the displeasure of five yeomen and two spinsters. On the other hand, John Freake, who appeared before the Assizes on 17th July 1645 would seem to have been an old-fashioned arsonist:

John Freake of Ashdon, labourer, on 20th July in the nineteenth year of the reign of Charles I [1642], there feloniously set fire to the house of John Buttoll. Pleads not guilty; guilty; to be hanged; reprieved after judgment.

The same, 1st June, in the twenty first year of the reign of Charles I [1645] there burnt a barn near the house of Cuthbert Matling, with two cart loads of hay worth 40s. and a cart worth 30s. Pleads not guilty; guilty; to be hanged on another indictment.

While it would not be unreasonable to link the various anti-social activities listed so far in this chapter and the pressures of poverty described in the last, there was one conspicuous feature in the sixteenth- and seventeenth-century social scene which would seem to have little to do with wages, prices or mounting unemployment: this was the campaign against witchcraft that was waged by Protestants and Catholics alike all over Europe. On the European mainland, according to H.C. Lea, 'witches were burned in scores and hundreds. A bishop of Geneva is said to have burned five hundred within three months; a bishop of Bamberg six hundred, a bishop of Würzburg nine hundred. Eight hundred were condemned, apparently in one body, by the senate of Savoy' (*History of the Inquisition in the Middle Ages*, quoted in G.G. Coulton: *Mediaeval Panorama*, C.U.P., 1947, p.118). The English judiciary were never quite so sanguinary. Of the considerable numbers detected between the middle of the sixteenth and the middle of the seventeenth centuries, half were prosecuted under the 1563 Act 'against Conjuracions, Inchantments and Witchcrafts' which laid down as the maximum punishment four sessions in the pillory and one year in a House of Correction. Half were prosecuted under the Act of 1604, made more severe as a compliment to James I, author of the rabid anti-witchcraft tract *Daemonology*. Under this new Act, it became a capital offence to 'entertain, employ, feed or reward such a spirit or any part of it — skin or bone — for purposes of enchantment or sorcery' or to indulge in any witchcraft by means of which anyone 'should be killed, destroyed, wasted, pined or lamed'.

The outstanding authority on these matters is Alan Macfarlane and he has amply demonstrated in his definitive *Witchcraft in Tudor and Stuart England* (Routledge, 1970) the considerable number of witches detected in the villages of Essex. In all, seventy four witches were executed in Essex between 1560 and 1645, as many as a quarter of these in the last year by the single-minded efforts of that most notorious of all witch-finders, the Suffolk lawyer, Mathew Hopkins. Because they were all detected before the end of the sixteenth century, the four recorded witches in Ashdon's history escaped both his ministrations and the full rigours of the anti-witchcraft laws.

The first of these in date is also the Ashdon witch about whom the most details are known. She was indicted at the Trinity Assizes on 4th March 1590 in the following terms:

> Juliana Cocke of Ashdon, spinster, on 20th March, 33 Elizabeth [1589] at Little Walden, bewitched 3 *caballos* [horses] valued at £6, 2 cows valued at £4, and 2 calves valued at 10*s*. of the goods and chattels of John Petite of which one horse and the cows and the calves instantly died. Pleads not guilty; guilty. Judgment according to the form of the Statute.

Her name next appears in the calendar for the gaol at Kingston-upon-Thames which took delivery of her on 4th June 1591. The records indicate that she died 'of plague' on 13th April 1592.

Of the three other Ashdon witches, rather less is known save the obvious fact that they were clearly all members of the same family. They first appear in the records of the Archdeacon's Court: in 1596, Joanna Rawe, wife of John Rawe, was presented by the churchwardens who had 'detected that she was a common wytch' and in October of that year, her name appears in the list of indictments drawn up by the clerk of Assize for the South East Circuit; what happened thereafter is not known. The same is true of Anna Rawe and Maria Rawe, each reported by the Ashdon churchwardens in 1598 'suspected to be a witch' and each on the South East Assize Clerk's list of cases to be heard in August of that year coupled with the observation 'stands excommunicated'.

Though the enthusiasm for witch-hunting was positively rabid during the century or so while it lasted, its principal victims in the English countryside were confined to one sex and one class: impoverished women who could arouse popular suspicion merely by living a solitary existence and manifesting even a faintly eccentric lifestyle. Since time immemorial, human communities of whatever size must regularly have produced minor eccentrics of this sort. It is a measure of the increase in our concern that they are now, at the very least tolerated and at best actively helped rather than haled before the legal powers and subjected to every sort of indignity.

A further indication of moral advance since the 'good old times' has been the progressive softening in judicial attitudes towards infractions of the Game Laws. Transportation ceased to be a legal punishment in 1853, no longer was it a capital offence to assault a gamekeeper and with the Ground Game Act of 1880, farmers were no longer in breach of the law if they killed rabbits on their own lands. The following sample of convictions for poaching offences in Ashdon at the turn of the century can be used as a measure of the distance travelled towards leniency if not compassion:

On 10th November 1896, Amos Harris and Ebenezer Richardson, labourers, were found guilty of trespassing in search of game on land in the occupation of Mr T. Hagger; they were fined 3s. 9d. and 6s. 3d. costs each. Gamekeeper Manning found six rabbits in the defendants' possession. On 10th May 1898, Frederick Barty, 24, retired inn-keeper (sic) and Charles Fitch, 13, labourers, Ashdon, were charged with setting snares to take hares at Ashdon, on 27th March. Frederick Reid, gamekeeper, knowing the snares were set, watched, and saw the defendants take them out of the hedge. Barty did not appear and was fined 8s. 6d. and 11s. 6d. costs. Amos Harris, 40, a thatcher, of Ashdon appeared again before the Justices, charged with setting two iron traps to take hares on land in the occupation of Major Pelly, Waltons Park, Ashdon, on 26th November, and also with assaulting Richard Purkis, a gamekeeper, at the same time and place. The defendant was fined £1 and 4s. costs for the trespass, and on the charge of assault was asked to pay 4s. costs. At the same Sessions, Amos Harris, 40, Arthur Marsh, 29, William Pearman, 34, and William Chapman, 31, were summoned for being in search of conies on land in the occupation of Mr E.B. Gibson, J.P., at Ashdon, on 1st January. Harris and Chapman were fined £2 and 4s. costs each, and Pearman and Marsh £1 and 4s costs each. Mr Gibson did not adjudicate in this case. On 30th December 1912, George Cornell and Thomas Marsh, labourers of Ashdon, were summoned on a charge of being suspected of coming from land on which they had been in search of game on 17th December; P.C. Cross stated that he was on the Ashdon to Bartlow Road at about 3.30 a.m. when he saw the defendants with two dogs going in front of him. He caught them up and, being suspicious, searched them, finding two rabbits and a ferret on Cornell. They were fined 5*s*. and 4*s*. costs each.

To compare these punishments with those meted out for similar offences only a few decades previously is to be reminded, not for the only time in the course of this chapter, of the fickleness of man-made laws and of the crucial distinction between good and evil on the one hand, and mere right and wrong on the other.

7

Unwillingly to School

> Train up a child in the way he should go; and
> when he is old, he will not depart from it.
>
> Proverbs 22 : 6

Evidence from a number of sources indicates that there were undoubtedly schools of sorts established in Ashdon in the first half of the eighteenth century. Replying in 1814 to a questionnaire sent by the National Society for the Education of the Poor in the Principles of the Established Church, John North, then Rector of Ashdon, reported that 'a Charity School for Reading, Writing and Arithmetic has been supported in this Parish for upwards of fourscore years past'. He added that his parish also contained 'two Day Schools kept by women, one for children beginning to learn to read, and the other for children of more advanced age'. Where these schools were located and who exactly they catered for must remain matters for speculation.

Some information about the nature of these early schools in Ashdon is provided in the rectors' replies to the Visitation questionnaire which regularly asked 'Have you any publick School in your Parish? Is it duly managed and attended, according to the Directions of the Founder, and the Canons of the Church?'

In 1723, the then Rector, Thomas Baron, replied:

> 'We have no publique School but a very good private one where all the children in the parish are taught, those that are able pay for the children, the poor ones are taught one halfe at the charge of the parish payd out of their Church Warden's rate, the other halfe of the charge is supplyed by a private hand'.

In 1766, the Rector, by now one D. Sampford, replied 'There is no Chapel nor public School. The Parish Clerk keeps a small school which is chiefly supported by myself.' There was an almost identical reply in 1778, when the rector commented that the Clerk of the parish kept a school 'supported chiefly by myself and the Parish', while in 1790, the Curate, replying on behalf of the incapacitated Rector, reported that there was a school 'for the benefit of poor Children supported by subscription.'

It is still not possible to say for certain where this 'dame's school' was situated nor when it was first established. From 1744 onwards, the Rector's account books contain entries like the following:

> Paid the Clerk for six children's schooling, half-year to Midsummer 1744 £1 · 0 · 0
> Paid the Clerk for six children's schooling, half-year to Christmas £1 · 0 · 0

Entries of this type are an annual feature and show remarkably few variations until 1767 when the following entry is made:

> Paid Tho. Larkin for schooling for 6 children to Mich 1767

In 1809-1810, the entry reads

> For schooling of 7 children, £4 · 4 · 0

and from 1811 to 1815, the following entry appears at six monthly intervals:

> To Jeremiah Howes for teaching seven children £4 · 4 · 0.

Since the 'poor children' are not specified by name, one cannot be certain that they were the same poor children, equally nameless, for whom a payment of fifteen shillings was made to the village teacher every quarter by the feoffees of the Ashdon charities. One can, nevertheless, confidently assume that in the last decades of the eighteenth century as in the early years of the nineteenth, Ashdon's one schoolteacher was not in danger of being over-worked. This is just as well because he ran no risk of being overpaid. Towards the end of official return compiled for the Justices in January 1801 by the Ashdon Overseers of the Poor, and listing those needy villagers who qualified for an allowance, occurs the name of 'John Darcy, schoolmaster'. The weekly earnings of the numerous 'labourers' on the list average ten shillings, bricklayers' wages average twelve shillings, wheelwrights average sixteen shillings and the weekly earnings of a 'higler' (or tinker) are given as £1 · 5 · 0. The schoolmaster's weekly wage is given as eight shillings.

As will later appear, there are grounds for believing that the schoolmaster has always occupied a distinctly lonely eminence within the village community being too impoverished to share in the leisurely pursuits of the gentry and, more often than not, being regarded with lingering suspicion and resentment by the labouring classes whose children he was expected to educate. It is arguable that even today, the schoolteacher like the policeman, is fated to exist in a sort of limbo, respected and admired if he does his job well but, because of the nature of his rôle in the community, always somewhat isolated. Many years later, Lord Wharncliffe was to provide a succinct definition of the social position of the country schoolteacher when explaining how government grants for building teachers' houses were to be utilized. He declared that schoolmasters 'ought to be provided with . . . a house by no means too large, so as to exalt him too much . . . but he should be taken out of a cottage and put into a decent residence . . . to make those persons lower than himself inclined to show a proper feeling of respect for the schoolmaster who teaches their children.'

At the beginning of the nineteenth century, country schoolteachers were more often than not persons who because of incompetence, infirmity or indolence, could find no other mode of employment. The first important movement towards something like respectability came with the founding of 'The National Society for the Education of the Poor in the Principles of the Established Church'. In the course of time, this enterprise made its mark on the life of Ashdon as it did on the majority of villages throughout the kingdom.

The National Society was found in 1811 and its principal aims were 'to train the rising generation to habits of religious and moral duty and thus qualify them to fill their respective stations, with decency and comfort to themselves, and with fidelity and satisfaction to their Employers'.

Not surprisingly, particular emphasis was placed on the religious instruction of the National School pupils. One of the key regulations stated:

> On Sundays, the School shall be regularly opened at 9 o'clock in the morning; at which hour, except for some cause to be signified to, and allowed of by, the Superintendent, all the Children shall, invariably and without exception, attend, for the purpose of repeating the Church Catechism, and of receiving such religious instruction as the Superintendent may direct; they shall from thence proceed in order and decorum to the Established Chapel; which they shall attend also in the afternoon, assembling in the School-room *not less than one hour* previous to the Service.

'Honest Industry' was especially to be promoted 'as well as useful religious knowledge' and it was unambiguously stated that 'the Girls in particular will be taught ... plain work, knitting and other domestic services, calculated to make them good and faithful servants'. Later in the century, this view that the social hierarchy was not only immutably but divinely ordered came regularly to be reiterated in one memorable verse of what is probably the most popular of all schooltime hymns, Mrs F.C. Alexander's *All things bright and beautiful*:

> The rich man in his castle,
> The poor man at his gate,
> God made them, high and lowly,
> And ordered their estate.

The idea that effective schooling might positively stimulate social mobility was not in the forefront of the minds of either the founders of the National Society or of the management committees entrusted with the task of putting its principles into practice. The available evidence also indicates that it was not a notion which occurred to the teachers either: as far as was possible, the poor were to be taught to read and write so as to cope with the increasingly more sophisticated demands of a world being transformed by technological advance and driven by economic competition, but the poor were to remain what they had always been, the hewers of the community's wood and its drawers of water. In this respect, the record of Ashdon School seems neither worse nor better than that of any of the countless schools serving the needs of rural society across the length and breadth of the land.

Ashdon's first National School opened on 12th April 1841, the money required having been provided partly by the Feoffees of the Ashdon charities and partly by benefaction from the Reverend Benedict Chapman, D.D., sometime Rector of Ashdon and eventually Master of Gonville and Caius College, Cambridge. A few years later, there was a visitation by the Rural Dean, who calculated that there werė at that time 898 people living in the parish and 190 separate families. He noted that the National School met at 9 a.m. and reassembled at 2 p.m. from Monday to Friday, and had on its registers 40 girls and 27 boys; there were no 'schools not connected with the Established Church' in the village, maintained by Public Funds. The Ashdon National School's record, simply in crudely statistical terms, was by no means negligible, given that many of the nation's children were receiving no formal instruction whatsoever at this period and that all but the very poorest parents were expected to pay a weekly fee for the privilege of having their children taught. Those unable to pay the fees could be helped from charitable trusts as is made clear by such entries as the following from the account books kept by the Trustees of Robert Freeman's Benefaction to the Parish of Ashdon:

1846
April 4. Paid Fred Ruse for teaching Hannah Chapman Writing 6^s; Jane Gowlett, reading, writing and arith. 11^s; Emily Smith reading 3^s; Matthew Ewin writing 3^s; Eliza Ford, reading, writing etc. 12^s; Charles Unwin reading 12^s; Allen Green do 12^s; Arthur Andrews reading, writing and arith. 3/-
£3 - 2
April 12. Bibles given to Eliza Nunn and Sarah Smith 7s
Eliz. Pearson for teaching Sarah Ford   12s
1847
April 5. Paid Fred. Ruse for teaching Eliz. Ford ½ year's reading and writing 2s. 6d.; Emily Searle do., ¾ 4s. 3d.; Charles Unwin reading 1 yr. 12^s; Allen Green do. 1 yr. 12s.; Emily Smith ¾ year reading & writing, 1 qu^r reading 15s. 9d.   £2 - 12 - 6
Bibles given on the 4th to Maria Marsh & Sophia Frost   6s. 6d.
Eliz. Pearson for teacing Sarah Ford   12^s

In each of these years and, for that matter, in every year which the Freeman account book covers, an annual subscription is also paid to the National School.

In Ashdon, the National School venture would seem to have prospered. In October 1847, a second building was opened on the same site at the top of Church Hill opposite the driveway to the parish church: it was built at the expense of Lord Maynard, owner of Waltons Park and used for the boy pupils; the older National schoolroom erected by the Reverend Benedict Chapman was used for the girls. Thomas Prior and his wife Harriet were appointed as Master and Mistress at an annual stipend of £50 per annum with an additional payment of £3. 10s. 'for the purpose of finding coals for the use of the schools'. In 1852, the Curate noted in the School's accounts book 'The Mistress, Mrs Prior, having obtained her certificate of Merit at the examination held at Norwich by the Rev. M. Mitchell Her Majesty's Inspector of Schools, in the Easter Week of 1852, and this circumstance being likely to prove of great benefit to the School, it was agreed to raise the Salary of the Master and Mistress to £60 per annum to commence from Michaelmas 1852'. The Priors were assisted by a pupil teacher to whom the Ashdon Charity donated one pound in 1853 as a contribution towards the expenses incurred at the Norwich Training Institution.

The School's income derived partly from annual donations of from one to two pounds from the local gentry — Lord Maynard being the exception who provided fifteen pounds — and partly from fees paid by the pupils' parents. This income regularly amounted to almost one fifth of the whole, and we would do well to remember that this had to be provided, in weekly measures of one or two pence per child, up to a maximum of ninepence per week per family. To a labourer who was expected to maintain his whole family on a wage of from twelve shillings to one pound per week, the school-fees were far from negligible. The 'monitors' referred to in the 'Disbursements' entry for 10th July were one of the most distinctive aspects of the so-called 'Madras' system adapted in all the 'National' schools. The monitors were paid a small stipend to assist the certificated teachers in the 'simultaneous' or 'mixed' instruction of often very large groups of children of widely varying ability. The experiment enjoyed very limited success, and the same must also be said of the slightly older 'Pupil Teachers' who subsequently replaced them. These were recruited at far too young an age, often as early as thirteen, their knowledge was inevitably limited and their previous training, by virtue of their status, was non-existent. Until the proliferation of the Teachers' Training Colleges, the 'Pupil Teacher' scheme was the regular way the nation's elementary schools recruited its apprentices and, not unnaturally, over this and other deficiencies, critics of the existing system waxed eloquent, few more so than W.E. Forster, Vice-President of the Council and brother-in-law of Matthew Arnold, when, on 17th February 1870, he introduced his momentous Elementary Education Bill in the House of Commons. What, he demanded, were the results of the nation's efforts to educate its children?

> They are what we might have expected; much imperfect education and much absolute ignorance; good schools become bad schools for children who attend them for only two or three days in the week, or for only a few weeks in the year; and though we have done well in assisting the benevolent gentlemen who have established schools, yet the result of the State leaving the initiative to volunteers, is, that where State help has been most wanted, State help has been least given, and that where it was desirable that State power should be most felt it was not felt at all. In helping those only who help themselves, or who can get others to help them, we have left unhelped those who most need help. Therefore, notwithstanding the large sums of money we have voted, we find a vast number of children badly taught, or utterly untaught, because there are too few schools and too many bad schools, and because there are large numbers of parents in this country who cannot, or will not, send their children to school. Hence comes a demand from all parts of the country for a complete system of national education ...'

The House voted to 'cover the country with good schools', these to be managed by locally elected boards of management which could, at least in theory, compel all children of school age to attend them; in practice, many of these boards seem to have lacked the desire or the nerve to enforce attendance and, as will be seen, a constant complaint of teachers for decades to come was that far too often, far too many truants and their parents went unpunished. For all that, various laws were put on the Statute Book to improve school attendance.

In 1873, the Agricultural Children's Act was passed under which no child under eight could be employed on the land unless it happened to be his father's own holding. From the age of eight onwards, a child could be employed part-time if, during the year preceding, he had attended school a given number of times. In 1876, it became the legal duty of parents to ensure that their children 'received efficient instruction in reading, writing and arithmetic'. In 1880, the School leaving-age was raised to ten and pressure soon began to mount to have this raised still further to twelve; the move was bitterly resented by parents, by the children it was supposed to benefit and by all manner of critics among the gentry who felt that money spent on over-educating the less well-off was money wasted.

For all that, there was one group amongst the poorer children of any village who needed to be taught the special skills that were vital to the community's prosperity: cordwainers (or cobblers) to shoe the labourers, blacksmiths to shoe the horses and repair the implements, bricklayers to build the walls of houses and carpenters to complete them and to keep the barns in good repair. The mysteries of some of these crafts, those of the blacksmith in particular were transmitted by word of mouth and by practical demonstration from generation to generation down the centuries. The same was largely true of bricklaying and Ashdon is typical of many a village in having had the same family (in its case, the Ketteridges) engaged in bricklaying from the sixteenth century to the twentieth. Carpentry, however was something of a special case, calling not only for manual dexterity but for a level of numeracy sufficient to carry out relatively sophisticated calculations. Just how sophisticated may be judged through reference to the handbook unearthed for me by Ann Alexander. It once belonged to her grandfather whose signature appears on the fly-leaf together with the date 'May 24 1813'. The work was published in 1761. The author is one E. Hoppus, 'Surveyor to the Corporation of the London Assurance', and the title of the book has all the grandiloquence of a lost expansive age:

Practical Measuring
Made Easy
To the Meanest Capacity
By
A *New* Set of Tables;
which shew at SIGHT

The *Solid* or *Superficial* Content (and *consequently* the Value) of any *Piece* or *Quantity* of *squared* or round Timber, be it *Standing* or *Felled*, also of Stone, Board, Glass &c, made Use of in the Erecting or Repairing of any Building, &c.

Contrived to answer all the Occasions of *Gentlemen* and *Artificers*, far beyond any Thing yet extant; the Contents being given in Feet, Inches, and *Twelfth Parts* of an Inch.

With a *Preface*;
Shewing the *Excellence* of this *New Method* of Measuring, and *Demonstrating*, that whoever ventures to rely upon those OBSOLETE Tables and Directions Published by ISAAC KEAY, is liable to be deceived (*in Common Cases*) 10*s*. in the Pound.

The book includes lists and prices of joiners' tools (augers, chisels, hammers, hatchets, saws) as well as of hinges and bolts. It provides considerable detail about 'the many sorts and great variety of nails' in which, in the author's view, so great Abuses and Impositions constantly occur. They are broadly divided into the categories of Brads, Hobbs and Nails and further sub-divided into classes such as 'Bill-Brads, Plain-Brads, Gunner-Brads; Clasp-Hobbs, Dye-Hobbs, Rose-Hobbs, Skidder-Hobbs, Thick-Hobbs; Deck-Nails, Flat-head-Nails, Flat-point-Nails, Drawe-Nails, Lead-Nails, Rose-Nails, Scupper-Nails, Sharp-Nails, Middle-Nails, Square-Nails, Prigg-Nails, Spike-Nails and Weight-Nails', and numerous examples are provided of how much a thousand of each variety ought to weigh if the cost per thousand is known. However, the bulk of the book, some hundred and eighty eight closely typed pages out of two hundred and four, is given over to column upon column of figures enabling the user to solve such practical problems as the following: 'Let the Length of a Piece of round Timber be 45 Feet and the Girth 44 Inches; one Fourth of which is 11 inches: I demand how much Timber this Piece contains?' or 'What is the value of ONE FOOT in LENGTH of a Piece of Timber, Stone &c whose Size or Scantling is 6 inches by 9 inches, at 18*d*. per Foot Cube?'

What is intriguing about the copy of the manual I have examined is not so much the quaintness of the prose or the minute particularity of the figures but the fact that it has clearly been regularly used; the pages are well-thumbed and the end-papers covered with rapid calculations in the original owner's hand. James Downham, who farmed Midsummer Hill Farm on the Ashdon-Radwinter border, was born in Saffron Walden in 1749 and his son Richard in Radwinter in 1827. The probability is that each received his initial formal education at the local school and that each left when he was no more than 12 years old. The fact that they seem to have been well able to use Mr Hoppus's '*Measurer*' may be taken to indicate something of the quality as well as of the content of the craft apprenticeship they received when their country schooldays were over.

But the chief concern of the education reformers in the second half of the nineteenth century was not so much the highly skilled artisan as the ordinary labourer who still constituted the great bulk of the population. Not every theoretician was persuaded that the spread of elementary education was necessarily a good thing. In 1861, when a Royal Commission under the Duke of Newcastle reported on the State of Popular Education in England, one of the assistant commissioners (the Reverend James Frazer, later to become Bishop of Manchester), frankly declared his misgivings:

> Even if it were possible, I doubt whether it would be desirable, with a view to the real interests of the peasant boy, to keep him at school till he was 14 or 15 years of age. But it is not possible. We must make up our minds to see the last of him, as far as the day school is concerned, at 10 or 11. We must frame our system of education upon this hypothesis; and I venture to maintain that it is quite possible to teach a child soundly and thoroughly, in a way that he shall not forget it, all that is necessary for him to possess in the shape of intellectual attainment, by the time that he is 10 years old. If he has been properly looked after in the lower classes, he shall be able to spell correctly the words that he will ordinarily have to use; he shall read a common narrative — the paragraph in the newspaper that he cares to read — with sufficient ease to be a pleasure to himself and to convey information to listeners; if gone to live at a distance from home, he shall write his mother a letter that shall be both legible and intelligible; he knows enough of ciphering to make out, or test the correctness of, a common shop bill; if he hears talk of foreign coun-

tries he has some notions as to the part of the habitable globe in which they lie; and underlying all, and not without its influence, I trust, upon his life and conversation, he has acquaintance enough with the Holy Scriptures to follow the allusions and the arguments of a plain Saxon sermon, and a sufficient recollection of the truths taught him in his catechism, to know what are the duties required of him towards his Maker and his fellow man. I have no brighter view of the future or the possibilities of an English elementary education, floating before my eyes than this. If I had ever dreamt more sanguine dreams before, what I have seen in the last six months would have affectually and for ever dissipated them.

The Reverend J. Fraser's pessimism, which grew out of a period of direct observation as a Schools Inspector, was evidently rooted in his belief that country children's intellects were as limited as their horizons and that they were congenitally incapable of improvement. Other opponents of the extension of elementary education were disturbed because they felt precisely the opposite: they feared that the better educated masses would waste no time in infiltrating their own entrenched positions of power and privilege. This is brought out particularly vividly in a set of minutes preserved in the Essex Record Office of a meeting of the Board of Guardians of Witham Union, near Chelmsford, on 13th March 1880. At this meeting, a certain Colonel Lucas proposed that the following composite resolution be presented to Parliament:

> That this Board views with alarm the greatly increasing cost to the County of the advanced compulsory Education enforced in the Elementary Schools;
> That admitting that it may be the duty of the Country to educate the masses in such degree as may fit them the better to fulfil the duties of the respective stations in life in which they are born, they consider that it cannot be called on to assist by grants of public money in elevating them beyond such stations;
> That it is unjust to compel the higher classes to supply the means by which the children of the lower classes shall be enabled to compete with their own children for employments for which they should seek;

That the compulsory detention of children of the working classes at School till they are fourteen years of age is detrimental alike to the employer and the employed depriving the latter of a considerable amount of earnings by the children themselves and the Mothers by which formerly they were benefitted and compelling the former to pay men's wages for many light works formerly performed by women and children;

That the advanced education now enforced in the Elementary Schools tends to dissatisfy the children in after years with their sphere in life whilst the prohibition against employment till the age of 14 years engenders habits of idleness which in after life cannot be overcome;

That the larger grants given for higher subjects Geography, Mathematics, Music, Drawing, Botany and other sciences tempts the Teachers to give their chief attention to the brighter children, for their own advantage and to neglect the duller whilst at the same time such sciences when taught are in the main worse than useless to the children of the labourer in after life.

Your Petitioners therefore pray that the children may not under any circumstances be compulsorily detained at School beyond the age of 10 years and that no public money may be expended in teaching in the Elementary Schools more than Reading, Writing and Arithmetic sufficient to enable them to pass the third Standard as it is at present framed, with needlework for Girls.

The motion was seconded by a Mr Beaumont and carried by sixteen votes to five.

Two years before this rearguard action was mounted in Witham, on 30th September 1878, the first Board School opened in Ashdon, built on a sloping site, near the centre of the village, purchased from one Thomas Cro, Innkeeper, for £100. From the outset, its fluctuating fortunes were recorded in the official School Diary or 'Log Book' in which the Headteacher was instructed to make 'at least once a week . . . an entry specifying ordinary progress and other facts concerning the school or its teachers such as the dates of withdrawals, commencements of duty, cautions, illnesses etc., which may require to be referred to at a future time or may otherwise deserve to be recorded'. Doubtless because this injunction was reinforced with a timely reminder that, on the occasion of his annual visitation, the Inspector would examine the Log Book and pronounce whether or not it had been properly kept, successive Headmasters observed the practice of making very full and occasionally fussy entries 'at least once a week'. The would-be compiler of any village history must be duly grateful because the product constitutes an invaluable record of the Board School's activities: who taught what to whom, when and in what circumstances. In this respect, the Ashdon Board School Log Books are models of their kind.

When the Ashdon Board School opened its doors in September 1878, a mere thirty five children were admitted. The number was small because the old National Schools at the top of Church Hill continued in existence until the Whitsun of 1885 and for seven years, the village enjoyed the rare luxury of providing two schools (or even three, if the National Boys' and Girls' Schoolhouses are allowed to count as separate entries!). The normal complement of staff for the Board School was the Headmaster and an Infants' Mistress supplemented by one other teacher (normally the wife of the Head if he happened to be married) and supported by one or two young Pupil Teachers. It was not until 1884 that the first Essex Training College (for female teachers of infants) was opened at Saffron Walden and, for several decades, Ashdon School persisted in the long-established practice of appointing young probationers and training them while they were in post. As will be seen, this procedure was occasionally fraught with difficulty, not least because the trainee teachers were only a year or two older than their senior pupils. The pupils came from Ashdon, from Bartlow Hamlet and from as far afield as Shudy Camps, a good three miles distant by winding road to the north-west. More often than not, pupils were admitted at the age of five though the records show that there were, on occasion, some mites well below that age in the Infants' Class, and they stayed on normally until they were into their twelfth year. Almost without exception, these pupils were the children of farm labourers. While the children of the local gentry were educated within the privacy of their own homes by a resident governess or far away from the village at a boarding-school, the regular practice of the Ashdon farmers and shopkeepers was to send their children into Saffron Walden to be taught either privately or at the Quaker Friends' School.

In keeping their children out of the Board School, the better-off Ashdon families were acting like the great majority of their kind all over the country. After his tour of a wide range of Board Schools, one of Her Majesty's Inspectors observed in 1877 that in most of them 'the farmer will not let his daughter — nor his son except in earliest years — sit beside the children of his labourers'. He also commented that he had often been told by country clergymen that over-education led to social discontent and to their wives having no servants or useless ones.

Though Ashdon's farm-workers were to establish something of a reputation for Labour militancy in the early part of the twentieth century, it seems unlikely that this can be attributed to their having been 'over-educated' at the village school. This is not meant as a slight on the staff who taught them in the first decades of the Board School's existence (indeed, all the evidence suggests they were both dedicated and conscientious); it is a comment rather on the content of the School curriculum which, on the face of it, was just about as likely to foment social discontent as a plate of cold porridge. Apart from providing basic instruction in Reading, Writing and Arithmetic, most of the teachers seem to have expended a considerable part of their time and energy in persuading their classes to sing what sound like particularly jolly songs (lists of which are faithfully listed year by year) and in stirring their patriotic emotions through learning by rote such poems as Macaulay's *Spanish Armada* or Tennyson's *Charge of the Light Brigade*. The opening entries in the very first Log Book could be said to establish the pattern of what was to follow for the next quarter of a century:

> October 1 1878: Gave a lesson on *England* to the first class consisting of second, third and fourth standards.
> October 7-11 1878: The girls take needlwork in the afternoon under the care of Miss Hex, Assistant Mistress.
> November 4-8 1878: Children learn a song 'Catch the Sunshine.
> November 11-15 1878: Girls recommenced needlework this week.
> November 18-22 1878: Began to learn a song 'Let the hills resound with Song'.

January 13-17 1879: Taught a new song, 'Lightly tread'.
January 20-24 1879: Taught a new song 'Whistling Farmer's Boy'. Received a globe for the use of the school.
February 3-7 1879: Taught a new song 'March away'.

While the Ashdon hills were resounding with all these songs and the lightly treading farmers' boys were merrily whistling, the infants were being kept active with a range of other activities, all designed, it would seem, to teach them to be more appreciative of the world around them and occasionally of worlds far away:

List of Lessons given to Infants, 1883
Natural History: Horse. Cow. Sheep.
Object Lessons: Coal. Paper. Wood. Bread. Butter. Meat. Sun. Moon. Rain. Harvest.
Lessons on Form and Colours:
Occupations: Building with Cubes. Forming articles with peas and sticks. Paper plaiting.

Infants' Lessons — year ending September 1884
Agriculture: Harvest. Haymaking.
Object: Basket. Bell. Book. Chair. Tables. Needles. Paper. Apples. Umbrella. Tree. Windows. Bread. Penny. Clock.
Natural History: Cow. Dog. Lion. Cat. Duck. Fly. Horse. Sheep. Elephant. Rabbit. Camel.
Natural Phenomena: Light. Seasons. Sun. Rain.

What the children made of these various activities must remain matter for conjecture but what one particular Headmaster made of them is made particularly clear in some of the observations of Mr F.J. Wyatt who took charge of Ashdon School on 7th January 1901. He took stock of the prospect before him on 29th March 1901 as he reviewed his pupils' performance in the recent Quarterly Examination:

> I found Standard 4 particularly weak all round and it is evident that as Standard 3 they received but little 'teaching'. Reading and Recitation are not yet satisfactory especially in

the first class of the Infant Department. I found these subjects extremely drowsy, expressionless and tiresomely monotonous. The knowledge of phrasing and stops was at the minimum.

I am making efforts to infuse more life into these as well as in all the other subjects of the curriculum. By combining the complementary subjects History and Geography, Object Lessons and Composition, by daily Nature — contact talks, by encouraging the children to take and make daily observations on the Sun, Moon, Clouds, Rain, Weather, Animal and Plant life, by getting the children to take an active part in the 'Object' lessons by providing outdoor specimens, I am endeavouring to tap the springs of Observation and Enquiry in order that the children shall learn to take a greater and wider interest in their surroundings and so awaken the whole of the Activities of Child Nature.

Six months later, after examining twenty three children newly promoted from the Infant Room, Mr Wyatt had to reflect more than a little ruefully that there was still a considerable gulf between the ideals to which he was aspiring and the reality in the classroom before him. The ages of the children he had just tested ranged from between six years eight months to seven years three months. He reported:

> One third have no idea how to read the tiniest words, several did not know letters and most of the others 'read' badly. One or two cannot talk. Nine children have not the slightest knowledge of simple addition and eleven could not take 4 from 15 or 36 from 37. In 'Notation' many wrote '50' for '15'. Several wrote anything, others nothing. Thirteen could not answer the simplest questions on 2 or 3 times tables. Out of twenty three, only seven children are in a satisfactory condition.

In spite of such setbacks, Mr Wyatt would seem to have persisted in his endeavour 'to tap the Springs of Observation and Enquiry'. On 12th March 1903, he lists the questions he had just put to Standards 5, 6 and 7:

> The questions are put to the children some days before, thus

giving them an opportunity of 'Finding Out' the answers themselves.

The following were answered today as a type:—
1. Explain 'M.D.', 'P.S.', 'P.M.'. 2. Why should a bird with long legs have a long beak? 3. What becomes of water when it 'boils away'? 4. Why does a person poke a fire? 5. Give date of 'longest' day and date of 'shortest' day. 6. What is the distance across a penny, the distance round? What are the marks etcetera on a penny? Why is a penny round in shape?

Some of the subjects given for Composition lately were:
1. What would you do in case of fire? 2. An application for a situation? 3. Kindness to animals. 4. How to keep your body healthy. 5. A letter.

I gave a lesson on No. 4 introducing the subject of Cigarette Smoking. Spitting, unclean habits and the consequences. Weak boy, weak man, irregular at work, loses employment — to dwelling especially on the body as 'Temples of the Holy Spirit'.

25th June 1903: Gave permission to a Mr Woods, after seeing references from Managers and Schoolmasters, to give an Entertainment (after 4 o'clock to the children) including talk on Natural History illustrated by fossils.'

What his pupils made of Mr Wyatt is not on record. That he should, on occasion, have thought so poorly of them is not altogether surprising nor is it uncommon in the Ashdon school Log Book. Like all the Headteachers in those early years, he was confronted with all manner of difficulties; any one of these must have been at the very least profoundly irritating; the combination of so many of them must have occasionally been so horrendous that each Headmaster in turn must surely have echoed Carlyle's adage that 'It were better to perish than to continue schoolmastering'. In addition to the daily penance of having to face recalcitrant children and the not infrequent ordeal of having to confront actively hostile parents, the longsuffering Headmaster had sometimes to try to solve the problems posed by the inexperience of his Assistant Teachers. Occasionally, these were simply too young or too incompetent for the job. Thus, on 15th February 1895, the Head confided in his Log Book that his new Assistant, who had only two or three months previous experience as a teacher, did not seem to have the slightest notion of how to teach and was totally ignorant of what the children were required to do. A fortnight later, he complained to the Clerk of the Board of Managers that his Assistant was unable to do the work required of her or to keep discipline 'even in Standard I'. On 11th April, he noted:

> The Infant Mistress guilty of disobedience in not carrying out the instructions given by the Sewing Mistress for the proper teaching of Needlework to Infant Girls. Reason given: 'It was so much trouble'. This is the third act of disobedience committed by the Infant Mistress, first detaining the children beyond school hours after the Master had told her to discontinue the practice and secondly not obeying instructions with respect to classification of the average attendance of 31 which she was told to adopt until the Board gave more help.

On 26th April, he reported that the Infant Mistress 'has no control whatever of Standard I. Owing to her inability to maintain discipline it is necessary for the Master to repeatedly visit the class to keep them in order for her. This Standard has gone back very much'.

A week later, on 1st May, he wrote to his Board of Managers pleading 'for the children's sake' that they take notice of his Assistant's inability to work efficiently or maintain any semblance of discipline. On 17th May, he once again recorded his displeasure and concern in the Log Book:

> Told Assistant to give Standard I a writing lesson on Blackboard. Found the children writing from Reading Books very carelessly. Gave lesson myself during part of recreation time while Assistant, according to the rules of the Board, went out into Girls' playground.
> At the close of recreation, Assistant returned to classroom and immediately left without permission giving no reason for so doing. She did not return in the afternoon. Since this new Assistant commenced duties on February 11th, Standard I instead of making progress has deteriorated very much indeed owing to her inefficiency, which serious defect has been aggravated by systematic insubordination.

> Master has written twice to the Board calling their attention to the true facts. On Wednesday afternoon, having set the boys to work (it being Drawing Lesson), I went into the classroom and found Standard I quite beyond her control. I told Assistant to stand in front of the Boys and simply see they kept to their work. Coming out of classroom shortly after and finding their Assistant was not giving the slightest attention to these Boys, I told her she had better go back to Standard I and try.

Instead of going back to her class, the wretched Assistant would seem to have gone home; she had still not returned three days later and on the fourth day, she resigned on the grounds of ill-health. Whether this was a real or diplomatic reason is beside the point: one does not need to exercise much empathy to experience her misery or her Head's mounting irritation.

Over the next three years, the Infants' teaching was in considerable disarray: the disgraced Assistant was temporarily replaced by a Monitress (one of the older pupils), then by a succession of Assistant Teachers who remained in post from one to three months only, one resigning because she found 'the standing too great a strain on her strength', another being dismissed by the Board for 'not being sufficiently experienced'. On 4th February 1898, the newly appointed Head complained that he had been without an Infants' Teacher for ten weeks. 'The Master has sole charge of 80 children in Standards III to VI. He has therefore not been able to give proper supervision to the lessons of the probationer Maggie Phillips.' A month later, he was able to note with some satisfaction that a properly qualified Assistant Teacher had been appointed 'taking Standard III and considerably relieving the Master'. Two months later still, however, on 6th May 1898, he confided in the Log Book that his confidence in the new appointment had been entirely misplaced:

> The Infants' Assistant has acted in an exceptionally eccentric manner this afternoon. On going into the room to look at the children's work, she commenced such a tirade of abuse as to cause me serious doubts of her sanity. The only reason I can discover for this outburst seems to be the fact that the Candidate for Probation — who acts as Monitress in the Infant Room — has, for the past fortnight, been taking lessons in

the upper room from 10 to 12 a.m. each morning, but as this is only in accordance with the Regulations in the Code and the Instructions of the Board, I can only put her present conduct down as part of the systematic defiance of the Master's authority which this Assistant has practised for many months.

On 17th January 1899, the Head had once again occasion to complain of the 'eccentric' ways of his Assistant:

> I again enter a protest against the conduct of the Assistant. On requesting her not to air any grievances before the scholars she said defiantly 'I shan't' and followed this up by threatening to throw something at me if I did not leave the room.

This seems to have been a short-lived altercation because although the Assistant absented herself from School for the next six weeks, she did not in fact resign her appointment until January 1901, a month after the Head was transferred elsewhere. Thereafter and until the present, no further complaints by successive Heads against their colleagues have been recorded in the Ashdon School Log Books.

The inadequacies of their junior colleagues were by no means the only difficulties of which the Ashdon Headteachers had to complain: there were in addition, any number of breaches of discipline committed over the years by recalcitrant pupils. The following are but a selection from many:

> (*Headmaster*: Mr W.T. Sutton)
> *1st June 1885*: Mr Ruddock visited me in rather a threatening manner respecting his son Albert being sent out of his class so often, and on my punishing him with two strokes on the behind when so sent out.
> *4th January 1886*: Punished E. Cooper with three strokes (sharp) on the behind for pushing a boy off the form.
> *14th January 1886*: Punished Ben Marsh with four strokes for inking the desk.
> *24th February 1886*: Punished whole of Standard III for repeated idleness by three stokes on the hand.
> *12th March 1886*: Punished T. Coote with one stroke then perceiving his insolent look called him back, told him to hold out his hand, which he did not do. Stood him aside for some time then called on him again and told him I should give him

double if I had to push him on the desk. He still refused. When I placed him on the desk I gave him two over the behind. He then picked up a slate and threatened to throw it at my head. I gave him four more strokes across the back of the legs as he persisted not to lay the slate down. Kept him back after school and his mother came and took him off without my permission.

13th April 1886: Had to severely punish A. Nutting for disobedience and unruly conduct during school hours.

20th May 1886: Punished A. Nutting and sent him home as he showed signs of determined resistance. I have written to his father to know what he intends doing with him as he is not only misbehaving himself but also influencing others.

21st May 1886: Received note from Mrs Nutting this morning thanking me for writing to them and telling me that his father had severely beaten him last night, also expressing a wish for his future better conduct.

A. Layzell (Pupil Teacher) was mixed up in this matter.

2nd June 1886: Punished A. Nutting severely for refusing to hold out his hand and have written to his parents respecting the matter.

21st June 1886: Have been obliged to caution A. Layzell (Pupil Teacher) respecting E. Cooper. Talking with her in class room contrary to my directions.

29th June 1886: Cautioned A. Layzell repeatedly about talking to the girls in school. Directly my back is turned I find the thing repeated.

30th June 1886: Similar thing repeated today.

10th August 1886: Nutting began his stupid conduct again this afternoon. I am inclined to think that the boy is regularly stupid. Punished him but does not appear to have much effect.

From this point onwards, the handwriting of Mr Sutton grows more and more illegible and it comes as no surprise to note that on 19th October 1886 he has been replaced as Headmaster by Mr John Smith. It did not take very long before he too was embroiled in disciplinary problems:

25th November 1886: Last evening Charles Cooper ran away from his last *task* but on visiting his home, he found firmness was certain to deal with him, and on my return from the village, I found him again in school performing his *task*.

9th December 1886: Punished W. Ford for offering *stolen* glue to the other boys as Toffy and also for insolence.

7th January 1887: On Monday evening received on leaving school some insolence from Ben Free, a boy not attending our school. I captured him, took him into my house, where he had to remain until he expressed his penitence.

19th February 1887: Punished a boy on Thursday named Walter Smith for stupidity in not answering how many eight-pences there were in two shillings.

11th March 1887: Frank Stock came to school this afternoon in reference to a knife which had been taken (rightly) by Miss Edith Cooper during school hours for playing with it. At 8.30 p.m. yesterday he accosted me about the knife and I promised him that I would, on the following day (i.e. today) deliver the knife to him, until he made use of foul language, when I stated that as he had made a threat on Miss Cooper's head, I should not deliver the knife until he appeared before the Board. He this day came at 2.25 p.m. to abuse me, and as he was so drunk, and continued to use phrases of the kind not fitted for school place, I sent for the Police Constable who saw him depart from the premises. After school, the Mother came but I refused to have anything to do further until I had seen the Chairman of the Board from whom I received the sympathy that I had done quite right.

19th March 1887: Went to Walden to try to get a summons on Frank Stock for his behaviour to me personally but was told I could not obtain one.

26th March 1887: Attended at Walden Court this day to support a Police Summons' Case against Frank Stock for being drunk and disorderly on the Highway in front of the Ashdon Board School. He was to pay fine and costs amounting to fifteen shillings.

25th September 1894: On going into Infant Room yesterday I heard Miss Fitch address a girl by her surname which surprised me much. I spoke to her this morning and find this custom has been usual. I told her that I could not allow any girl to be addressed by her surname.

Conflicts with incompetent staff, with contumacious pupils or with aggressive parents were by no means the only tribulations of the early Headteachers of the Ashdon Board School. Almost from the outset, as the Head adds up the number of attendances and the amount of pence taken by the end of each week, he complains of the total of absentees which he judges to be excessive, and this lament is sounded all too frequently through the pages of the Log Books right to the outbreak of the First World War.

On a significantly large number of occasions, the absences can be attributed to ill-health or to inclement weather:

> *9th-13th December 1878*: Several children absent this week through severe weather and colds.
> *12th-16th May 1879*: A very wet day on Thursday lowered the numbers considerably.
> *21st-25th July 1879*: Monday and Tuesday exceedingly wet: many children absent whole week in consequence.
> *10th-14th November 1879*: Whooping cough beginning to make itself felt.
> *17th-21st November 1879*: Heavy fall of snow on Friday kept many children away.
> *22nd September 1882*: Reopened school this week with a very small number. 13 only present out of 77 owing to gleaning and an epidemic of measles and scarlatina.
> *June and July 1891*: Influenza rife in village. Many children absent.
> *29th June 1891*: Scarlet fever has broken out in the village.
> *18th December 1891*: Attendance very bad this week. A great number of children suffering from mumps.
> *17th June 1892*: Whooping cough prevalent in the village. Many children absent in infant room.
> *25th February 1895*: Dr.Armistead, Medical Officer of Health, visited school and ordered that it must be closed owing to the prevalence of Diphtheria and Whooping Cough until he give instructions that it be reopened.
> *25th March 1895*: School reopened.
> *11th November 1895*: Epidemic of measles has spread very quickly through village.
> *16th November 1895*: Medical Officer instructed Master not

to reopen School until the epidemic is quite gone.

9th December 1895: Master attempted to re-open School this morning. As only 3 children came it was necessary to close again.

1st July 1903: 57 absent this morning, over a dozen cases of Whooping Cough. With the exception of less than a dozen all the rest are ill also. Most of the children attending have colds and the coughing is very bad.

10th July 1903: 45 children absent all week: quite 40 have the whooping cough.

20th August 1907: School closed because of Measles epidemic.

5th March 1908: School closed for fortnight on account of Fever.

18th June 1909: Four children have been excluded with ringworm of the scalp.

9th July 1909: Another case of ringworm in the head this week. I think I shall be justified in excluding all boys who have this complaint, even if they wear skull caps.

13th December 1910: I sent two children home this morning. Suspected scabies.

It is not altogether surprising that the schooldays of an Ashdon pupil were so regularly interrupted during the first three decades of the Board School's life: the classrooms were inadequately ventilated and so poorly heated that the ink regularly froze in the teacher's inkwell; for those children prepared to brave the worst of the weather, there were no facilities for drying clothing; the lavatories for boys and girls consisted of buckets in the primitive outhouse (and these served as the 'toilets' until after the Second World War). Comments on the shortcomings of the primitive conditions of the School are occasionally to be found in the Log Book: in 1891, the visiting Inspector observed 'there should be a supply of water other than a cask of rainwater on the school premises'; in 1893, the Inspector commented, 'Care should be taken that the offices (lavatories) are well supplied with earth'; on 16th January 1901, when William Tuck first took over the School, his very first entry in the Log Book was about the extreme cold of the building: 'The infant classroom was very cold, 40°F. The children were blue and I asked Miss Simmons to cease lessons and warm them by the fire'. Given these factors and

Ashdon village schoolteachers in 1904: the Misses Day, Smith (later Mrs Eason) and Greengrass with Mr and Mrs Tuck

what were often cramped and confined conditions at home, one should marvel not that there were so many disruptions because of illness but that there were so few. And I marvel also that all the Ashdon villagers I interviewed old enough to have been pupils at their Board School at the first decade of this century recalled the time they spent there not with bitterness but with serenity and often affection.

These, however, were not the sentiments with which successive Headmasters regularly viewed the depressingly large numbers of absences which had nothing to do with the pupils' ill-health.

15th-20th June 1879: Several Camps children away all week Carlick (leek) picking.
6th-10th October 1879: Very thin school: harvest not finished.
26th-30th July 1880: A bad week. Flower show in Ashdon on Tuesday. Sunday School Treat at Walden on Wednesday: school closed. Thursday very poor school. Children too tired to attend.
20th-24th December 1880: Very poor school this week. Tuesday — nearly all the children away seeking Xmas gifts.
23rd December 1881: Very thin school on Wednesday (St. Thomas's Day). Children away 'boxing'.
15th January 1884: 3 children left School this week in consequence of the Uncle being summoned by the Board for employing the boy.
4th October 1889: Attendance bad again during the week. Gleaning not yet finished. The irregular attendance greatly interferes with work especially the class subjects. The children seem to have forgotten. Must concentrate with their subjects. The Inspection being just after harvest is a great drawback, it being almost impossible to make up lost ground.
6th November 1891: Louisa Pettit received a Special Prize she having been present at all School meetings during the year.
4th November 1892: Many of the children away gathering acorns. Unless a better attendance is enforced it is useless to expect good enough results to obtain the Higher Grant.
17th August 1894: Harvest work has now been going on a fortnight. Several of the older boys are away leading horses.
24 July 1895: 30 children absent gathering Wild Flowers for Ashdon & Bartlow Show tomorrow.
8th September 1896: Attendance extremely bad. A number of boys are being employed in the harvest field; a still larger number of both boys and girls are away gleaning. For the absence of a third considerable number there is no adequate excuse.
30th October 1896: The attendance is very irregular. Children are called upon to assist in various kinds of outdoor work as acorn-gathering, potato-picking, root-pulling and sheep-minding.
9th August 1897: Very low attendance this afternoon. 63 children absent. Of these only 5 are harvesting. For the re-

mainder there would appear to be no adequate excuse.
21st January 1898:   A meet of the hounds at Waltons took away a number of children this morning.
10th February 1898:   40 absent. 13 are suffering from colds, which are very prevalent. The remaining 27 are merely 'wanted' to help at home.
20th May 1903:   Arthur Barker absent on Monday last and Tuesday morning. This boy since 1st October 1902 has been absent 107 times. His mother writes me 'I kept Arthur at home as I am Spring-cleaning as I have no one else he is a great help to me'.

One can sympathize both with the parents and the continuously frustrated teachers: for many of the parents, who till 1891 still had to provide the 'pence' for their children's schooling, the temptation must all too frequently have been irresistible not merely to save the fee-money but positively to add to the paltry family income by putting the children out to work; if the mother were ill or a newly born baby needed nursing, there was sometimes no other option but to keep one of the older children at home. The teachers were no less understandably agitated at seeing so many absences not only going unpunished but, on occasion, being actively encouraged by the local squirearchy. What is abundantly clear from the Log Books is that their agitation was only partly occasioned by the thought of regulations being flouted or educational opportunities going to waste: a much more pressing reason for their alarm and despondency was the dread prospect of the annual visitation of Her Majesty's Inspector of Schools.

What was at issue on the occasion of the Inspector's visit was not merely the teacher's personal reputation over the job he had been doing in the months preceding. What was at stake was the financial well-being of the School itself. The School's annual grant was calculated on a number of factors: on the average attendance, at four shillings per pupil plus one shilling for singing and another shilling for organisation and discipline; each pass-mark in each of the 'three-Rs' was rated at three shillings and there were four shillings for each pass in two other subjects (such as grammar, history, geography and needlework). The last two amounts were for children of seven and upwards who had made 250 attendances in the course of the year. Grants were also paid for Pupil Teachers.

This 'payment by results' system must in large measure account for the Ashdon teachers' abiding preoccupation with absences and with breaches of discipline but also with the ambitious repertoire of songs they obliged their pupils to learn. It doubtless also explains why, on surveying the School he had just taken over, each new Ashdon Headteacher in the 1880s safeguarded himself by recording in the Log Book that his predecessor had presented him with a particularly backward collection of children. In this respect, no Ashdon head seems to have been more agitated than the hapless Mr D.G. Smith who was appointed on 9th January 1888:

> The children are very backward. Some in Standard I I scarcely know how to write or read.
> *27th February 1889*: Examined the First Standards: they were unusually backward when moved into this class. Find that they have made scarcely any progress. The Pupil Teacher seems to have greatly neglected her duty, have on several different occasions spoken to her about the matter, this time very strongly.
> *8th March 1889*: Pupil Teacher has been absent all week. Unwell.
> *15th April 1889*: The Infants are very backward. The needlework of the boys so badly done it is necessary to discontinue it for the present as there is no possibility of sufficient improvement to secure a grant. The other work requires *so much* attention.
> *10th May 1889*: The Assistant complains greatly of the backward state of the Infants and not without cause: it is evident they have been greatly neglected.

These early Ashdon School headteachers would seem to have worried themselves unduly over the verdict of the dreaded Inspectors. In the event, year by year, the Inspectors were as appreciative of the teachers' achievements as they were sympathetic towards their many problems, and even when they found some feature to criticize, they did so in kindly and helpful fashion:

> 1879 — An excellent beginning has been made here. The premises are admirable and the Discipline and Instruction

are most creditable. The Needlwork is excellently taught. 1882 — This is a very good school. The Instruction and Discipline are satisfactory throughout and the Infants are particularly well taught. 1885 — The new Master maintains the very high standard of efficiency which the School had previously reached ... The Infants' needlework like most of the elder girls is excellent. 1886 (after the merger with the Ashdon National School) — There has been a considerable increase in the numbers of this School during the past year. The attainments of the children continue very satisfactory. Arithmetic deserves special praise: for the second time the whole school has passed in this subject. ... The Infants are well taught but their discipline is not perfect. They are now numerous and a Certificated Teacher for them is desired. A.J. Layzell, Pupil Teacher, a Failure. 1887 — There has been a serious decline in the efficiency of this School since the last Examination. The spelling of the third and fourth Standards is particularly weak. English may just be classed as 'Fair' but Geography was a failure. Needlework is very good. The Assistant has worked well but the Pupil Teacher does not seem to have received proper instruction ... The infants are at present very backward. 1888 — Mr Smith found this school in lamentable condition but all the teachers have worked hard and the improvement does them much credit. 1889 — The irregularity of attendance in this School continues to form a great drawback to the teaching, but it seems that the Board find it difficult to procure convictions when they prosecute ... Some of the Infants' work is now good but there is an unusually large proportion of children who have attended so irregularly that thier attainments are very low. 1890 — Attendance in this school continues very irregular. There seem to be a few families in this parish who much neglect their duty in this respect. Considering the difficulties which have to be met the attainments are decidedly creditable. 1893 — The attendance at this school is still unsatisfactory and it would appear that several children have been allowed to leave School before attaining the required standard. 1895 — In spite of a severe epidemic, the attainments in this school, which had fallen last year to a very low level, have decidedly improved.

1896 — Mr Fowler found this school in a poor state owing partly to changes of teachers. He and Mrs Fowler seem to have effected some improvements but attainments are still low . . . Miss Simmonds teaches and manages the Infants with skill and gentleness and has accomplished creditable results; but she should certainly receive the permanent aid of at least an efficient Monitor in her task of teaching 40 or 50 Infants. 1897 — Mr and Mrs Fowler have worked hard to improve this school and the results are now on the whole satisfactory . . . Miss Simmonds teaches the Infants with much zeal and care: their numbers are still increasing . . .

The Inspectors' report continue in similar strain right up to the present: year by year, the Infant Mistresses are praised for their care and gentleness, and the Head and his Assistants in the upper school are commended for their dedication in conditions 'that have never been easy' and for seeking to give their children a confidence in themselves, a respect for others and an interest in the world around them. The extent to which they succeeded may, in part, be gauged from the accounts provided by some of their former pupils in the chapter that follows.

8

Edwardian Summer

> How strange are the tricks of memory, which often hazy as a dream about the most important events of a man's life, religiously preserve the merest trifles.
>   Sir Richard Burton: *Sind Revisited*

The writer who seeks to conjure up the more recent past is much less dependent, as he was for earlier ages, on the leaden prose or bare statistics of bureaucratic documents. All manner of other aids are at his disposal from the 'potency of cheap music' to the evocative prose of old advertisements. Consider, for instance, the following examples, culled from the pages of the 1911 Saffron Walden Directory in which Ashdon features. 'R.A. Williams, Royal Mail Contractor. Job, Livery and Commission Stables. Buses, Brakes, Waggonnettes, Victorias, Broughams, Open Carriages, with and without Rubber Tyres, of every Description for Hire on Reasonable Terms. Wassington Car and Mourning Carriage for Funerals. Distance no Object. Superior Horses Supplied for Gentlemen's Own Carriages, which can be hired by the Week, Month or Year. Horses taken in at Livery. Good Loose Boxes. Terms Strictly Moderate'. 'W. Windwood. Universal Hair Cutting and Shaving. Saloons and Fancy Repository. Walking Sticks in Great Variety. Families waited upon at their own Residences. Schools attended. Ladies Combings made up. Razors and Scissors Ground and Set'. 'J. Wright, Motor Works. Sole Agent for the District for the well-known Cars: Humber, Swift, Flanders, Belsize, Austins, B.S.A., Daimler, Rover, Unic, Arrol-Johnson, Crossley. Tyre-stockists for Dunlop, Michelin, Continental, Wood-Milne, Mackintosh'. 'Dobson's, Tobacconist, Hairdresser and Perfumer. Cigarettes always stocked, including Virginia, Turkish,

Egyptian, Havana, Algerian, Russian, Swiss and Brazilian Cigarettes. Also: *Sure Shot. The leading* 2^d *smooth. You will enjoy this Cigar until it Burns your Fingers'*. All of these powerfully evoke a vanished world that, for all its imperfections and inequalities, feels somehow more spacious than our own.

Old photographs cast an even more potent spell and the chronicler of Ashdon is specially blessed in this respect because in the first decade of this century, it was privileged to have its very own photographer, as prolific as he was proficient. This was Willie Smith, son of one of the two village shoemakers, who had been left crippled by an accident and would range across the district on a tricycle with his tripod strapped behind him. Thanks to the generosity of Ashdon villagers, I now have almost a hundred copies of his photographs in my possession, and they constitute both an eloquent tribute to a devoted practitioner's skills and a graphic record of a lost era: there are images of Ashdon's many beauty spots in all seasons, bathed in sunshine and buried under snow, views of woods and of fields and of Church, School and of every other building of significance; there are views of Ashdon folk at work or at play, of the Edwardian cricket team, comprising eleven good Ashdon men and true, including both the blacksmith and the squire, of the local Fire Brigade, attired in resplendent if ill-fitting uniforms and of a handful of ordinary villagers, sitting at their picnic amongst the new-mown hay beneath a sun which for them will be always shining; there are records of important local events such as the Army manoeuvres of 1912 with troops smilingly rehearsing for a drama that would all too soon be all too real, such as the freak hailstorm of 1913 which devastated all the greenhouses at Waltons Park and smashed the straw boater of a local publican, such as the array of coachmen, in their rosetted livery, assembling on Crown Hill to convey the favoured guests to some gala occasion over at the Big House. As one surveys these assorted images, tears are never far away and one hears oneself readily echoing the refrain of *MCMIV*, Philip Larkin's elegy to that lost era: *Never such innocence again.*

And there is material more evocative and more moving still, the spoken words of survivors from that devastated world, a number of whom I was fortunate enough to be able to interview when the century was in its early seventies and most of them were in their early nineties. The first of these was *Florence Anderson*, whom, in 1971, I met one afternoon, purely by chance in Ashdon Churchyard, and who there and then invited me into her immaculately kept cottage beside the ancient Guildhall. I interviewed her on three separate occasions and this is what she told me:

I was born in Caledonian Road in London in 1880. My father was a policeman and, at the time I was born, he was the station sergeant. To start off with, we lived above the police station. He was a wonderful man. He was born on the Earl of Cadogan's estate, near Bury St. Edmunds. The eldest boy of each family on the estate was always sent to the Bluecoats School and my father was sent there too when his time came. He always told us that he hated it there. He'd say, 'If you want to understand why I hated it in that school, just you read *Tom Brown's Schooldays*'. He always said, 'I happen to be Tom Brown'. In the end, he ran away. He had his bright mustard stockings and his shoes with the silver buckle on and his long frock coat. He had a little money with him and he got rides in all sorts of different carts to get up to London. He ended up with one of his cousins who kept a small butcher's shop in Whitechapel, and he worked there for a while till he joined the police. He'd had a very good education for those days and he got on very well. He finished up as an inspector.

My mother's name was Struggett but *her* mother's maiden name was Pearman and there have been Pearmans living in Ashdon for three hundred years and more. I can't tell you what *all* my ancestors did but I know that my grandmother Pearman was nurse-maid to the family who lived in the big mansion at Audley End. She married the head coachman at Audley End and they moved to a little house in Halt Lane to look after her mother, my great grandmother, that's to say. She used to look after children, and one of the boys she was once nursemaid to became the Rector here, and he used to teach my mother and her brother over at the Rectory. Because of that, they was able to get places with good families, very good families in fact. My mother was married from a big house in Berkeley Square when she was in service and I think it's rather nice to be able to say that. But what's nicer still is that I was actually christened here in Ashdon village church. Ashdon's always been a really special place for me and I'll try and tell you why.

Because Ashdon was my mother's home, we always came down here for a month in the summer holidays. We never missed a year all through the 1880s and 1890s and for years and years afterwards too. One of the loveliest of my memories is having tea from the Sunday school, out there in the fields. There used to be all sorts of lovely races for boys and girls and we always had this great big picnic-tea afterwards. And there was a very special tea-party in June 1902 when King Edward was crowned. They gave us all a special coronation mug. I've still got mine. I'm afraid it's been roughly used because I've often put flowers in it but now I'm old, somehow, I've come to value it more than I ever did in my younger days. Just to hold it and stroke it makes all sorts of other memories come back to me.

I remember we used to go fishing in the Bourne with the boys. We used to catch little shiny fish and we'd cook them outselves in the meadow over a bonfire. We'd no salt and no bread but we just used to eat those fish and think they tasted beautiful. We smelt all fishy when we got home. And I remember having to go across the fields to Goldstone's Farm to fetch mother a little bit of butter and a drop of cream. We'd never have to buy a mushroom for ourselves: that meadow beside the Church was full of them and we'd come back with our aprons laden. They'd all go into the meat pudding or else be made up into ketchup. But what I liked best, and what I remember most, was coming home from Church with father and mother and calling in at somebody's cottage and having a sip of lemonade wine while the men perhaps would have a smoke. And in the field here, next to the Church yard, the old horses used to be put out to rest. We'd go into somebody's garden and we'd help ourselves to a few carrots. It didn't matter whose garden it was as long as it wasn't Uncle's! And if there was lump sugar on the table, we'd sneak a few lumps and rush round to feed them to the horses. Fine behaviour for a station sergeant's daughter, wasn't it just! And the horses would bend down so we could get up on their backs, and when we used to ride down the meadow the Queen herself couldn't have been more proud.

Our Sundays in Ashdon were very happy. While we were in Church for the morning service, the potatoes would be baking back in the house in the space underneath the fireplace. The fire would have been made right up, you see, and there'd be a huge, big meat-pudding that had been in the copper, boiling along while we were at the service. As soon as we got home, we'd have our dinner right away. Before we started, though, the potatoes would be taken out and burst open, and some of the gravy out of our meat-pudding would be ladled over them. Then the potatoes would be closed up again and quickly wrapped up in a bit of flannel and brown paper and then popped into a box. And after our meal, my brother and I would take the box with the potatoes from Ashdon Church over to St. James Workhouse in Walden where usually there'd be two or three poor old people. We loved doing that. It was a long walk for us but we loved walking along the country road and smelling the hedges and flowers. Back we'd come, mostly slow but sometimes with a hop, skip and a jump, and we'd have tea and then be off to Church again. That might not sound very exciting to you but we were quite content. There wasn't so much wealth around in those days but I'm sure there was more happiness.

I don't suppose you can have any idea of how poor old people had to live in those far-off times. Well, I *saw* and *I* can tell you. For instance, there were these three old ladies — friends of my grandmother, they were — and they all lived in the one little house. There was just the one room down and the one room up, always polished bright and clean as clean. They had two shillings a week to live on, just *two shillings a week*. Oh, and a loaf of bread a week besides: I mustn't forget that loaf of bread. Sometimes they'd have a slice of pork, or else somebody would catch them a rabbit and they'd always invite me in to dinner with them. We used to do what we could to help them along. We had a set of scales and we used to divide up a packet of tea into little two ounce packets. And we'd make up little twist-packets of sugar and put all those packets in a shoe-box and take it in. They'd *always* give us a bit of cake and a drop of their homemade wine. What they'd regularly do was go out and pick dandelions and make their wine with some of the sugar mother used to give them. Two shillings a week was all those old ladies used to get but I still feel those old people were the three happiest people I ever knew. Today, we've all got so much more and yet nobody seems satisfied.

My brother and I didn't leave all the helping to our parents. We used to go into people's gardens and steal potatoes and bring them special to our old ladies. It probably sounds very naughty to you but those potatoes were perhaps being grown to feed someone's pigs and we thought our old ladies came first by rights. So we'd collect a few potatoes in my brother's cap and run off. And they'd be cooked in their jackets by our old ladies and then they'd skin them and mash them. They used to say, 'You shouldn't do that, you know', but they'd eat those potatoes, you know, and so would we. There were never no potatoes to taste like those we stole.

Now, if you're thinking my father and mother didn't bring us up properly, you'd be very wrong. We were always taught to talk properly and always to be very respectful. We had to learn our collects and learning our hymns was something that simply had to be done. When we were here for our holidays, we always had a penny to put into the Church collection-box. My brother and I always went on ahead of our parents and on the way, there used to be a little tiny window where old Mrs Maynard would sell sweets she'd made herself. And we'd spend a ha'penny on those sweets and put just a ha'penny in the collection-box. We did that several times before we got caught. It wasn't me so much as my brother. I *had* to do it because he did it, you see. But I never told tales. We got caught because we were eating the sweets in Church. After that, we never had our pennies given us till we were *inside* the Church.

We had a strict upbringing, I'd say, and even when we were little we had to help with the housework. My mother was very delicate and we all had to help her. Mother would sit there in her armchair and tell us exactly what had to be done. My brother Will had to clean the boots and the outside of the windows. My sister and I had to clean the inside of the windows. We had to dust the tops of the picture-frames and we had to do the ironing too. Mother also showed me how to goffer and I've still got my goffering-iron today. I'm the only person now in Ashdon who knows how that's done and I still goffer the crimped collars for the Church choir. My sister had to bath me and then I had to bath her. We'd light up the boiler in the scullery and we'd have our bath in there. Always there'd be plenty of hot water and it would be warm as toast up beside the boiler. My brother Will would have to have his bath the night after and he'd also have to bath our younger brother. That's how we were brought up: helping ourselves by helping each other. I'd say you couldn't have better training for later on in life.

We learned other things from our parents. How to be kind to others, how to spend our money wisely. Never waste. What *you* throw away, someone else surely needs. When we had potatoes, we'd always boil up the skins and things like apple cores together, to feed to the birds. I taught my daughters to make their dolls' clothes and how to wash them, just as my mother taught me. And we were taught whatever money we might have, always, *always*, to put a fraction of it away and never touch it, come what may. That was just about the best advice I ever had — as you shall hear tell.

Those are the things I learned from my parents at home. Where I went to regular school was in London but I also had lessons here in Ashdon. Some of us used to go for special lessons to Dr. Swete, the Rector at that time. He was a very clever man and he went on to be a real Professor over at Cambridge. He was also my godfather. He gave us extra lessons in England and arithmetic. My cousins didn't seem to learn much at the village school and they left very early. So Dr. Swete did his best to polish them up and help them read and write better. And, of course, I used to go along too. I used to love that. Of course, I always beat them: I was a *London* child. But what I think I remember best about Dr. Swete's was the big copper he used to have in his kitchen. It was a huge thing and it was made out of real copper: that was a real *copper* copper, that was. The gardener used to bring in rabbits, the Rector might get half a calf's head, and twice a week, that was all put into the copper with perhaps a chicken as well. When the Glebe Field was being cut at harvest-time, just in front of the Rectory, the men used to come to the kitchen. They had only small little cottages and hadn't got a copper of their own. And us children would take it in turns to get up on the little ladder that stood beside this huge great copper and we'd dip in our finger and suck. If I close my eyes now and really think hard, I can still taste how good that tasted then, and that was more than eighty years ago. And that dear old copper is still in our village today. Years later, the Rectory kitchen was altered, and they gave that copper to me. And what I did was polish it up inside and out and then it was put on my White Elephant stall. Brigadier Collins bought it off me and now he has it over in Ashdon Hall to store his logs in.

And *still* I haven't finished with the things I can remember from the time I was a little girl in Ashdon. From my cousins but, most of all, from those poor old ladies we used to take the tea and sugar to, I learned all sorts of what you'd call old wives' tales, about what brought you good luck and what brought you bad. You were supposed to wear your new clothes for the first time on a Sunday and if you didn't, then sorrow and sackcloth would follow. It was bad luck to turn your mattress or to change your sheets or to cut your nails on a Friday or on a Sunday. It was bad luck if you were going to market and chanced to meet a cross-eyed person. Should you do so, you were supposed to go all the way back home and start out all over again. And a bride should on no account be married in green. There were all kinds of things to do with the moon. When the first sign of the new moon was seen, women ought to curtsey towards it and men ought to turn over any coin they might have in their pocket. If the moon was seen lying on its back, that was a sign of bad weather, but up on its tail, at harvest-time particularly, was sure sign of good weather. And they always used to say that if you sowed seeds under a new moon they'd grow best of all. Strange tales, weren't they, for a London girl to carry in her head but, then, I've always felt I was part of Ashdon too.

*   *   *

Another of Ashdon's nonagenarians I was lucky enough to interview in 1971 was *Emily Ford*, mother of the so-called 'Dry Bread' Ford of whom Spike Mays makes somewhat spiteful fun in *Reuben's Corner*. She was as annoyed over this as she was over the fact that she had recently broken her leg and was temporarily unable to cycle in to Saffron Walden and back for her shopping:

I can remember when we went to school in Ashdon in the 1880s that the new school hadn't long been built. The oldest child in each family had to pay twopence a week for schooling and the younger ones had to pay a penny each. Every Monday was the paying-day. That was hard for my mother to find some of the times. My father worked on the land and when we were going to school, his weekly wage was nine shillings. There was four children in my family, so that was fivepence every week going out on schooling.

I'd got an old grandmother still alive then and the Parish was supposed to be keeping her. She used to get two shillings and a loaf every week. Mr Drane, the Relieving Officer, would come over from Radwinter to give that out. I used to have to get that for her once a week from a shop behing Mr Moss's. Often that Parish loaf just wasn't fit to eat. She couldn't eat it sometimes it was so bad. Must've been made out of stinking flour, people said. People complained so much about it that in the end, it got done away with altogether and they just had the money.

Mind you, our Granny was luckier than some poor people. She was living with us then same as I'm living with my daughter-in-law now, and our mother always used to bake her own bread. Her mother taught her how to do it and my mother taught me. That's something you don't ever forget. We used to have a bushel of flour every week and we children would have to fetch the yeast all the way over from Linton before we went off to school. That was four miles there and four miles back again. We'd bake enough to see us through the week in one go. I can remember it like it was yesterday how she'd go about making her bread. She'd first of all mix her dough and knead it good and proper in her 'keeler'. That's what you'd call a trough, I suppose. That would be like the night before the baking part of it. All the old water and flour and yeast would all be mixed in together and over the top would go the lid of the keeler. And I'll tell you something you might not believe. She'd put little bits of sack on top of that lid for to weigh it down but still, next morning, that lid would have been pushed right up by that old mixture rising. The next thing would be to shape up the dough and get it ready for goin' into the oven. And all this time the oven would be gettin' stoked up ready for the dough to be put in. In those times, you wouldn't have no thermometer on the outside to tell you when it was hot enough. What you had built into the oven was a 'watch-and-tell-tale'. Don't expect you've heard tell of that, have you? Well, that was a special little old stone from off the fields and that was in the side of the oven wall. That little stone used to change colour when the oven got hotter and hotter. When it turned real red then you'd know it was the time for to put your dough in. You'd rake out those hot old embers into the space underneath and give the floor of your oven a quick goin'-over with a sort of mop arrangement. You'd have to be sure to use lots and lots of water. Then you'd push them old loaves in, one at a time, always on the end of a long wooden spoon. And after that, you'd just wait for them loaves to be done. The smell was wonderful as they was a-bakin' but the taste, the *first* taste, was nicest of all. When the loaves was ready to come out, she'd slide them out, one at a time, neat as you like, and put them on our table to cool down. And as they was cooling, perhaps she'd pop a few potatoes in the embers to bake. That was as good as a feast, that was.

My father's money was small but we always managed somehow. We got enough to eat and that was good natural food. Cottage people in those days used to have an iron bar go across the opening of the chimney, and they always used to have what you call a trunnel on that. That's like a chain and hook. And they'd have a boiler and that'd be hung on this hook. All your meals would be cooked in that old boiler: your meat and your vegetables, and those vegetables would all be cooked in a separate bag. That way, you always got all the goodness of the vegetables naturally. Things was a bit cheaper in them days, of course. There was such a time when I married, just after the Boer War ended, when you could get, say, mutton for fourpence a pound, beef for sixpence a pound, and pork for about fivepence a pound. Round about that time, rents were about half a crown a week.

Half a crown a week was quite a bit out of a working man's wages then but, at least, we was lucky to have a house at all. In those days, there used to be no end of people on the roads, walking, walking, walking. Whole families of them just travelling on, from nowhere to nowhere, just nomads. They'd no home, no job, nothing, nowhere. They used to go to St. James's Workhouse at Walden. That was called the Union then. They'd go there for the night and then they'd have to be on their way the next day, another fourteen miles, to spend the night after at Kedington. None of us liked it when they came through Ashdon. They used to beg on the roads, you see, beg for a scrap of bread or hot water for a cup of tea or even for some coppers. That was a mistake to give them anything if they was to knock at your door. Give anything to a nomad at your door and you might as well open it to the whole tribe.

They talk about the 'good old days' but they wasn't all that good for a lot of folk. Mind you, I don't want to complain myself. I've had a long life and it's often been a hard life but I don't know that I've got a lot to regret, not really. I wouldn't want to go back to the start again, though. I think all the changes there've been have made life easier for ordinary folk. One thing that seems to have dropped out, though, are the things you did on special days, same as on St. Valentine's Day, when girls would put bay leaves under their pillows the night before, like, and they'd hope they'd have a dream of the boy they was going to marry. Nowadays, they might get a fancy card from Woolworth's but it isn't the same. And on Good Friday, we was always told you wasn't supposed to use nails or iron tools because it would mean bad luck. Nowadays, nobody bothers. We was always told that it was good luck to step on the first daisy of the year and bad luck to cut holly. And rosemary growing outside the house meant the woman there was the boss of it.

They're asking me to keep going till I reach a hundred but I always say I don't feel I want to be a hundred, really, I don't want to let all my feelings, all my knowledge slip away. I don't want to be deaf and I don't want to be mental. I want to know who I am and where I am. And I'd like to ride to Walden on my bike again.

Emily Ford died in 1973.

*   *   *

In that same autumn of 1971, soon after the death of her husband Walter, one of the greatest heroes of the Labour group in Ashdon, I interviewed *Hilda Marsh* in her trim little cottage beside the Labour Club Hall she'd helped to build and spent much of her life in helping to run:

One of the big differences, I'd say, between the old times and now is how much earlier the day used to start. When I started going to the village school here at the turn on the century, I remember my father had to get to work by five in the morning to mow the barley. They'd start so early because it mowed easier with the scythe when the dew was on it. Sometimes they'd still be working out there by moonlight.

Another difference between then and now, I think, is how much more children was expected to do in the home compared with now. When I was still quite a little girl, I recall I had to do all the dusting and I'd have to get the kindling sticks ready for next morning. I had also to fetch the milk from Newnham Hall farm before I went off to school. It was nearly a mile for me to go up Dorvis Lane and a mile back. You had to go whatever the weather, even if there was snow on the ground. I'd fetch it in a tin can which held about a quart and we used to get that nearly full for a penny. I can still see the old lady skimming the milk in her farm-dairy. There'd be a great round pan full of milk with all the cream on top. The cream used to be skimmed off with a skimmer which was a round ladle with little holes in it, and that cream would be put on one side to make butter. But the milk that was left was just as good as any milk you'll drink today. Mother used regularly to make us a nice rice pudding from that and that's something we all enjoyed.

Money was scarce for working people before the First World War but none of us starved in the country. You'd be all right if you knew how to manage. Some families would try to keep a pig which they'd buy from the farmer. They'd buy the meal to feed it from the farmer also but they weren't always able to pay for that, so when the pig was ready for killing, it would have to be sold back to the farmer to pay for the meal. My mother was a good manager and when father bought our pig, she found ways of keeping down its food bill. She'd boil up the very small potatoes and the peel and the cores of things to mix with the meal. When it was fat enough, weighing about seven or eight stone, it was killed in our home by the village butcher, Mr Arthur Moss. He was very particular and clean. The pig would be hung on two large hooks in the kitchen and the next day, Mr Moss would come back and cut it up into pieces. Some of these we'd sell to pay the rent. Mother always managed to keep back at least a quarter. She'd cure a nice ham and a nice piece of bacon; there'd also be the head, the pluck and other odd bits and pieces, all of which was a great treat to us. When they'd been cured, the ham and bacon tasted much better to anything you'd eat today.

We learned a lot just watching Mother but she also taught us things. She taught us cooking and she also taught us needlework, my sisters and me. I can remember we used to have to sit there of an evening, by the fire, and she'd give us some old pieces of rag and tell us to hem that round for a duster. That's how we were learned to sew. We'd be sat around sewing for hours. One of my sisters, she didn't like it, so Mother said, 'Well, if you don't do that, you'll just have to go to bed.' And she'd go to bed: she *wouldn't* do it.

I wouldn't say my parents were strict, really, but we used to have to do what we were told. Our mothers had to obey the rules also. If they was to meet the rector or gentry out in the village, then they'd always have to curtsey. On Sunday, us children had to go to Church three times: we'd have to go with Grandmother in the morning; there'd be the children's service in the afternoon, and then we'd have to go again with Mother at night. We couldn't get out of it, no matter how hard we tried. We *had* to go.

At Christmas, we didn't have all the presents children have today. If Mother bought us anything special, it'd be something. We had a new frock once in two years and if you should tear it between times then that just had to be patched or mended. She used to fill our stockings — well, they was never really *full* — she used to put a few nuts in, an orange and an apple, and, if we were lucky, perhaps a chocolate mouse. On Christmas Day itself, we'd have a good plum pudding and a nice piece of beef. They were happy times.

I think we were more happy growing up than the children are now. We made our own pleasure. We knew it was no good wanting the moon because we couldn't have it. So we didn't need to fret.

*   *   *

Up on the hill beside the village church, set far back from the road behind a rampart of trees, stands Ashdon Hall, home of *Brigadier Thomas Collins*. I interviewed him many times either in the drawing room, beside a deep-set log fire, or in his oak-lined dining room, hung with oil portraits of his family:

I was born in London in 1905 but I feel my roots are in Ashdon because we moved here when I was three years old and Ashdon Hall has been our family home ever since. I've no direct recollection of that first arrival but, it would appear, my parents drove over from Audley End to Ashdon in a Victoria four-wheeled carriage. When this got to the foot of Chalk Hill, on the road from Saffron Walden, they got out to make life easier for the pony. The driver at this point seemed to forget about his passengers because he proceeded steadily on his way. My father naturally shouted to attract his attention but it was a waste of breath: the driver was stone-deaf. My parents walked the rest of the way.

To what extent this particular incident affected my father's subsequent thinking I wouldn't care to estimate, but he it was who, not long afterwards, took the initiative in making the trains stop at Ashdon. When we first came to the village, such trains as there were used to go straight through along the single track between Saffron Walden and Bartlow Junction. My father decided it would be a good plan for the train to stop at some convenient access-point and selected the level-crossing where Fallowdon Lane and the railway-track inter-sected. He approached the Great Eastern Railway authorities who came up with the idea that would-be passengers should contribute twelve pounds each towards the cost. The other villagers weren't exactly overjoyed at this part of the scheme so, in the end, my father paid the bill himself. In addition, he guaranteed that he would travel first-class (which was his wont, anyway). The outcome of these dealings was *Ashdon Halt*. It consisted of a short stretch of platform, about twenty yards in length, a disused railway carriage, minus its inner partitions, which served as a shelter for the passengers, and two oil lamps inscribed with the name *Ashdon* on the inside of the glass. My father used the Halt every day of his working week and it would be accurate to describe hime as the very first Ashdon commuter.

He needed to commute regularly up to London because he had a solicitor's practice there. He was a perfectly competent solicitor but I don't think his heart was ever really in the Law: he often omitted to send accounts to his clients and never seriously stirred himself to make a great go of it. What he passionately would like to have been was a professional soldier and I'm convinced he'd have been an extremely good one. To his lasting disappointment, however, this was not to be. His father had been a professional soldier — a doctor-soldier, in fact — so he wasn't especially wealthy. There were five sons and the eldest of these decided to go into the Army too. In Victorian times, this inevitably meant that the family had to provide a deal of financial support and it was just not feasible for any of the other sons to follow a military career. Another son, again senior to my father, became the family artist. As you might suppose, he too had to be propped up with family funds though he, in fact, became commercially successful. I still have the most successful of his books in my library, *Cathedral Cities of England*, *Cathedral Cities of Spain* and what have you, all painted by him. He was a very competent watercolourist and quite popular in his day, without a doubt. However, in my opinion, my father was really the better artist. Some of his drawings are quite exquisite and he was particularly good at illustrating the letters he sent me when I was away at school.

He never really lost sight of those two careers which were denied him so it's somehow appropriate, I suppose, that he was a volunteer in the Artists' Rifles. He communicated his lifelong enthusiasm in both these areas to me, as well as his considerable knowledge about wine and all of this has undoubtedly enriched the quality of my life.

It's probably no accident that a certain number of the clearest memories of my Ashdon childhood have a distinctly military flavour. We were relatively isolated here as we grew up because there weren't many children close at hand with whom we associated: there was nobody at the Rectory and Eric Pelly, at Waltons Park, was already at University. However, once every two or three months, we might perhaps go into Saffron Walden for a children's party. We'd invariably travel in our wagonette, a splendid four-wheeled vehicle with a removable top which was raised or lowered from a pulley in our coach-house. I can remember a summer fancy-dress party at Walden Place which was then the home of the Tukes, the big banking family. I think I must have been about six years old at the time and I was dressed as a Grenadier Guardsman. The uniform was an absolutely meticulous reproduction down to the last particular because my father had a genuinely scholarly interest in military uniforms (something I've tried to keep up myself) and insisted that it should be just right. My sister went as a *vivandière*, one of those ladies who attended to the needs of French soldiers wounded on the battlefield and her gear was authentic too. We were both awarded prizes which, at the time, rather astounded us. I remember that I was also dressed up in military uniform when we 'drilled' and 'paraded' the boys at the local Waifs' and Strays' Home here, an occasion which, I think, was enjoyed by all, as the saying goes.

My sister and I used to go out regularly for walks, usually round the outskirts of the village, with our nursery governess and I still remember with great clarity one particular walk when I must have been quite small. We were going along the Glebe, the large field which stands between Ashdon Hall and the Rectory. A soldier came marching towards us. He was dressed in bright scarlet which, in those days, was the standard colour of the walking-out uniform. He must have been a local man home on leave. I remember that the clouds were massed in the sky behind him and their particular formation looked, to my child's eye, just like a fort. In fact, I thought it really *was* a fort and that the soldier was marching out from inside it. The next day, we went for another walk along the same path and our governess was somewhat nonplussed — as, indeed, I was — to discover that the fort was no longer there. I couldn't understand where it had gone.

Not *all* my early memories of Ashdon have a military flavour. Other memories, interestingly enough, have to do with *water*. For years, we always used to draw water from our own well which is something like forty eight feet deep. There's an even deeper well in the Church yard, next door, which is said to be eighty feet deep. In this part of the village, the water comes up through a deep layer of gravel and it's quite the most beautiful water I've ever drunk anywhere. At the hottest part of the summer, you'd pump water up which straightaway frosted the outside of the jug: it was so cold.

When we first came to Ashdon Hall, the moat was quite overgrown. It was thick with bullrushes and full of very deep mud. If you had big enough waders, you could have walked straight across it. Way back, you see, this stretch of water served not only the original manor house but also the earliest village. Then the villagers decamped because of the Black Death, and the moat was reduced, in the course of time, to being a feature in an ornamental garden. A reverend gentleman called Mr Hammond made a really determined attempt to lay out the gardens half a century before we arrived here: he transformed the former manor orchard into a lawn, he planted a number of splendid trees which still flourish, he built walls here and there and he generally got the place into shape. My father decided to carry on Hammond's good work — just as I hope I've done in my turn — and soon after our arrival here, he decided that the moat needed to be reclaimed and that the way to do this was to mobilize the local work-force. The first move was to summon the village Fire Brigade. Five splendid chaps arrived in their Keystone uniforms, gleaming brass helmets, long blue coats and all, and brought with them a hand-pump. In the course of three evenings' vigorous activity, they got most of the water out and revealed an impressive display of the most splendid mud. To cope with this, a force of some twenty five chaps from the village was deployed. They put rows of planks across the mud and up the bank and they wheeled their barrow-loads into the adjoining meadow where it was dumped in little heaps all over the place. It was wonderful stuff, as good as Bassett slag. I remember watching those men performing: a most impressive sight it was. The chap who impressed me as much as anything was a Mr Chapman. There seem always to have been Chapmans in this village. They were always dark and strong and sinister, the Chapmans, a cheerful lot, and this particular representative of the breed was a particularly rough, tough creature who seemed to me immense. He really did impress me and seemed to have everyone and everything under control except for a brief moment, when one chap, somewhat less impressive than Mr Chapman, parted company with his wheelbarrow on his way up the planking. Anyhow, they dug the whole thing out. I don't think it took very long and I'm sure it wouldn't have cost all that much. At any rate, the operation was quite clearly on in those days. Now that nature's trying to claim the moat back again, the operation will, equally clearly, never be on again. The moat doesn't seem likely to have much of a future.

I can still recall, quite vividly, the great hailstorm which struck the village in May 1913. Thick, black cloud built up directly overhead and we heard a dull rumbling noise approaching steadily from the distance which built up into the most colossal crescendo mingled with the sounds of shattering glass. Those hailstones were phenomenal, some were a good five or six inches round. Greenhouses were smashed to pieces all round the village and there's a photograph on record of a hole that was driven through the straw hat of a local publican who would, I hope, have temporarily discarded it. As soon as the storm had passed, my sister and I ventured forth to pick up some of the prize hailstones and my mother came out

Dorothy and Tom Collins displaying hailstones after the great storm of 1913

and photographed us. The photograph was printed in *The Daily Mirror* on 29th May 1913, the only time, I believe, we've graced the pages of that particular paper.

I have some rather less dramatic memories of Ashdon before the First World War. Going to Church on Sundays was a weekly ceremonial for the whole village. It was very much a social occasion, with everyone on parade, and everyone dressed in their Sunday best. Most of the villagers walked a very long way. One simply had to be there. I wasn't, at that time, all that keen to attend myself. I looked on it as something of an ordeal and I used to march in, behind my parents, with a fair degree of diffidence. Mr Banham was our parson in those days, admirable at his job in many ways if rather tedious in the pulpit. He sang in a very fine bass voice and the village schoolmaster, Mr Tuck, was a superb tenor. The choir was quite excellent, larger and better, I suppose, than it's ever been since: there were always a dozen boys from the Waifs' and Strays' Home and at least a dozen men. They put a great deal into their singing then; I'm told that choir practices used to go on into the winter till the lady organist's fingers were just too frozen to play another note. I'd dearly like to hear their music again because I suspect I'd appreciate it more now than ever I did then.

What I did appreciate at the time, and what I still clearly remember, was the village Flower Show. This took place once a year, always in high summer, and it was staged over in the ground of Waltons Park. You'd see handbills advertising the forthcoming event on display around the village for weeks before the event. Everyone hoped it would keep fine. The village Fire Brigade would turn out in all their finery and would invariably give a demonstration of how you squirted water at things. I can't remember whether they were ever called upon to put out a fire, or how they responded to such a call if it came, but they *looked* very splendid. There was a thing called the 'greasy pole' which was something like a telegraph pole fixed into the ground and liberally coated with thick grease of some sort: if you managed to climb to the top, you won, I believe, a leg of mutton. There was also a greasy pig, a small specimen covered in the same thick grease which was let loose at the appropriate moment. It inevitably ran into the crowd and the ladies always screamed as the men dived about trying to catch the pig which became the property of whoever managed to cling on to it. Then there was 'tilting the bucket', when a rider, in a wheelbarrow was armed with a long pole, which he had to drive, while being pushed in a sitting position, through a ring fixed beneath a bucket of water suspended from a frame: the water invariably came cascading down over wheelbarrow, rider and pusher alike. There was the usual racing for the village children, a tug-of-war match for the men and, of course, since it was supposed to be a *Flower* Show, the judging of the flowers and vegetables. There was always an atmosphere of great gaiety about that day: I've no doubt that this had everything to do with the fact that the participants were actively creating their own amusement and not passively observing amusement served up by other people. At all events, it now seems part of a vanished world.

For all that, the village wasn't *always* quite so united or quite so peaceful. Politics regularly made the temperature rise in those days, more so, perhaps, than it does today. On polling day, one decked oneself up as a matter of course. The big rival parties then, of course, were the Conservatives, whose colour was blue, and the Liberals, whose colour was yellow. We were Conservatives, as you might suppose, and I can remember how we used to drive in our pony and trap into Saffron Walden to hear the result of the poll announced. There'd be a bright blue rosette on the whip, one on either side of the pony's head collar, bright blue rosettes in the men's button-holes and along the side of the trap. If you happened to meet a group of Liberals along the way, sporting their yellow favours, they booed you and this caused the pony to behave in an unsatisfactory manner. On the other hand, if you should pass a group of Conservatives, they cheered you, and this had exactly the same effect on our pony which was a highly-strung creature. Going to the poll in these circumstances was, you'll therefore appreciate, a surprisingly hazardous undertaking.

It wasn't necessarily any less hazardous travelling by motor-car when politics were involved, at any rate here in Ashdon. When I was a boy here, there was only one motor-car in the whole village. It belonged to the Pellys at Waltons Park and was a rather splendid machine. It was a Rolls Royce, as you might expect, and what I particularly remember about it was the immensely strong running-boards on either side of it. After our election meetings down in the centre of the village, the locals were inclined, in those days, to be somewhat rougher than they are today: *they threw stones*. Because of this, when the car set out on its way back up the hill towards Ashdon Hall, certain precautions had to be taken: the men in the party — my father, Major Pelly and two others — stood, two at each side, on the running-boards while the chauffeur prepared to negotiate the hill. The men remained standing on the running-boards all the way back here to ensure that if stones were thrown in the direction of the car, the ladies sitting inside wouldn't be showered with broken glass.

All of this was, you might say, part of my *general* education. My more formal education also began in Ashdon because we were taught, in the first instance, at home by a succession of nursery governesses. They taught us writing and arithmetic and, needless to say, French, for which a series of French governesses were engaged. We were obliged to talk French throughout meal-times and on other occasions too. We didn't react altogether creditably to this. French governesses are, I suppose, a reasonable target for tiresome children and my sister and I were tiresome enough in all conscience. We became progressively more obstreperous in fairly short time and in 1913, I was sent off to a very good prep. school called Roydon Hall, at Diss, near Norwich. There, I quickly discovered that the other boys knew no French at all. This made me feel ashamed at having learned so much so I proceeded to drop it very smartly indeed and to pretend I knew no French at all. I've long been convinced that I spoke very much better French in Ashdon, at the age of seven, than I've done anywhere else ever since.

*   *   *

Anybody tempted to make some ideological point about the obvious contrast between the Ashdon childhood of Brigadier Collins and that of the other villagers so far considered would do well to ponder the lifetime he went on to spend in the public service. After further education at Haileybury and Sandhurst, he was commissioned into the Green Howards, served as a Staff Officer in the Second World War and, like so many of his kind, on leaving the Army, devoted himself to local government at both parish and county level. He has put back into the community rather more than he has taken out of it and the same is true of his sister Dorothy who worked for years as an *aide* to the Duke of Norfolk before returning to Ashdon as a long-serving local Councillor. I interviewed her in her old-world cottage near the reputedly haunted Lady Well:

We didn't have what you'd call a large clientèle of domestics at Ashdon Hall at any one time. My mother was very good at training girls, so, you see, they'd stay for a little while, be trained and learn to better themselves. We had a succession of these and we had a succession of French governesses. As far as I remember, only one of these was really any good, the first one, and I learned what French I still know from her. I still believe I probably learnt more French than my brother did. He rather left things to me. He didn't make much effort to *read* French because I was able to manage the reading instead. There was very much a feeling that I wanted to show off and so I learned to read rather quickly when we were very young so that I could perform my party piece.

We were packed off to boarding-school rather early. On reflection, I don't think that's *quite* the way I'd like to put it: we weren't exactly 'packed off', we weren't hauled away kicking and screaming; we were quite keen to go, in fact. There weren't any children of our age in the village to associate with on anything like a regular basis. That's not to say we felt lonely: there was always plenty to keep us busy and happy. No, it was rather that my brother, at the ripe old age of eight, decided he couldn't be taught by any more females. 'Mam'selle's no good', he said, 'she doesn't know the difference between a partridge and a pheasant.' So off we went to boarding-school — Tom to Diss, and me to Norwich. I'm still very grateful to my parents for sending me away because one really did appreciate one's home when one came back to it.

I appreciated coming back to the village too, then as always. I was very much aware of Ashdon being there as we were growing up even though our home wasn't altogether in the centre of it. As children, we used to go out for a walk regularly with our governess every day, and the views of the woods and fields somehow become part of you. Things I remember specially clearly are the different tools they used for farm-work in those days: when they threshed beans in our barn here, up at the Hall, they'd use a flail — a couple of sticks with a thong between, and when they mowed the hay, there would be a team of men, advancing steadily, one behind the other, each with a scythe.

* * *

One of those scythes might well have been wielded by *Herbert Farrant* whom I was fortunate enough to be able to interview on three separate occasions in 1971 and who provided a particularly full and detailed account of what it was like to be a young farm worker before the turn of the century. He was the very first Ashdonian I interviewed, in the tiny cottage he'd occupied for fifty years. It was a most inexpert interview from the technical point of view and his rich Essex accent is sometimes barely audible above the ticking of his clock and the purring of his cat:

Now Wal Marsh is gone, I'm supposed to be the oldest man livin' in Ashdon. I weren't born here, though. I were born in Bumpstead in 1883 and I come to Ashdon when I started school. Can't rightly till you much 'bout when I was *that* small but I remember my grandfather used to take me to Camps Fair. We used to *have* to see that. That were a three day pleasure-fair. Some of 'em would make a real feast of it. Used to buy a pig at sich a time in the season so's they could kill that for the Fair. If you was one o' them *lucky* ones went the right time — get me? — ye'd get yer beans, yer potatoes, yer plum pudden and yer pork.

My father never said much about when he were a boy hisself. Did say as how his own father's wage on the land was six shillin' a week. One mornin', his mother give him half a farthen and sent 'im down road for to get a quarter of a farthen's worth of tea. When he got there, he forgot whether it was half a farthen or a quarter 'e was to git. Thought 'e'd best git the half to make sure. When he got home and put that on the table, his mother swore 'e should've got just the quarter. Got his father's belt fer that, then 'e 'ad to go back and get that changed. that were a way to live, weren't it? Don't suppose you ever see a quarter or a half a farthen? Had the quarter for years and years till someone had it from me box. Give the half to me granddaughter. Be worth a bit more'n that today.

My father was a shepherd. When I was small, I remember he used to wear his smock. That were made out of linen. Two big pieces on't sewed up each side o' him. And he'd go off wi' his old crook. That had a long wooden handle, that did, and there was this old curved iron bit at the end. Lambin' time was one of his busy times. Sometimes then he never did come back home. Slept out in the fields then, he did. Had a little hut. But the shearin' time was his *real* busy time. Course, that was like his harvest-time, worn't it?

I went to school chiefly in Ashdon. School was never no trouble to me. Happen we had been in the second standard twelve months. When we shifted up, I had learnt more'n the other, so I jumped a class at the finish. My mother and father used to say I could go to school till I was twenty if I wanted. I said, 'How you goin' to keep me?' 'Well', they said, 'we keep you now, we can keep you then, surely!' But I didn't want to. I was crazy to start work, couldn't grow up quick enough. Smokin' a pipe, my mate and I was, when we was still at the school in Ashdon here. Must've been all of eight or nine. We used to have to go to the railway arch in Rectory Lane to fetch the newspapers fust thing in the mornin'. Threw 'em off the train they did in a bundle. In the bushes they'd go regular. My mate come from Church End. He always was there first. He'd light up the pipes so mine'd be ready drawin' when I got there. Got larruped for it once. Someone must've told on us. Mother said, 'No tea for you', she said, 'you can get to bed. Your father'll be up directly.' He was too, belt'n all. But I lived to tell the tale!

When I was thirteen, I started work at Broadysh Farm out Radwinter way. That were two miles there, all winds and weathers, and that were two miles back agin at night. Six in the mornin' I had to be there till six at night-time. I walked twenty four miles a week and when I held out my hand for my pay on Saturday night, I had the large amount to come of two shillings. That's what it stayed till I got to sixteen and then it went up to three shillings and six. That were a way to live, worn't it! A farmer I went to once, he said that it didn't matter how good a man you was and you was single, if you was workin' beside a married man, he would always get a shillin' a week more than you. Get married and you get your shilling more. That's to say, a wife is worth one bob a week. That's how they looked at it. Country life!

After I was three or four years at Broadysh we all went to work at Belchamp St. Paul's. My father was to be shepherd and my brothers and me was ploughmen. The foreman had offered us another shillin' a week to go there. We all went over, but when I started there, this foreman said, 'Herbert', he said, 'I can't give you your extra shilling a week because it's the winter. I've altered me mind', he said, 'and you'll just have to put up with it.' So I did for a time. Straight off, I had to plough twenty five acres of bean-stubble up. I didn't go off so early as the others. I had to get one of my horses with cart-harness on to fetch a load of straw out of the stackyard. Then I had to uncollar that again and get ready to plough. This old foreman said to me, 'You know where you left your plough, Herbert." He said, 'You'll see where that's stood by the road. You can't go wrong if you stop where your horse stops.' Well, my owd horse goes off and I lets it keep a-goin' and the first place it stops by itself is the public house. What I din't know was this foreman had been followin' us on behind in his own pony and trap. He come in behind laughin'. He said, 'I'll pay for that pint of your'n'. He said, 'You done just what I told you to do.' Had a glass of bitter, he did. Paid for mine 'n all. After he'd finished, he said, 'Well, I'll be a-goin. You won't make that mistake the next time.'

There weren't no next time. No with he. Come up to my father few months after. He said, 'Shepherd', he said, 'if the gov'nor come round to you any time and ask how many lambs you got, don't tell him the proper amount. Jest say, 'somewhere about twenty or thirty lambs.' He said, 'I'll have the rest meself.' My father told us he said to that foreman, 'I've been a shepherd all my life', he said, 'and I never been asked that question before.' 'And I shan't do that now to please *you*." Foreman said, 'You won't?' 'No', father said, 'no I shan't.' He said, 'That ain't been my way, never.' Know what that foreman done then? Put 'is 'and in 'is pocket, give my father a month's pay and the odd days what 'ed got to come and give him the sack straight away. My older brother come — he's under the dust now these ever so many year — he told me they'd got the sack too. He said, 'He's coming up to see you next.' I said, 'I don't care if he do.' I said, 'Time I tied these two bits of wood up, I said, I can get a job anywhere on a farm.'

He did come for me then. I stopped on for five weeks more. You see, there were plenty of houses I knew in the village where there was always a spare bedroom. The owners would take in lodgers. This poor owd girl I stopped with, she had an allowance from the parish. She could keep a lodger for the one month but not longer. I durstn't stop any longer in case they took her allowance off. What'd I do then? I don't want to say that wrong . . . Well, then I went up to London. I trained to be a slater and tiler. I only did about a quarter of my apprenticeship. I done so well they put me on a fully-fledged worker. The furthest out I went was Fleet, other side of Aldershot. I was putting tiles on a bank they built there. There hadn't been one in the place. We could see the soldiers paradin' from up where I was workin' and there were old tram-lines there right down one side of the road to fetch the soldiers backwards and forwards. Never thought to be a soldier myself. Came back to the land after a couple of year because I was broke.

Soon after that it was I met my wife. Met her at Camps Fair where my grandfather used to take me. I went to that fair to see some old mates. I was havin' a good chin-wag with one and he asked me to go to a pub with him. I said, 'Not now.' I said, 'I'll just walk round the fair first. I'll see you in quarter of an hour.' Quarter of an hour? Half a day more like! On the way round, I first met Minnie. She'd been working in a little tuck shop in Watford then her old mother asked if she'd come back home to Camps. I said to Minnie, I said, 'You had to come here from Watford to meet me, and I had to come back from London to meet you.' Like it was all arranged.

We was courting for four years and we was married in Camps. The regular owd parson was on holiday when we got married but he come to see us when we'd been married about six month. I looked out of the window and I said, 'Here come the Rev. C.H. Pearson. Comin' *here* by the look on't.' He were in his pony and trap. I stood still at the window then, just afore he stops, I goes out in the road. I ties up his pony to the fence. I ask him in and I ask him to sit down. He done so. We sit and talk a little while then he says, 'Minnie, I've come to bring you your marriage fee back because you've been a good girl.' That meant she weren't in trouble when she were wed. Many's the baby what's arrived just in time for a slice of his mother's weddin' cake. They reckon that were a disgrace to the parish. Minnie was all right, though, so she had her ten shilling and she could buy what she liked with it. Can't rightly recall what she spent that on. Grub, most like.

After we come back to Ashdon for good, I worked on the farm mostly. Did a bit of diggin' over at Bartlow once but I din't go much on that. Diggin' in the churchyard, we was, me an' Fred Rawson who lived at the 'Bonnett' pub. Had to go down nine foot, we did. They wanted to put three coffins in. The pick we took over there, that got bent, so you know that were tough enough. And we got seven skulls out of that one place. 'Course, there'd been a war there, they do say, years and years ago. We reckoned they'd just been dumped in there. I got one out whole. I said to my mate, I said, 'I'll jest see if I can get that one out.' I did too. He got a full set of teeth in. That was somethin' to dig out, warn't it? And the man what done 'em afore us, he opened a grave where there'd been a corpse put in. Hadn't been put down deep enough so his tool went right through the top of this coffin. Course, all the wossname spewed up all over him, out on it. And he never done no more. That put he off. He told us so hisself. That's how we come to get that job. *I* didn't stay long neither.

Mostly I did farm-work. I'll tell you what I said to a farmer once when I asked him for a job. He asked me what could I do on the farm. I said, 'Anything on the farm bar one job and I wouldn't do that at no price.' 'Oh', he said, 'and what's that?' I said, 'Go in the house and serve your missus' . . . Get me? Servin' the mare, I meant . . . In my time, I did just about everything else on the farm. At the start, I'd have to clean up the ploughs and the harrows. Sometimes I'd have to polish up the harness. Them little old brass studs had to shine. Crikey, they did! Weedin', hedgin', ditchin', hoein' — I done all those. Done my share o' ploughin' too. I walked many a mile to plough an acre. For to plough an acre, I reckon I'd have to walk about ten mile. I found out the length o' one furrow, see, then I worked that out. Ploughin' was never no trouble to me. I liked walkin' behind my pair of horses: the one would always walk up the unploughed bit of land, the other would walk along your furrow. And that one would allus go nice and dainty, real neat little old steps. Like a little owd maid goin' to Church.

Sowin' I didn't reckon much on in the old times. Knew you'd done a day's work after that. You'd have to go backwards across the field with your dibbers. Dibber had a handle, about three foot long it was, and that's what you made your holes with for your seed. Two lines o' holes you made at the one go, right 'cross the field. As you went across, one of the others would follow you across and drop the old seeds in your holes. Then that had to be covered over with your harrow. I remember once the rain tipped down about twenty four hours. I'd been harrowin' this ground for barley. When he went on it after that rain, there was nothin' there to cover the barley up with . . . All been washed off. So they had to skim it over again. You'd a' said it was ploughed where they'd pulled that owd cart. That come up in the end, though. Somehow . . .

Threshin' was one of the big winter jobs. Sometimes you was lucky to be took on. The farmer could pick and choose then who he liked. Different from harvest — *then* he could never get enough on us. I've threshed with a flail in my time and I'd like to have a pound put in my hand for every day I've threshed with a *drum*. That was hard work but you may depend that warmed you up in the winter. Hard work never killed me. Used to like when hay-making come round. Way back, we used to go out like a team. All in a line we'd go, slantwise 'cross the field. The front one was leader. When he stopped to sharpen his scythe, you'd all stop. You'd all be a-sharpenin' together. Real bit of rough music, that'd be. I remember when Tilbrook lived up at Goldstones Farm before Furze come. (There used to be an owd windmill up there in the old days. There was the wooden post-mill that still stands and there was this other one. Made of brick that was. There was a long belt to drive it and the engine stood over in a dry shed. They used to say there wasn't enough wind in Ashdon to drive the *two* so that one had to have its engine.) I was workin' in one of the fields next to Tilbrook's stackyard. He looked over the hedge. He said, 'There's eight on you there', he said, 'and there's only two good scythesmen out on the lot of ye.' I stopped just then. I said, 'What's that you say, Master Tilbrook?' I said, 'If I come up to your house, will you get me some beer?' He said, 'Get you some beer? You come up here', he said, 'and you'll get this stick more like.' Anyway, I *went*. I knew I was one of them two scythesmen he'd meant. I went up with a two-gallon bottle. He stood out on the road. Just afore I got there, he give me a sign to go on round the yard. There's still the door there now where they used to pull the beer . . . Know what he done? He give me a pail of beer for me to drink the time he was drawin' them two gallons. I see some of the others was a-comin', so I got a move on and by the time he drawed the two gallons, my pail was empty . . . Like givin' an old sow swill, warn't it? I kind o' gave a half turn when I went back down the road but I kept on a-goin' till I made it back into the field. Anyway, when he come down the field an hour later, I was still a-mowin'. I showed 'im!

One of his men used to brew the beer once a year. That stood a year afore they put the tap in the barrel. He used to say, 'If you can stand and look in and see your photo in it, you may depend that'll be a drop o' good stuff.' That was too! Regular old brew that was. That used to *keep*. Don't get that with Benksin's now. Where's the malt gone they did the brewin' with then? Never did me no harm, that home-brew. *And* I was never in the Cage. The Cage was near where the telephone box is today. Like a little old garden shed, that were, but instead of walls it had these owd bars. The policeman'd lock 'em up in there all night sometimes if they'd drunk a bit too much. Sometimes he'd jest let 'em go in the mornin'. Sometimes they'd be took off to Walden.

There'd be extra beer at hay-makin and when you used to take the harvest. That'd happen this way. What happened was we'd choose our Lord of the Harvest. He had to make the deal with the farmer and he had to show us how fast we was to cut and when to stop for our grub. He was the one who kept all the largesse money. The one under him was called the Lady. He was your second in command as you might say. Come July, the team would get together and the Lord'd work out with the farmer what the deal was to be. The two on 'em would go round the fields, see if it was laid an' that, and fix a price for the harvest. That's what the price would be no matter how long it took. I remember owd Mrs Smith at Hill Farm always used to bring out half a Cheddar cheese. All the beer you could drink and you helped yourself to your cheese. I remember one day we settled the deal and we went up to where the beans was and we sat ourselves down all that day. Complained to her son about us, she did. 'Don't want to fret about *they*', he said, 'they never works the *fust* day'. We did the next day, though. Lord had us up there at five o'clock!

The best harvest I ever had I got on my own. Didn't need no owd Lord to make that deal. I were on my bicycle over at Camps one evening arter tea. It were just afore this farmer was to start his harvest. And he said, 'You want a job, hubby?' Wondered what he wanted *me* for. I got off my bicycle, real slow, and I walked back, real slow. He said, 'That'll be a cartin' harvest', he said, 'and that'll last about a fortnight. Come to £14.' I said, — not too fast, don't do to look *too* willin' — I said, 'Well, I think I'm goin' to take that. I know no one'll give me £14 over in Ashdon.' So I weren't in any Ashdon team *that* year. D'ye blame me?

When I started work fust, there weren't such a thing as a binder. You cut the corn with a scythe. You'd go over in a line, like for the hay-makin', with the owd Lord givin' the time. There'd be a woman or two behind each man and they'd tie that cut corn into shocks. About six of those shocks'd be stood up together and the owd sun and the owd wind ud dry it out. Then, after a bit, you'd cart those shocks over to the stackyard. They'd stand there till the tackle come round for the threshin'. Used to like to see those stacks all lined up. Looked better'n field of burnt stubble!

All the time we was workin' at the harvest, we had these rules to help us get the largesse money. You'd got to be there on time in the mornin' or you'd have a fine for that. You had to stand so far off if you wanted to wee, and if you blew off, you had to go so far off. And if you wanted to do the other part, you'd got be further than ever away. You hadn't to swear neither. If you broke any of those rules, you had to pay a fine. One old chap said he reckoned as how anyone who went on the booze and had to stay at home the next day when other folks was workin' should pay ten shillin' a day. Do you know, he was the fust one what went an' done it. Din't like it when he had to put out the ten shillin' hisself. He had to, though. That had been made a *rule*. If we saw someone we didn't know going along past the field and we was near enough, we'd all go over to the hedge and holler 'Largesse!' They was supposed to pay. The farmer was supposed to put something in the largesse kitty also. Old Mrs Smith never give us nothing one harvest. So we wished her the best of luck and said we hoped she'd have a good crop of thistles. She did too! Next time round, she couldn't pay up quick enough. (I'll tell you another tale about she. This was jest afore she was selling up. Her husband had been dead over two year. I stood talking to her near the house at Hill Farm. A few poor old hens come round us. They was these Light Sussex, you know, with the speckled necks. 'You poor dears', she said, 'I brought you here from Bowsers Farm right the other side of Ashdon thirty five years ago, and now I've got to sell you!' She never set those chickens up in proper coops you see. Those chickens of hers used to set theirselves out in the hedges. The new chicks come that way, the old uns died off all year round. Did she think they lived *forever*? And she was still hoping that one of those owd hens, creepin' about, might lay her one more egg. Something to wait for, wasn't it — *one* more egg!)

In the *real* old days, before the First World War, that's to say, we'd always celebrate the end of the harvest. That would start out on the field. When the last stock got pitched up on the cart, someone would holler '*That's* the Horkey one!' Then we'd take the harness off the trace-horse. We'd tie a bit of rope round its collar. The other end we'd tie to the bough of an owd tree. Oak was best if there should be one handy. That owd horse'd give a heave for us and as like as not you'd get a bit of bough off. That was your Horkey Bough. We'd sling that up on top of that last cart-load. We'd drink to that last sheaf and we'd drink to the Horkey Bough also. Then we'd go marchin' off back down to the stackyard. That's all gone now, of course. Been gone these many years. The Horkey Feast has gone too. That was what your largesse money was spent on, see? There'd be one feast at 'The White Horse', one at the 'Rose and Crown', one at 'The Fox', one over at 'The Bonnett' like as not. You could go to whichever one you liked. They used to cook the grub for it and dish it up. Always more'n enough to go round. There'd be plenty of beer, bread and cheese. There'd be a big bit of boiled bacon. If we'd got a tidy bit in the kitty, then there'd be a nice bit of beef or pork. There'd be a mouth-organ or a melodeon, maybe, you know, the old squeeze-box. No end of songs, there'd be. There weren't two songs alike. At the end, we used to finish up with an old hymn tune. Something about 'The day thou gavest, Lord, is ended . . .'

That was like the *year* not jest the day was ended but course, it weren't. Started off all over again then. At the start of the proper New Year, fust Monday after year started was Plough Monday. We collected like largesse money again then. We used to take our plough on a cart round the farms and the big houses. That owd plough'd be done up in ribbons. One would have a whip to crack and the rest on us would join in a chorus or two. I once or twice seen some on 'em dance. Once we went up Ricketts Farm, up Rectory Lane there. Tom Hagger was farmer there, that time. Said he wouldn't give us nothen. We give *him* somethin' though. Set our plough in the top-side of his front lawn and ploughed a furrow out, right down to the gateway. Don't suppose he forgot that in a hurry.

There's lots I've forgot and there's lots I remember. I don't reckon there's a man left in Ashdon now who's seen all the sights I seen. A powerful lot of changes on the farm there's been. A lot easier, you may depend, but it must be a lot lonelier, I reckon, shut up in one of them modern tractors. Lonely's somethin' I *never* was. I've had a good life. I allus remember when I was at Liverpool Street Station gettin' my ticket to come back here. Ticket clerk said, 'Where to mate?' I said, 'Ashdon Halt.' '*Ashdon?*' he said, 'Gawd help you!' Well, lookin' back at it all, I reckon He '*as!*

Herbert Farrant died in 1973.

Additional details were supplied by *Mary Goodwin*, a near contemporary of Herbert Farrant's, interviewed like him, in 1971, in her council house opposite the church:

I was born in Linton in 1884 and I went to the village school there till I was thirteen. Then I came to Ashdon and started work. My first job was at Old Sandon's Farm and I did the housework there for Mr and Mrs Smith. I used to live in at the farmhouse and my wage was one shilling a week. I stayed there till I was married five years later. My husband, John Goodwin, was the farm horse-keeper. We moved out to a two-up two-down cottage in Rock Lane. That's where we reared our family. We had six sons and six daughters and all but one of those children grew up. We lived in that cottage for sixty years and my son has it now. If I've got one ambition left now it's to move back out of this council house and back down to my cottage again. I expect I will.

You had to work real hard for your money in those days. My husband was horse-keeper to Mr Hagger at Hill Farm and he had to work extra long hours. Horses have to be looked after seven days every week, you see, week in and week out. And they'd be long days too. He'd have to get up at four in the morning and he'd go out at half past four. He had to feed and groom those horses ready for the men to take them out into the fields at six o'clock. His wage in those days — I'm talking about just before the War in 1914 — would be fourteen shilling a week. The other men would then have been getting twelve shilling a week.

My husband's money wasn't really enough for our size of family to live on so we used to do extra jobs, me, that is, and sometimes some of my children. For instance, I'd go out all day thinning mangolds. A tough old job, that was. You'd have to leave them just six inches apart and that had to be done with your bare hands and you'd have to go crawling along those rows on your knees. Mind you, we'd make things a little bit more comfortable by padding over our knees with bits of old sacking, like. Another weeding job we'd do was getting out docks. You had to get those old roots right out and that took a bit of doing when that ground was hard. And what you'd do was collect them in the front of your apron. And when that was full you'd take them over to the edge of your field. They'd all be heaped up and they'd be burnt.

Another way of getting just a few extra shillings was stone-picking. What you did for that was take a tin pail and go over the fields when the corn was just about two inches high and pick up all the big stones and middle-sized stones. And when your pail was full, you'd empty that on to your own special heap. It took a tidy lot of pails to make a load, something like eighty. The farmer paid you half a crown for every load and that was used for road-mending. I used to go nights as well as days to do stone-picking. The children would come sometimes and help me when they come out of school.

What I could do as well was strawberry-picking at Mr Charlton's place at Springfield near our cottage in Rock Lane. I think he was the first round these parts to try fruit-growing. I used to get up at four o'clock in the morning and I'd come back to the cottage to get my children off to school. I'd go back out in the fields after they'd gone to school and do more picking till it was time to get dinner for my husband and my boys. Then I'd pick some more in the afternoon.

Like lots of other people round about, I also went out gleaning. The first thing to remember was that you weren't to go into the field till the farmer had done carting and raking. If he meant for you to keep out, then he'd leave a big old stook stood standing out there in the middle of his field for you all to see. That was to warn you away and that was called the 'Policeman'. If there wasn't no 'Policeman', then you'd know it was all right to start the gleaning. But you didn't just start off anyhow. There was a special way of doing it. We'd have to choose a sort of foreman called the 'Queen' and that 'Queen's' job was to see we all started and finished at the same time and all had a fair crack of the whip. The 'Queen' would ring a bell for us to start off at about eight o'clock in the morning and we'd work on round till near on seven at night. And when the bell rang again, we'd all have to stop. Not that we needed much telling at that time. In the middle of the day, some of us would have to go back to get the men's dinners. But grans and children stayed out in the fields.

Most women would have a special sort of apron over their ordinary clothes and they'd collect up their corn in that. And some women had what we called a 'totty bag'. If you was collecting *long* heads of corn, you'd tie your stalks round with a special sort of knot. And you'd make a pile of these little tied-up bundles at the side of the field. And when the gleaning was done, the corn you'd got up was ground into flour. Some went to the local mill in Ashdon itself. We used to take ours to Barker's mill at Linton. We always found the gleaning flour came out brown so we'd mix it, half and half, with other flour we'd get from the bakery. We always baked all our own bread in those days and we used our own flour for it. Seemed to have a taste all its own. Must have been part of our own sweat, I shouldn't wonder.

Mary Goodwin died in 1974

*   *   *

My second-ever interview was with *Elsie Allgood*, also inexpert, because it took place in the Baptist Hall as preparations were busily in train for that evening's 1971 Harvest Supper:

I wish I could tell you more about the old times but I really don't remember *very* clearly. I can't even tell you the exact year I was born. Must have been around 1890 or so. Now, I *do* know mother had ten children, that I do know, and I know one died when he was just a baby and one died at five. So that left eight of us and I was the fourth one. My two eldest brothers had to pay a penny a week when they went to the village school here but *I* didn't have to pay. I loved schooldays best, simply loved them. My father's name was Pettit and he was shepherd to Mr Hagger. His wage was ten shillings a week most times but he got two shilling more if he worked Sundays. He'd get a bit more again at lambing time. That was threepence an hour, that was. I think there was something like three hundred sheep to look after in those days. He was always busy. A tidy number of lambs would always come round Christmas time so we'd sometimes not see him at home at all. Said he'd go nearly a fortnight without taking off his clothes or his boots. Had to stay out in the cold with his ewes and his lambs. They'd have been warmer than what he'd be, shouldn't wonder. And he'd know where they were born and when they'd been born. I must have been real hard work but I *know* he loved it. 'A good shepherd shears his sheep', he used to say, 'but it don't do to *flay* 'em.' Another thing I remember his saying was 'Good pastures make good sheep' or was it the other way round? Mostly he'd have to feed the sheep on things like turnips but he always reckoned those sheep would feed the ground back. The farmers must have thought so too because sometimes he'd have to take them miles away, right outside this village, to feed. He was a hard-working man and he was a good-living man. 'I get up with the lark and I go to bed with the lamb.' It did him no·harm at all. He was 94 when he died. Now he's gone and the sheep have gone too. Ashdon's never been the same without 'em.

Elsie Allgood died in 1973.

*   *   *

To interview the next witness, nonagenarian *Richard Eason* I had to travel to the outskirts of Bournemouth, where he retired with his slightly older wife in the early 1930s. Like him, she was born and brought up in Ashdon and together they recalled what it was like to run the Ashdon village store at the turn of this century:

My father's name was Richard Charles Eason and he was a tradesman all his working life. He started out as an apprentice to an outfitter's in Wallingford, Berkshire, and he moved to Ashdon and took over the village store when he got married in 1885. I was born in 1889 and I was the second son. My mother died when my sister was born and for quite a number of years we had a housekeeper who had a daughter who helped out in the shop. My father eventually married again to the widow of Mr Moss, the village butcher who broke his neck when he was going too fast in his horse and cart.

My older brother Vic was sent to a grammar school. He started out as a clerk on the line and he ended up working for Barclay's Bank. Spike Mays speaks in *Reubens Corner* of *Vic* Eason's shop but he never worked in the shop. I was the one who worked in the shop and, looking back, I think I was always meant to. There was no grammar school for me but, mind you, my father did all he could to see I had a good education. I started off in Ashdon Village School but then I went to have private lessons with my brother up at Ashdon Hall with someone called Mr Scher. After that, I went to a private school in Saffron Walden round about the turn of the century. I wasn't there for very long and I don't recollect much about the lessons. All I can remember is that there were about ten or twelve of us at that school, mostly farmer's or shopkeeper's children, and that I used to go there and back in a donkey-cart. I left school for good when I was fourteen to work full-time in the shop.

Mr Eason's General Store

We ran a general store and we sold just about everything that was needed in village life in those days: clothes, food, hardware, well nigh everything you can think of. We used to sell boys' and men's suits and these came in just the three sizes for off-the-peg — four, five or six — with your four being the most popular. There were three-piece suits, coat, waistcoat and trousers, and the complete rigout would cost fifteen shillings. The men would wear these suits for Sunday best but for their every day, they used to wear corduroys: corduroy trousers, corduroy waistcoat with cord front and drabbet sleeves; your corduroy jacket would sell for about twelve and sixpence. We'd sell a lot of hobnailed boots from ten shillings to twelve shillings a pair. What we sold a powerful lot of, in the men's line, were buskins. Your buskins were like shin-pads made out of leather, stretching up to the knee, with straps at the top and bottom and three buttons at the side. All the labourers wore those to protect their trousers and they mostly always had another pair in reserve. They'd sell for five or six shillings a pair and last for years if they was kept up to the mark regularly with blacking or dubbing. For the ladies, we used to sell print dresses and material at sixpence a yard which they could make up into blouses. Also in the drapery line, we sold lots of unbleached calico for sheets and pillow-slips: the double width was about a shilling a yard and the single width was threepence a yard. It was marvellous stuff, that unbleached calico. Everyone made their own sheets in the village in those days and we've still got some sheets today, seventy years after, that we made then. We used to have a special kind of wool, in packets, called 'Perseverance', which came in one pound boxes from Spencer, Traill and Boldrow's in London. Our other drapery supplies came from Saffron Walden, from Haverhill and from Eaden Lilley's in Cambridge. I can still remember the regular routine when that Cambridge traveller used to call. Every three months, he'd stop by to see what we wanted to order up. He'd go out into the warehouse behind the shop with my father and they'd always finish up going next door to the 'Crown' for a bit of bread and cheese and a pint of beer. All this while, his old horse would be stood there in front of our shop. That traveller always used to take a fourteen pound weight out, put it down on the road, and tie it with a long lead to that old horse's harness. That knew that was going to stand there for a good two hours and more and that old boy weren't bothered one little bit.

We used to sell lots of candles, usually half a dozen at a time, and plenty of paraffin oil which used to come from a big barrel that had to be kept out of the back in the shed because of fire regulations. We also sold lots of lamp-glasses. Everyone's light came from oil-lamps in those days and the glasses for these would be stored out in our warehouse on shelves which were partitioned off every so often. There were little lamps with long, thin chimneys, your ordinary lamp with a double-burner which needed a glass with a small bulge, and your single-burner, which needed a round glass with quite a big bulge. We had three big lamps in our shop, one in the centre and one in each window, all with big double-burners. It was quite a business getting them going in the long winter nights and quite a business keeping them going; if you got a really frosty night, bang would go the glasses. People take bright light for granted nowadays: just press the switch and you've got it. Same with water: nowadays, all you do is turn your tap; for quite some time in our village, you had to get your drinking water from the village pump and big tubs and tanks outside to store the rainwater for washing with. You were somehow that bit more thankful for it.

We stocked all the basic groceries. Sugar was twopence a pound or penny three-farthings if you bought more than two pounds. It used to come in two-hundredweight bags and we had to fetch that in our pony and trap from Bartlow Station, two miles along the road; those bags then had to be carried from the cart and out into the warehouse and, you may depend, two hundredweight is a fair old weight to move at any one time if you're not used to it. In the shop itself, the sugar was stored in some of the little drawers that went all the way round the walls: there was a special drawer for the granulated, a drawer for the demerara, another for brown, I could have found my way to any of those drawers blindfolded. Then there were other drawers for soda, drawers for currants, for raisins, for sultanas, everything had its regular place. Tea was fourpence or sixpence a quarter; it came in thirty- or forty-pound boxes lined with silver foil and that all had to be weighed out and done up in our own little packets; the best-selling tea was always Mazawattee. Butter was something else we had to weigh up ourselves; we didn't make our own, it had to come from Whitens Mere Farm and one of my regular jobs was to take one of the big slabs of butter and make it up into pound or half pound packs with my two wooden butter-pats; after I'd shaped it up with the pats, I'd always put our own trademark on it with a little seal. My favourite butter came from further afield. It came over from Ireland in six-pound boxes and was called Bullrush Blat; I've never tasted butter like it before or since, it was gorgeous stuff. There was no marg. in those days but there was plenty of lard; it used to come in small round tubs and after I'd cleaned them out, I'd paint them up nice and bright, put flowers in them and line them up on the outside of the shop, along the ledge above our name-board. I used to get those flowers from Brocklebank's estate over at Bartlow and they used to look lovely on parade there in their pots, the petunias especially: a lovely picture.

   We didn't stock milk which people had to fetch themselves from one or other of the local farmers: it was penny a pint new, in my time, and halfpenny a pint, skimmed. What we did stock in the drink line was beer. We used to sell it at twopence a pint, the ordinary, and threepence a pint our special Old Brown. We used to sell the beer loose, that's to say, our customers would call to fetch their measure in a jug. We used to sell sweets too, four ounces for a penny: humbugs, boiled sweets, pontefract cakes, sherbet bags, sticks of liquorice, home-made toffee, and we sold cigarettes — Woodbines at five for twopence and Players at twenty for elevenpence halfpenny. Meat and bacon was another of our lines. Bacon rashers were tenpence to a shilling per pound and the rolled shoulder, done up with string, was eightpence a pound. Each week we'd have either a New Zealand lamb or else a hind-quarter of beef (I remember that very well because I once put the hook through my finger). Pork, we'd get regularly from the village people. Most of them used to keep their own pig, sometimes two. They'd buy them as piglets and rear them up. It was nearly always pay as you go with us. If they wanted something special, we'd come to an arrangement about their pig. The village butcher would kill the pig for them and then we'd take a quarter or maybe a half for the goods they bought. It suited us and it suited them. We'd spend the whole of Friday morning cutting that up and we'd sell it off as fresh meat or as sausages; we'd use the whole leg and forequarter for those sausages and we made fifty pounds regularly every Friday morning.

My father was very much liked by everybody around the village. He was very fair all round; he never did anybody out of so much as a halfpenny. To help people get a little bit put by for Christmas, he ran a clothing-club: folks would put in so much each week, just whenever they could afford it; sometimes it was just a few coppers but this gradually mounted up and about a fortnight before Christmas, when they took out that club money, it could come to a tidy few shillings as like as not. We didn't forget our special customers when Christmas came round: they'd get a calendar, a pound of fruit and a bottle of port. If anybody should ask for something that wasn't in stock, then my father would get it for them from Haverhill or Saffron Walden. There was another general store as well as ours in the village, that was Purkis's, as there was no real need in those days to go much further afield for your shopping. Nearly everything you needed could be got right here in the village itself.

Some years after our shop had been going, the Post Office was added. Letters were brought out to us twice every day from Saffron Walden. They'd be delivered on foot by a big chap who'd been in the Army. He'd march out from Walden to Ashdon and back again twice a day on weekdays, and once on Sunday, winter and summer, come rain or come shine. I can see him still with his big sack and always with his little stick. At first, people used to have to come and collect their mail but, after a while, I had to go round delivering. There wasn't a corner of the village I didn't visit: I'd go right out almost to Hadstock in one direction to deliver to the Bowsers' Farms,

Great and Little, I'd go up the long lane past Sandon's and on over the fields to Winsey, and I'd go up hill and down dale to Water End. If I had a pound for every mile I walked in Ashdon, I'd be driven around everywhere today by a chauffeur in his uniform. Mind you, I did earn myself a bit of extra money when it came to delivering telegrams: I got sixpence for every telegram I delivered if the distance was over two miles and twopence if the distance was less. The only time I thought I stood any chance of making my fortune out of this was when Miss Pelly got married from the big house at Waltons Park. She had a telegram every half hour. When she was still a-courting, her young man used to send her a wire to start her day, first thing in the morning, and he'd send her to bed with another wire at night. That was a real love-match.

We didn't start to get daily papers regularly in the village till round about 1902. These would be delivered in the first instance by train. The guard used to make a bundle of five or six, put a big stone in the middle and throw the lot out from the railway bridge where it crosses Rectory Lane. If you weren't there when the train passed over you had to hunt around to find them and, of a dark winter's morning, you could take a good half hour to do that. We had a paper regular and a few of the farmers did too. We got our news from the outside world real slow in those days. My wife's brother was wounded and taken prisoner in the Boer War at Pretoria and nobody knew about it for months and months. The first any of us knew was when I read his name in the paper one morning, 'Private A.W. Smith, wounded, taken prisoner by the Boers at such and such a time.' We really were in a little world of our own.

Our shop used to be open from eight in the morning till eight at night, Mondays to Fridays, and on Saturdays, we were open till ten o'clock at night. On Sundays, we'd be open for Post Office business only from eight in the morning till about ten. My father was a very keen churchman and I loved singing in the choir: we wouldn't have missed Church for anything. For the rest of the week, I had a fairly regular routine. On Mondays, I'd have to weigh up the sugar, tea, dried fruit, soda, tobacco and pepper. These would all have to go in their little paper 'cups', as we called them, which we had to make ourselves, twiddle around and pop into their own particular drawer. It was only after a good few years that the bags were made for us. I also had to clean out the stables and look after the pony and cart. On Friday afternoons, I'd be out all round the village getting the orders and on Saturdays, I'd be out delivering. It was a quiet life, if you like, but comfortable and very satisfying. We felt we were appreciated and we had a real sense of belonging: you can't put a price on what that meant.

Every customer was treated as an individual and some were wonderful characters. We used to have one old lady who'd march in, every Friday afternoon, as regular as clockwork. she was the wife of Mr Pearson, the horse-keeper at Bowser's Farm, two miles from our shop. She used to stump along in a long, black skirt, right down to her ankles; she'd have a shawl round her shoulders and a veil on her hat which came down over her face. And she always wore slatey coloured plimsolls, whatever the weather. She'd come in every Friday afternoon and you could lay forty pounds that her order would always be the same: always started off with a quarter of pound of shag for her old man, which would cost her a shilling, and then the usual groceries like butter, lard, tea, sugar and so on. I don't know why to this day but my father never liked to serve her. He'd always find some job that desperately needed doing when Mrs Pearson was due to arrive. 'Time I made myself scarce', he'd say, and off he'd slip. It was like the little man and the little woman on the weather house: you'd never see the two of them on view together. And every Saturday night, always dead on half-past nine, in would come this mother, daughter and granddaughter: you could set your watches by them. And the stories they used to tell: we were all propped against the counter laughing come the end. Then there was Mossy Harris. He was a thatcher and hay-tyer by trade and he was reckoned to be just about the best poacher in the whole of Ashdon, which is saying something for those days. He used to ride a penny-farthing bike and the more he had to drink, the better he seemed to ride. It was better than the circus. There was another old boy from Church End they used to call 'Pipe' and when he'd had a drink too many, which was often, he'd go along singing 'When the fields are white with daisies.' He wouldn't have hurt a flea; all he wanted to do was sing that song, at the top of his voice, happy as a sandboy.

I still feel I'm part of Ashdon and that Ashdon's part of me. I grew up there, I married an Ashdon girl and we were married in Ashdon Church on 2nd June 1915 when I was a Lance-Corporal in the Essex Yeomanry. When we finally left the village in 1935, the people presented us with a silver tea-set and the choir presented us with a silver inkstand plus a book with the names of everyone who'd donated. Many of them have gone on now and I don't suppose there are that many left now who'll remember Richard Charles Eason in whose memory the lectern in the village church was given. And I don't suppose many folk will understand what's behind the name of our little bungalow here in Bournemouth. We've called it just 'Ashdon'.

Richard Eason died in 1979

*   *   *

Richard Eason's impressions of a community that, in so many respects, was almost self-supporting, were confirmed by *Len Martin* who, in his working lifetime exemplified the spirit of all round endeavour by serving as both village baker and village coalman:

I should say just about the biggest change there's been in Ashdon during my lifetime here is in the number of goods and services you used to get in the village in the old days compared with today. We was like a law to ourselves then and we all sort of linked up. My father had his baker's shop where the Labour Hall stands today, there was my uncle in the centre of the village, there was Martin Marsh up Dorvis Lane, and there were two other bakers besides that who'd come in from Linton and Walden. I started work in my father's bakery soon as I left school when I was thirteen. I must have been about fifteen or sixteen when I baked my first loaf entirely on my own. We all used to be up at about five o'clock, my mother as well beause she made the fruit cakes. We'd spend the morning delivering bread and then, in the afternoon, we'd switch to delivering coal. We'd fetch it over in a horse and cart, half a ton at a time, from Bartlow station yard. Bread and coal, the black and the white.

Of course, we had our butchers and our general shop and our blacksmith and a shop that sold saddles and bridles and that, right in the centre of the village that was, Levi Archer's. Then there was the shoemaker's, an old chap called Bob Matthews. He was also one of our firemen because we even had our own Fire Brigade in those days with their special uniforms. Fred Karno's, we called them. Anyway, when we was boys growing up, we played up poor old Bob Matthews something shocking, I can tell you. In the winter-time specially, we'd congregate in his little shop of a night, where the village Post Office is today. We'd lark about inside the shop or else one of us would get up on the roof and put a slate over the chimney to stop the smoke getting out. In the end, he'd chase us out on to Crown Hill with his whip. Don't know why we picked on him, really. They do say there wasn't one to touch him for hand-made boots and buskins.

The Ashdon Fire Brigade

At one time, there was the two cobblers at the same time working in Ashdon. Old Harry Smith was the other one and he had a son called Willie. Now Willie was something I bet lots of other villages never had. He was a photographer. He'd go all over Ashdon on his tricycle and take photos of everything. A real professional he was.

Another thing we had in Ashdon was fairs and fêtes. There was always a big Flower Show in July over at Waltons Park. As well as flowers and vegetables on display, there'd be a band and all sorts of comic competitions. I remember there was a comic boxing match where one of the boxers would dip his gloves in flour and the other one in soot. Black and white again. I remember they held a fair once right by the centre of the village when there used to be a pub called 'the Fox' next to the butcher's shop. The fair was in the meadow at the back and I bought a coconut for the girl I was a-courting. I didn't

dare hand it in at her door so I just left it on the steps. That's just about the only thing we couldn't produce for ourselves in Ashdon in those times, *coconuts*. As far as everything else was concerned, we were like a world on our own.
Len Martin died in 1980.

*   *   *

That feeling of being in a world of their own was expressed more graphically by his great friend, *Frank Moss*, who once said to me 'Before that First World War, Ashdon was our *Castle* — and we was nice and snug inside that, I can tell you'. He was to become the village postman for thirty years but, before the First World War, he and his parents were very much in 'Trade':

I was born in 1898. My father's father worked as a carpenter in the village but my father set up on his own as a butcher. He did very well at that and when you saw the words 'High Class Butcher' over his shop those words really meant something. He used to make real lovely pig's cheese — what they call brawn nowadays — but most of all, he was a first-class killer. He could kill anything, he was real good at that and he was *clean*. People for miles around reckoned he was the cleanest butcher going.

At that time of day, butchers did a lot of killing for their customers. Ordinary village poeple would keep their own pig and after it was killed, they'd put the ham up the chimney and smoke it. The cottage would have a great big open grate and there'd be nails going half-way up the chimney for them to hang that ham on. Now, if that wasn't bled right, the blood would congeal and that'd go bad. Half the battle was in the hanging of the meat and the other half was in the killing and the bleeding. To get the blood out, you had to take hold of the pig's hind legs and pump them backwards and forwards. Every time you done that, the old blood would shoot right out. My father used to make me get hold of the pig's hind legs and pump for him. Used to frighten the life out of me, that did: the blood would go right across the room. I knew that I'd never make a butcher myself.

As I say, my father had a very good name locally as a butcher so he made a good living. Those were the days when the village was our castle. For most people, there was never any call to travel far afield: you could get all you wanted here. It was good to be in trade. My father did well enough out of his butchering to be able to take on a pub and the money wasn't in short supply there either. They used to drink down the beer like water in those days — except it was a good deal stronger than water, I can tell you. The pubs used to open up at six in the morning and they'd stay open right on through till ten at night. They didn't go short of customers. Old Peter Richardson who used to live here in this cottage before we had it, now he was the man for the beer. Many's the time I've heard him say that when they used to go mowin' the barley, there'd be twelve or fourteen of 'em with their scythes, all in a row. What they'd do was to put the youngsters in the middle of the line and the old 'uns at each end. The old 'uns could cut real good and the young 'uns, who wasn't used to the scythe, well, they just couldn't lag behind. And Old Peter said, 'We'd always empty a niner before breakfast.' A 'niner' is a nine-gallon barrel and that'd be drunk by twelve to fourteen men. *Before breakfast*. And they'd get down a sight more before their day was done.

They'd have other things as well as beer, of course. They used to have a great big slice of cold pork on a bit of bread. Nothing else. You know, proper *fat* port. That's what they lived and worked on round here: fat pork and beer. When we had the public house, they'd come in with sixpence. They'd have a pint of good strong beer for twopence, a half ounce of tobacco for three ha'pence, a box of matches for a ha'penny and tuppence worth of bread and cheese. That was their sixpenny worth. So that was a good meal, a good drink and a smoke afterwards. That was their regular thing, dinner-times, and most of 'em lived to a ripe old age. My father didn't manage to, though.

At that time of day, a butcher's one pride and joy was his horse and cart and the faster they could go, the better they liked it. They had these high steppers, you see, and they did go like merry hell. Well, my father always went to Haverhill market on the same day as this local farmer, Mr Pearson from Bowser's. They'd start out in their carts together and the one who got to Haverhill first was stood his beer and his dinner by the other one. Same on the way back. And there and back they'd go like bats out of hell. Well, that particular day, December 5th 1906, they was racing back from the stock market at Haverhill home to Ashdon. It was real foggy by the afternoon and they'd a fair bit to drink. By the time they'd got to the top of Camps Road there, my father had caught the farmer up, and from there on, that's all downhill and straight into Ashdon. So they put the reins down on the horse's neck and said 'Go on, now, boy.' Well, it just so happened that an old miller was coming up the hill at that time, on his way back to Haverhill from Ashdon Mill with a load of pig food. That was so foggy by then that he was walking at the horse's head, and because he couldn't see the side of the road, he'd taken the lantern off from the side of the cart and was carrying it in front of him. My father came down at such a lick in that fog that when he saw that light close up, he must've thought he'd gone past the cart. So he pulled over and the shafts caught the cart and the horse and the whole lot went over. Bill Smith, the old blacksmith's son was with him at the time. He happened to be a peace-time soldier, in the Army Veterinary Corps, and he was saved from going over because he was wearing his spurs. My father was flung straight out and broke his neck.

That was about six o'clock when they brought him back home. Of course, he never came round and he died next morning. A man like that, he wouldn't make a will. His bank manager regularly said, 'Now see here, Mr Moss, if you're not going to make your will, why don't you invest that money of yours. You don't want to keep it all in the house.' But that's just what he done: kept it all in the house. 'If I want it, it's all here', he always said. And so that was. But he couldn't take that with him when he went. That will run into four figures, at the time of day when a pound really was a pound, and he was only 36 when he was killed. He'd made that all on his own. What wouldn't he have been worth if he'd lived!

Frank Moss died in 1982.

*   *   *

Details of how other Ashdonians used once to spend their leisure-time were provided by two of their liveliest nonagenarians. Firstly, *Herbert Farrant:*

One of the things I done a lot of when I weren't workin' was to bicycle. The longest ride I ever done was Ashdon to Yarmouth and back. In a *day* we done that, two on us. *And* we had a nice time down there too. But the *fastest* I ever rode on a bicycle was when our boy Harold was about two: I know he was in his pushchair. My wife and he was goin' up Tottenham on the train and I was bikin'. They got the train at the Halt, a stoppin' train that was that picked up workmen along the way, dropt 'em off here and there. There was a feller I knew goin' south that day. Regular racin' cyclist 'e was and 'e was goin' to Croydon. So I says, 'Well, I'll keep up with you far as Tottenham.' I did too. Twenty five mile an hour we went. *And* I had a suit of clothes on. Minnie's uncle come to meet her at the train and he says, 'Well, you come by motor-car, then?' 'No', I said, 'I've come on my bike.' That were 'nother hour and half afore the train come in. Lost a bit o' sweat that day. Went all over on my bicycle, I did, all over. Always liked a mate with me and we never used to get off, no walkin' up hills or nothin'. We never learned that trick.

Like everyone else, I did a bit of poachin'. Never bothered with the nets or nothin', just took my gun. Used to 'ave me poacher's pocket inside me coat. They never caught me. Nearest I come to bein' caught was up on the Radwinter Road. I got what I wanted one time but I heard the sticks a-rattlin' behind me when I were comin' away. Turned me head and there's a man there. I guessed who he was. Had his bowler hat on. So I packed up my gun, hid it in my pocket. Then, when I went to cross the lane, there's this policeman a-comin' up the hill on his bicycle. I was just on the footpath, see, so I went back in the field, got down low, went all the way down the field real low. Hid me stuff afore I got *right* down into the village then walked the last bit real slow out on the road, a-whistlin', walkin' real slow, just like as I were comin' out of the Church. No, they never did get me. That were the nearest they come to it.

Then what I also done was keep bees. Done that for years and years. That never took me long to make a hive, I can tell you. Never got stung much, leastways not on my *head*. Used always to keep my cap on. Sometimes stung me old feller, that's true. Looked a rare fine soldier then, when he was swelled up, I can tell you. All you needed for him was a helmet and a strap. I used to work for old Stanley Hagger, used to live up Hill Farm there. He used to keep bees too and once they stung him there too. Pulled it out to let me see. He said, 'Whatever we goin' to do with this, Farrant?' I said, 'It ain't no use askin' me', I said, '*I* can't do nothin' about it.' I said 'Why don't you go in the house', I said, 'and see what your wife's doin'?' He said, 'You bloody fool, you.' I said, 'Well, she could always put a poultice over it if that were hard enough.' Courtin' tackle!

But bees is peace-lovin' really. They don't reckon they'll stay with folks as is forever argufying. And you ain't to say swear-words when you're near the hive and it's best always to talk to 'em nice and gentle when you're workin' 'em. And I'll tell you somethin' more. When someone die in your family, you have to take a bit of old crepe out to the skeps after the sun's gone in. Pin that on the skeps. Tap the skeps, gentle like, and then you has to tell 'em. Tell 'em who it was who's died. They reckoned if you didn't tell 'em that, the bees would go away for good. Or just die themselves ...

Secondly, *Mabel Eason who died in May 1988, aged 101:*

Some of the younger poeple I meet seem quite convinced we couldn't have known how to enjoy ourselves all those years ago before the 1914 War before we had films or television or motor cars: they're quite wrong, you know. There was plenty of amusement in and around Ashdon in those days, at any rate: there was the Church choir, for example, which everyone used to enjoy; there were the rehearsals and the performances and once a year, we had an outing to Clacton-on-Sea or to Great Yarmouth and — just fancy! — there would be a saloon carriage pulled through from Bartlow Station all the way to the seaside just for the Ashdon choir! Then there were the handbell ringers who'd go round each Christmas to all the big houses of the parish; they'd play outside on the lawn and then get invited in for drinks and mince pies. I mustn't forget my Girl Guides too but best of all, I'd say, was the dancing. Ashdon was a great village for dancing and we had some really lovely times which I've still not forgotten sixty years afterwards.

Before and soon after the First World War, we used to have a dance once a week in the Conservative Club from eight o'clock till midnight. Lots of young folk used to come from Ashdon and from other villages like Radwinter. We could always count on forty or fifty; for long nights, we'd get as many as sixty. In his book *Reuben's Corner*, you'll find Mr Mays says that *I* was the one who started dancing classes in the village and that I wouldn't let anybody in wearing hob-nailed boots. That's just not true. All I used to do was play the piano for them. I've never given grown-ups dancing lessons in my entire life. He's mixing me up with Mrs Tuck who was the wife of the village Headteacher. She taught waltzes, polkas, schottisches, the Lancers. She really was strict about certain things: the men weren't allowed to dance unless they had the proper shoes and unless they came wearing the proper white gloves. I remember once, a real, old farm labourer called Patrick Smith from Rogers End arrived wearing a pair of woollen gloves and she created something shocking. He took it all in good part, though: he loved his dancing. We all did.

Twice a year, my husband and I would go into Saffron Walden for really special occasions, the Tradesmen's Ball and the Conservative Ball. That really was posh and we thought we were simply *it* when we went there. Not *everyone* was invited to that, you know. The dance would be in Walden Town Hall with the carpet up. There'd be a four- or five-piece band and something like twenty four dances with an interval in the middle. We'd travel in from Ashdon by pony and trap, Mr and Mrs Eason in front, my husband, Rich, and I in the back, with a big umbrella to shelter under if it should rain. We *were* swells: the men wore tails and bow-ties; I remember I had a lovely pink frock, with tiny puffed sleeves and three or four frills; there was a light chain-attachment which you put your arm through and which you used to hitch your long skirt up from the dance-floor. The ladies had little cards with a pencil attached and the men came round and booked you up. To have more than two or three dances with the one partner wasn't supposed to be proper, you understand. I'm afraid I was a culprit, more than once. I can hear the music yet. Dance on and on till two or three in the morning, we would, and not feel the least bit tired. I remember once we got back to Ashdon and Rich just had time to change and then go straight out on the early morning post-round. Lovely, lovely times, those were. Riding back in the pony and trap, we might still be humming 'After the Ball was Over'. Prince Charming and Cinderella weren't in it! You mustn't believe that all everyone did in Ashdon in the old days was just work and drink.

*   *   *

The point is well made and, as is true of so many of the older Ashdonians' reminiscences, is made with a quite remarkable lack of rancour. Nevertheless, one is bound to observe that the public records reveal rather darker areas which individual private memory has unwittingly suppressed. The Log Books show how unpleasant it must so often have been to attend Ashdon School at the turn of the century while over the first decade, in two particular areas, the one parochial, the other international, gathering storm clouds cast shadows over the sunlit Edwardian scene. These were two distant sets of relationships, between local farmers and their labourers on the one hand, and between the major powers of Europe on the other: how the sharp deterioration of each so dramatically threatened Ashdon's centuries-old life-style is the subject of the following two chapters.

9

The Ashdon Labourers' Strike

Says the master to me, 'Is it true? I am told
Your name on the books of the Union's enrolled;
I can never allow that a workman of mine,
With wicked disturbers of peace should combine.

I give you fair warning, mind what you're about,
I shall put my foot on it and trample it out;
On which side your bread's buttered, now sure you can see,
So decide now at once for the Union, or me.'

Says I to the master, 'It's perfectly true
That I am in the Union, and I'll stick to it too;
And if between Union and you I must choose,
I have plenty to win, and little to lose.

For twenty years mostly my bread has been dry,
And to butter it now I shall certainly try;
And though I respect you, remember I'm free —
No master in England shall trample on me ...

Anon: *My Master and I* (Union song of the 1870s)

The wide gulf between Ashdon's rich and its poor which, as we have seen, divided the village community for hundreds of years, seemed just as wide as ever at the beginning of the twentieth centry. Three different sets of data will serve to bring this out and the first of these is a simple comparison between the estate agent's description of the Maynards' Ashdon properties, which were put up for sale in 1898, and an article about farm labourers' cottages in Ashdon published in a local newspaper a few years afterwards. The description of the Maynards' Estate reads as follows:

It is seldom the opportunity occurs to purchase so fine a

Residential and Sporting Estate as the one now brought before the public and its long association with the Maynard family should commend it to the attention of anyone seeking a really first-class Property.

The situation is one of the best and prettiest in the County of Essex, very healthy and commanding beautiful views . . .

The Mansion House is exceedingly well-placed and comfortable, with very convenient Stabling and Offices.

The Property would make a capital Residential Estate for a gentleman of means and fond of sport. The Coverts are excellent, and the country round, including the Estate, abounds in game; it is also within easy reach of Newmarket Heath, either by road or rail.

The Essex and East Essex Foxhounds hunt the district, and the Essex Staghounds are also accessible. There are also several Coursing Clubs in the neighbourhood.

There is a Trout stream on the Estate, and good fishing is obtainable in the River Colne, which is easily reached by road or rail.

It will, I hope, prove instructive to set this beside the following anonymous article which was printed in the *Essex County Chronicle* in February, 1907:

The Cottage Problem is to the fore at Ashdon. The writer of an article in the *Country Gentleman* some time ago stated that if this problem were ever to be solved it would be done by the £150 cottage, but he had taken the average wages of the agricultural labourer to be from 12*s*. to 14*s*. per week whereas the average in this village and others akin to it is less than 12*s*. We will take the case of a most steady man in Ashdon who is in constant employment and has been so for years on the same farm; yet his weekly wage is only 12*s*. He has a wife and four children (girls) dependent upon him. A £150 cottage means a rental of £8 per annum, or a fraction over 3*s*. per week. Therefore if he paid 3*s*. per week for rent he would only have 9*s*. left to feed and clothe a family of six, on 1*s*. 6*d*. per head per week. If this man could not pay a rental of 3*s*. how much less could a casual worker do so? And let it be borne in mind that in costing the above average no account has been taken of wet days (when no work is done and no wage is paid) which sum up to a considerable number in the course of the year ... There is a scarcity in house room. Therefore depopulation ensues. This causes a scarcity of labour which is affecting the farming interest, and to the depopulation of our rural districts one may ascribe the deterioration of our race ...

The second comparison is between two sets of attitudes, across the social divide, to the centuries-old subject of game. As it happened, I recorded the conversations from which the following extracts have been selected, in the course of the same afternoon and evening in the early summer of 1973. I thought then and think still they make their point without the assistance of any commentary from me. First, Brigadier Collins describes how his father used to organize his Ashdon shoot at the beginning of the century:

My father's shooting-rights, before the First World War, took in pretty well everything between Ashdon and Radwinter, including the Great and Little Bendysh Woods, Sandon's Farm, Goldstone's Farm and The Grove — Griggs, Longmead and the Bourne. It was all organized by the keeper, Mr Phil Day, a splendid character and a very tough number who looked after the shoot throughout the year. He'd collect the beaters for the day's shooting, twelve or fifteen of them as a general rule, plus a few boys. Several of the guns regularly came from my uncle's regiment, the East Lancashires stationed then at Colchester, and each was entitled to bring guests. My father, naturally, regularly had a gun, and his younger brother, who was learning to be — or playing at being — a solicitor in London frequently joined the party too: he was an excellent shot. Occasionally, Major Pelly would come across from Waltons Park to join our shoot, and, occasionally, my father would be invited to go over and join their shoot. This, of course, was how country gentlemen used to pass — still do pass — much of their leisure-time.

My mother, my sister and I, plus any other wives who might happen to be about (and there weren't usually very many) used to take the lunch out and set it up in some barn at one or other of the big farms. We'd drive out in our wagonette which, more often than not, had its roof removed during the day-time and was covered, normally, only in the evenings when the ladies went out to dances. Our gardener-coachman, whose name was Riley, used to wear our livery. This consisted of a top hat and a great big buff coat (which I still have) adorned with silver buttons and scarlet facings on the collar and cuffs. When he first turned up in this with the lunch-baskets, it somewhat startled the beaters, and he himself was immensely embarrassed about the whole business, as you might suppose. However, when they got used to it, it came to be expected. I well remember diving out in the back of the wagonette behind Riley in all his splendour when, on one famous occasion, the cork flew out of an enormous keg full of ginger beer we were taking out to the beaters. There was a tremendous pop and I can see it still, sailing away through the air in a great fountain of froth.

We shot great quantities of partridges in those days, starting on 1st September when it was legally correct to do so. Nowadays, alas, they've been decimated by modern methods of farming, there are no hedges for them to nest in, and you see scarcely any at all on our local heavy soil. Years ago, they were here in abundance. There'd probably be five drives before lunch and, say, two or three afterwards. You walked everywhere in those days, of course, and there were always sufficient partridges for the guns to drive one way and then turn about and drive back again, in the opposite direction, over the same ground. The thing about partridges is that they don't like going away from their home. Once they've pitched, they won't go on; they'll turn, one way or the other, and return to where they started from. That is why you should always have *short* drives and that is why it was a simple matter to bring them back again. You were taking with you a new lot of birds plus all the old ones, who'd come out in the original drive, and wanted to go back, anyhow. When you walked everywhere, it was a normal expedient to do a reverse drive. Nowadays, everything is mechanized. You proceed from one drive to the next in a Landrover, the beaters follow on tractors, you travel anything up to two miles between drives and you only drive in the one direction. The reverse-drive is quite unheard-of now. Mechanization is all very well but I'm not sure that it can be said to have much improved the quality of shooting.'

Later that day in 1973, I had the first of several most rewarding conversations with *Bill Albon*, the Waltons Park gardener, the bulk of whose reminiscences will be found in chapter 10. He spoke not only of his own gardening exploits but of the great poachers from his Ashdon past:

I reckon the best known poacher in these parts in my time was old Fuller Smith. The daddy of 'em all, he was reckoned to be. Course, the police knew what 'e was up to and this time they really made up their minds to catch him. Well, this night, they was all a-watchin' round at the front of 'is cottage, waitin' for 'im to walk back in through the gate with the stuff on 'im. He didn't reckon much to that, not old Fuller, so what 'e done was to come in the *back* way. Mind you, the old river was in flood just then so 'e 'ad to swim across, boots round his neck and all. His wife Liza had the light on upstairs that night and when 'e got back in, drippin' all over the shop, he says, 'Don't you put that bloody light out, gal.' He says, 'Let the buggers wait out there all night.' And that's just what they done. He *was* a poacher, 'e was. But then, who weren't a poacher in those days.

I'll tell you another trick they used to get up to. The old keeper's cottage used to be over the other side of the brickyard, over near the old railway track there. When there'd been a shootin' party on the estate earlier in the day, old Stewart the keeper would be fair gone in, tuckered as you might say. Old Fuller Smith and old Jim Marsh ud peek in at the window of the cottage and they'd see that old boy sittin' by the fire with his slippers on. Course, those old poachers wasn't tired. They hadn't been out beatin' all day. They was on *night* shift. Away they'd go into the big wood there and get themselves a nice bag of birds easy as you like. No trouble for anyone who wanted to get a brace of pheasants in those days for three or four bob.'

A fuller account of the poacher's skill was provided in the evening of that same day by Bertie Bartram, a well known Ashdon Labour stalwart, for reasons that will not be difficult to deduce:

'I came to Ashdon when I was just six months old and I've lived here all my life. I've lived in just the two houses, in one of the old cottages by the Church yard for years and years and now in this Council house just across from the Church. That's the furthest I've ever been, across the way there and now here, that's the furthest I been. I went to school in the village and I left when I were thirteen. I went to work at a local farm in the village here. The farmer was a real hard man, on that you may depend. I went there and worked from half past six in the morning to half past five at night. No Saturdays off. Just the two shillin' a week.

They was real hard times, I can tell you, real hard. At one time of the day, I tell you the truth, when I just was a little boy, all the ordinary women used to have to curtsey to the gentry ladies in the street. That's God's truth. Reckon they had us where they wanted us then. Same as if you'd took the harvest. I mean, once you took the harvest and fixed the price, they had you. You took the harvest for five pounds or eight pounds, say, and that was the price for the job no matter how long it took. If that took you twelve weeks, you still only got the five pounds. You had to work for your money right enough. I remember one week, I was due an odd ha'penny on my wages. The farmer had a penny in his hand and asked if I had the change. I said "No, I haven't." He said, "Well, I'll just go and see if the servant's got any." He wasn't giving anything away, *he* wasn't.

Lucky for us there was always the rabbits. We always used to keep a couple of dogs as well as a couple of ferrets. People knew I was good at catching rabbits, there was never any secret about it. I'd had several rabbits off a farmer's field, up on what we call the Downs, and then one day he sent me a letter saying I was to go up and see him. When I got up there, he said, "I've got a job for you to do, Bertram. I know you can do it all right." "Oh, and what might that be?" I said. "I want you to catch all the rabbits that side of the river. You can take a gun, take what you like, but I want 'em caught." That's what he said. Well, what I did was go off to Walden and get fifty snares. I caught twenty five to thirty straightaway that first night. I kept on at it. Next year, when they cut his corn, there was only three rabbits in it. The year after that, there was just the one. And in the winter-time after that, he came up to me and he said, "If you don't get off my beet-field", he said, "I'll put a bullet in you. You was only meant to take the rabbits *the once*!"

Don't know what we'd ever have done without our rabbits and that's a fact. On Saturday, I'd go out with my old friend Arthur Mallyon. He used to live at Halt Cottage and we used to do a stretch of the railway line from Walden to Bartlow. Arthur would have his gun and his dog and I'd have my two ferrets. We'd go out at, say, two o'clock of a Saturday afternoon and come back about six. I'd gut them all and I'd open the door here and sell them or take them down the pub and sell them to the customers there. They'd always be ready for 'em. It wasn't just rabbits we got either. I remember one Boxing Night, old Wal Marsh and I went out into the woods over there. I took the light, he had the gun and we had nineteen pheasants when we'd finished. That took a bit of doing but it wasn't always as hard as that. I remember once the Braybrookes had a cage set up. They was gathering up the pheasants to cart them over to another wood. Right, I said. Nonethemore, I got my bag, just broke the necks and put them in my sack. Two gamekeepers come down the wood just then but I done them all. I didn't run away. I tell you what I done. I just lay down in the ditch with my dog beside me. I heard one of them say "He's gone down this way somewhere." Mind you, I didn't use to care about *nothin'* then. That was as near as they got to catchin' me.

A powerful lot of poaching used to go on in Ashdon in the old times. There was those who worked more in a sort of team, like, and there was some as worked on their own more. If you was in a gang, you might sometimes get one or two letting off their guns now and again in one part of the wood, see, and the rest would be doin' the real business very quiet somewhere different. Me, I liked to work on my own or with just the one mate along. Sometimes I'd use a net. I'd have a sort of wooden frame like for pictures only instead of a picture it would have a net across it which had to be made out of real strong twine. That frame used to fit real neat across the gateway to the field. Your dog would drive the field and the hares would come leaping across to get away from the dog and end up in the net. No trouble at all. What you could also do was use your ferret instead. You'd see the rabbit-holes along the bank, like, and what you did there was block up nearly all the holes and just leave one or two. You'd put your small nets over those and when you was ready you'd put your ferret in. The rabbit would pop out double-quick and that would be that. I don't reckon that made *real* criminals of us. You'd get to do something, you see. There wasn't much meat to be had. There *was* meat, of course, for those who could pay for it. The trouble was not all of us had the money to pay for it. The rabbit was the saving of us. The working-man's best dinner.'

The third variation on this theme of social difference in Ashdon is the most dramatic of all, nothing less than an out-and-out strike of the village labour-force. It took place in the summer of 1914 but the train of events leading up to it effectively begins almost a century before.

In the course of the nineteenth century, the squires, parsons and wealthy landowners finally lost their age-old power over Parliament. Three bitterly contested Reform Bills grudgingly extended the franchise to electors who had never before been allowed to vote: in 1832, to certain members of the middle and professional classes who possessed the requisite property qualifications; in 1867, to male workers in the towns; finally, in 1884, to male labourers in the country. This last Bill also ended the tradition of constituencies returning two members thereby allowing the electorate the occasional luxury of being represented both by a reactionary and a radical, and elections became increasingly bitter as a result. Some indication of this is provided by the campaign literature circulated in 1885 by the Liberal candidate to the electors of the Saffron Walden Division of Essex, a constituency of which Ashdon has always formed a part.

The candidate in question, one Hubert Gardner announced his intention of making the current agricultural depression his prime concern, of devoting his especial attention to abolishing tithes, of protecting the tenant farmer, of strengthening the Army and Navy (while condemning War as the enemy of civilisation and the chief source of the National Debt), of providing free education for all classes of the Nation, of strongly supporting Free Trade, of resisting to the utmost any attempt to Tax the Bread of the People, of backing the Deceased Wife's Sister's Bill, and of curbing the great and dangerous power of Mr Parnell (thereby helping to solve the Irish Problem). Like any candidate of whatever political party before any British poll, he proclaimed that 'The General Election we are about to take part in is perhaps the most important this country has ever seen.' The by now familiar cliché was rather more apposite than usual of the 1885 election because English farm-workers were about to vote for the first time in history. So unfamiliar were they with the electoral system, in Gardner's view, that he felt it necessary to get a special poster printed by Hart and Sons of Saffron Walden and have it distributed throughout the constituency. The Ashdon electors would have seen prominently displayed on Crown hill the following 'Warning to Farmers and Labourers':

WARNING
TO
FARMERS & LABOURERS.

It having been rumoured that certain TORY FARMERS have been intimidating their Labourers by threatening a REDUCTION of WAGES if the LIBERALS GET IN,

WARNING IS HEREBY GIVEN

to such persons that they have transgressed "The Corrupt Practices Act," and are liable to

IMPRISONMENT FOR TWELVE MONTHS

WITH HARD LABOUR,

and will certainly be prosecuted.

Every Labourer is FREE TO VOTE as he PLEASES, and any one INTERFERING with his RIGHT of Voting, WILL BE PUNISHED with the UTMOST RIGOUR OF THE LAW.

HART AND SON, PRINTERS, SAFFRON WALDEN.

> It having been rumoured that certain TORY FARMERS have been intimidating their Labourers by threatening a REDUCATION of WAGES if the LIBERALS GET IN, *WARNING IS HEREBY GIVEN* to such persons that they have transgressed 'The Corrupt Practices Act' and are liable to *IMPRISONMENT FOR TWELVE MONTHS* WITH HARD LABOUR and will certainly be prosecuted.
>
> Every Labourer is FREE TO VOTE as he PLEASES and any one INTERFERING with his RIGHT of Voting, WILL BE PUNISHED with the UTMOST RIGOUR OF THE LAW.

Whatever the foundation for the rumour, the poster-campaign evidently did nothing but good for Gardner's cause because the new electorate returned him by 4755 votes to his Tory opponent's 3005.

Also returned at the 1885 General Election (for the North-West Norfolk constituency) was Joseph Arch, a leaflet by whom had been distributed to the Saffron Walden district labourers reminding them that the Tories had opposed all moves to give them the vote. 'You have the vote', he declared, 'and now the Tories who did their best to keep you out of it are trying to make you believe that they are your best friends.' Arch himself had no doubts on this score. His Warwickshire background had given him ample knowledge of the pressing need to improve the labourers' lot. His own family were more fortunate than most labourers because they owned a cottage of their own and were in no danger of being evicted because of Arch's blunt views, regularly expressed at public meetings with the vehement conviction of a Methodist preacher. His compassion for his fellow-labourers inspired him to compose his famous Grace:

> O Heavenly Father, bless us,
> And keep us all alive;
> 'There are ten of us for dinner
> And food for only five.

His reputation as an embattled orator drew him into trade union activities which had been forbidden under threat of imprisonment by the Combination Act of 1800 and were were not given final legal sanction till 1875. He was particularly effective in activating the union cause in East Anglia and it was as a result of his pioneering campaigns in this regard that the Ashdon strike took place in the high summer of 1914.

Of the Ashdonians who were growing up or already out at work in the village before the First World War, I met very few who did not have at least one clear memory of the agricultural strike of 1914. The slow-burning fuse was lit elsewhere in East Anglia in the two years preceding when more and more farm labourers came to believe that they could best improve their working conditions by joining the National Agricultural and Rural Workers' Union. The East Anglian headquarters of the Union was at Fakenham, in Norfolk, and when, in October 1913, a branch was formed in Helions Bumpstead, just over four miles east of Ashdon, forty one men joined. By the New Year, this number had doubled, and since the total labour force of the area was only one hundred and thirty, the local farmers had good reason to feel alarm.

Confronted by what they saw as a distinct menace, some of the Bumpstead farmers reacted as their Suffolk predecessors had done before them in the 1870s, when the labourers' union movement first began to spread into East Anglia. The owners of Copy Farm and Helions Farm announced that unless their employees surrendered their union cards forthwith, they would promptly lose their jobs and the tied cottages which went with them. The men's response was to walk off the farms there and then, declaring that their price for returning to work was a rise of two shillings per week on the basic wage. What began as an employers' lock-out became an employees' strike and in the following months, this spread sporadically out into parts of the surrounding district. In June 1914, ballots were held in Ashdon, Birdbrook, Helions and Steeple Bumpstead, Ridgwell and Sturmer. In each village, the labourers voted overwhelmingly to join the strike and at midnight, and again at daybreak, they broke the news to the world and his drowsy wife with a serenade of rural 'rough music': ringing bells, blowing whistles and beating on tin cans or whatever other cacophonous container came to hand. Close on four hundred men were now out, ninety five per cent of the entire labour force in a region which relied exclusively on farm produce for its wealth. Of the small minority of labourers who remained at work, nearly all were those who had animals to tend, the horsemen, the stockmen and the shepherds.

Considering the labourers' wages and working conditions in East Anglia at the beginning of the twentieth century, it is surprising that the strike had not come earlier or been more widely spread: a thirteen year old farm lad was paid two shillings for a sixty-hour working week while for the same amount of work, a sixteen-year old received three shillings; the standard weekly wage for a grown man was thirteen shillings but, in the winter months especially, bad weather could cut this figure by half, and out of this amount, the men were obliged to buy their own tools. Certainly at this period, the average rent for a cottage was as low as half a crown per week but the tenants of tied cottages could be summarily evicted as was the case in Helions Bumpstead with the first sign of confrontation in February 1914.

I was not fortunate enough ever to speak in person with Walter Marsh, the last surviving folk-hero of the Ashdon strike but before he died, in the Spring of 1971, he had more than one memorable conversation with the Reverend Walter Lane, Rector of Ashdon from 1947 to 1973. 'What impressed me more than anything else about Walter Marsh', he told me, 'was the man's *dignity*. I remember him speaking about the start of the strike in the summer of 1914. There was no aggression as he spoke, no hint of bitterness. His voice was deep and slow. "When the farmer gave me a week's wages just afore we struck", he said, "I threw it at his feet. A man can't live on wages like that (I said), I'd sooner work for *nuthen*".

The official demands of the rest of the strikers were, however, for something rather more substantial: sixteen shillings per week for labourers, eighteen to twenty shillings per week for stockmen and one pound per week for horsemen; one half-day off each week and holidays on Christmas Day, Good Friday and on public Bank Holidays; overtime at sixpence per hour; harvest rates to be standardized at £8 for four weeks of work and five shillings per day should the harvesting take longer; all tied cottages to be on a three-month tenancy.

Each side gave vent to the ritual utterances that have become part of the ceremonial of every industrial dispute: the workers insisted that they would not settle for a penny less while the employers were adamant that they could not offer a penny more. Neither side was in the mood to yield or, for that matter, even to enter into negotiations, in spite of entreaties from such dignitaries as the Bishop of Chelmsford. The hay harvest in the strike-bound areas was completely lost. Such green grass as had been cut rotted where it lay, the uncut grass was scorched and wilted, and the time for the corn harvest was inexorably approaching.

James Coe, of Castle Acre in Norfolk, was the Union official controlling the strike and he paid out ten shillings strike-pay every week to each of his members involved. The Dockers' Union contributed £20 each week to the strike fund, and prominent speakers and suffragettes came from London to encourage the labourers to fight the good fight. In Ashdon, such speech-making took place in front of the 'Rose and Crown' and impromptu concerts were staged in the field behind the 'Fox'. Broad Essex voices were regularly raised in choruses of the 'Red Flag', banners were waved and there was occasional chanting of the slogan 'No surrender!'.

The Reverend A.W. Smith, son of the Reverend T.H. Smith, who was Baptist Minister in Ashdon from 1895 to 1920, recalled that when he first arrived in the village, before the turn of the century, 'the labourers and their wives were docile, subservient to vicar and squire, bowing and curtseying whenever they happened to pass them in the village street.

In a little cobbler's shop in the village was a poor lad who for a long time had lain on his bed unable to move, the victim of a pennyfarthing bicycle.

My father used to visit him and hand him newspapers and magazines, and in time he became quite intelligent. It occurred to my father that he could procure him an invalid carriage and the fresh air would do him good, which proved to be the case. The stages of his recovery were remarkable. First he was able to get about with the aid of two sticks, then on a tricycle. What he had read and learnt on his sick-bed he imparted to his friends . . .

When the strike got under way, the men no longer wore a hangdog look but walked about with the boldness of a Goliath! They demanded their rights and refused to be downtrodden by vicar or squire. They held up the police who tried to interfere; no blackleg was allowed to work on a farm. On one occasion, they barricaded themselves behind beer barrels in the 'Rose and Crown' yard, arming themselves with staves and threatening any who tried to interfere with them. My father, a staunch Liberal, but with great sympathy for the poor and much beloved by them all, tried for an agreement between masters and men. It was a pitiful sight to see the cripple one Sunday morning, leading a procession of labourers to the village chapel. Feeling ran high, and the spirit of worship was absent that Sunday morning".

A particularly detailed account was provided by *Frank Moss*, who was born, lived all his life and died in Ashdon:

I was fifteen years old at the time of the famous Ashdon strike in 1914 but I can remember very well some of the things that went on. Poor old Arthur Thake was horse-keeper up at Goldstones and he just kept on working. They all laid in the ditch beside Thake's cottage at Midsummer Hill, of a morning, you see. 'Come on out, you old blackleg, you. Come on out, you old blackleg. We'll have you this mornin'.' What they didn't know was that he was having all his meals across at the farm, on the other side of the road, and he didn't go home for a whole week. And, of course, when that got light, he'd be going up the fields with his horses, a-ploughing or a-drilling, whatever that was. They couldn't figure out how he ever got past them.

Major Pelly over at Waltons Park once tried to get the farmers and workers together. And he had them all over there up at the Park, in the big hall. He put out spirits and wine and beer and that. The farmers could have a drop of whisky and the men could have all the beer they wanted. And the men came outside the front door and they piddled everywhere, all over the porch and round the garden; they never asked for the proper place to go. They'd had just about as much as they could take, you see. They didn't want to settle the strike, you see; they never took no interest in that meeting. The Major was so disgusted that he closed the meeting. He sent them all out, the farmers went home and the strike just went on same as before.

One Saturday night, they had Ben Tillett come down from the Dockers' Union in London. He spoke out there on Crown Hill. 'Well', he said, 'I don't know how many of you have got your Sunday joint for tomorrow. Not so very many of you, I don't suppose. Well, I see there's a butcher's shop there and there's a grocer's shop there. Help yourselves! You've got no money but you don't need no money. Help yourselves!'

And at that same big meeting, he said, 'Now, I want all of you to parade here Sunday night, tomorrow that is, at six o'clock. I want you all to march up the hill to Ashdon Church. You've all got to be there. And I want you all up there in the men's gallery . . .' That's the big gallery that could hold a hundred and fifty to two hundred people. And they all filed in there and, sure enough, they'd got the red flag flying. But the verger, old Walter Williams, he said to them, 'You can carry *that* under your arm. You're not meant to bring that into Church. Just you carry that in under your arm.' And that's just what they did. And then we had *our* procession, and we marched in singing 'Onward, Christian soldiers'. Those were the days.

There was a bit more excitement that same Sunday night. At that big meeting on the Saturday, the speaker had said 'There's plenty of sheep and lambs in the field. All you've got to do is take one and kill it. No need to go hungry.' Well, after that Church service, old Reuben Ford made a bee-line for this flock of sheep along the road at Newnham Hall. The shepherd had got wind that something might happen to the sheep so he and the farmer, Harold Smith, were keeping watch in the ditch. Old Reuben was so anxious for a bit of mutton, he got over into the pen. He was just about to get hold of a nice little lamb for hisself when Harold Smith couldn't hold hisself back no longer. He jumped out and caught hold of Reuben. Of course, he hadn't got hold of the lamb at that time and he said he'd been taken short and he'd come in there to do a job. And, course, there was no real proof either way. He still got summonsed with intent to steal. He *had* been taken short in a way, though, hadn't he, come to think on it? *Taken short with hunger.*

The most dramatic episode of the Ashdon strike was the arresting of eight of the strikers. Incensed at the sight of a labourer who had the temerity to continue with the hay-harvest, they burst into the field where he was working and wrenched his hay-fork from him. They were arrested, charged with trespassing and convicted. Two were fined £2 with costs; the other six £1 with costs. All eight decided to serve a month in prison rather than have their fines paid out of their Union's funds. Escorted by some two hundred of their fellow-strikers, bearing hay-rakes and forks, waving their banners and singing the 'Red Flag', they marched the five miles into Saffron Walden to surrender to the police. At the police station, a nonplussed superintendent would have none of it, so the convicted men and their retinue marched back in procession to Ashdon. A few days later, in the small hours, when Ashdon was asleep, policemen picked up seven of the men from their beds, took them along the road to Bartlow Junction and transported them to Cambridge Jail. Their names were: Samuel

The end of the Labourers' Strike, 1914

Chapman, 'Sunny' Chapman, Walter Marsh, Walter Simmons, Charlie Smith, George Thake and Harry Webb.

Demonstrations continued. Daily meetings were held at which, as Frank Moss so clearly remembers, outside speakers urged the strikers to take the law into their own hands. The wilder exhortations were disregarded but some hayricks were set on fire and wagons were overturned. On at least one occasion, Mr Furze of Goldstones Farm, not one of the most popular farmers in the district, found his homeward way barred to his pony and trap because of a rough barricade of assorted agricultural implements set up across the road. Just occasionally, verbal warfare between the opposing camps would give way to physical violence, as Herbert Farrant, then aged thirty one, was still able to recall fifty years later:

That was a time! We hadn't had our union long then and the farmers thought they would see us out, you see. But they couldn't. We hadn't much money in the bank when we started out and there were two thousand pounds in the bank when we finished. All gift stuff, you know, all gift stuff. In the end, we won wer deal, but what a do that was!

There were as many police as there were of us! There were a hundred and twelve here on strike and there were as many as seventy six policemen about Ashdon somewhere. Quite a lot of those police came from London down here, they said. Flippin' super came after us from Walden. We was supposed not to come down by the footpath we was on. 'Do you know where you are?' he says. 'I know fine where I am', I says, 'I was here before Furze was.' At the finish, this super says to me, 'Well, if you ent satisfied with the police you've got here now', he says, 'I can soon send you some more.' 'The more the merrier', I says. He turns his flippin' horse round and off he went to Walden real quick. If he'd stopped another two minutes, he'd've gone somewhere else right enough.

There was some police used to be at the 'Crown' here all day and night. Used to be drunk. I remember one come out of there once when I was a-comin' by. I wasn't doin' nothin', I was just walkin'. Nobody with me. He was goin' to hit me across the head with his wosname. I walked down the brook a little way, opposite the school there, and I cut a stick up. He came arter me. Stood there shakin' like a fart on a pin. Then we set to. My stick got in afore his wosname did. Fair bent his old helmet! I got a hold on the strap and fair wrapped that helmet round his neck. I mean ter say, he was asking for trouble that one was. Just a-walkin', I was, that's all.

For all that, violence seems to have been the exception rather than the rule. Even when allowances have been made for the compulsion to strike an attitude before the novelty of the camera, it is a mood of calm, even of ritual, that is now held captive in the various photographs which record selected moments of the strike for posterity: labourers and their womenfolk, attired in their Sunday finery, stand side by side impeccably uniformed policemen, and there isn't a menacing truncheon or clenched fist to be seen; the faces are quietly smiling or, at worst, blandly impassive.

The Farmers' Union finally gave way on 3rd August 1914. The strikers were all reinstated on a basic wage of fifteen shillings per week, harvest-men were henceforth to be guaranteed not less than eight pounds for four weeks' work, and the labour-force was no longer to be laid off without wages in bad weather. It was a victory for social justice and also for common-sense because by this time, the Ashdon corn stood golden in the fields, ripe for the cutting.

A few days before the farmers surrendered, the imprisoned strikers were released from prison. The reason had nothing to do either with the rights or wrongs of their cause or with the dictates of the waiting harvest. While the opposing factions had been hurling abuse and the occasional missile at each other in the seclusion of Ashdon, Europe's leading statesman had brought their countries to the very brink of war. The convicted strikers, all reservists, were allowed little time to celebrate their release and, in the event, did not return to their farms. On 4th August, Britain declared war on Germany, and they were marched away to the more sinister harvest that would shortly be reaped in the battlefields of Northern France.

10

The Threat of Invasion

On the idle hill of summer
Sleepy with the flow of streams,
Far I hear the steady drummer
Drumming like a noise in dreams.

Far and near and low and louder
On the roads of earth go by,
Dear to friends and food for powder,
Soldiers marching — all to die . . .
    A.E. Housman: from 'A Shropshire Lad'

The history of human conflict is not only of the development of more and more devastating weapons but also of the progressive involvement of more and more of the nations' citizens. In this respect, Ashdon can be seen as representative of country life in general and a microcosm of England as a whole: for centuries, it provided a token handful of its young men to fight in fields far away; with the approach of the modern age, the village itself became more and more embroiled to the point of being threatened with total destruction.

Any researcher anxious to discover which of the ordinary citizens of his chosen district were involved in bygone wars is regularly advised to study the Muster Rolls of the sixteenth and seventeenth centuries which usually give the names of the able-bodied men between the ages of sixteen and sixty likely to be of military use and usually the kind of weapon they should provide. Unfortunately, the Muster Certificates for Essex, particularly for years when they are normally most informative such as for 1569, are not at all revealing because they give figures for several 'hundreds' combined together and not for individual parishes. It is not, therefore, possible to name the Ashdon men who were called to military service in Tudor times.

The Essex Assize files do, however, provide the record of at least one Ashdon man's being called to the colours in this period. On 19th February 1600, in 'the two and fortethe of her Majesties Raigne, Rob. Skynner of Ashden was pressed for her Majesties Service into Ireland' and delivered to Lieutenant George Brown. On 30th June 1600, he was indicted at the Chelmsford Assizes for having deserted. For later ages, however, a few documents have survived which show that even a community as remote as Ashdon could not entirely escape the effects of war. One such document is a petition from an Ashdon man which was sent to the local magistrates at the Petty Sessions of 1651-52:

> To his Excellency the Lord Generall Cromwell,
> The humble peticion of Jeremiah Maye.
>
> Showeth, that aboute 7 yeeres since your peticioner with one John Wyeburne, Sir Timothy Middleton's man did take a Cavalleere with his horse & arms at Stansted Mount Fitchett, and hee offered them his horse & 40 li (£) in money to lett him escape, But they refused the same, Not longe after your peticioner was imprest at Ashdon in the County of Essex for the Parliament service & served under the command of Captain John Smith in the Regiment of Sir William Waller at Basinghouse where he received divers hurts & wounds in his Body, As by certificate will appear, The which hath altogether made him unfitt for future service & noe waies able to mainteyne himselfe & languishinge family beinge nowe in a most ald & deplorable condicion.
>
> Humbly beseechinge your Excellency to take the premisses into your wise consideracion and to bee pleased to grant your Excellencies Warrant directed to the honorable Bench assembled in Essex to afford your peticioner a pencion or some other Releife what they in their wisdomes shall thinke fitt.
>
> And hee shall ever pray for your Excellency.

On the back of the paper is written:

> Whereas the Bearer hereof Jeremiah Maye the peticioner was wounded in the service of the Parliament and thereby unable to follow his calling as appears by the annexed certificate.

These are therefore to require you to permit & suffer him quietly to passe to Ashdon in Essex his former aboad without molestacion. And I desiere the Justices of peace for ye said County to allow unto the said Jeremiah May a competent weekly pencion for his releife & maintenance according to the late Act. Given under my hand & seale the 10th of January.

To all officers & souldiers under my command & others whom it may concerne.

(signed)
O. Cromwell

It is doubtless a measure of social progress that while the serving soldier has since time immemorial been expected to pay for wars in currency of flesh and bone, the civilian has been asked to make an ever-increasing contribution in pounds, shillings and pence. This trend can be clearly if modestly discerned in the Ashdon records: thus, in 1759, during the Seven Years War, £2. 9s. 0d. was paid by the Ashdon Guildhall Charity 'for George Taylors discharge from being a soldier', while in 1816, a public subscription held in Ashdon for the 'Poor Widows and Orphans' of those who lost their lives in the Battle of Waterloo raised £14. 11s. 6d. paid by forty five different contributors. Appeals to the charitable conscience of the individual parishioner was not, however, the only way of meeting the financial consequence of war. For centuries past, as for example, with the Lay Subsidy of 1327, the nation's rulers traditionally had recourse to fiscal measures to pay for military campaigning and these devices were employed on an increasing scale as England became more and more embroiled in the wars with first Republican and then Napoleonic France.

When William Pitt went to war with France in 1793 he made two important miscalculations: he believed the war would be short-lived and that it would be inexpensive. He was seriously wrong on both counts. Four years after the outbreak of hostilities, with peace seemingly as far way as ever, the country was faced with a deficit of £19 million. Pitt had no other option but to increase 'assessed' (or direct) taxes, on such luxury items as carriages, race-horses, hair-powder, dogs and clocks. On 25th January 1797, the Secretary of the Bank of England blithely announced:

> The Public are informed, that in pursuance of an Act of the present Session of Parliament, for granting to his Majesty an

THE THREAT OF INVASION

Aid and Contribution for the Prosecution of the War, Books are opened at the Chief Cashier's Office, in the Bank of England, under the following Titles:—
1. For the Payment of Assessed Taxes.
2. For the Payment of Assessed Taxes with a Surplus intended as a Voluntary Contribution.
3. For the payment of Voluntary Contributions.

There was an enthusiastic response to this appeal in the northwest corner of Essex: in Saffron Walden, where in 1795, rioters had forced merchants to sell corn-stocks, meat, flour and cheese at prices listed on a board nailed to the market cross the corporation resolved to suspend all public entertainments and donate the money saved to the war effort; the following list of voluntary contributors was opened in Ashdon, headed by the Rector and completed by nineteen of his parishioners in a variety of styles of handwriting some bold, some distinctly wavering:

Revd. John North, Rector in addition to his assessed Taxes	£15-15-0	Wm. Haylock	£2-2-0
		Wm. Hales	10-6
		Jeremiah Howes	2-6
Edmund Goodwyn M.D.	£25-0-0	Susannah Bowtell	1-0
Revd. William Bushell	£3-3-0	Sarah Cro	10-6
Thos. Giblin	£1-1-0	Wm. Smith	£1-1-0
Robt. Blackman	10-6	Tho. Whisken	£1-1-0
Wm. Bacon	5-0	Robt. Maskell	1-0
Saml. Brooks	10-6	Henry Freeman	£0-2-6
Daniel Kent	10-6	Joshua Ruse	10-6
Edmund Nerville	2-6	Thomas Green	£0-2-6
		Jas Ruse	£0-2-6

Beneath the subscription list the following handwritten instruction appears:

The Parishioners who are willing to contribute for the Defence of the Country are desired to pay their Contributions into the Hands of the Rector and Churchwardens within the present Week, in order that the Amount of the Contributions of the Parish may be transmitted to the Bank of England with all convenient speed.
Amount of whole   £54-7-6

If this was the typical response from a small rural community, the Government ought, by rights, to have been most impressed. The average weekly wage of a farm worker at this time was a mere ten shillings. But to raise funds in this manner was not an entirely satisfactory way to finance a major war, and it was not feasible to go on raising 'assessed' taxes indefinitely. Accordingly, in the middle of 1798, Pitt introduced a new scheme for paying for the war, graduated income tax levied on anyone who earned more than £60 per year.

Being cajoled or being legally obliged to hand over more and more money to the Government was not the only contribution civilians were called upon to make to the prosecution of the war with France. It was seriously envisaged that very much more and much worse was going to follow because, as the eighteenth century neared its end, there seemed to be a distinct possibility that Napoleon's forces were going to invade England. Essex with its flat coastline seemed just as likely to become a battle-zone as Kent with its natural bulwark of high cliffs and the county authorities began to make all manner of contingency plans. Had the French forces established a bridgehead and driven inland they would have encountered scenes of total devastation because the official policy at the time was to 'drive the country' and remove or destroy all resources likely to succour the enemy: bands of volunteers would have driven away the livestock, burnt the standing crops, destroyed roads and bridges. It was anticipated that a major cooperative effort would be required to feed the defending British Army and an official questionnaire was sent to the millers and bakers of every parish, accompanied by a leaflet giving advice on how the normal production figures could be increased. Ashdon is one of the few Essex parishes for which the questions and answers have survived intact and they make instructive reading.

The millers were all asked to complete a printed form which was worded as follow:

> WE, the undersigned MILLERS of the ... of ... in the County of ... having taken into Consideration a Plan recommended to our Attention by ... Lord Lieutenant and Custos Rotulorum of the County aforesaid,
>
> For ensuring a regular supply of Bread to His Majesty's

Forces, in the ... District, during the Continuance of the Present War, in case it should become necessary to assemble large Bodies of Men, in one or more given Points, for the Purpose of opposing an Enemy.

Do hereby declare our entire Approbation of the same. And we do most readily and faithfully promise and engage to deliver such Quantities of readymade Flour as we may happen to have in Hand, over and above the immediate wants of our Customers; and also to prepare, and deliver such Quantities of dry, sweet and clean Flour, made of good marketable ENGLISH Wheat, out of which the Bran shall have been taken by means of a Twelve Shilling seamed Cloth, as are expressed opposite to our respective Names, whenever we shall be required so to do, the whole in the manner, and upon the Terms, and Conditions specified in the Plan herein-before mentioned ...

Subscribers Names	Names and State of Water Mills	Names and State of Wind Mills	No. of sacks of flour of 280lbs net each, to be furnished by each Mill every 24 hours	Will the Subscriber provide the Wheat or not? Answer Yes or No.

Written in longhand in the first column were the following instructions:

Those who cannot engage to deliver the flour within 10 miles of the Mill should add to their names these words 'At the Mill'. Those who are not possessed with 12s. seamed cloths should add to their names these words 'No cloth'.

Two Ashdon millers replied: Stephen Philpot owned a water mill 'of no use only in very wet weather and then can do 4 load pr. week'. He also owned a windmill which was 'a very good one. Can do (if wind) 10 load pr. week'; Richard Kent had a windmill 'in good condition can if windy grind 4 load per week'. Both millers answered 'no' to the question 'will the subscriber provide the wheat or no?' but in the first column of his return, Richard Kent commented that he could deliver flour 'at any distance'. The return is signed by the Parish Constable of Ashdon in 1798, Jeremiah Howes, the official responsible for the correct completion of the form.

The wording of the Bakers' questionnaire showed some differences from that of the Millers: They 'most readily and faithfully' promised and engaged 'to bake and deliver such quantities of good, wholesome well-baked Bread, in Loaves of Three Pounds, as our stock of Flour in Hand at the Time may enable us to furnish, over and above the ordinary consumption of our Customers . . .' The printed form was divided into eight columns as follows:

Subscribers names	Number of Loaves of Three Pounds to be furnished by each subscriber every 24 hours			Number of additional Journeymen Required	For what kind of Fuel the Ovens are calculated	What Quantity is requisite for 24 hours to keep each oven constantly at work	Whether fuel is abundant or not? Answer YES or NO
	By their usual number of hands		By the help of additional journeymen for a constancy				
	For a constancy	On an emergency					

The two Ashdon bakers replied as follows:

Name	Usual	Emergency	Extra help	No. required	Fuel	Amount	Abundant?
Stephen Philpot	280	500	960	Two	Wood	3½ cwt	Yes
Edmund Nerville	85	191	383	One	Wood	1¾ cwt	Yes

Again the return is countersigned by Jeremiah Howes, the Parish Constable.

The corresponding return from the parish of Elsenham, also in the Saffron Walden area, will help set the Ashdon bakers' replies in some sort of social context. The single reply is from one Alexander McWhinnie who declares

> There is not a Baker properly Qualified for the Business in the Parish. Every Body Bakes their own Bread, only some of the Poor who can't always purchase Flour nor Wood. The

above subscriber is no Baker only for his own Family, and sells the Poor a little when they are in need, as Farmers and others do, betimes.

As long as the threat of invasion seemed real, officialdom continued to insist on the accurate and prompt completion of its questionnaires. 'At a General Meeting of his Majesty's Lieutenancy holden at the Shire-Hall Chelmsford on Friday the 8th Day of July 1803' . . . it was:

> Resolved,
> That as the very particular and critical Situation of the Country at this Time, and the Apprehension of an immediate Attack by the Enemy, require every Exertion of the Inhabitants of all Descriptions, and his Majesty . . . having directed certain Returns to be immediately made by the Constables of all the Parishes throughout the Kingdom . . . that it be earnestly requested of them that they do give their Assistance, and use every Means in their Power for such Returns to be made to the Subdivision Meetings with all possible Accuracy and Dispatch.

On August 12th 1804, a set of Regulations were promulgated 'for the preservation of Good Order to be adopted in case of Actual Invasion in each county of Great Britain'. The Magistrates of each County remaining at Home were 'to sit daily at a Place to be appointed in each Division for that Purpose; the 'trustworthy Housekeepers and others' were to be persuaded to enrol themselves as Special Constables whose particular function was to be 'the prevention and quelling of Disturbances' and the taking up and conveying of Offenders to Prison'. In addition

> If, contrary to Expectation, any Impediments should occur in the regular Supply of the different Markets, every Assistance to be afforded to the Persons who are accustomed or who offer to supply them, and Escorts to be granted in Cases where it may be necessary for the secure Passage and Conveyance of Cattle and Provisions.
> The Constables within each Division, assisted by Patroles of Volunteers, if requisite, to see that all Public-Houses within the same are orderly and regularly conducted, and, if thought

necessary by the Magistrates, to be shut at such Hours as they may direct; and to bring all unknown Persons, who cannot give a satisfactory Account of themselves, before the Magistrates . . .

Clearly the concept of 'total war' was beginning to take root and, as hostilities proceeded, even the trees were enlisted. The records of the Maynard Estate reveal that between 1807 and 1809, nearly four hundred oaks were taken from Shadwell Wood to aid the nation's war effort.

*   *   *

If Napoleon had proceeded with his plan to invade England, the population would have been alerted by blazing beacons, the traditional warning-system which was first devized in the days of the Spanish Armada. Between 1796 and 1798, the east coast was provided with advanced new equipment, the semaphore telegraph, a large frame with six shutters which could be opened or closed to form a range of patterns and which could be observed from a considerable distance through a telescope. Further inland, however, the more primitive system had still to be employed and in August 1803, the Lieutenants of each of the County Divisions were asked to ensure that adequate quantities of furze or other combustible materials should be heaped 'on such eminences in the Interior of the County as may appear best adapted for the purpose'. It was believed that 'a Boy of sufficient Discretion may easily be found, at a very trifling expence' to watch from each church tower, and hoist a large red flag when he saw the nearest beacon alight.

The links in the chain of Primary Alarm Signal Stations from the east coast to the north-west corner of Essex were Brightlingsea, Colchester, Earls Colne, Cosfield, Thaxted, Sewards End (on the western boundary of Ashdon) and Littlebury. How effective the system would have been had it been found necessary to put it into action is open to considerable doubt. On 14th November 1803, the system was partially tested by lighting nine of the beacons. The official verdict was that 'they did not answer the expectation that had been formed of them'. The Lord Lieutenant of Essex, Lord Braybrooke reported in December 1807:

I made and attended the largest beacon (at Littlebury) and

watched in my neighbourhood the corresponding one at Sewers [sic] End (4 miles away), and notwithstanding a great flame and smoke our beacon was not seen by our neighbours nor could we distinguish theirs.

He was not particularly impressed by the efficiency of the corps of observers:

The soldiers who watched (or rather who were ordered to watch) at the signal houses behaved disorderly, ran in debt in the neighbouring villages, and never were seen in their duty — but were heard of as poachers.

Improvements were thereupon ordered by Lt. Colonel J. Birch, Assistant Quarter Master General of the Eastern District and these were accepted by the general meeting of the Lieutenants of the County held on 27th May 1808. The signal stations were henceforth to be guarded by 'some careful person near the spot' who would be paid three shillings per week out of army funds and would 'see that no depredations are committed on [them] by idle people and that the station is always kept in a state to be occupied by soldiers should circumstances require it'.

In 1811, when it was clear that the threat of invasion had finally receded, payments ceased, at which juncture Lt. Colonel Birch commented 'as the Huts will remain standing, it is hoped that the Proprietors of Land will afford to them such protection as may enable their being reoccupied at a future Period ...'

How effectively these hopes were heeded it is not possible to estimate but what is abundantly clear is that throughout the century which followed the defeat of Napoleon, the imagination of the English people continued to be excited by the prospect of military invasion from across the sea: so much is evident by the remarkable number of novels and stories which were sold in vast quantities and inspired considerable attention as well as numberless imitations abroad.

Tales of imaginary wars played the same role and enjoyed the same spectacular commercial success in the late nineteenth century as science fiction has achieved in the second half of the twentieth. From 1880 to 1914, the British, French and German publics were able to gorge themselves on a seemingly never-ending feast of fiction in which their country was over-run by but eventually victorious over one of its near neighbours: a British best-seller like Erskine Childer's *The Riddle of the Sands* could be matched in France by Emile Driants's *La Guerre Fatale* or in Germany by August Niemann's *Der Weltkrieg* but the most spectacular success of them all was *The Invasion of 1910* which was published in book form in 1906. It sold over a million copies throughout the world and was translated into twenty seven languages including Arabic, Chinese and Japanese.

Its author was William Le Queux, Queen Alexandra's favorite novelist who had established his earlier reputation with such highly charged romances as *Hushed Up*, *Stolen Sweets* or *Indiscretions of a Lady's Maid*, all published in Newnes Sevenpenny Series at the turn of the century. *The Invasion of 1910* was fresh territory for him but ground which had been trampled over by whole battalions of bellicose novelists in the previous decades. The great majority of these writers had been quick to express the centuries-old Francophobia of the English by reviving traditional fears of invasion by the French or to exploit latter-day suspicion of what was felt to be a dastardly French plot with the plans to build a Channel Tunnel which were given very wide publicity in the 1880s. William Le Queux's novel was one of the first to appear in England after the signing of the *Entente Cordiale* in 1904 and one of the first to make the Germans rather than the French the villains of the piece.

The novel first appeared in 1905 as a serial in the *Daily Mail* and was marketed with considerable flair. Special advertisements were placed in the London dailies and many provincial newspapers consisting of a map showing the district the Germans were due to invade the next morning. Sandwich-men, dressed as German soldiers, paraded through London to remind the public that the progress of the great Invasion was being reported only in the *Daily Mail*. Attempts were made in the House of Commons to suppress the story altogether, it was condemned by Campbell-Bannermann and R.C. Lehmann declared that it was 'calculated to prejudice our relations with the other Powers'. All that happened immediately was that publishing houses of 'the other Powers' very rapidly brought out translations, sometimes spectacularly altered so as to display their side in the most favorable possible light. Two hundred pages were cut out of the German edition which in the original version described how the English snatched victory from the jaws of defeat, rose up against the common foe and put them to flight. The opening chapters, however, remained substantially unaltered. A vast German army, transported by one hundred 3,000-ton steamers and a host of lighters, barges and tugs, lands on the Norfolk coast on 3rd September 1910. East Anglia is rapidly over-run, there is desperate fighting across Essex, in and around Colchester and Chelmsford, and for a brief while, the line is held between Saffron Walden and Royston. (Ashdon does not merit a mention, doubtless because featuring it in the action would not have won all that many additional readers for the *Daily Mail*). The German hordes sweep irresistibly towards London which is ferociously bombarded and triumphantly occupied; they are finally overcome by a *levée en masse* of the whole population and by a strenuous urban guerilla campaign.

The novel, which lacks any strongly drawn individual characters and which reads like an extended series of newspaper *communiqués*, was a flagrant piece of propaganda. William Le Queux made no bones about this in his preface in which he declared 'To be weak is to invite war: to be strong is to prevent it. To arouse our country to a sense of its own lamentable insecurity is the object of this volume.'

He drove his point firmly home with an outspoken conclusion:

> The British Empire emerged from the conflict outwardly intact but internally so weakened that only the most resolute reforms accomplished by the ablest and boldest statesmen could have restored it to its old position ... Germany emerged with an additional 20,000 miles of European territory, with an extended seaboard on the North Sea fronting the United Kingdom at Rotterdam and the Texel ... Practically the whole cost of the war had been borne by England ... As is always the case, the poor suffered most. The Socialists, who had declared against armaments, were faithless friends of those whom they professed to champion. Their dreams of a golden age proved utterly delusive. But the true authors of England's misfortunates escaped blame for the moment, and the Army and Navy were made the scapegoats of the great catastrophe.

Just how faithfully Le Queux had expressed the popular mood of his day and just how close real life came to re-enacting his lurid fiction can be measured by three samples of evidence from Ashdon's more recent history. That the Imperial pride he voices was being assiduously maintained even at the humblest level is confirmed by the following extracts from the Log Book of Ashdon Village School:

24th May 1906: In order to commemorate Empire Day a few songs etc. had been learned by children. The Managers were represented by the Rev. T.H. Smith and Mr Ben Smith. All joined heartily in singing the National Anthem. The song *Flag of Britain* was then rendered by the children. The Rev. T.H. Smith then addressed the children for a few minutes on our duties and responsibilities which was keenly listened to by the children. After the reciting of Kipling's *Recessional* and the singing of *God Bless our Native Land* the school closed for the day.

25th May 1908: Empire Day was observed today. The following managers attended: Rev. D.B.R. Banham (Chairman), Rev. T.H. Smith (Vice Chairman), Major Pelly & Mr J. Hagger. Mrs Pelly was also present.

The proceedings were opened by the singing of the National Anthem followed by *The Flag of Britain*. Mr Banham then gave an interesting address on Christian duty and responsibility. Major Pelly told the children to keep the flag unsullied, and pointed out that only by manliness and courage could this great Empire of ours be held together, and to illustrate this point gave a graphic account of the battle of St. Vincent. Mr Smith also addressed the children and said that in our duty as citizens of a great empire we must not be haughty in our pride but loving and forbearing towards each other and to all nations, remembering always that we are not only children of an earthly empire but also children of God. After the singing of a few patriotic songs, the morning session closed, and a holiday was granted for the afternoon.

The British Army's attempts to ensure that Le Queux's fictitious catastrophe was not repeated in reality are recorded by Thomas Collins, who went on to become a Brigadier in later life, but was just a boy of seven when Ashdon and the whole of the surrounding district was taken over by the military:

THE THREAT OF INVASION

I can still remember quite vividly a number of scenes connected with the great Army manoeuvres of September 1912. The whole of the British Army was involved. The Kaiser came over from Germany and the King was out observing too with the whole of his entourage. The Third and Fourth Divisions from Tidworth and Colchester, respectively, took on the First and Second from the Aldershot Command. One side wore white hat-bands; the other side had no special distinguishing marks. They fought all around this area, we went out every day to watch — my mother, my sister, and I in our pony-cart, my father following behind on his bicycle — and it was the greatest possible fun. I suppose the thing that interested us most of all was the sight of the aeroplanes, all monoplanes, the first aeroplanes we'd ever seen. There were also four airships — the Alpha, Beta, Gamma and Delta. They consisted of a large cigar-shaped balloon with a gondola underneath for the crew. They never flew at more than five hundred feet and you could see the observer peering out with his field-glasses as plain as anything as it sailed majestically overhead, no doubt saying to his colleagues, 'Do you think *those* could be the enemy?" I don't know whether anybody down below ever thought of firing a round or two upwards in their direction. As targets go, those airships were pretty prime.

The fighting mostly took place on a line between Horseheath and Radwinter, about three miles north of here. There was a tremendous Cavalry Brigade camp over at Linton which we went over to see. In those days, if you got caught up in a supply-column, you went along at the proverbial snail's pace. They were all horse-drawn carts; as far as you could see, ahead and behind, were wagons and, of course, there was no overtaking unless you were prepared to go at a gallop and this was considered to be bad form. However, on one famous occasion, we got into a field below Ryder Hill which stands above Linton and now sports a prominent water-tower. Our pony was a thoroughbred which is always rather inadvisable. My mother was a first-class whip; she used to drive in London before she was married and she really knew what she was about. She needed to on that particular day. Our pony was ambling quietly along when a calvalry regiment passed him at the gallop. As you might suppose, he wasn't prepared to let that happen. Up the hill we went in our cart, over the stubble, at full gallop. There was no holding him. We were all convinced the cart was going to turn over. Somehow, we managed to get to the top of the hill where, fortunately, the cavalry regiment halted, otherwise I'm quite sure, we'd have ended up leading the charge to Lord knows where.

These manoeuvres took place in September when the shooting season was getting underway. My uncle, who was a major with the Eleventh Infantry Brigade from Colchester, found himself defending Great Bendysh Wood, to the south-east of Ashdon. This contained some of our prime shooting territory and, naturally, he was extremely keen that this shouldn't be disturbed by the blank firing. He tied a handkerchief round each arm which made it look as though he was an umpire, and he went straight across the line over to the other side who were then about six or seven hundred yards away. He approached one of the top ranking officers there and he said, 'I say, old boy, this happens to be our best cover. Do you mind awfully not attacking it?' 'Oh, not at all, not at all,' came the prompt reply. 'Quite understand, old boy. We'll go *round*.'

I can remember when the Cease-Fire went, there was tremendous cheering along the whole length of the front. I thought, in my boyish innocence, that the soldiers were cheering because they'd won. As an ex-soldier, I now know there's no question that they were cheering because the damn thing was over and done with. Or *was* it?

The Cease-Fire for this particular battle went very suddenly and, as things turned out for the defending army, in the very nick of time. It was quite dramatic. We were observing things from our pony-cart over near Radwinter, and we suddenly saw a detachment of cavalry approaching at a gallop. They drew up under some cover at a place called Plumtree Grove. There was an atmosphere of intense excitement. I don't know how this was conveyed to us but I remember it to this day. There was a sort of silence, infinite care was being taken to use ground and keep low and so on. One felt Something was just about to happen. Reading the accounts afterwards, I subsequently discovered what that Something was: if the Cease-Fire hadn't been sounded at that particular time, the Headquarters of the Southern Army would have been captured by those cavalry without the shadow of a doubt. They'd broken completely through and the prize was there for the picking. We didn't know this at the time, of course, because we were mere on-lookers, but there, close to Ashdon, in 1912, they'd achieved the really decisive breakthrough they were always trying for on the Western Front throughout the 14-18 War. When it came to the real thing, it never happened ...

Brigadier Collins was also provided details of a scenario in which Ashdon was to have enacted a role as dramatic as any conceived by William Le Queux. These details are contained in a set of documents preserved by his father, Captain J.A. Collins, and demonstrate that had the Kaiser's army advanced across Essex in the early stages of the First World War, the village of Ashdon would have had to be destroyed by the villagers themselves.

British defensive strategic planning had not radically altered since the Napoleonic Wars. It was still assumed that an invasion from the European mainland was as likely to be effected across the flat Essex shore as over the cliffs of the south-east coast and in 1914 as in the 1790s, the chief response to such an eventuality was going to be to 'drive the country', to clear the civilians from the path of the armies and to destroy all supplies and all buildings likely to be of use to the advancing enemy. Something of the atmosphere of those stirring times is conveyed in the General Instructions issued by central government to Local Committees and to Inhabitants IN CASE OF INVASION.

> An invasion is improbable. But an invasion is not impossible and hence the civil population must be prepared and organised for it.
>
> In case of an invasion in the Division the business of the civil population will be:—
> (1) <u>To destroy everything that might be of service to the enemy</u>
> (2) <u>To evacuate the Division entirely.</u>

If an invasion occurs, the civil population will know for the first time what war really means. All conditions will be altered; things which previously had great importance will suddenly cease to have any importance and martial law will be in force. The supreme duty of every citizen will be calmly, promptly, obediently, and with the utmost good will, to do his share in the general scheme of operations. Citizens who lose their heads, or refuse to obey instructions, even though such instructions may seem harsh, will be helping the enemy, and endangering not only the lives of their fellow citizens, but the safety of the Empire.

Under the heading THE ORDER TO EVACUATE, a supplementary sheet provided minutely detailed instructions that were expected to be carried out to the letter should the Emergency Committees' worst fears be realized.

One sub-section is entitled 'Getting the inhabitants away':

> On receipt of the order to evacuate all helpers must be instantly summoned by a prearranged method and the general alarm given.
>
> The Church Bells may be rung violently.
>
> No matter what method of alarm is employed, the danger of a false alarm, with all its regrettable consequences, cannot be entirely eliminated. Every precaution should be taken against it.
>
> Helpers on bicycles or on horseback must go to warn outlying parts of the parish.
>
> One or more helpers with bicycles or horses should be kept at hand for special unforeseen work.
>
> All inhabitants must understand that the motto is not 'Each for himself' but 'Each for all'.
>
> Owners of vehicles will have the first call on their vehicles, but every vehicle must pass through a given spot for inspection, and no vehicle must leave the parish until it is fully loaded with people. In vehicles, preference must of course be given to the aged, invalids and mothers with small children. If the supply of vehicles is insufficient, all persons, men or women who can walk, or ride a bicycle, should do so.
>
> Travellers should take with them nothing but clothes, blankets, money, jewellery, and food and drink for forty-eight hours. It is expressly forbidden to take away furniture or other belongings, as all available space in vehicles will be required for people.
>
> Helpers should empty bicycle shops and provision shops and distribute such of their contents as travellers may desire to take, destroying or rendering useless the remainder.
>
> The doors of deserted houses, though they may be closed, must not be locked. This rule is made because it has been found that in other countries the enemy has more or less respected the contents of houses deserted but not locked up.

THE THREAT OF INVASION

Another sub-section is headed <u>Destruction</u> and clearly shows how determined the authorities were to make life difficult for the invaders:

> The sole object of destruction is to make it impossible for the enemy to live on the land.
>
> All live-stock must be destroyed. The best way to kill cattle is to shoot them. Carcasses should not be bled, nor disembowelled. It is absolutely forbidden to use poison.
>
> After the destruction of live-stock, all firearms of every description (except antiques) should be collected so far as possible, and handed over to the police.
>
> All grain stocks must be destroyed, unless contrary instructions have been received from the General Officer Commanding, or unless their destruction would involve the destruction of buildings.
>
> Grain in stack need not be destroyed.
>
> Hay stacks and straw stacks must be burnt, unless their destruction would involve the destruction of buildings.
>
> Petrol must be either taken away or run off.
>
> All liquor, especially in hotels and public-houses must be run off.
>
> All vehicles not employed in the evacuation must be rendered useless by breaking the wheels.

Preparations to implement arrangements for the evacuation of the civilian population and for destroying livestock and materials were entrusted to emergency committees which were set up at parish level. The Chairman of the Ashdon Emergency Committee was Captain J.A. Collins whose planning was as meticulous as his record-keeping. Still preserved amongst his papers at Ashdon Hall and dated 13th February 1915, is the return he made to his District Co-ordinator providing minutely detailed replies to the specific questions that had been put to him. On the face ot it, every man, woman and child then living in Ashdon is accounted for as well as every animal and piece of equipment.

On the computatations of Captain Collins, there were in the parish at that time 170 horses in all, of which 15 are described as 'Riding' (2 under 4 years and 13 over 4 years), 16 were described as 'Light Draught' (3 under 4 years and 13 over 4 years) and 139 'Heavy

Draught' (47 under and 92 over 4 years). There were 384 cattle, 505 sheep and 698 pigs. There was an estimated 526 quarters of grains to be threshed, some 2,830 quarters of threshed grain in store, 534 tons of hay, 1,120 tons of straw and 5 tons of flour. The total number of vehicles in the parish was 167: this total was made up of 41 wagons, 80 farm carts, 46 'other horsed vehicles', 1 motor car, 2 motor bicycles and 17 pedal bicycles. At this time, the number of gallons of petrol stored in the parish was nil. In the columns headed 'Implements' are listed 35 picks, 76 shovels, 60 spades, 28 felling axes and 58 handsaws. The number of 'Male Employees' is given as 106 of whom 17 are described as 'cattlemen or drovers', 88 as 'labourers' and one as a 'Motor Traction Engine Driver'. The parish included no foresters, no carpenters, no farriers and no 'men accustomed to the use of Explosives'. No Farms or Estates in the district possessed a telephone. To the question 'Would the destruction by Fire of Stacks involve destruction of buildings?', there were 26 answers in the 'Yes' and 7 answers in the 'No' columns.

In these columns of carefully calculated totals completed in the same detail for all twenty nine of the Emergency Committees in the Petty Sessional Division of Saffron Walden there is much to marvel at: there is that seemingly insatiable appetite for statistical information displayed in English public life from the Domesday Survey onwards which has made scholarship profitable not to say possible for all manner of social and economic historians; there is a vivid panorama of a rural community's agricultural resources in the early dawn of the age of the internal combustion engine; most haunting of all, there is the prospect of a real-life holocaust more horrendous than anything in the apocalyptic war-fiction of the turn of the century.

The impression of impending catastrophe is powerfully intensified if one allows one's imagination to linger over the remainder of Captain Collins' return in which he tabulates the roles that would have been allocated to Ashdon's men, women and children. Ten of the villagers are named as special constables, six designated for Point Duty, fourteen selected as Dispatch Riders and eight as Guides; four are picked as Collectors of Tools, five as Drivers of Stock and twelve as Slaughterers; as many as eighty one are listed as Trench Diggers. More dramatic still is a fifteen-page document which sets out the Evacuation Plan in minute detail, listing the vehicles and their owners, the names of the drivers, the pick-up point and the names of the passengers assigned to each conveyance. The bulk of the convoy would have been made up of farm-waggons but all manner of other vehicles are listed also, providing a sensitive index to the village's social hierarchy. The majority of the farm labourers' wives and children, together with the proletarian elderly and infirm were to have travelled in waggons: old Reuben Ford, made famous by *Reuben's Corner*, was to have driven a waggon supplied by Alfred Hagger, and to have picked up from the 'Bonnett' public house out at Steventon End, three Mrs Smiths, two Mrs Coopers, Miss Cooper and four children. While the rector, most of the farmers and the shopkeepers would have set out in pony and trap, some of the gentry and the wives of some of the farmers, and their maids, would have been conveyed by dog-cart; the village's one motor car would have set out from *The Clays*, one of the more impressive private residences in the parish, bearing the very well-to-do owners Mrs and Miss Duchesne. The entire procession would have consisted of the single motor car, two waggonettes, three dog-carts, twelve ponies and traps, thirteen carts and forty waggons, each of which would have transported seven or eight passengers.

Captain Collins had prepared a typed set of instructions on pieces of white card to be issued to each driver once the order to evacuate had been received. The *recto* side of the card is set out as follows:

Instructions to Drivers

Driver
Waggon No.

—

On Mr — instructions you will take your horses to Mr — providing:-
  forage
  food for yourself
  rugs (or blankets)
  a bucket
  a lantern and matches
  extra rope and shoulder chains
harness as Mr — directs and drive to — where you will pick up:-

The *verso* of each card outlines the northward route the convoy was to follow once the inhabitants had been assembled from the far ends of the parish and the work of slaughter and destruction had been set in train:-

Route

Drive to Great Chesterford Park crossing the railway near the Halt and the Hadstock Road at Mitchell's.

Through Little or Great Chesterford to Ickleton and on to Chrishall Grange.

The route is marked by arrows painted on gates etc.

As the months passed, it became more and more obvious that the spectacular breakthroughs achieved in pre-1914 manoeuvres belonged to a bygone era of military history. As had happened in the course of the even more protacted Napoleonic wars, the threat of invasion receded and in August 1916, the central government announced from London:

The original Emergency Scheme is entirely cancelled . . . In view of changed conditions —

The Military Authorities, conjointly with the Home Secretary, have decided that in the event of an emergency arising —

(1) It will not be necessary to evacuate the civil population.

(2) It will not be necessary to destroy live stock or supplies.

Captain Collin's emergency plans were filed away in his desk at Ashdon Hall, the village work-force did its best to meet the nation's demands for higher and higher yields of corn and families with fathers or sons in France went on praying that the dreaded telegram bearing dire tidings from the distant Front would not be delivered to their door. For years after the Armistice, white arrows still stood out on walls and gates in the village and throughout the surrounding district to tantalize the young and recall to those old enough to remember the horrendous prospect of what might have been. For my part,.I have never ceased to marvel over the fact that while I was directed to my beloved Ashdon because of the Second World War, it could well have been destroyed by the First.

11

The End of an Era

> Oh let us love our occupations,
> Bless the squire and his relations,
> Live upon our daily rations,
> And always know our proper stations.
> *Charles Dickens:* The Chimes

The First World War left its indelible mark on Ashdon as it did on every single community in Britain, large or small. The names of its dead are inscribed on the small but dignified War Memorial which stands opposite the School where they learned to fight the good fight. In that same school, as in every other throughout Britain, on each 11th November for the next twenty years, the pupils stood in stilence from 11 a.m. till 11.02 and then proceeded to sing 'O God our Help in Ages Past'. Apart from that, and apart from the bereaved or the maimed, really tangible evidence of the direct effects of the First World War on Ashdon life is remarkably hard to come by. The great bulk of the working population of the village was still involved, as it always had been, in agriculture, employed by a score or so of farmers whose ranks were augmented by a few newcomers from the north of England, and the squirearchy, as it had done for hundreds of years, remained in its three principal bases: the Rectory (home of the Lord of the Rectory Manor), Ashdon Hall (home of the Lord of the Manor of Ashdon) and Waltons Park (home of what, through marriage and conveyancing, became the combined Manors of Steventon End and Newnham Hall). Compared to many a Stately Home, Waltons is of modest dimensions but to most Ashdonians, it is recognised as the Big House, the place where they habitually come together for such communal activities as the annual fete or a royal jubilee and within its grounds, throughout this century, have been sited the pitches for the thriving village soccer and cricket teams. Between the wars, its *châtelaine* was Mrs Leila Luddington, and her active interest in Ashdon affairs, both large and small, is recalled with amused affection by many of the older villagers. The three following witnesses are both representative and instructive. Firstly, *Kitty Vinall*, who served for many years as Ashdon's District Nurse:

'I first arrived in Ashdon in 1944 and this is how it came about. It was the war which led me into nursing, really. I felt I ought to do *something* and I thought about joining the Women's Land Army. I thought about the hard work and being out in the wet and the cold and I quickly decided that wasn't for me. Quite funny, that reasoning, the way things later turned out . . . Well, I belonged to the A.R.P. and the local Red Cross in the Sussex village where I'd been brought up and it so happened that I'd done exceptionally well in the various First Aid tests. No doubt with that in mind, the vicar's wife suggested I should possibly go away and take up nursing professionally. So that's what I did. I did three years of General Nursing training and after that, my midwifery-certificate. In those days, you either paid for your midwifery training yourself or you did it under contract by doing your two years in the County which provided the training. I chose the second method and the county I was trained in was Essex. I owed them two years. I did one year in Leytonstone and Stratford and then it emerged that Ashdon was desperate for a nurse. I was rather boggled off to Ashdon to pay back the second of the two years I owed and I've worked here ever since. That should give you some idea of whether I like it here or not!

For fifteen years, I lived in a little cottage beside Waltons Park. The cottage was owned by Mrs Luddington who also thought she owned the nurse! She rang me up *every* morning to see what was on my list for that day and she also had the right to inspect my books at any time. We were always on the best possible terms. It was a two-up, two-down little cottage which, when I first arrived, contained a very beautiful Aladdin lamp and precious little else. There was no electricity and no conveniences of any sort. It was as good as most people had, though, and in fact I was absolutely thrilled with it. I felt I was really getting somewhere: so soon after I'd started, to have the tremendous responsibility of the health of a widespread area *and* a house thrown in was more than I'd dreamed of.

Mrs Luddington more or less kept me to start with. I'd got very little money and she provided me with eggs, fresh vegetables, tomatoes and soup. She really was an exceptionally good Lady of the Village: one of the old school. She certainly did everything that was humanly possible as far as I was concerned. For a long time, midwifery services had been organized on a county basis but *general* nursing was under a local Sick Committee. The County Council paid something towards midwifery services but nothing for General Nursing. The money for this had to be provided by the local community itself and some part of this was regularly raised through whist drives and all sorts of communal efforts. I *hated* those whist drives: I had to go along to give out the prizes and regularly show willing. Each month, I'd go along and they'd say, "Well, we've just about raised enough to pay your salary *this* month. We're not sure about next month. Expect something'll turn up." It didn't seem all that amusing at the time! I also had these village Associations in which the villagers paid twopence a week: that entitled them to free nursing-services. If people didn't belong to the Association, they paid me three shillings for each visit I made to them. This sometimes proved very tricky. You might well be visiting a household which hadn't had the foresight to pay into the Association. Sometimes, you'd feel that

Mrs Luddington distributing prizes at the 1948 Annual Flower Show

another visit was medically advisable but would certainly be financially burdensome. What did you do? Well, in fact, lots of visits were made without payment at all but then you'd be under the eagle eye of the village Association Treasurer. Sometimes, one of these treasurers would stop you and say, 'Now I *know* you've paid six visits to that house. They haven't contributed. Where's the money for all the calls?' So I had to be a little bit cagey about extra visiting and not letting too many people know about it. This state of affairs lasted from 1944 to 1948. When the N.H.S. came in, of course my salary was assured. Nurses no longer had to hold their hands out for their money. After that, it came regularly through the post. There were no more funny looks, no more Treasurer's spy-system, and, for me, no more dishing out the prizes at the monthly whist-drives!

* * *

Secondly, *Mrs Eileen Buncombe*, who moved to Ashdon in 1947:

When we took stock after moving in, we had a very positive feeling that we'd come into a genuine community. For example, with just a single once-a-week excursion into Saffron Walden, I found we could satisfy all our shopping needs within Ashdon itself: you could get marvellous home-baked bread from the village baker's, the butcher was very good and there was an exceptionally good general stores. We felt that the community was very positively a caring one and it all seemed embodied somehow in the person of Mrs Luddington who was then very much the Lady of the Village. She called on me very soon after we got here and then she called again as soon as I'd had my baby. My husband's former housekeeper came over to be with me when I was having the baby and because, apparently, I was having a rest, she wouldn't allow Mrs Luddington to cross the front doorstep. She had to make contact with me by letter saying she hadn't been able to get past my Dragon. Normally, she didn't find it so hard to get a sight of the new-born babies of Ashdon. There wasn't a baby born in the place in those days but Mrs Luddington wasn't there the next day to see it. She really did *look* at it, it wasn't just a question of flowers and a card from the Lady of the Manor. She went right into the houses and I'm sure almost all the villagers would tell you they never minded. She didn't look closely at the curtains or inspect to see if there was a hole in the carpet. She really knew how to *in-*

troduce. She was a very good person and to my way of thinking, her going meant the start of the disintegration of the old village community.

Of course, I realize there's a lot more to it than that. There's been a general levelling in society all round. I'm not sure that those who used to be on the receiving end of the Lady of the Manor's benevolence would be quite so welcoming today. The anonymous Welfare State has taken over most of the duties of the old-fashioned squire and such largesse as there is now quite impersonal. Before that particular piece of social evolution took place, Mrs Luddington played her part admirably here and did a lot, I believe, to hold things together when various forces were threatening to pull the community in different directions.

*   *   *

Much the same point was made by *Arthur Kemp*, headmaster of the village school for a quarter of a century:

The great person in the village when we arrived here in 1950 was Mrs Luddington. She was the Lady of the Manor and took up residence at Waltons Park in the First World War. Her age, I think, is strikingly shown when I tell you that when she was presented at Court it was to Queen Victoria. She fulfilled her manorial role in the traditional liberal way. She's a person for whom I have an enormous respect even although all my class-prejudices ought to be against all she stands for. She was friendly and welcoming, she used to take me to drawing classes at Linton, we'd be invited to the big house at Waltons and so on. The great thing about her, I remember, was the fact that whenever a child was born in Ashdon, she gave it a Savings Stamp to start it off in life. When our third child was born, Mrs Luddington approached us and said she hoped we wouldn't take offence but she proposed to do exactly the same for our daughter who was born in Ashdon Schoolhouse. She was a splendid institution: one day she could go into a derelict cottage where a family of up to a dozen children might be living on a labourer's wage, and she'd sit in their kitchen and talk away, and the next day, she might well be at a Buckingham Palace reception. She had this wonderful gift of being equally at home with everybody. This aspect of paternalism was something quite unexpected to people like my wife and myself, coming as we did from our urban, organized, trade-union, working-class background. To be quite honest, I'm bound to concede that we were impressed, though I think this had everything to do with the personality of Mrs Luddington herself. We ought to have resented the feeling of being patronized but somehow we didn't and weren't!

*   *   *

I was able to interview a number of the members of Mrs Luddington's domestic establishment and from their different accounts one can assemble quite a detailed picture of what below-stairs life was like at Waltons Park between the wars. What struck me with particular force was that if Mrs Luddington's employees were indeed latter-day survivals from an ancient feudal era, they all found satisfaction, if not authentic pride, in their calling. *Mrs Threadgold*, Mrs Luddington's cook for thirty years was genuinely surprised when I asked her if she at any time resented being a domestic servant:

'It was a very good position to be the cook at the Big House in the village. There's many who'd have liked it in those hard times. I never thought twice about going into service, it seemed the most natural thing in the world. My father was a gamekeeper, my mother was in service, their parents were in service before them, so my sisters and I were put into it too. I was thirteen when I left school in Hatfield Forest in 1908 and I wasn't home round about five days before my mother got me a little job looking after an elderly lady. It was a sort of little apprenticeship for me. I used to go to her mornings only just to start and come back home afternoons. After that, when I was about fifteen, I went with my three sisters down to Eastbourne to work for a gentleman who had a big tea plantation in China. I was a housemaid for two years and then, when I came back to Newport, Essex, I got a better position as parlour-maid. That was another rung on the ladder, you see? Round about that time, I met my husband. He was a gamekeeper in Takely Forest and he'd been lodging with her all the time I was away in Eastbourne. After that, when we were thinking of getting married, my mother said, "Well, now, look. If you're getting married, you've got to learn cooking. I want you to go into a place where they'll learn you to cook." So that's what I did. I went to a family in Bishops Stortford who had a big shop and I was their cook. The first thing I ever had to cook there was sausages and the lady had to show me how that was to be done. I've learned quite a bit since then, of course, but that was the way of the start of it. I wasn't the cook at Waltons straight away. I had to work up to it. I only got to be the number one cook after Mrs Luddington's first cook left. Been with her over forty years, she had, so you see it wasn't too bad a life, was it? Nobody would stay forty years in one place if they didn't like it. In any case, it meant you had a place to live and you didn't want for food or for warmth and such. But there was more to it than that. You came to feel you were part of a family, if you know what I mean. You weren't sort of swallowed up in the crowd. You had your place and you knew your place, you might say. No, looking back, I wouldn't say they were bad times. Mrs Luddington was never any bother to me in my kitchen. She'd come in once a day to tell me what she wanted and then left me to get on with it. Which I did. And when you'd done that particular job, there was always something to show for it. It might be a pie or a stew or a cake or a tray of scones. I enjoyed my time at Waltons and when it was burned down like that it was all very sad. What a waste!

*   *   *

A similar sense of satisfaction in a job well done was expressed by *Lawrence Bidwell* who, before he took over the only garage and petrol station in Ashdon in the late nineteen-forties, had been in Mrs Luddington's employ for nearly a quarter of a century:

'I can't say for sure when first I got interested in machinery but it *seems* as though I've been mechanically-minded all my working life. Certainly I was working with machinery before we came to Ashdon which was in 1917. My father was Major Luddington's manager over at Littleport and I worked there too for about a year on the steam engines they had over there and also on the first tractor they ever had. When they sold out and came over to Waltons Park, we were brought over with the establishment and we lived at Place Farm which is the home farm, as they call it, of the estate. I continued with tractor driving and doing mechanical jobs around the estate until 1921 which was the year Major Luddington died. That meant a complete change in the Luddington style of life. Up till then, they'd had a big car and a full-time chauffeur as part of the establishment. When the Major died, they had to lay up the car and the chauffeur had to go. It was only after the legal affairs were settled and Mrs Luddington resumed a more normal life, as you might say, that she bought another car and I started in private service.

I had two main jobs at Waltons Park. I used to look after the central heating and the electric light charging-plant. They had a form of central heating at Waltons from before the 14-18 war. There were at least two old boilers situated in the cellar. In the cellars, I should say by rights, because there was a regular ramification of cellars there: cellars and underground passages all over the place. You used to go down into one cellar and there'd be a passage leading round into another cellar; to your right, there'd be a group of three or four cellars and to the right *of them*, another lot still, going right out under the courtyard at the back. Someone, sometime, must have spent no end of time down there burrowing into the earth. There was supposed to be a passage going underground all the way to the parish Church but that I never did discover.

As well as the mechanical handyman, I was also the chauffeur. In those days, we went everywhere by car and we had a fair selection in the time I was there. We had a Buick Tourer for about a year, a bit on the draughty side and not quite the style of car Mrs Luddington wanted. Next we had an Austin four-cylinder limousine with an open front, after which she went for an Austin six-cylinder effort, all enclosed, which we had for eight years. Then she bought a Buick Straight Eight. Now that really *was* a car, lovely to drive and never a mite of trouble.

As I say, we used to drive all over the place. At least once a week, we'd drive up to London. Mrs Luddington would stay at her club at Hyde Park Corner while I'd lodge with an aunt of mine at Putney. When she went abroad, which she was able to afford just about every other year, she always used to go to Italy, and I'd drive straight from Ashdon to Victoria Station. Traffic was light in those days and driving through London was no bother at all. Twice a year regular, she'd go down to Pembroke to paint and again, we'd drive all the way, stopping overnight at Ross-on-Wye. All that came to an end with the Second World War. There wasn't the petrol to go around so the big Buick was laid up for the duration. I've no cause to regret my years at Waltons Park. I was left very much to my own devices, was boss of my own domain as you might say, and was engaged in a job I liked doing. That was more than many a man could say in the twenties and thirties. I've no complaints at all ...

*   *   *

A rather more detailed account of domestic service life was provided by *William Albon* who, before becoming head gardener at Waltons Park, learned his craft at the rather more opulent establishment of Bartlow House, a mile or so distant across the Cambridgeshire border. This same William Albon, incidentally, is the Bill Albin (sic) described in *Reuben's Corner* as having a big casket of a head containing 'but a meagre treasure'. I can only report that I found his company wholly engaging and readers may judge for themselves from the account that follows whether the judgement of Mr Mays is altogether to be trusted:

'I was born in Bumpstead. I was an only child. I went to school in Bartlow. Used to get the stick occasionally. The Churchwarden, whose name was Gibbs, was also overseer at the school. Anything wrong we done, he used to come in. We had a schoolmistress and old Gibbs had to be sent for to punish us. It was hold your hand out and you'd get six nasty raps. Can't say I cared much for that.

I stayed at that school till I was thirteen, then it was time for to start work. I started work as houseboy to Mr Brocklebank at Bartlow House. That was the biggest house in the village and Mr Brocklebank was the top gentry. The Reverend C.H. Brocklebank was his full title and he was powerful rich with it. Used to breed greyhounds. That was his great passion. Dreamed of winning the Waterloo Cup, they used to reckon. Funny sort of hobby for a right reverend gentleman but greyhounds was his pride and joy.

As I say, he has this great big house and estate at Bartlow. Kept it like a squire. There was a tidy sized staff to run it. Twelve maids, all told, a butler, a footman and a page-boy for the Reverend Brocklebank. I was houseboy. My jobs were to clean the shoes, clean the knives and forks, get in the coal and sticks, that sort of thing. I'd have to start at seven in the mornin' and leave off at five at night. Then I'd go back home. For that, I picked up the princely wage of five bob a week.

After that, I went into the blacksmith's shop alongside my father. He was the blacksmith on Rev. Brocklebank's estate. He wanted me to be a blacksmith also but I never had any interest. I didn't mind the iron work side so much: that was real craftsmanship. It was the horses I didn't much care for. They'd come off the land all dirty in that time. Sometimes I reckon they come straight in off the plough: greasy legs, all old hair, mud up to here. Didn't fancy having *that* between my legs. It wasn't for me. All I ever wanted to be was a gardener.

They wouldn't give me a job as gardener straightaway. What I used to do was go back up the estate in the evenings and go round with the vegetable head gardener. They had two head gardeners, one for fruit and one for vegetables. The vegetable one was a Swiss. He was a very clever man but a bit of a cure. He had a terrible temper and used a lot of bad words. He taught me a lot. About gardening, that's to say. There wasn't nothing I don't think you put in front of him that he couldn't grow.

It was always hard work in the gardens but we had our funny moments too. One Sunday morning, I went up to help him water the peach-house. He was a-leanin' over with the can to get come water from the pool. The water-level was a bit low, he leaned out a bit too far and over he went. He was a bit crotchety when I pulled him out. There was another time when he got into hot water, as you might say, and that were a Sunday mornin' also. The old butler at the big house told him the lady was going to be away for the weekend. This old Swiss man thought that would be a fine time to have his all-over bath in the greenhouse. So what he did was get out the big tin bath, drawed the water from the boiler what heated the greenhouse, took off all his clothes and got into the bath. Presently, Mrs Brocklebank walks in at the other end to collect some carnations . . . He never did tell us what they said to one another.

Another story concerning him was when we got a boy digging over a round flower-bed. He started on the outside and just kept on a-diggin' round and round. Next thing was he finished up plumb in the middle. Didn't see *how* he was to get off. All the other blokes right took the mike out of 'n. The old man was over by the greenhouse, stood watching. He came right over and said 'Ach. The mike you have took. You take it again, you buggers, and it's the damn sack you shall have!'

The worst scrape I ever got into myself was when I put the mower into the brook. It happened this way. I was a-cuttin' along the riverbank and the river had about four or five foot of water in it. There'd been a little shower in the early afternoon and I must've been a mite too anxious to get on with it. Should've waited for things to dry. Anyways, I didn't and consequent, the wheels skidded and down she goes, wallop, in the water. She spent all night under water. The gov'nor came over the little wooden bridge that night and went back out over the bridge next morning and he never see her. I'd have been in the brook myself or out on my ear more like if he had done. As it was, we got her out next morning, George Bennett and I. Washed her in petrol and away she went like a bird. Kept going for years and years after that did that old motor-mower, long after I'd left Bartlow.

I suppose the next scrape I got myself into that, you might say, was the First World War. I wanted to be in it so I joined up at 17½. I put down my age as 18 to get in. Didn't do myself all that good, mind you. Just two days before the cease-fire, I got hit by a piece of shrapnel in the back of my neck.

After the war, my father was still powerful keen for me to work beside him in the blacksmith's shop. He was a real craftsman, my father. He had to do plenty besides shoe the horses. He made all sorts of things for around the estate and for the Church. Though I say it myself, he made things with his hands that no workman could turn out today, acetylene welding-gear and all. In particular, he made a pair of gates for the Bartlow Estate that are decorated with flowers and tulips all in iron. I never could have done that. For me, it had to be real flowers, real tulips. I *had* to be a gardener. And so it turned out.

After the Great War ended, I became head gardener to the Rev. Brocklebank. My wages was thirty shillings a week. To be accurate, twenty nine shillings and threepence, with ninepence off for my insurance stamp. I don't think I paid any income tax. Six months after starting that job, I got married. I'd first met my wife when we was thirteen years old. She worked for Brocklebank's also. We was twenty seven when we was married so you could say that was a fairly steady courtship. Mind you, I used sometimes to talk to other girls too. I was well placed to give them flowers. But it was never serious like.

I stayed as head gardener at Bartlow for eleven years till the Brocklebanks sold up and moved away. Mind you, I was lucky, though. Not long after, I got the job as head gardener to Mrs Luddington at Waltons Park, and there I stayed for thirty year till the end of my workin' life.

I enjoyed my time at Waltons Park. It was hard work but with gardening there's always something to show for it. There was a great big staff to start off with: all the staff for inside the house as well as carpenters, painters and the like, and three or four of us to do the gardens. As time went by, this staff had to be cut down. The full-time gardeners became part-time. Come the end, I was the only one left to do those gardens.

Growing fruit and flowers was always what I liked doing best of all. I didn't much care for diggin' and weedin'. Mrs Luddington loved her flowers. She'd absolutely fill the house with them. Geraniums were one of our specialities: not the little ones down near your ankles but big standards, right up to your shoulders. We'd have to pinch the tops out so as to make them nice and bushy. What a picture they made when you'd set them out. We also grew quantities of chrysanthemums, three or four hundred potfull. There'd be two or three hundred primulas and the same number of cinerarias, freesias and bulbs every year. Beautiful growing soil, those gardens had. It would grow just about anything.

We used to grow fruit also. As well as the usual sort, we grew any amount of peaches and grapes. We'd grow the grapes in the big greenhouse, always about eight or nine lines of 'em. I suppose we used to average about three hundred bunches. They had to be kept thinned out, about a foot apart. It would take about an hour to thin a bunch properly. You'd have a little stick in one hand, just to part the leaves, and a special pair of grape-scissors. Then there were the peaches. Lovely peaches we used to grow, although I say it myself. The secret is to keep the leaves good and moist in the summertime. Many's the time I've gone back into them after Sunday evening Church to make sure they had their drink. Let them leaves go dry in the sun and you get red spider, sure as sure. It's goodbye to your peaches, then. When I first started out as a gardener, little did I dream that ever I'd be able to grow juicy round peaches like that old Swiss used to. Howsoever, I did. That was a dream come true.

I couldnt get away from horses altogether. The times I had with them was mostly good ones. When I was with Mrs Luddington, the mower would be drawn by a pony. He'd have to have special shoes made out of leather. Albert Bassett made those. He were another blacksmith craftsman, like my father. I didn't have to lead that pony none. I could start him on that big front lawn and just leave him to it. He'd keep a-goin', round and round on his own and that whole lawn would end up cut as smooth as smooth. He wouldn't miss a mite and that's God's truth. Lovely old boy, he was, name of Tommy. Mind you, if you had him to pull the brougham or the damned old four-wheeler then he'd go like a bat out of hell. Many's the time I had to drive Mrs Luddington down the Carsey on the way to Linton, to the Board of Guardians, and that old pony would go as if the devil hisself was after us.

When the 1939 War came, the Royal Air Force took over Waltons Park and used it for an Officers' Mess. And a right mess they made. Mrs Luddington had just a few small rooms left to her for her own use. Strange, isn't it, that that big house should have been spared right through the War and then burnt down after it was all over. Bartlow House got burned down too. Like as if there's a sort of curse on these fine big old houses.

I don't much like to think or talk about it but I must admit I won't forget till my dying day that terrible fire. 22nd of February 1954, it was, with the trees all bare. Mrs Luddington was away painting in Cornwall and I'd been left in charge. We came back up the road from the Church where I always sang regular in the choir. I'd been in and seen the windows was all shut. That would have been something like four in the afternoon. Everything was in order. Half-past four next morning, the police came and got us out of bed. 'Come on, Bill, quick', they said, 'the Park's on fire!' And by God, it was too! My wife and daughter and I went out as quick as we could. We showed the firemen where the pool was by the rookery. 'Tweren't no use. At six o'clock, the roof fell in. I wanted to go in to save what I could. The police wouldn't let me; they wouldn't let nobody near. Mrs Luddington's clothes had been laid out all on the spare beds in the spare room, all ready to be packed. She was due to go off to Cyprus the following week. She never did come back here no more. Must have fair broke her heart.

What dam near broke mine also was all the questions they kept on putting to me, straight after the fire, the Police and the Norwich Union. Was I *sure* I'd checked everything? Could I have left a cigarette burning? I've never ever smoked in my life. To think anybody could think I had anything to do with what happened fair chokes me. I

Waltons after the fire

love that place like it was my own. In a way, it *was* sort of my own. You could see what the fire had done from our cottage window here. No leaves on the trees that time of the year. Made you feel sick and ill deep down inside, what you saw then, and what you smelled. I couldn't smell my flowers for ages afterwards but, course, that come back in the end. That had to didn't it?

I always worked all the hours God sent. I'd be up at five in the morning and as like as not it'd be close on ten before I come back at night. I never grudged those hours. I loved making things grow and making places beautiful for other folk. I used to decorate the Church at Ashdon at Easter, Christmas and Harvest Festival. And up at the Big House I'd regularly do the floral decorations. Pity is, my decorations will never last like dad's iron flowers. *His* floral decorations anyone still can see, though he made them all those years ago.

I need two sticks to get about nowadays but I can just about manage to yet. Guess what I like doing most now I've retired? making my own garden grow.

* * *

Bill Albon's account can be complemented with one equally detailed provided by his late wife Constance who was so determined to get the record straight that she followed her interview with additional reminiscences she subsequently set down in a small exercise book:

When I left school in Haverhill, it was two months before my thirteenth birthday; I don't know how I managed that but I *did*. I went and got a little day-job at the station-master's house at Haverhill. I got a shilling a week to start with and when I'd been there six months, she gave me a sixpenny raise. I used to go at nine and stay till five. I'd have my dinner there mid-day but no tea. I had to do all the different chores: polishing, scrubbing, washing-up. That weren't too hard. That wasn't a very big place, you see. That was just two rooms downstairs, a hall and three bedrooms upstairs. Good apprenticeship for the rest of my life, as it turned out.

My mother fixed up my next job. I suppose she was glad, really, to get me off her hands. Anyway, on 5th March 1914, off I went to Bartlow House, and that was just two months before my fourteenth birthday. I started off as under-housemaid. There were four housemaids all told and ten more domestic staff as well. As well as that, there was an outside staff of six for the flowers and vegetables. My duties were all to do with cleaning. I was forever clearing grates, emptying slops, scrubbing doorsteps, polishing brass-work. There seemed to be no end of it.

My day would start just after six a.m. with the old alarm clock waking me up. I'd begin by making tea for the other housemaids and calling Grooby, the Upper Housemaid with her hot water. Then I'd be off downstairs to make a start on my various cleaning jobs. There was any amount of water-carrying to do. You see, there was no wash-hand basins in bedrooms in those days, no running water. Everything had to be carried in pails and emptied down the toilet. Most gentry had baths in their bedrooms: the ladies had hip-baths, the gents had big round baths with a lip attached. You'd scoop out the bath-water with a chamber-pot, pour that into a pail and so on. Backwards and forwards, up and down those old stairs till all the water was gone.

Then, of course, you had to fill the baths up all over again when the time come. The hot water had to be carried in large two-gallon brass cans, and when these were in use, they had to be cleaned and shined up every day. You also had to put a brass quart can in each basin and cover it over with a hot-can lid. You'd have to do this first thing each morning and again in the evening when the gentry was getting ready for eight o'clock dinner.

When I was under-housemaid, another of my regular early morning jobs was to clear out and re-lay the grates. Downstairs, there'd be the sitting room, box room, billiard room and the big hall when they had a fire there, which wasn't often; upstairs, I'd probably average four or five bedrooms a morning. You'd have to cart your paper, sticks and coal upstairs and lug the ashes down. That wasn't no picnic. Cleaning the carpets was another job. That was different than nowadays. There was no hoovers, no mechanical gadgets. When you turned out a room, you took tea-leaves which you'd previously washed and then put through a sieve and dried out. You'd sprinkle these dried tea-leaves over your carpets and then three of you would each take a big bass broom and sweep the carpet right across to the skirting-board. All tea-leaves and fluff it would look like but those carpets would come up a treat. And if we didn't have enough of the tea-leaves, then the trick was to use old newspaper, soaked in a bowl of water and then squeezed out. You spread that all about and pressed all over that.

Your doorsteps had to be scrubbed every morning, right through the winter. Winter didn't make no difference as far as they was concerned. I've seen us scrubbing when the ice was a-forming. One door in particular, out on the Camps Road there, regular used to freeze over as you scrubbed it. And there didn't have to be a spot in the vestibules. Bright little red tiles, there were, all over, and there daren't be the least little spot seen anywhere. You could be a-sittin' having' your breakfast and Grooby would just march in and say, 'May, there's a *spot* there! Go and clean it off! At once!' And off you'd have to go, there and then. You'd have to be specially particular with your doorbell. There'd be a round brass disc with a key attachment, of brass also, like a thick ring, and you'd turn that to make the bell ring. That had to be polished up like billy-o. That wasn't runny metal polish like today. That was all thick and mucky, more like jelly it was, and if there should ever be the tiniest spot of that left on, then woe betide you! And there mustn't ever be a bit of polish left on those varnished doors. I've been called back to it over again more than a few times. That had to be done just right. Of an evening, we'd be sat in the housemaids' sitting room a-mending household linen. I was a fair darner so I come in for my share and more. There again, Grooby was most particular. That had to be just so and so you just didn't bodge it.

In the Spring, we'd start house-cleaning. The gentry would be most always away, out of England altogether as like as not. That would give us the chance to give the main rooms a real good going-over. That was when the decorators would come in. As for us, we'd have all the carpets up and out on the lawns for a good beating with cane bats. The footman and the hall-boy helped at this so we had to be very much on our guard. What I mean by that is that we didn't have to say a word out of turn or we'd very soon be in trouble with our uppers. The upper *servants*, that's to say, who saw we kept our place in the order.

In the autumn, the game-shoot would begin: September, the partridges; October, the pheasants. We'd have a full house for five days each week. The guests would come in on Mondays. There'd be shooting on Tuesday, Wednesday and Thursday, then they'd leave on the Friday. Lunch used to go out in large baskets, by horse and cart to special sheds around various parts of the estate. The ladies would lunch out with the shooters, and the butler and footman would always be in attendance. In the afternoon, the ladies would come back in and rest. Then they'd put on their tea-gowns which had already been laid out for them by the maids. They'd wait for their gentlemen to come back in for tea, and this, they'd take in either the drawing room or else the billiards room. Dinner was at eight in the evening and, as like as not, several extra butlers would wait at table, some even staying in the house as well as the guests. The table was always most elegant with a different colour-scheme each night. The Lady was real gifted at flower-arranging. The billiards, cigar-smoking and port-drinking would go on to the early hours of the morning.

The food was good: nice meat, veg. from the estate gardens, a fresh sweet every day. Eggs, milk, chickens, mutton and lamb all came from farms on their own estate. Butter and bread was all made in the house and so was all the jam from the fruit in the estate gardens. We never went without ourselves. Always had plenty to eat while plenty of poor devils round about could only get by with poaching. I remember the old Swiss gardener would come up to the kitchen window at strawberry time, and he'd say to Cook, 'These strawberries would suit you, yes?' He was the *vegetable* gardener, really, he was but he thought that was right, he being the head, to bring that fruit up to be passed fit for table.

There was a right way and a wrong way when it come to our own meal-times. The four housemaids and footman had their meals together in the servants' hall. The cook, housekeeper, the lady's maid and the butler had the best part of their meals in the housekeeper's room or 'Pugs' Parlour', as it was called. The kitchen-maid, scullery-maid and hall-boy had theirs in the kitchen. There was a place for everybody and everybody had to keep in the right place. The head housemaid, Grooby, must've been about fifty year old and must have been there for nigh on twenty year before I come. She ruled with a rod of iron. We were told what to do and what we was not to do. There was never any answering back. You'd be sitting there at table and you'd very soon be told *you* weren't being spoken to and you weren't to chime in. You respected your elders and betters. You might well be seen but there was no call for you to be heard.

The staff from the housekeeper's room had their meat and veg. course with us but when they'd eaten that we'd all have to stop. Down our knives and forks would go, the butler would say grace, and off they'd all troop to their own special room for the sweet. Sir Philip Reckitt from Colman's mustard was on a visit one day, and his chauffeur came in to dinner with us domestic staff. After the grace was said and the top staff was going out, he said he'd never seen anythin' like this in all his born days, and he was close on fifty year old. Wanted to know what century we though we was livin' in. That was the middle of the nineteen twenties and he didn't know the half of it. There was *always* a set way of doing things. Same as the way we dressed. In the mornings, we wore print dresses, white aprons and starched caps. In the afternoons, it'd be black dresses and aprons. The washing of all this stuff was done in the estate's own private laundry by two maids who lived in a real cosy little cottage just next to the laundry.

Sundays was always special. The whole place would be like out on show. First of all, though, you'd have all your usual cleanin' jobs to do but after that, you'd all have to go to the morning service at eleven o'clock. You'd have to wash and change into your outside uniform. You had to wear a tiny little black bonnet, trimmed with velvet ribbons and strings. That sat right up on the top of your head like it was a balancing act. The upper maids had to wear toques. We'd all parade to Church. The gentry would sit in the front pew on the right. The upper servants would sit in the front pew on the left; that would be the first cook-housekeeper, the maid and the housemaid. Us little tweenies, the unders, would sit all in a row in the second pew. After the service, we'd all march out, real stately-like, then there'd be a real rush to get back and into our uniforms.

We had no set time-off in the week. If the gentry was away, you might just get out after tea for about an hour, but the only real time you'd have off was every other Sunday. We were free from about half-past two in the afternoon until nine o'clock at night when it was supper-time. We'd come back as far as the gates, just before nine, when I was courting, till all of a sudden, that old supper-bell'd ring. You'd have that long old yard to run up, go upstairs, take your hat and coat off and get dressed for supper in your black rig-out and in your white overall. Down you'd go then and outside to the servants' hall. You should've seen the black looks we got if we were as much as a few minutes late sitting down to supper. We simply had to be there and no two ways about it.

My first year with the Brocklebanks saw the start of the First World War. Our footman was called up, the third housemaid went and left but otherwise we carried on much the same. One thing, though: we did a lot more knitting in the evenings. And I remember the Lady was very busy with Red Cross parcels and hundreds were sent out to the prisoners of war. She did a lot of work also for the wounded soldiers. There was a lot of wounded in the hospital over at Linton and they used to get invited over to the estate for tea and a taste of a different life than they were used to. Must've tasted sweet.

After nearly thirteen years in service with the Brocklebanks, I finally got married. I'd actually first *met* my husband when we was both thirteen years old and he'd just started work as houseboy. We started courtin' then but we left off. We only began courtin' again when he come back from the war and was workin' regular in the gardens. We was a-courtin' proper for nearly six year. We was twenty seven when we wed. I stopped being a domestic servant then but I really kept on a-workin' for the Brocklebanks. I used to help my husband in the garden. After the First World War, the garden staff was cut right down. All told, there used to be six when I first lived in single. Later, this got cut down to just the two. I used to work in the gardens afternoon and evenings, weedin' mostly. My husband lived for his gardening but he never much cared for the weedin' side of it. So that's what I used to do. I helped with the weeding, on and off, for nigh on ten year, and the only reward I ever got for all that weeding from the Brocklebanks was a handbag. That come from one of those big London shops and that was pale fawn and that got a zip on the top. That's the only penn'orth I ever got from the Brocklebanks after I left domestic service. We never had nothin' extra at Christmas and there was never nothin' for our little girl. And he was supposed to be a millionaire!

Mind you, they didn't exactly throw their money around when I worked regular for them. My wages in my first year was five shilling a week plus my keep but I had to pay for my mornin' and afternoon uniforms. Worse than that, I even had to pay for my little Sunday bonnet. That cost ten shillings when I was getting five shilling a week. My mother had to have it made up special at the milliners and when they told her the price she just about had a fit. After ten years' service, they give me a £5 note and a £5 rise in my wages. After thirteen years' service, my yearly pay packet come to £32. It was just as well, perhaps, that after that, I used to find bits of money when I was a-weedin' them onions. When you was a weedin', specially like after a storm, we'd be forever pickin' up little old coins. *Real* old coins. We'd hand that over and we'd get ten bob a time for it. The good Lord looking after his own, I suppose you might say, except that he didn't look after it all *that* careful. That was all put in a big old case in Bartlow Church and that got stolen about a year ago.

When I look back, I'd say I've had a hard life, especially early on, but a good life also with my husband here. Forty six years of married bliss, you could call it. We've always been real partners. Those bunches of grapes he grew when we come to Waltons Park: *I* was the bloke who used to thin them out. He never had the patience whereas *I* did. We was always partners and always worked real hard. If there was money to be made from tins of elbow grease, I'd be ridin' in a coach and pair seven days every week.

THE END OF AN ERA

When I first visited Waltons Park, in September 1947, I did not meet nor have I any recollections of even seeing Mrs Luddington: it was the occasion of the annual village Fête and Flower Show and I was a mere visitor amongst the crowd. When I finally met her, in September 1971, she was ninety four years old and being cared for in The Hope Nursing Home in Cambridge. On the occasion of our meeting, she was mentally alert but physically frail so it was not possible to conduct a protracted interview. Her remarks are, for all that, in my view, well worth recording, evoking as they do an era now virtually beyond recall:

My father was Chief Constable of Caernarvonshire so I spent a lot of my early life in South Wales. I've still many friends there. I never went to school ever: I was taught by governesses. Can't remember that. I can remember meeting my husband, though. I went to a dinner-party after a friend of ours was married: Captain James Luddington. On his part, he said, it was love at first sight. I can't remember what my first feelings were. Anyway, we were married in the lovely old chapel at Hampton Court. My godmother had Ann Boleyn's room, up a little narrow staircase ... Very very haunted ... I wonder how many years since I was married. Must be years and years ago. My daughter is over sixty. Must be years and years ago. We went to India for a five-month honeymoon. We went to stay with my brother who had a house in Nepal, then we went on to an uncle, at Delhi, I think it was. Then there was a cousin who'd married a Governor of the Punjab, so we had a lot of introductions. It was the year Curzon entertained the King and Queen. I went back twenty years afterwards, after my husband died, this time to Afghanistan. Very exciting it all was. I've travelled about quite a bit. We had a little house in Rome. I took my daughter there to educate her instead of going to Paris. Everywhere I went, I painted in water colours. I loved my painting. I used to paint in Rome and in Wales and I painted in Ashdon too. What can I remember about Ashdon?

Well, we moved to Waltons from Littleport, from an old house called Plantation House. I planted a lot of trees there, that was my great hobby. I planted any amount of trees at Waltons too, a tremendous lot of walnut trees. That was a very profitable crop. I had to do what was best in the way of crops because the soil is rather heavy for other sorts of farming on that estate. Gardening was my great hobby at Waltons. I made a lovely rose garden and behind the Library was what was called the Nuns' Walk. On each side of it, I planted yews, little Irish yews, to bring out the mystery of the place. I always thought that was a very haunted place. Sometimes I don't believe in ghosts, sometimes I do. It was easy enough to believe in them in Waltons: it had been there for hundreds of years. Tansley, my husband, found a priest's hiding-hole in one of the big chimneys and there was an underground passage going out from Waltons to Cherry Tree Cottage. Sometimes, I'd be sketching by the pool at the back, and perhaps a kingfisher would flash over and I'd feel a Presence. You don't seem to see kingfishers any more . . . I also felt the presence of something beside the Lady's Well in the field near the Rectory. Ashdon is an old, old place.

Of course, moments like those happened just now and again. Mostly it was much more down to earth. I had to keep my eye on the village, it was expected of me, you see, and I had the estate to attend to. There was a reasonably sized staff most of the time. There was a butler, a housekeeper, a cook, a couple of housemaids, a couple of gardeners, the chauffeur, the gamekeeper. My husband brought up pheasants and that sort of thing but we lost a lot of game at one time. They told me afterwards that one of our keepers was one of the worst poachers. We took him out of the Fens, so I suppose we had ourselves to blame. We had our share of entertaining in our time. The Countess of Warwick would come over from Dunmow and offer to sell me paintings of my own Waltons at enormous prices: I didn't buy any. We used to entertain the Brocklebanks from Bartlow but we fell out over something or other and he never spoke to me again. If we ever passed each other on the Bartlow road, he'd take good care to look the other way. What an *odd* way for gentry to behave!

What else can I remember? Well, I recall that the different farms used to paint their carts in their own individual colours. The carts at Overhall Farm, as I recall, were royal blue. Ashdon Place carts were much closer to azure. Our carts at Waltons were always beige. The wheelwrights used always to mix their paints themselves — to our specification, of course.

The war changed all that. The *most recent* war, I mean. The Air Force commandeered us. They left me with just one small room and kitchenette. They made a mess-room out of our hall. We used to hold dances there, in that hall, long ago. A hundred people could dance there. The coaches would crunch as they came up the driveway on to the courtyard. I remember the music and sometimes see those dancers. All gone now ...

I haven't been back to Waltons since the fire. I couldn't bear it, you know. Nearly all my paintings gone. The end of a world ...

* * *

And the end of a world it has proved to be though it would be simplistic to relate it exclusively to that one incident, or to the departure from the village scene of that single individual. No one person in Ashdon has ever been able to exert quite that degree of local influence, not even one as wealthy as Edmund Vesty, joint head of the vast Vestey Organization, who had Waltons Park rebuilt to his specifications, has made it his main English country seat since 1960 and now owns nearly half the farmlands in the whole parish. Over these, he regularly casts a perceptive, professional eye — his farming is emphatically serious business for him, not a light-hearted hobby — but the close involvement of a Luddington-type figure in village affairs or in the private lives of individual villagers is a thing of the past, most of it taken over by the State, by a network of local committees, and by the qualified social worker.

However, the most striking difference between present-day Ashdon and the centuries-old community analyzed in earlier chapters is that it is no longer dominated by agriculture. The reasons for this are various and doubtless include the widening of horizons brought about by two world wars and by the mass media, the great increase in privately owned motor-cars, the seductive lure of higher wages and the greater creature comforts offered by the towns, but the major single factor must surely have been the spectacular changes in farming technology. This has been as rapid as it has been dramatic. In the nineteen twenties there were still some two million heavy horses in service on the land in Britain. When I helped with the Ashdon harvest in the mid-forties, the binder, the tractor-drawn cart, the stook and the stack were still conspicuous features of the late summer scene. It was only in the course of the nineteen fifties that the combine-harvester became a standard item of equipment on every farm in the area and farmers could effectively manage with three or four labourers where their predecessors of less than half a century earlier would have needed four or five times that number.

Progressively throughout this period, the diminution of the agricultural work-force has been matched by the run-down of local specialists supplying goods and services to the work-force: the blacksmiths, shoemakers, millers and bakers has quietly vanished away, the number of public houses have gone down from six to three and the number of general stores, unable to compete with supermarkets easily accessible by car, has been reduced to one. The old closed community — what Frank Moss called Ashdon's 'castle' — is closed no longer, even though the local railway link was severed in the early nineteen sixties and the provision of bus services has been drastically curtailed. At the turn of the century, a visit even to nearby Saffron Walden was something of an event (indeed, a fifty five year old labourer with whom I harvested in 1947, had made the journey there just once in his life): in the nineteen-eighties, the advent of the motor-car has brought much more distant towns and cities within range and, in Ashdon, as elsewhere, one does not need to be well-to-do to take one's holiday in Spain or Greece. The majority of the many Ashdonians who work for their living often do so far beyond the parish boundaries, in Saffron Walden, in Cambridge or in Haverhill while a score or more commute each day to London. The more affluent of these are professional people who, as like as not, live in what used to be the farmhouses owned by independent farmers. In the twenties, there was an influx of these from Scotland and the North of England. Over the last three decades, these have all been bought out by the Vestey Organization which has resold the farmhouses on the open market while adding the lands to its inexorably expanding estates, thereby reverting to the eighteenth- and nineteenth-century pattern when the greater part of Ashdon's farmlands was owned by the Maynard family.

In one other important respect, present-day and nineteenth-century Ashdon are significantly different: the numbers of what would once have been classified as 'gentry', never large in the locality, are now much increased both in quantity and importance. In the early nineteen seventies, out of a total population of just under seven hundred, the village could number the following among its inhabitants: the late General Sir Geoffrey Scoones, former Commander of the Fourth Army Corps in Burma, whose victory over the Japanese in the Imphal Plain was described in his Times' obituary notice as 'one of the most remarkable battles of the whole war';

another distinguished staff-officer, Brigadier Thomas Collins, who played a leading part in sustaining the smooth flow of men and materials along the roads of Southern England up to, then during, the invasion of Normandy; two circuit judges (Sir Joseph Cantley and His Honour Judge Michael Chetwynd-Talbot), a prominent merchant banker (the late Walter Brandt), and an active novelist and former winner of the John Llewellyn Rhys Memorial Prize for Poetry (Morwenna Donnelly). Of those — like Ralph Baignard, Lord of one of the Ashdon manors at the time of Domesday — two also achieved eminence on the County scene: Brigadier Collins was for several years Chairman of Essex County Council while Edmund Vestey has served his turn as High Sheriff of Essex.

As distinguished in his own particular sphere as any of these was yet another eminent figure who chose to end his days in Ashdon, Sir Eric Thompson who became the world's leading authority on the ancient Maya civilization and who till his death in 1976 carried on writing his books on their history and culture in his neat modern bungalow close to the village school. As eloquent as any indication that Ashdon lives in changing times is that to help him prepare the index of his definitive study of Maya hieroglyphics, he enlisted the services of Michael Swan who carried out the work in the winter evenings after completing a full day's work on Goldstone's Farm. Not so long ago, he would have had to be described as a farm labourer but this seems inadequate for somebody who is called upon to service and operate machinery costing tens of thousands of pounds.

For all the impressive present-day evidence of increased prosperity, Ashdon still shows signs of its chequered past. Evidence of age-old tensions and continuing divisions is not hard to come by: the Council Estate high on Church Hill makes an obvious contrast with the scattered grace-and-favour private residences behind high hedges or at the far end of a winding drive; the village school can now offer flush toilets, neat playing fields and, as it always did, imaginative and dedicated teaching, but the Ashdon professional classes tend, almost without exception, to send their children out of the parish for their education; in Canterbury Cathedral, the Archbishop of Canterbury may kneel in prayer beside the Pope, but in Ashdon, the villagers still worship separately in either church or chapel; there are, in fact, as many as *four* separate halls where the adherents of various groups can socialize: a Church Hall, a Baptist Hall, a Conservative Hall and a Labour Hall. Since 1973, a completely new group has added a distinctive new strand to the village's colourful tapestry: the premises which for so long served as the Children's Home now house a Kham Tibetan House directed by the Lama Chime Rinpoche, born in Pema Tang (the Plain of the Lotus) and brought up in the Buddist monastery of Benchen of which he subsequently became Abbot.

As noteworthy as these examples of ways in which the Ashdon community is divided are instances of how it comes together. Sport is a case in point: there is a well-supported Tennis Club, a football team (called — as one might expect — Ashdon Villa) and a village cricket team drawn from all social classes: this still plays all its home fixtures, as it has done throughout this century, in the grounds of Waltons Park, and the annual high spot is the match against a touring team of Old Etonians. For years, there has been a thriving drama club and its satirical revue, staged each December in the Labour Hall, and full of allusions incomprehensible to the outsider, invariably plays to packed houses. The committee members of a particularly active Ashdon Labour group readily concede that in recent times no single individual has worked harder or achieved more in practical terms for the village than Brigadier Collins, the most prominent and articulate of the region's Tories. In 1969, the bells of Ashdon Church rang out once again in full chorus for the first time in almost a century. One bell had been cracked for the whole of that time and the other five were hopelessly out of tune. Edmumd Vestey paid for the cracked bell to be recast, the five to be retuned and two extra new bells to be cast and hung. On each of the two new bells were inscribed the names of two of the four Vestey sons. On one of the older bells were inscribed the names of the then Churchwardens, Len Martin and Lionel Bartram, son of the inimitable Bertie and dedicated Secretary of the local Labour Party:

'That tells you all you need to know about Ashdon', he said to me in the course of our interview. 'Mr Vestey's a big, big Capitalist, as big as you'll find, and he's no more likely to vote Labour than I'm ever likely to vote Tory — Hell will freeze over first — but there's my name and his name up there on those bells, and those bells will ring for us when they pop us in the Churchyard and go on ringing long, long after, on that you may depend'.

Further evidence of the narrowing of the ages-old gulf between

Ashdon's distinctive groups will readily be found on the farming scene. The mechanization of the agricultural industry has resulted not only in a markedly smaller but a markedly more skilful workforce; the labourer may still, on occasion, have to wield a fork or a spade, but he is much more likely to be manipulating a spanner or a battery-charger as he services the sophisticated machinery entrusted to his care; his working day will start not, as it so regularly used to, with a series of imperious commands, but as my interviews clearly established, with a round-table conference in which his employer will discuss with him how next to proceed and why. He is, as like as not, able to take his extended holiday abroad, and to drive in his own car to spend his Sunday watching the Essex County Cricket team in pursuit of the John Player Trophy.

A view of the newly evolved Ashdon community conveyed to me by a number of the modern villagers was perhaps best expressed by John Double, an admirable example of the newer-style country policeman. Like Michael Swan, he is an articulate, well-read ex-grammar schoolboy and he was also able to provide some very useful comments on the subject of village law and order:

By and large, the Ashdon community in the nineteen eighties is fairly law-abiding. There's not the *public* violence there used to be in days of old. No doubt there's the occasional punch-up inside this home or that — the occasional bit of husband-battering is bound to crop up more or less by the law of averages — but it's not something which is very often brought to my notice. We have our small quota of alcoholics — no community would be complete without them — and they're a little more evident in a little place like this but they're more tolerated and better cared-for than I think they'd ever be in a town ... There's still a certain amount of poaching in the village but by and large it's at a level that can be tolerated inasmuch as Edmund Vestey doesn't want pheasants and the like on his big estate at Walton's — just a few to keep the foxes interested. So we don't have breeding grounds for the vast quantities of game which would attract the professional teams up through the Dartford Tunnel from Kent. Some of the locals help themselves to trout from the dammed-up part of the stream here as they've no doubt been doing for centuries, but it doesn't seem to be done on an excessive level. If somebody got too greedy, I'd know which door to knock on. The fact of the matter is, people no longer have to poach to survive as they used to here in the wild old days. Our local poachers have been bred to it. Their fathers were poachers before them and their ancestors before that. It goes in families. It's a trade, really ...

If you want a word to describe the sort of community we are today, I'd say that word was 'caring'. Everyone here seems to have an adequate circle of friends. There isn't, as far as I'm aware, anyone who's so alone as to have to depend *exclusively* on the professional social worker. Because we're a small community, we're very quickly alerted to what's going on. By some group or another, I'd say that everyone in need is being cared for or, more accurately, *being paid attention to*. That distinction's worth making. Once people feel they're being 'cared for', that's it: they stop caring for themselves. Better to keep an eye on them and let them know you're not far away. I'd say that was the predominant attitude in this village. Be concerned but don't be too impatient to get too involved. If they're able to, they'll soldier on that bit longer. A little sympathy as and when. That's our way of it. You can't really be a full-time hermit here. In Ashdon, folk *do* want to know and they *do* care. That's what village-life is all about.

'Caring', while by no means inaccurate, is not the only epithet to characterize present-day Ashdon. Inevitably, as, one by one, the older Ashdon natives go with their memories, into the grave, the village looks and sounds more and more middle-class. The large families of labourers in their small cottages are now part of history. Now, more often than not, as those cottages are vacated, they are refurbished in a style and at a price that only the affluent and the upwardly mobile can afford. The 'Rose and Crown' now takes pride not only in its display of authentic Jacobean panelling but in its scampi and chips or its chicken-in-a-basket; the delicatessen opposite offers an impressive array of cheeses as well as salamis, pizzas and other continental delicacies, the annual satirical revue produced by the Ashdon Players and the glees and madrigals sung by the Ashdon Waits are a fairly far cry from the now extinct Horkey Supper; as well as thriving branches of the W.I. and the Mothers' Union and a very active 'Over 60's Club', there is now a lively W.E.A. Study Group — but all these are, it would seem to me, signs of a healthy new mode of life rather than symptoms of decline. Those who mourn for the lost poetry of Ashdon's rural past rather too readily forget that for far too long, too many worked too hard for too little and that the villagers of the present are incomparably better fed, better housed and better provided for.

I hesitate to speculate on how long the present life-style of the Ashdon community is likely to endure. Much will clearly depend on how the technologists respond to the growing problem of dwindling supplies of oil. If no adequate substitute is found, it does not seem to me too fanciful to foresee a return to an age of horse-drawn vehicles, to dramatically shortened lines of communication and to a mode of rural living that, for the moment, seems all but extinct. Be that as it may, the most important single factor in the life of the Ashdon community will surely remain what it has always been, the bounty of its land, giving generous sustenance to the living and, when time has run its course, providing a last resting place for the dead. To these, with whom this work began, I must now return.

12

Death and the Countryman

> In my beginning is my end. In succession
> Houses rise and fall, crumble, are extended,
> Are removed, destroyed, restores, or in their place
> Is an open field, or a factory, or a by-pass.
> Old stone to new building, old timber to new fires,
> Old fires to ashes, and ashes to the earth
> Which is already flesh, fur and faeces,
> Bone of man and beast, cornstalk and leaf.
> Houses live and die: there is a time for building
> And a time for living and for generation
> And a time for the wind to break the loosened pane
> And to shake the wainscot where the field-mouse trots
> And to shake the tattered areas woven with a silent motto.
> T.S. Eliot: *East Coker*

My earliest recollections of Ashdon are, like my latterday resolve to write this book, closely connected with mementoes of death. I was dispatched to Ashdon in the very first instance only because the Second World War was being waged and the nation was short of unskilled farm workers. The peace of Ashdon had been brutally broken some time before my arrival on the scene. In September 1940, a German land-mine exploded at Church End and shattered several cottages up on the hill-top, an incursion as dramatic and rather more sinister than the fall of the famous meteorite which fell in a wheatfield at Ashdon Hall Farm on 9th March 1923 with a crash that was clearly heard in Saffron Walden. While we schoolboys played our lowly parts as sheaf-carriers in the ageless drama of the harvest, the air resounded to the roar of aircraft engines. We could count the combat planes taking off on their sorties from the wartime airfield at neighbouring Hadstock and note that the same number did not invariably return. Three months before I first arrived at Sandons Farm in August 1944, Mrs Betty Everitt had been blown up just a couple of miles away, trying to rescue the crew from a blazing Havoc fighter-bomber which crashed soon after taking off from Hadstock. She was killed when its load of bombs exploded. When she was buried a few days later, in Ashdon churchyard, a flight of U.S.A.F. Mustangs swooped low over the old Church tower in salute; and in February 1945, her four year old son was taken to Buckingham Palace to receive her posthumous Albert Medal from King George VI. After the war, in my long years of exile from Sandons, I came fully to appreciate the force of George Eliot's dictum that 'in every parting there is an image of death'. Accordingly, while Ashdon came to represent for me The Land of Lost Content, my dreams of it were never purely wistful. From the outset, there ran through them, like some chilling refrain, that reminder of mortality inscribed on the tomb which features in many of Poussin's paintings: *Et in Arcadia ego*—'I am in Paradise too'. The speaker, I have always assumed, is not a fellow-outcast from felicity but Death itself.

Emblems of Death are among the oldest features of the Ashdon scene. Some of the Bartlow Hills still stand to mark the burial place of the Romano-British noblemen whose last sight of this sublunary world must have been the woods and fields of Ashdon. Ironically, their remaining worldly goods, which had laid undisturbed in the Bartlow Hills for something like one thousand, seven hundred and fifty years, did not long survive in the light of nineteenth-century days. The ornamental glass and the decorated bronze were removed to Lord Maynard's home at Easton Lodge, near Dunmow, where they and the stately home perished together in the fire of 1847.

Later Ashdon men of rank were equally frustrated in their bid to leave some vestige of their earthly existence behind them. Prominent among the fourteenth-century lords of the manor of Newnham Hall were the Cloptons and as late as 1631, when J. Weever surveyed the fabric of Ashdon Church, they were still dramatically commemorated in stained glass. Weever reported:

> In the south aisle of this Church and in the south window thereof, there are seene severall Cloptons kneeling in their compleat Armour with their several Escutcheons of Arms upon their breasts (being S, a bend *Or* between 2 cotizes dauncitee or) of which the first is Sir William Clopton there mentioned to have died in the fifth year of King Edward the Third

[1331-32]. The second Sir Thomas Clopton knight mentioned to have died the second yeare of the raigne of King Richard the second [1378-79], and the third Edmund Clopton, the yeare of whose decease is there set down to have been the thirteenth yeare of the said King Richard [1389-90]. And it is very likely the said Edmund lieth there buried under the window ...

Of that picturesque stained-glass window only a few fragments now remain and though 'Cloptons' survived for hundreds of years as an alternative name for Newnham Hall, all visible traces of the once prestigious family have long since vanished.

One presumes, with Weever, that they lie buried, together with generations of poorer Ashdonians, on the south side of the parish Church. In the Middle Ages, one entered the churchyard from the south between the east end of the Guildhall and where a cottage now stands. In olden times, what is now an unbroken wall was pierced by the lich-gate (*lich* being Anglo-Saxon for 'dead body') and it was there that the bearers would rest after carrying the coffin from the dead person's home before entering the Church through the north entrance, regularly referred to as the 'Devil's Doorway'. After the funeral service, the coffin would be carried out through the south doorway (then the principal entrance) for interment in the consecrated burial ground. This is therefore the most ancient part of Ashdon churchyard and many gravestones have been so ravaged by wind, sun and rain that the inscriptions have entirely vanished and one cannot tell whether they once commemorated lord or labourer.

Inside the church, safe against the depradations of the weather, the attempts by a few former parishioners to remind posterity of their existence have proved marginally more successful. Between the North-West Chapel and the north aisle of the church is a fifteenth-century archway. Its wave mouldings merge into the widely splaying jambs and on these splays are some tantalizing graffiti. There is a mask, probably from the fourteenth century. There is a shield across which, from top left to bottom right, runs a diagonal adorned with three paty crosses (the arms being nearly triangular, very narrow where they meet and widening towards the extremities); in the top right hand corner of the shield are the block capital letters R.W. V. Pritchard, an authority on English mediaeval graffiti, suggests that this most likely commemorates a member of the Weller-

Poley (or Pooley or Polhill) family of Boxted Hall, some sixteen miles from Ashdon, whose lineage shows some lineage with Essex families. Also prominent is the signature Robert Cole, a cousin of William Cole, who was born in 1714, lived at Milton, but went to school at Linton. According to Dr. W.M. Palmer, Robert was 'probably a corn chandler in a large way of business'; he lived at Linton and often acted as a churchwarden there. One can only assume that if he is the Robert Cole commemorated on the chancel arch of Ashdon Church, he must have carved his name there before attaining the age of discretion: carving one's name on the fabric of another church was not normally listed as part of one's official parochial activities.

Within the confines of Ashdon Church there have been more grandiose and more official attempts to impress one's name on posterity. In the north-east corner of the sanctuary, stands the altar tomb to Thomas Tyrrel of Warley and to Ann (née Wolley), his wife. The tomb has been seriously mutilated, the top slab does not fit the sides and its inscription plate is missing, but the two sides which are visible are cusped and panelled with the heraldic shields of the Tyrrel and Wooley families. Fixed to the church wall above the tomb, set in a deep moulded frame, is an elaborately shaped shield announcing the achievement of arms of Richard Tyrrel in 1566. A further attempt to stress his social distinction is to be found in the Parish Register of Baptisms and Burials for the period 1553-1595. On the page for 1566, the Rector or Curate of the day had inscribed the name Magister Richardus Tyrrel in letters seven times larger than those of the humbler parishioners that follow.

On another of the Church walls is a memorial tablet to another of Ashdon's past worthies. It caught the attention of a contributor to *The Gentleman's Magazine* who, on 6th September 1791, wrote to the editor as follows:

> Mr Urban,
> I send you an epitaph on the late Mr Salter ... fitted up on the South wall of the chancel at Ashdon Church, in Essex, on a tablet of black marble, in a frame formed like a Gothic arch; designed and executed by Mr Robinson, mason, of Saffron Walden.
> Here lies the body
> of the Rev. NATHANIEL SALTER, A.M.

who died March 7, 1791, aged 87 years,
  late rector of this parish,
and for many years a constant preacher
  in this church;
and being dead, still desires to speak
  to his beloved parishioners;
and earnestly exhort them to have
  a special care of
  their souls;
and to that end
constantly to attend upon the worship of God,
frequently to receive the sacrament, and
diligently to observe the good instructions
  given
  in this place;
to breed up their children in the fear of God,
and follow peace with all men,
  and holiness,
without which no man shall see the Lord.
God give us all a happy meeting
at the resurrection of the Just.
  Amen.

Mr Salter's death was occasioned by his falling down the stairs of his cellar, the decay of his sight preventing him from seeing that the door was open. He was admitted of Caius College, in Cambridge, where he proceeded A.B. [i.e. Bachelor of Arts] 1724, A.M. [i.e. Master of Arts] 1729, and was presented by that Society to this rectory 1748. He repaired his chancel 1790, and inhabited an excellent modern-built parsonage-house, finely situated on a rising-ground, with a delightful prospect, about a quarter of a mile North from the church. He bore an excellent character in his neighbourhood.
  Yours &c.,
  R.G.

This may be somewhat fulsome for contemporary taste but it is the very model of terseness and diffidence compared to the funeral inscription to be found a few miles distant in the church of the neighbouring parish at Little Sampford. In the north aisle stands a monument twelve feet high hearing an effigy lying on a mattress. Above this is a scroll with a Latin inscription of which the following is a translation:

> Under this marble is deposited as much as *could* die (the comeliness, namely, the beauty, and the perfectly elegant, accomplished and symmetrical figure) of Bridget, that choicest and indeed unrivalled model of a woman; who had for her husband William Peck, for her father Morgan Randyle, esquires; the latter of Chillworth, in the County of Surrey, the former of Sampford Hall, in Essex; of both of whom, while living, she was the pride and delight. Now she lies, alas! the object of their long and anxious desire, by all lamented! If, however, the obsequies of her, whose were these more than thousand endearing *virtues*, must be observed with tears; *they*, destined ever to survive, shall frequently by the lips of all repeated, whose ears they have either already reached, or are doomed hereafter to greet. For this lady was qualified, at it were, from above, for the discharge of every duty in life, in admirable conjunction, whether they related to God, to her neighbour, or to herself; at once the best of daughters, wives, parents and mistresses. Wonderful was her suavity of temper; wonderful was her ingenuousness of mind; and what is seldom to be found in the tenderer sex, wonderful, whenever circumstances required, was her fortitude of soul in the education of her children. A prudent at once and a fruitful mother (for she left at her death two boys and eight girls) she applied herself to toils not ungratifying, with others still more in prospect. Engaged in such pursuits, neither desirous of nor dreading the grave, being at length ripe for heaven, she, in obedience to a summons from thence, departed on the 14th of June, A.D. 1712, aged 31.
>
> Reported in T. Wright: *History and Topography of the County of Essex,* Vol. II, 1836.

This sort of portentousness does not seem to me faithfully to represent the countryman's attitude to death. I would not want for one moment to suggest that he feels the pangs of bereavement any less keenly than the town-dweller but, because, his whole life long, he is directly involved in the pageant of the seasons, he is that much readier to accept death as part of the endless cycle of seed-time and harvest. From the countryside came that archetypal legend of resurrection, the body of John Barleycorn, laid in the earth in the dark season of the year and returning unfailingly to life at the touch of the sun. For this reasons, it seems to be wholly appropriate that while Ashdon Church is the oldest building in the village, surrounded with mementoes of mortality in the form of its ancient gravestones, the most durable relic within, much older than the walls around it or the roof above it, is the octagonal bowl of the font in which the parishioners have been christened since the days of the Normans.

In a place where people have lived for hundreds, if not thousands of years, one would expect to find at least some accounts of hauntings, of visitations from parishioners from the long lost past. Ashdon, in this respect, is not disappointing: it can provide two 'happenings', the one, part of local village-lore; the other, authenticated by no less a dignitary than the former Vice-Chairman of the Churches' Fellowship for Psychical and Spiritual Studies.

The local tale, recounted to me by several of the older Ashdonians now dead, is of Lady Well, the pond beside what used to be the Baptist Manse. It used to be surrounded by willows and tall elms before these were smitten with the dread Dutch disease, and is reputed to have been the spot where a well-do-do lady was drowned when lightning caused her pair of horses to bolt and so overturn her carriage. The former carriage-way has dwindled to a mere footpath but the phosts of the frightened horses and their terrified driver are, or were, believed to haunt the spot. It was also believed that Lady Well was the only pond in the whole of ashdon where moorhens were never seen but on the truth or the significance of this I am unable to pronounce.

On the second 'happening', rather more detail and an authentically authoritative view can be brought to bear. Both are provided by Canon John Pearce-Higgins who was invited, in the mid 1960s, by the then Rector of Ashdon, Walter Lane, to investigate what was thought to be a case of paranormal manifestation in one of the very oldest houses in the parish. He was kind enough to supply me not only with a full account of his investigation but to set it in the context of modern thinking about psychic phenomena in general:

> We have to get right away from mediaeval thought which actually

believed that people could swallow demons or devils, as is seen by the many old illustrations of 'exorcisms' which depict scores of little Satans, complete with horns, hooves and tails, emerging from the mouths of the (usually female!) patients being exorcised by the priest. No psychic researcher ever finds anything of this sort. What we invariably find are the dead, discarnate, former living beings who have become earthbound after shedding the physical body, who, because of a variety of factors (such as ignorance of the real nature of death, a sensual and materialistic outlook on life or inhibiting traumatic memories) have failed to progress forward, and have remained close to the scenes of their former existence. Apparently, if they find an 'open door' in the psyche of some still living individual, they enter in and use the mind and body of such a one for their own ends and the gratification of sensual and other impulses. Why some people have this 'open door' is not fully understood, but it seems that severe illness and resultant nervous debility, stress or—very commonly—a blow on the head or some emotional trauma can be among the causes of a breakdown of the normal defences ... Heaven and Hell are states of consciousness in the soul of man and if we have been earthly-minded while in this body, we shall continue so after death's shedding of the physical body ...

To turn now to the particular case of psychic disturbance at Ashdon. I went there in 1969 or 1970 but I think I destroyed all the documents relating to it because of the unsatisfactory outcome of my visit. Let me try to construct from memory what happened.

I was giving a lecture on parapsychology to a small group in Cambridge where I met a lady who was in the process of getting divorced from her husband. He had, apparently, offered her the chance of buying the family home (a rather old building) if she wished it. She was in two minds whether to do so owing to the atmosphere of the place which appeared to be having a deleterious effect on her children and on a son in particular.

I went to the house with medium. To the best of my recollection, we did a recce of the house and he said that there were entities present, especially in the big downstairs room, and also in a small room upstairs at the far end of the passage. We also went around outside and he discovered a tombstone with a name which he said was that of a former occupant of the house — a female — and I rather think he suggested she was still earthbound in the house. He also discerned traces of battle in and around the churchyard. We finally finished up in the church and in the side chapel on the north side, he went into a trance and appeared to be controlled by a mediaeval monk who spoke some words in Latin to which I replied suitably: I think he said, '*Dominus tecum*', to which I politely answered, '*Et cum spiritu tuo*' and bade him depart in peace. We then went back into the house where I conducted a Requiem Mass (in English) in the main room. Present were the medium and his wife, the lady who'd contacted me in Cambridge and two — or possibly three — of her women friends.

Later, after we had had a picnic lunch, the medium went back into the house and said that he must go alone into the upstairs room as what was there was somewhat violent. He came back perhaps ten minutes later and said it was pretty grim, that there was an almost maddened monk there who appeared to have had his hands cut off. Whether he invented this just to satisfy us, I do not know. However, it appeared to exhaust him, and I can certainly remember the drive back to London during which we were both completely exhausted. This sometimes happens after a service of cleansing (I will not call it Exorcism because it is not a cursing service but a Requiem, designed through our prayers and the invocation of the ministry of Angels to remove any spirit from any place and help him or her on and up into the realms of light). I know we stopped at a pub for a stiff whisky and I was so tired I insisted on fifteen minutes sleep in the car before I felt able to go on.

The medium said we would need to go back again as we had not cleansed everything from the house but again I was not sure for I had begun, by this time, to note that he nearly always asked for a second visit in order to get a second fee! (I never charge anything myself except legitimate petrol expenses.) In fact, we never paid the second visit because the husband intervened. Owing to delay on the estranged wife's part, we paid our first visit almost when the terminal date for her option on the property had been reached. By the time we'd arranged to go back again, the date has passed and I felt it necessary to contact her husband. He was not willing for me to go again and, therefore, the case was closed. I was sorry because it seemed to offer interesting possibilities.

I would say from my now much greater experience from dealing with scores of claimed hauntings (by no means all of which are genuine cases) that this was genuine enough: there was *something* there and it is quite probable that the service cleared it — it normally does, provided there is something there to clear — and I would adduce, in addition, our extreme exhaustion as a sign that this was so. I find after a service of this sort to clear someone away that I am usually pretty well laid out for about twenty four hours. I am not psychic myself which is why I often use a medium to enable me to know just what we are dealing with, but it seems as though I am drained of a great deal of psychic and spiritual energy — I'm used as a sort of battery! But it is the actual service and the prayers and *not* the medium which clear the place. I believe the clearance is done by the

'Brother' Joslin in 1953

celestial civil service — alias Angels, messengers, guides (wingless variety) — and I have hundreds of feet of tape-recordings testifying to this.

The Rector of Ashdon was not very enthusiastic about our findings at the house. He opined there was nothing there because there had been long periods when nothing was sensed. This does not prove anything: a non-psychic family will feel nothing; as soon as someone psychic lives in the house, all hell may be let loose!

*   *   *

Mercifully, death for the countryman is commonly a much less traumatic affair than any of this, and his attitude to death is, to his everlasing credit, much less portentous than that expressed on the funeral monuments to Nathanael Salter or to Bridget Peck. Much more characteristic, and, at the same time, more dignified and more moving, in my opinion, is the following account provided by Hilda Marsh of the last days of her husband Walter, one of the last surviving heroes of the Ashdon farm workers' strike of 1914:

My husband worked hard all the time he could. He couldn't bear to be idle. Before the First World War, he used to work with his two brothers, James and Nipper, making or mending hurdles for the sheep-fields. They always had the five bars across, like a gate, and put end to end, they made up a fence to keep the sheep inside their field. There was a lot more sheep around in Ashdon before 1914 than there's ever been since. Those hurdles were always in demand and they needed always to be made out of ash trees, out of the saplings. Wal and his brothers made these for all the local farmers and they got quite a name for it, I know.

We were married the year that First World War broke out. That same year was the one he went into prison in Cambridge. That was because of the famous strike of the labourers. They let him out to join up. Because, you see, he was an old soldier, on the reserve, and he was needed to join his regiment. I didn't know he was being let out. That day, he just appeared. They had a party for him down at 'The Fox' and then we went off to the war. He went right through the war. Had his feet frozen in the first winter over there. Said they froze to his boots. That was a specially cold winter, that one. Very sharp. I remember the Bourne was frozen right over and the children used to slide right the way down to the school. Never known it to freeze like that before.

When he came back from the war, there wasn't the same call for sheep-hurdles as there'd been before. Tried to get the business going again but it didn't seem possible somehow. So he worked on the land, labouring jobs here and there. Sometimes he helped over at Waltons Park with Mr Albon. He always did his best. And he had a great bit allotment ourselves. He always dug that all up himself but if he should want any help, I helped him out.

On Easter Monday 1971, he said to me in the morning, he said, 'I fell so well this morning, I think I'll get on with digging that garden'. He said, 'That's a nice day for that job'. So I said, 'Well, don't you stop out there *too* long and get yourself tired'. But he stopped out there all day. He just came in and had his dinner and went right back out again. Then, about four o'clock, he took the dog for his run. He always took him twice a day and off they went together as usual. In the meantime, I had a nephew call to see me. And I'd got arthritis in my leg and it was so painful, I thought to myself, 'I wish you hadn't come *today*'. Anyway, Wal came back and he was sat in there and I thought to myself, 'I think you've done too much, you do look tired'. But he said he wasn't. Now because of my bad leg, I'd got afraid to bring in a tea-tray with all the things in it, so when we was on our own I used to bring things in one at a time. When I said to my nephew I'd get him a cup of tea before he left, my husband said he'd fetch in the tea-tray. I went out to the kitchen and Wal began to follow me out. When we got as far as the door, he sort of fell against it. And I looked at him and I said, 'You're not well, are you, Wal?' I said. And he said, 'I'm all right'. And I said, 'No, you're not'. I could see what was happening. He'd had a stroke. I tried to hold him up but couldn't really. So I said to my nephew, 'Help me with him to this chair'. Which he did. And I got him a little drop of brandy but he couldn't swallow it. So I knew there had to be something wrong. So I sent for my son and he came and we got him on that comfortable chair. He didn't seem as if he would talk. So we got the doctor and, of course, when he came, he said that was a stroke right enough. He'd lost the use of his side and he couldn't swallow. But Dr. Anderson said he wasn't suffering no pain. And he said to remember Wal could hear all we said even though he couldn't talk. Well, he couldn't talk very *clear*. He could just mumble. I had a job to understand him.

Before that, we used to talk about how it might end because you know that's got to happen sometime, sooner or later. He always said he wanted to be the first to go. And he always said, 'Well, I've had hard times when I was young, but I've enjoyed life'. And again near the end, he said, 'I've had a good life'. And when he said that, it sounded as though he didn't mind really. The poor old chap lasted till the Friday, so that wasn't very long. I was very glad he didn't suffer long. He went as he wanted to go. He was ninety years old and we was married fifty seven years!

*   *   *

After the death of Walter Marsh, Herbert Farrant was the oldest man left alive in Ashdon when I interviewed him in the autumn of 1971. He too spoke without rhetoric or sentimentality of the death of his life-long marriage-partner, though in his account, one might say, there was something of a sting in his tale:

That Tuesday mornin', she was set on that little chair there. Low off the ground that had to be because she'd god short legs. I always used to go down to the shop on Tuesday mornin', you see, about half-past ten for to draw the pension. She'd got the shopping-list wrote out and the money was on the table because I wouldn't interfere with the pension. She said, 'Well, you could do two or three little jobs before you went or you could do 'em when you come back. You please yourself, bor.' 'No', I said, 'I'll finish they *first*.' I done so. Then I went. Well, when I come back, 'bout an hour after, the doctor was there. I let he down the yard first and he went on in to see her. I'm puttin' the things in the other room when the doctor comes in to me. He said to me, 'Mr Farrant', he said, 'she's dead.' Just lay there she did. Must've been real quick. Doctor said he didn't think she'd been takin' her tablets regular. She'd left two and she ought to have had those two afore she died. That's what he said to me. For the weight, it was. Weighed thirteen stone when we was courtin'. That wasn't all bone. Poor old gel. Fifty four years we was married ... Well, I went down to tell the bees. They had to be told, you see. You always has to tell your bees if there's someone just died in the house ...

*   *   *

Herbert Farrant may have been unique among the Ashdonians I met in responding to bereavement in the particular way he did but he was by no means alone in sensing that death demanded some special ritual communion with the earth. Richard Eason died at Wallisdown, Bournemouth, aged ninety nine, in March 1979, having left Ashdon over forty years before; his widow brought him back for burial in the village where they had been born, grown up and were married in 1915.

The Reverend Walter Lane had much more regular contact than I did with Ashdon folk close to death and he contributed some most perceptive comments on the subject of death and the countryman as well as fascinating account of the last days of Herbert Farrant who died some eighteen months after my final interview with him:

Even today the parson regularly finds himself in the proximity of death. The village grave-digger is frequently close to death in the physical sense, and so also, for obvious reasons, is the doctor or the nurse, but the parson, too, has still a very special role to play at the end.

I've found that the attitudes of people to death vary enormously: it's a very personal thing and, for most people, a very lonely thing. To bring true comfort may not always be possible. Some people relate to death in a very deep way, a way I would have to characterize as 'religious': the very simplicity of their relationship with it is quite different from the fatalistic view of 'when you're dead, you're dead, and you might as well face up to it'. Herbert Farrant is a case in point.

I don't suppose there was any period in Herbert Farrant's life when he made a point of going to Church with unfailing regularity! But I had a long relationship with him after his wife's death. He lived alone and I made a point of going to see him. For a long time, we never talked about religion at all and it was a long time before I suggested that he might care to have a blessing before I left. This became a regular feature at the end of my visits. He had been ill, on one occasion when I called on him, but he insisted he was better again. Then he said, 'I want to tell you something', and he went on to tell me that someone had constantly been coming to his cottage in the night, at about two o'clock, and tapping on the window and the door. He said his first thought was that somebody was trying to get it. He regularly called out 'Who's there?' but there was never any answer. He said, 'So I got out my old gun and I kep' it close by my bed. And the next time they come, there was a tapping and a knocking on the door and again I said, "Who's there?" and this time, they said, "It's me".' He said 'Do you know who that was?' 'Yes', I said, 'I know who it was.' He looked at me in some surprise and he said, 'Who was it, then?' ... I said, 'It was Minnie' (that was the name of his wife). He said, 'Yes ... it was.' I said, 'How nice that she should be around. You're not the only person who's had this kind of experience in Ashdon.' 'Oh' he said but I didn't tell him of the other experiences either then or subsequently.

After a few months, he fell ill again and it was from the moment that he'd told me about Minnie coming and tapping on his door that I became quite convinced that he wasn't going to live long. When I heard that he was ill again, I went once more to see him and I found that really his 'sickness' was nothing else than that he had had enough of life and was preparing to take his leave. I stood beside his bed. He was weak but in no sort of pain at all. And he said, 'Know where I'm goin'?' I said, 'Yes, I think so.' He said, 'I'm goin' home.' I said, 'Yes, you are.' I said, 'I knew that when Minnie knocked on the door and you said it was she that it wouldn't be long before you joined her.' He died twenty four hours later.

As I intimated to him, his experience wasn't unique. For people who live close to nature and being, close to the earth and its teeming life, with real awareness of the constant cycle of life and death for such people, I'd say, death is accepted as an integral part of an unending process. This means that what you might choose to term 'manifestations' are recognized as being entirely natural. Let me instance another Ashdon man who'd also lost a close relative. In this case, one of two brothers had died. The surviving brother told me that the dead one had been seen not just once but at frequent intervals, perhaps of a month, then six weeks, then three weeks. Some manifestation would take place on these occasions which made him aware that his brother were still around. The living brother's reaction to the manifestation was, I think, every bit as interesting as the form of the manifestation itself.

He said, 'One night, my brother gave me such a start. He brushed his hand right across my face and when I looked, there was my brother and my mother too. And the place was light, it was full of light.' And I said, 'It's nice to know they've got you in mind.'

DEATH AND THE COUNTRYMAN

Now in his particular case, this was quite a regular occurrence. He was an ordinary countryman, of the earth earthy. He talked about the experience not with awe or wonder but in a perfectly matter-of-fact way as though it was part of normality. He wasn't surprised that it had happened, he didn't regard it as spooky. When he said his dead brother had given him a start it was the suddenness of his arrival he had in mind rather than the fact that his brother was back inside him.

*   *   *

The passing of another of Ashdon's great twentieth-century 'characters' was described by Donald Elsdon who served as the village's Baptist Lay-Pastor in the second half of the nineteen sixties:

We were sometimes present right at the end or were called in immediately after a death. Our role at such times was to comfort those near the point of death or console those who'd been left behind. The first funeral I ever conducted in Ashdon was that of 'Brother' Joslin, the famous thatcher and one of the most memorable Ashdon characters of this century, so I'm told. Unfortunately, I never knew him in his prime. I never saw him on his famous tricycle. I never saw him in his full regalia of top hat, tail coat, wing collar and pin-stripe trousers fastened with bicycle clips. I never saw him standing on his head up on top of a stack or on top of a cottage roof after he'd finished his job of thatching. I'm told that when people swore in his presence, he'd at once drop down on both knees and pray for their endangered souls. At other times, so I'm assured, when the mood was on him, he'd ring his handbell and summon a crowd to one of his hell-fire sermons. I missed all that. But I didn't miss him at the end. He'd been immensely strong in his prime, although he was slightly built, but when I made his acquaintance, in the Old People's Home at Linton, he was a frail little old man. I can't claim ever to have got truly close to him but certainly, he knew who I was, knew that I came from Ashdon and was touched to know that the village still remembered him. They remember him still as a man of parts. He always reminded me of a little old child ...

With that sense of the wheel coming full circle and our End being in our Beginning, I leave the final words to Florence Anderson, whom I first met in the little cemetery beside Ashdon Church, and who said to me in the same matter-of-fact tones with which she remarked on the chill of the late September afternoon, that her husband felt it was high time she went back into the cottage to brew her four o'clock cup of tea. We were standing beside a grave as we spoke and it was only in the course of the ensuing conversation that I realised her husband was inside it:

After my childhood years were over, I never once forgot Ashdon. To me, it was always the loveliest place on God's earth. I'd think about it in my good times and in my bad times. I used to think about it when I was in domestic service in Yorkshire where I was eleven years serving-maid to Lady Downe. And I used to think about it when I was in London in the First World War when food was so terribly scarce and a friend of mine used to put my baby girl and hers in the same pram so as to be sure of getting a share of the rations. And, of course, I often used to talk about Ashdon to my husband. He was my brother's best friend and I first met him when I was only seven years old. His mother died when he was quite little and his father, who had a greengrocer's business, married again. His stepmother wasn't too fond of him and he became the regular little sweeper-up so he ran away from home and joined the Navy. All the time he could, he spent at our house and we got married when I was twenty seven. He was a very clever man and did very well in the Navy. He did the electrical work in submarines and when he came out, worked for years on Mr Tiarks's estate at Chislehurst. When the time came for him to retire in 1936, there was only one place we thought of, naturally — Ashdon. With the money we'd regularly been putting by, we were able to buy this lovely old house from the Rector and as the years went by, we've gradually done it up. My ancestors used to live in this selfsame house two hundred and thirty years ago so I suppose it's a sort of miracle that I'm living back here again now.

My times here has been very happy: they were all I'd hoped they would be when I used to dream about coming back. When we first retired here, there was the same sort of family feeling at this end of the village as I remember from those childhook holiday times. I'm *sure* I'm not imagining it. We were such a happy crowd in these old buildings beside the churchyard and everybody helped everybody else. You'd never believe all the help I got when we first retired here and our garden was still a wilderness. Somebody would bring me in a cabbage, somebody else would bring new potatoes just dug out of the earth, a third person might bring in some beans or a little marrow. We were never allowed to go short. And when the Second War was on, I used to go round collecting for War Savings and, do you know, by the time I got back home, I could scarcely walk in a straight line. Every house I went to, they'd offer me a glass of wine. I've never been a great drinker but I just felt it would be rude to refuse. I'd walk back into our house as dignified as I could and Dad would say, 'What *have* you been drinking?' And I'd try to reckon up and I'd say, 'Blackcurrant wine, elderberry wine, sloe wine, wheat wine — what other wines are there?'

God has been very good to me. I've always had a good time, good people around me, good friends and neighbours, a good husband and three good daughters. I've only two daughters now. They're both District Nurses nearby and I'm really proud of them. My youngest daughter would have been a nurse too but she was killed in the London blitz. A bomb fell on her cousin's house just four hours after she'd gone back from us here in Ashdon. That bomb came down and everyone in the house was killed. She was such a clever girl, Joan. I think that was the first tragedy for this village in the Second World War. The whole village was upset. We had her body brought down from London and her cousin's too. We didn't want them to go into a communal grave up there, so my husband went up and brought the coffins back here and they were put first of all in the Sunday School and then brought over to the Church. And, do you know, every little child in Ashdon picked a little nosegay and did each one up with a little doily. You couldn't see the grave for bunches of violets.

My husband's buried over in the Churchyard now too and that's where I'll go myself. That'll round everything off very nicely, I think, to be buried in the same place where I was christened. That will be a nice end, to be buried in the place you've always loved best of all. That's what I say to Father sometimes when I'm out there tidying his grave. When my time comes, I'll be with him again here in my lovely Ashdon. People needn't feel sad for *me*.

*   *   *

Florence Anderson died in 1973 and is buried in Ashdon Churchyard beside her husband and her daughter and close to the farmer and his wife to whom this book is dedicated. Around them lie most of the elderly villagers I was privileged to interview and many of the

Ashdonians who feature in its earlier history, folk of both high and low estate, no longer divided by class or by time, now all as one in the welcoming earth.

Where are Ella, Kate, Mary, Lizzie and Edith,
The tender heart, the simple soul, the loved, the proud, the happy one?
All, all, are sleeping on the hill.

Select Bibliography

Ashby, M.K.:	*The Changing English Village*, Roundwood Press, Kineton, 1974.
Bagley, J.J.:	*Life in Mediaeval England*, Batsford, 1960.
Barley, W.M.:	*The English Farmhouse and Cottage*, Routledge, 1961.
Baseley, G.:	*A Country Compendium*, Sidgwick & Jackson, 1977.
Blythe, R.:	*Akenfield: Portrait of an English Village*, Allen Lane, 1969.
Bourne (Sturt) G.:	*Change in the Village*, Duckworth, 1912.
Brinkworth, E.R.C.:	*Shakespeare and the Bawdy Court of England*, Phillimore, 1972.
Brown, A.F.J.:	*English History from Essex Sources 1750-1900*, Essex Record Office, 1952.
Brown, A.F.J.:	*Essex at Work 1700-1815*, E.R.O., 1969.
Brown, A.F.J.:	*Essex People 1750-1900*, E.R.O., 1972.
Butcher, T.K.:	*Country Life*, Batsford, 1970.
Chambers, J.D. & Mingay, G.E.:	*The Agricultural Revolution 1750-1880*, Batsford, 1966.
Clarke, J.S.:	*Voices Prophesying War*, Oxford University Press, 1966.
Edwards, A.C.:	*English History from Essex Sources 1550-1750*, E.R.O., 1952.
Emmison, F.G.:	*Archives & Local History*, Methuen, 1966.
Emmison, F.G.:	*Elizabethan Life: Vol. I: Disorder*, E.R.O., 1970.
Emmison, F.G.:	*Elizabethan Life: Vol. II: Morals and the Church Courts*, E.R.O., 1973.
Emmison, F.G.:	*Elizabethan Life: Vol. III: Home, Work & Customs*, E.R.O., 1976.
Evans, G.E.:	*Ask the fellows who cut the hay*, Faber, 1956.
Evans, G.E.:	*The Farm and the Village*, Faber, 1969.
Evans, G.E.:	*The Horse in the Furrow*, Faber, 1960.
Evans, G.E.:	*Where Beards wag all*, Faber, 1970.
Ewen, C.L.:	*Witch Hunting and Witch Trials*, Kegan Paul, 1929.

Fussell, G.:	*The English Rural Labourer*, Batchworth, 1949.
Gill, R.:	*Happy Rural Seat*, Yale University Press, 1972.
Girouard, M.:	*Life in the English Country House*, Yale University Press, 1978.
Grieve, H.E.P.:	*Examples of English Handwriting 1150-1750*, E.R.O., 1954.
Groves, R.:	*Sharpen the Sickle*, Porcupine Press, 1949.
Hair, P.:	*Before the Bawdy Court*, Elek, 1972.
Hammond, J.L. & B.:	*The Village Labourer*, Longmans, 1912.
Harrison, W.:	*Description of England* (ed. G. Edelen), Folger Library, N. York, 1968.
Hart, C.:	*The Early Charters of Essex*, Leicester University Press, 1957.
Horn, P.:	*Education in Rural England 1880-1914*, Gill & Macmillan, 1978.
Horn, P.:	*The Victorian Country Child*, Roundwood Press, Kineton, 1974.
Hoskins, W.G.:	*Local History in England* (2nd edition), Longman, 1972.
Jennings, P.:	*The Living Village*, Penguin Books, 1972.
Laslett, P.:	*The World we have lost*, Methuen, 1965.
Macfarlane, A.:	*Witchcraft in Tudor and Stuart England*, Routledge, 1970.
Mays, S.:	*Reuben's Corner*, Eyre & Spottiswoode, 1969.
Mays, S. & Ketteridge, C.:	*Five Miles from Bunkum*, Eyre & Methuen, 1972.
Mingay, G.E.:	*The Gentry*, Longman, 1976.
Mingay, C.E.:	*Rural Life in Victorian England*, Heinemann, 1977.
Morant, R.:	*History of Essex*, London, 1978.
Newcourt, R.:	*Repertorium Ecclesiasticum Parochiale Londinense*, G. Bateman, 1710.
Page, R.:	*The Decline of the English Village*, Davis-Poynter, 1974.
Parker, R.:	*The Common Stream*, Collins, 1975.
Pugh, R.B.:	*How to write a parish history*, Allen & Unwin, 1954.
Reaney, P.H.:	*The Place-Names of Essex*, Cambridge University Press, 1936.

SELECT BIBLIOGRAPHY

Richardson, J.:	*The Local Historian's Encyclopaedia*, Historical Publications, 1975.
Rose, W.:	*Good Neighbours*, Readers Union, 1943.
Rowley, N.:	*Education in Essex 1710-1910*, Seax Portfolio No. 6, E.R.O., 1974.
Rowley, N.:	*Law and Order in Essex 1068-1874*, Seax Port folio No. 3, E.R.O., 1970.
Rowley, N.:	*Relief of the Poor in Essex*, Seax Portfolio No. 4, E.R.O., 1971.
Samuel, R.:	*Village Life and Labour*, Routledge, 1975.
Stenton, D.M.:	*English Society in the Early Middle Ages*, Pengin Books, 1952.
Tanner, J.R.:	*Tudor Constitutional Documents 1485-1603*, Chivers Ltd., Bath, 1971.
Tate, W.E.:	*The Parish Chest*, Cambridge, 1946.
Thompson, F.:	*Lark Rise to Candleford*, The Reprint Society, 1948.
Ward, J.:	*The Essex Lay Subsidy of 1327*, Essex County Council, 1986.
West, J.:	*Village Records*, Macmillan, 1962.
Wilson, S.:	*The Mayor and the Matron*, Precision Press, High Wycombe, 1972.
Wilson, S.:	*Saffron Crocus*, Precision Press, High Wycombe, 1971.
Wood, R.G.:	*Agriculture in Essex*, Seax Portfolio No. 7, E.R.O., 1975.
Wood, R.G.:	*Essex and the French Wars 1793-1815*, Seax Port folio No. 9, E.R.O., 1977.
Wright, T.:	*History and Topography of Essex*, G. Virtue, 1836.

INDEX

Persons and places

A

Abingdon: 122
Aethelred (the 'Unready'): 15
Ailid: 34, 56, 79
Albon, Constance: 303-8
Albon, William: 253-4, 297-303, 329
Alexander, Ann: ix, 178
Alexander, Mrs F. C.: 174
Alfred, King: 12
Allgood, Elsie: 233-4
Alvric: 40
Anderson, Florence: 130, 202-8, 333-6
Arch, Joseph: 259-60
Ashdon Hall: 9, 10, 34, 37, 69-71, 77, 96, 138, 213, 216, 221, 289
Ashdon Halt: 67, 213-4, 230, 246
Ashdon Place: 34, 35, 55, 81, 295, 310
Ashdon Street Farm: 9, 130
Ashingdon: 17, 18, 19, 20, 21, 22, 23, 26, 27, 28
Audley End: 50, 67, 203, 213

B

Baignard, Ralph: 69-79, 313
Bakewell, Robert: 46
Banham, Rev D. B.: 280
Baron, Rev T.: 171
Bartlow: 11, 12, 22, 26, 43, 49, 63, 82, 141, 225, 237, 241, 247, 255, 264
Bartlow Hamlet: 38, 45, 49, 53, 63, 183
Bartlow Hills: 13, 14, 21, 23, 25, 30, 319
Bartlow House: 81, 134, 297, 301, 303
Bartram, Bertie: 254-6
Bartram, Lionel: 314
Battlesbridge: 25, 26
Baynards Castle: 69
Bede, the Venerable: 7, 33
Belchamp Walter: 122
Bendysh family: 70, 73
Bendysh Hall: 72, 73, 78, 139, 140
Bendysh Woods: 11, 252
Betts, William: 65
Bidwell, A. L.: 62
Bidwell, L.: 295-7
Blythe, Ronald (*Akenfield*): 5
Boggis, Isaac: 121-2
Boleyn, Anne: 79, 309

Bonnett, The: 10, 225, 287
Bourne Farm: 74
Bourne, River: 11, 12, 36, 40, 62, 67, 204, 242
Bowsers Farm: 9, 11, 12, 43, 56, 229, 238, 240, 244
Brampton, Keling: 140, 163
Bramston, William: 71
Brandt, Walter: 313
Braybrooke, Lord: 29, 50, 52, 256
Brazier, William: 110-1
Bricklayers' Arms, The: 10
Brocklebank, the Rev C. H.: 134, 237, 297, 299, 307
Brocklebank, G. C.: 12
Brown, A. F. J.: 89
Brights Wood: 10
Bryght, Roger: 123
Buncombe, Eileen: 292-3

C

Cambridge: 8, 11, 12, 65, 93, 236, 309, 312, 325, 326, 328
Camden, William: 20, 21, 22, 23, 30
Canewdon: 25
Cantley, Sir Joseph: 313
Carr, John: 93-5
Castle Camps: 10, 63, 74
Chapman, the Rev Benedict: 52, 67, 81, 131, 175
Chapman family: 65, 216, 264
Chapman, Mary: 110-1, 119
Charles (or Chalne), John: 130
Charles I, King: 76, 153
Charles II, King: 107
Chaucer, Geoffrey: 149
Chelmsford: 5, 108, 275
Chetwynd-Talbot, Judge Michael: 313
Childers, Erskine (*The Riddle of the Sands*): 278
Christy, Prof Miller: 23, 24, 29
Church, All Saints: 9, 14, 15, 26, 43-4, 204, 205, 206, 218, 254, 263, 296, 302, 314, 320, 324, 333, 335
Church End: 10, 223, 318
Clays, The: 9, 287
Claydon (or Cleydon), John: 123, 143

PERSONS AND PLACES

Claydon (or Cleydon), Robert: 123, 145
Claydon (or Cleydon), William: 44
Cliff, James: 2
Cliff, Mabel: 1-5
Clopton family: 72, 73, 84, 319-20
Cnut, King: 15-17, 18, 19-20, 24, 28-9, 30
Cobb, Stephen: 73
Cocke, Juliana: 168
Coe, James: 262
Coke, Thomas: 46
Colchester: 122, 281
Collins, Dorothy: 217, 221
Collins, Captain J. A.: 213-4, 220, 252, 283-6
Collins, Brigadier Thomas: ix, 207, 213-20, 252-3, 280, 281-3, 313, 314
Cooper, Rev William: 89-91, 96, 119
Cowell, John: 114, 145
Cowell, Phoebe: 103, 104
Crabbe, George: 124
Cro, Thomas: 182
Cromwell, Oliver: 269-70
Cromwell, Thomas: 69, 74, 79, 84
Croxton-Smith, P.: 30

D
Darcy, John: 172
Dayrell family: 91-2
Dayrell, Rev Thomas: 50, 52, 92
Debden: 65
De Badlesmere, Bartholomew: 84
De Bousser, Robert: 84
De Bradenham, Simon: 70
De Burgh, Elizabeth: 42
Deedes, Mr: 92, 93
De Lacy family: 72-3
Deradour, Thomas: 136
De Storteforde, Nicholas: 41
De Vere, Aubrey: 39, 40, 73, 74
Donnelly, Morwenna: ix, 313
Double, John: 315-6
Downham, James: 180
Driant, Emile (*La Guerre Fatale*): 278
Duchesne, Mrs Matilda & Miss: 287
Dunmow: 34, 49, 69, 76, 77, 90, 319

E
Eadric: 17, 21, 29
Eason, Mabel: 247-8, 331
Eason, Richard: 234-41, 331
Easton Lodge: 90, 319

Edith Swan Neck (Edith the Fair): 56, 73
Edmund Ironside: 16, 17, 18, 29, 30
Edward I, King: 40, 84
Edward III, King: 41, 70, 81, 104, 158, 319
Edward VI, King: 69, 105
Edward VII, King: 77, 78, 204
Elizabeth I, Queen: 76, 98, 105
Elsdon, Donald: 333
Elsenham: 77, 274
Ely: 28, 33
Eustace of Boulogne, Count: 72
Evans, George Ewart: 5
Everitt, Betty: 319

F
Faraday, Michael: 13
Farrant, Herbert: 221-30, 245-7, 265-6, 330-2
Farrant, Minnie: 225, 330, 332
Fitz-Gislebert, Richard: 70
Fitzwalter family: 70-1
Florence of Worcester: 18
Ford, Emily: 130, 208-11
Ford family: 65
Ford, Reuben: 264, 287
Forster, W. E.: 177
'Fox', the: 230, 242, 262, 328
Frazer, Rev James: 180-1
Freeman, Prof E. A.: 25
Freeman, John: 62, 130
Freeman, Richard: 111-2
Freeman, Robert: 131, 175
Freshwell, Half-hundred of: 41, 42
Frodo: 39
Furze, F. M.: 227, 265

G
Gage, John: 13, 14
Gardner, Hubert: 257
George II, King: 102
George III, King: 86
George VI, King: 319
Giblin, Hannah: 55
Giffard, Ralph: 41
Gobion, Thomas: 41
Goldstones Farm: 9, 55, 74, 123, 204, 227, 252, 263, 265
Gonville and Caius College, Cambridge: 50, 69, 81, 131, 134, 175
Goodwin family: 65
Goodwin, Mary: 231-3

341

G

Gough, Richard: 23, 25
Great Chesterford: 288
Great Hales Wood: 10
Green, Angela: 6, 23
Green, J. R.: 23
Green, Martha: 55
Gregory, Pope: 15
Griggs Farm: 242
Guildhall, the: 9, 123, 203, 320

H

Hadstock: 27, 28, 29, 238, 318
Hagger, Alfred: 231
Hagger, Stanley: 246
Hammond, J. L. & Barbara: 108
Hammond, Rev William: 52, 77, 216
Hanson, Edward: 63
Harlow: 34
Harrison, William: 6, 7, 51, 71, 85, 88-9, 93, 106, 144-5, 159-61, 163
Hart, Cyril: 28
Haverhill: 8, 238, 244, 245, 303, 312
Haylock, Elizabeth: 55
Haylock, William: 86
Hempstead: 65
Helions Bumpstead: 73, 122, 260
Henry I, King: 70
Henry III, King: 69
Henry V, King: 74
Henry VII, King: 161
Henry VIII, King: 69, 79, 98, 104, 105, 115, 163
Henry of Huntingdon: 7
Hervey de Hispania: 73
Hewston, Henry: 56, 65
Higden, Ranulf: 7
Hill Farm: 67, 74, 229, 231, 246
Hinxton: 122
Hockley: 26
Holden End: 10
Holinshed, Raphael: 21, 25
Hooley, Ernest: 78
Hoskins, W. G.: 44
Hustler, Devereux: 57

I

Ivytodd Farm: 9

J

James I, King: 60, 76, 100, 153
Jones, Rev William: 80
Joslin, 'Brother': 327, 333

K

Kate's Lane: 9
Keene, Rev Charles: 52
Kemp, Arthur: 293-4
Ketteridge, Christopher: 4
Ketteridge family: 56, 65, 66, 178
Kham Tibetan House: 314
King Family: 71
Knox End: 10

L

Langley Wood: 10
Lane, Rev Walter: 261, 324, 331-3
Lady Well: 221, 310, 324
Lee, Rowland: 79, 84
Le Queux, William (*The Invasion of 1910*) 278-9, 280, 283
Lewes, Priory of: 69
Linton: 63, 81, 122, 209, 231, 233, 241, 281, 293, 301
Little Easton: 76, 77, 90
Little Hales Wood: 10
Littleport: 295, 309
Little Sandons: 8
Luddington, Mrs Leila: 31, 289-311
Luddington, Major Tansley: 295, 309, 310
Lustwine: 33

M

Machen, Arthur: 30
Malet, William: 70
Mallet, William: 70
Marsh family: 65
Marsh, Hilda: 211-3, 328-30
Marsh, Walter: 211, 222, 256, 264, 328-30
Martin, Len: 241-3, 314
Maye, Jeremiah: 269-70
Maynard estate: 250-1, 276
Maynard family: 76, 77, 90, 91, 250
Maynard, Lords: 12, 50, 52, 65, 71, 76-8, 91, 176
Mays, Spike (*Reuben's Corner*): 4, 208, 234, 247, 287, 297
Middleditch, Thomas: 61-2
Midsummer Hill: 2, 57, 197, 263
Mill Field: 131
Miller, Richard: 94-7
Miller, Robert: 112
Millicent, Lady Susan: 75
Millicent, Sir Robert: 75-6
Mortimers (Mortivaux): 73
Moss, Arthur: 212, 234, 243-5

Moss family: 65
Moss, Frank: 243-5, 263-4, 265

N
Nevill, the Hon R. C.: 12
Newcourt, Richard: 22, 80
Newnham Hall: 32, 38, 57, 72-3, 143, 211, 264, 289, 319, 320
Niemann, August: 278
North, Rev John: 51, 82, 93, 125-9, 171, 271

O
Oliver, John: 25
Overall, John: 103-4
Overhall Farm: 9, 310

P
Palmer, Dr W. M.: 6, 13, 31, 34, 75, 91, 92, 321
Parker, Archbishop Matthew: 80, 81
Pattrick, Thomas: 99-100
Pearce-Higgins, Canon John: 324-8
Peck, Bridget: 323, 328
Pelly, Major: 219, 220, 263, 280
Pentlow: 33, 34
Pitt (the Younger), William: 270-2
Pledger, Philippe: 99, 100
Prior, Thomas and Harriet: 176
Pritchard, R. W. V.: 320-1

R
Radwinter: 6, 8, 11, 41, 43, 72, 73, 78, 88, 106, 139, 180, 208, 223, 281, 282
Ratcliffe family: 70, 71
Rawe, the witches: 168
Reaney, P. H.: 23, 24, 74
Rectory Manor: 9, 51, 69, 79, 83, 133, 215, 289
Richard I, King: 158
Richard II, King: 44, 72, 104, 320
Richard III, King: 15
Richer family: 71
Ricketts farm: 9, 230
Ridducks Hill: 11
Rock End: 10
Rogers End: 10
'Rose and Crown', the: 8, 9, 52, 67, 230, 236, 262, 266, 316
Rothe End: 11, 73
Royston: 279
Ruse, John: 67

S
Saffron Walden: 8, 9, 10, 43, 59, 60, 61, 63, 125, 140, 180, 183, 210, 211, 213, 215, 219, 229, 236, 238, 241, 248, 255, 257, 259, 264, 266, 271, 274, 279, 292, 312, 318
Salter, Rev Nathaniel: 86, 321, 328
Sampford: 43, 65, 322
Sampford, Rev D: 172
Sandons Farm: 9, 74, 231, 239, 252, 318
Saward, Thomas: 130
Scoones, Sir Geoffrey: 312
Scutt, John: 101
Shadwell Wood: 11, 276
Sherbrooke, Edmund: 130
Shudy Camps: 10, 59, 91, 92, 183
Simeon of Durham: 18
Simmons, Walter: 264
Smith, Rev A. W.: 283-4
Smith, Fuller: 254
Smith, Rev T. H.: 280
Smith, Sir Thomas: 158
Smith, Willie: 202, 242
Steeple Bumpstead: 65, 222, 260
Steventon End: 10, 38, 39, 67, 287, 289
Stigand, Archbishop: 19, 20, 28
Sutton, W. T.: 190-1
Svarti, Ottar (author of *Knutsdrapa*): 24
Swan (or Swann) family: 65
Swan, Michael: 313, 316
Swete, Rev Dr H. B.: 27, 28, 81, 132-5, 207
'Swing, Captain': 129

T
Thaxted: 34, 78, 89, 96, 276
Thickhoe: 11, 73
Thompson, Sir Eric: 313
Thorne, Anthony: 4
Threadgold, Mrs: 294-5
Thurkill the Tall: 29
Thurstan: 28, 34
Tihel the Breton (Tihel de Helion): 73
Tillett, Ben: 263
Townley, Rev C.: 29
Townshend, Charles, Viscount: 46
Tuck, William: 194-5, 218, 247
Tyrell family: 74, 75, 321
Tyrrell, Richard: 69, 75, 147, 321

U
Upton, John: 80
Uttlesford, Hundred of: 41, 42

V

Victoria, Queen: 293
Vinall, Kitty: 290-2
Vestey, Edmund: ix, 311, 312, 314, 315

W

Walker, Rev Matthew: 60
Walton family: 74
Waltons Park: 9, 34, 35, 38, 43, 50, 56, 65, 70, 74, 78, 91, 176, 215, 219, 239, 242, 251, 252, 253, 263, 289-311, 314, 329
Walton, Sir Richard de: 74
Warbeck, Perkin: 70
Ward, Jennifer: 41
Warwick, Countess of: 77, 78, 310
Water End: 9, 10, 40, 239
Webb family: 66
Webb, Harry: 264
Webb, John: 44
Weever, J: 319
Wesley, John: 60
Westlake, H. F.: 123
'White Horse', The: 8, 95, 230
Whitehead family: 157
Whitehand, Ellen: 134-5
Whitelock, Prof Dorothy: 16, 24
William I, King: 15, 36, 68, 72
William II (Rufus), King: 74
William III, King: 108
William of Malmesbury: 17, 19
Willingale Spain: 73
Willowes family: 162
Willowes, William: 44
Wilson, Stanley: 78
Wimbish: 28, 33, 34, 65
Winsey Farm: 57, 74, 239
Wolsey, Cardinal: 79
Woodley family: 66, 103
Wornham, Mary: 104
Wright, T: 11, 323
Wyatt, F. J.: 185-7

Y

Young, Arthur: 127, 128

Subjects

adultery: see fornication
agriculture: 34, 40, 45, 46, 54-5, 57-8, 98, 125, 311, 317
Agricultural Children's Act of 1873: 178
ale, legislation re: 142-3
apprentices: 113, 116-7
archaeological discoveries: 12-14
Archdeacon's Court: 99, 148-157
Army manoeuvres: 281-2
Assandun, Battle of: 15-32
   Anglo-Saxon Chronicle account: 16-17, 18, 19, 24
   eleventh century monks' chronicles: 18-19
   arguments for Ashdon as battle-site: 19, 21, 22, 24, 27, 30, 32
   arguments for Ashingdon as battle-site: 17, 18, 19, 20, 23, 25, 27
   etymological evidence: 23-5
   Cnut's *mynster*: 19, 20, 25, 26, 28, 29
   Hadstock as likeliest site of *mynster*: 28, 29
   human skin on church door: 28-9
   oral tradition: 30, 33, 225
Assize files: 161-7, 269

Baptists: 10, 56, 60-3
Baronets: 76
bastardy, attitudes to: 98-104
Bawdy Court: see Archdeacon's Court
Bayeux Tapestry: 19, 72
beacons, warning: 276
bee-keeping: 38, 246-7, 330
beer-drinking: 47, 142, 224, 227, 244
beggars, attitudes to: 104-7, 117-8, 210
bell-ringing: 93-6, 155, 314
birthplaces of Ashdonians: 63, 64
Black Death: 43, 44, 104, 216
blacksmiths: 116-7, 297, 298, 299, 300
bread, legislation re: 142-4
bread-making: at home: 2, 209, 241; in Napoleonic Wars: 273-5
bridges: 66-7
butchering: 243-4

carpentry: 178-80
Catholics: 59, 60
census-returns: 45, 53
Chantry Commissioners' Report of 1547: 44

SUBJECTS

Chapel: 61, 174, 313
Charities: 123, 130-1, 172, 174-5
Children's Home: 133-6
Church, financial accounts of: 47-8, 146-8
Church-going: 58, 205, 212, 218, 307
Churchwardens, duties of: 146-7
Common fields: 50-3
Compton return of 1676: 58
Constables, duties of: 143-6
Cottage-spinning industry: 121-2
Court Baron: 137-8, 143
Court Leet: 139-40, 143
Country cooking: 204-5, 210-2
Country customs: 207-8, 210-1, 225
Crime and punishment: 86, 87, 143-70
  arson 166-7; Forest Laws 84; Game Laws 86, 169-70; hue and cry 144-5; indecent exposure 155; misappropriation of land 138; murder 165-6; offences against the person 165-6; offences involving crops 162-3; poaching 169; punishments in Tudor period 159-61; stealing animals 161-2; theft of goods and chattels 164; 'Tyburn tickets' 148
cycling: 245-6

dancing: 76, 247-8, 310-1
death, premonitions of: 331-2
deforestation, fears re: 163-4
Dissolution of the Monasteries: 69, 98
Domesday Book entries: 36-40, 49, 50
domestic service: 56-7, 203, 221, 294-308

earliest settlements: 12, 21, 22
Ecclesiastical Census of 1851: 45, 63
Enclosure: 45, 51-3
Esquires: 71
exorcism, act of: 325-6

family names of Ashdonians: 65-6
flooding: 12, 67
fornication: 149-52, 156-7
fruit-growing: 88, 232, 300, 306

gardening: 88, 297-303
gentry: 56, 68-97, 181, 203, 213-21, 309-11
gleaning: 232-3
Gilds: 123-4
graffiti in Church: 320-1
Guildhall Charity: 130, 270

harvesting: 211, 226-30
haunted house: 325-6
health: 193-5, 290-2
Hearth Tax returns of 1664: 65
horse-keeping: 231
housing problems: 251-2
hunting: 51, 83-8, 251

Inquisitiones post mortem: 69
invasion, threat of:
  in Napoleonic period 276-7;
  The Invasion of 1910: 278-9;
  in World War I, plans to evacuate and destroy village 283-8
inventory of Ashdon Church goods: 81-2

Justices of the Peace, duties of: 158

keeping the Sabbath: 62, 153-5
King's Book of Sports, the: 153

labourers, legislation re: 113-4, 126
labourers' strike of 1914: 78, 249, 257-67, 328
land-ownership: 36-40, 49-50, 52, 68-79
largesse money: 229
Lay subsidy return for 1327: 40-3, 65
Lay subsidy return for 1524-5: 44, 65

manorial rights and customs: 79, 137-8, 143
manorial system: 69
mechanization: 55, 311-2, 317
milling: 233, 272-3
mobility of Ashdonians: 65-6, 255
motor cars, early: 201, 219, 287, 296
Muster rolls: 268-9

parents and children: 212-3, 214, 222, 297-8, 303
paupers: 57, 120-1, 124, 205-6, 208
place-names: 24, 74
ploughing: 226
poaching: 87, 169, 240, 246, 254, 310, 315
political divisions: 219, 220, 257
Poor Relief: 115, 120, 125
population changes: 44-5, 53-58, 120-1

Quakers: 58-9
Quarter Sessions cases: 158-67

railway: 67, 213

345

INDEX

rectors: 47-9, 52, 63, 79-83, 171-2, 175, 328, 331-3
Reform Bills: 257
religion: 58-63
roads: 66-7, 139-41

Schooling: 171-221
  absenteeism: 193-7
  Board School, opening of: 182-3
  Charity-assisted schooling: 171-2, 175
  curriculum: 184-5
  dame's School: 172
  disciplinary problems: 190-2
  Elementary Education Bill of 1870: 177-8, 181-2
  Empire Day celebrations: 280
  fees: 175, 197, 208, 233
  illness of pupils: 193-5
  Inspectors' visits: 197-200
  Log Book entries: 182-200
  monitors: 176, 189
  National Society for Education of the Poor: 173
  National School: 174-6, 183
  private sector: 183-4, 203, 220, 221, 234, 309
  pupil teachers: 176-7, 187
  teachers' living conditions: 176, 194-5
self-sufficiency of Ashdon: 56, 239, 241, 243, 292, 312

settlement, Laws of: 107-113
shepherding: 222-3, 224, 233-4
shooting: 252-3, 305
social structure: 34-6, 40, 56-7, 98, 250, 255, 286-7, 289, 311-7, 321
sowing: 226
Speenhamland system of poor relief: 121, 128-9
stonepicking: 232

taxes for war-purposes: 41, 270-2
terriers of Church property: 51, 82, 83
Tithe Commutation Award: 45, 49
tithe payments: 46, 47, 48, 49, 257

vagabonds: see beggars
Village Flower Show: 218-9, 242, 309
Village General Store: 235-41
Visitation questionnaire of Bishop of London: 59, 60, 171-2

wages: 49, 172-3, 176, 210, 222-3, 231, 233, 251, 255, 261-2, 266, 272, 299, 303, 308
war: 15-33, 51-5, 249, 266-7, 268-88, 318, 335
windmills: 227, 273
witchcraft: 167-8
workhouse: 106, 123-5, 210
wurzel-thinning: 231

346